Katja Triplett
Buddhism and Medicine in Japan

Religion and Society

Edited by
Gustavo Benavides, Frank J. Korom,
Karen Ruffle and Kocku von Stuckrad

Volume 81

Katja Triplett

Buddhism and Medicine in Japan

—

A Topical Survey (500–1600 CE)
of a Complex Relationship

DE GRUYTER

ISBN 978-3-11-076295-2
e-ISBN (PDF) 978-3-11-057621-4
e-ISBN (EPUB) 978-3-11-057556-9
ISSN 1437-5370

Library of Congress Control Number: 2019951645

Bibliographic information published by the Deutsche Nationalbibliothek
The Deutsche Nationalbibliothek lists this publication in the Deutsche Nationalbibliografie; detailed bibliographic data are available in the Internet at http://dnb.dnb.de.

© 2021 Walter de Gruyter GmbH, Berlin/Boston
This volume is text- and page-identical with the hardback published in 2019.
Printing and binding: CPI books GmbH, Leck

www.degruyter.com

Contents

Prologue —— VII

Acknowledgements —— IX

Conventions —— XI

Introduction —— 1
- Scope of the Book —— 4
- Medicine and Religion in Japan —— 6
- "Buddhist Medicine" as a Field —— 11
- Outline of the Book —— 16

1 **Buddhism, Medicine and Magic: The Boundary Problem** —— 20
1.1 Mysteries of "Buddhism" and "Medicine" in Premodern Japan —— 24
1.2 Modern Views on Premodern Medicine —— 32
1.3 Terms and Concepts for a Survey of Buddhism and Medicine —— 38

2 **Operating with Buddhism** —— 44
2.1 Operating with "Buddhism" in Modern Academic and Popular Accounts —— 47
2.2 Incorporation of Buddhism and Chinese-style Medicine into Japanese Society —— 52
2.3 Historiographies of Buddhism, Medicine and Healing Rituals —— 58
2.4 Licit and Illicit Talismanic Cures, Rituals and Incantations —— 64

3 **The Eye I: An Organ as a Site of Empowerment and Healing** —— 70
3.1 The Eye in Buddhist Texts —— 71
3.2 Eye-Opening Ceremonies —— 73
3.3 Medicinal Treatment of Sight-Related Diseases —— 78
3.3.1 Buddhism and Cataract Surgery in Japan —— 80
3.3.2 Nāgārjuna Bodhisattva's Ophthalmological Treatise —— 87

4 **The Eye II: Buddhist Healing and Living with Visual Impairment** —— 92
4.1 Development of Monastic Ophthalmology in Japan —— 92
4.2 Monks as Doctors, Patients as Pilgrims —— 98

4.3		Miracle Healing of Blindness in Early Japanese Buddhist Records —— 102
4.4		Musicians, Ritualists, Healers: The Professional Lives of the Visually Impaired —— 106
5		**Women: Care of the Reproductive Female Body —— 111**
5.1		The Female Body as an Obstacle to Becoming a Buddha? —— 113
5.2		Care of the Reproductive Female Body —— 121
5.2.1		The *Essentials of Medicine* (*Ishinpō*) on Women's Health —— 122
5.2.2		Religious Regulations and Spells in the *Essentials of Medicine* (*Ishinpō*) —— 125
5.3		Care by Buddhist Women and Female Spiritual Practice —— 127
6		**Plants: *Materia medica*, Medicinal Gardens and Panaceas —— 134**
6.1		Medicinal Gardens —— 136
6.2		Global Trade in Medicinal Drugs: Evidence from the Shōsōin Repository —— 142
6.3		Japanese Compendia of Incense and Drugs —— 145
6.4		Buddhist Panaceas Made from Potent Plants —— 150
7		**Horses and Equine Medicine —— 163**
7.1		The *Scroll of Equine Medicine* (1267) —— 168
7.2		Horse Medicine of the Anzai School —— 177
7.3		A Temple Hospital for Horses —— 182
7.4		The Horse-headed Kannon as Protector of Animals —— 186

Conclusion: Boundaries, Maps and Types of Othering —— 189
    Distinguishing between Buddhism and Medicine —— 190
    Types of Othering —— 195

Timeline —— 197

List of Images —— 204

Bibliography —— 205

Index —— 240

Prologue

The *Spellbound: Magic, Ritual & Witchcraft* exhibition at the Ashmolean Museum in Oxford that I visited not long ago explores forms of "magical thinking" with a focus on Europe and local English customs and beliefs. Among the exhibits are scientific instruments used by physicians in Europe in the fifteenth and sixteenth centuries to calculate favorable times for bloodletting according to the moon's position and diagrams that express a medical, religious and psychological interpretation of the relationship between humans, their bodies and the cosmos. According to the makers of the exhibition, magical thinking is universal and based in both positive and negative human emotions. These emotions infuse rituals. If such magical thinking is indeed universal, the yearning to control unseen powers and entities must underlie much of ritualistic action in all human cultures. As is well-known, the emphasis on monotheism in Christian Europe led authorities to condemn practices relating to demons, ghosts and other supernatural beings believed to cause disease and misfortune, and such practices were regarded as criminal acts even punishable by death. Eventually, the existence of such entities was denied in Christian Europe and 'superstitious' acts were no longer punished as before. These entities were, instead, relegated to the realm of childhood fantasy or insanity.

What counts as natural and supernatural is not only specific to each culture but also within each culture, in itself a shifting and hybrid value system. Is this, however, all based in a universally existent human condition of magical thinking? I think adherents of the esoteric, or tantric, form of Buddhism that shaped much of premodern Japanese culture would agree that human emotions are central. Their rituals were designed to harness these very emotions of fear, hate or desire and transform them so they could eradicate obstacles to practicing Buddhism. In Japan, many who were empowered in the highly hierarchical initiatory system of esoteric Buddhism and trained to conduct various complex rituals also engaged in practicing medicine as a form of compassionate action. I encountered this historical circumstance when working on late medieval and early modern Buddhist narratives in which the motif of healing blindness occurred, and, in 2005, started to explore the topic of Buddhism and medicine in more detail.

I was drawn to this topic because it was not well researched at the time although, in my view, it was central to understanding premodern Japanese culture. On a more personal level, I grew up surrounded by relatives who were involved in medicine in different capacities and medical topics were discussed at length at the dinner table. Given these inspiring discussions (though many guests did find them off-putting!), it is no coincidence that two of my siblings work in health-related professions.

However, I have always been more interested in the analysis of the concerns expressed following medical discoveries and the cultural and social impact of these discoveries. It was striking that when news channels reported that bimaternal mice, created by applying a human-made biochemical tool to the genetic structure of embryonic stem cells, had survived to adulthood and had had offspring of their own, the question of the applicability of this method to humans immediately popped up. What would change in human society if two women could be joint biological parents? Or two men? Or any number of individuals, increasing parenthood from two to three or more? Ethical concerns such as these are a dimension of religion, as I see it, and the discourse regarding these concerns a viable topic within the academic study of religions.

Some have described this genetic manipulation by scientists as a miracle. I think that the evolving discourses on the sensation of creating bimaternal mice by editing genes is, above all, a testimony to the human creative spirit. Humans, whether guided by altruistic motives or self-interest, will always strive to make their endeavors appear reasonable and meaningful. While surveying premodern sources dealing with topics such as how to treat those with physical and sensory impairments, or how to increase a man's social capital by enabling women to participate in monastic business or by providing care for abandoned domesticated animals, I encountered ideas that I found inspiring and others that were difficult to digest. Because of the selection of topics this book is, in a way, my own processing of particular concerns. However, I sincerely hope that the reader will observe that the topics chosen show prevalent trends and important continuities and disruptions in the relationship of Buddhism and medicine in the history of premodern Japan.

Göttingen, November 12, 2018

Acknowledgements

I owe thanks to many colleagues and friends for their help with this book. Anna Andreeva, Barbara Gerke, Almut Barbara Renger, Martin Repp, Pierce Salguero, Yoshinaga Shin'ichi and Jan van der Valk, among others, provided helpful suggestions on earlier versions of some of the chapters that appeared as separate publications before being included in part in the book. Lucia Dolce, Ramona Jelinek-Menke, Elizabeth Kenney, Karénina Kollmar-Paulenz, Benedetta Lomi, Antonio Manieri, Jens Schlieter, Lena Springer, Michael Stanley-Baker and Robert Wittkamp generously shared resources and information during joint conference projects or on other occasions. Julian Triplett and Wang Xiaojing graciously assisted me with some of the translations. Colleagues and audience members at presentations during my fellowships at the Humanities Center of Advanced Studies "Multiple Secularities – Beyond the West, Beyond Modernities" at the University of Leipzig, funded by the German Research Foundation (DFG), offered useful questions and comments on various aspects of the book. My particular gratitude extends to Johannes Duschka, Katrin Killinger, Christoph Kleine, Elisabeth Marx, Hubert Seiwert, Monika Wohlrab-Sahr and Judith Zimmermann of the Leipzig Humanities Center of Advanced Studies. I am indebted to Sarah Eaton and Katja Pessl who facilitated my research at the Center for Modern East Asian Studies (CeMEAS) at the University of Göttingen in recent years. The teams at the Berlin State Library (Staatsbibliothek zu Berlin) and the Bodleian Japanese Library at the University of Oxford as well as Steffi Rüger of the Department for the Study of Religions at the University of Leipzig deserve special appreciation for their unbureaucratic proficiency that was essential to my research. I am grateful to Thandi House, David Law and Birgit Piegeler who accompanied me during the phase of making the language of this book evident. All mistakes and errors are mine. My heartfelt thanks go to my family and to Laurent for their encouragement and care.

In this book, the following publications will be republished in revised form with permission from the editors and publishers:

Triplett, Katja. 2010a. "Gründungslegenden in der Erinnerungspflege japanisch-
    buddhistischer Tempel am Beispiel des Tsubosakasan Minami Hokkeji." In *Geschichten
    und Geschichte: Historiographie und Hagiographie in der asiatischen
    Religionsgeschichte*, edited by Max Deeg, Oliver Freiberger and Christoph Kleine.
    Historia religionum 30, 140–180. Uppsala: Almqvist & Wiksell.
Triplett, Katja. 2010b. "Esoteric Buddhist Eye-healing Rituals in Japan and the Promotion of
    Benefits." In *Grammars and Morphologies of Ritual Practices in Asia*, edited by Lucia

Dolce, Gil Raz and Katja Triplett. Ritual Dynamics and the Science of Ritual 1, 485–497. Wiesbaden: Harrassowitz.

Triplett, Katja. 2012. "Magical Medicine? – Japanese Buddhist Medical Knowledge and Ritual Instruction for Healing the Physical Body." *Japanese Religions* (Special issue: Religion and Healing in Japan, edited by Christoph Kleine and Katja Triplett) 37.1–2, 63–92.

Triplett, Katja. 2013–2014. "Hippiatry and Ritual Healing: Considering Japanese Buddhist Illustrated Manuscripts on Equine Medicine". *CSJR Newsletter*, 26–27, 21–23.

Triplett, Katja. 2014. "For Mothers and Sisters: Care of the Reproductive Female Body in the Medico-ritual World of Early and Medieval Japan." *Dynamis* 34.2, 337–356.

Triplett, Katja. 2016. "Wissen und Wunder: 'Erleuchtung' und das Bild des asiatischen Buddhismus im 19. und 20. Jahrhundert." In *Erleuchtung: Kultur- und Religionsgeschichte eines Begriffs*, edited by Almut-Barbara Renger, 367–95. Freiburg: Herder.

Triplett, Katja. 2017. "Using the Golden Needle: Nagarjuna Bodhisattva's Ophthalmological Treatise and Other Sources in the Essentials of Medical Treatment". In: *Buddhism and Medicine: An Anthology of Premodern Sources*, edited by Pierce Salguero, 543–48. New York: Columbia University Press.

Triplett, Katja. 2019. "Potency by Name? 'Medicine Buddha Plant' and Other Herbs in the Japanese *Scroll of Equine Medicine* (*Ba'i sōshi emaki*, 1267)." *Himalaya* (Special issue: Approaching Potent Substances in Medicine and Ritual Across Asia, edited by Barbara Gerke and Jan van der Valk) 39.1, 189–207.

Conventions

The pinyin system of romanization (without the tonal marks) is used to render Chinese terms; the modified Hepburn system is used for Japanese terms and the International Alphabet of Sanskrit Transliteration (IAST) is used for Sanskrit terms. Spelling differences in quoted book titles or citations go back to differences in the authors' romanization styles and inconsistencies in their use of diacritical marks.

Chinese and Japanese names are written in line with the East Asian convention of writing the family name followed by the given name. The only exception to this occurs where an author with a Chinese or Japanese name published in a European language. In this case, the European convention of writing the family name last is followed, and the name is used as it appears in the publication in question, meaning usually without diacritical marks. The Japanese convention of using only the personal name of a famous personality is followed here as well. For example, I refer to Manase Dōsan as "Dōsan", his personal name, instead of Manase. It was customary for members of the elite to change their names or use several names simultaneously in the course of their lives. Sometimes, the reading of the character or characters making up their names differed too. Some men and women were only known by the palace or temple where they lived, or their title. I use only the most known and recognizable names. Other conventions regarding Japanese were adapted from the 2018 *Monumenta Nipponica* style guide.

Terms and names that form part of the American English lexicon such as sutra (for Sanskrit *sūtra*), shogun (for Japanese *shōgun*) or mantra (for Sanskrit *mantra*) only appear in transliteration when they are part of a non-English compound or title that is not part of the lexicon, for example *Vimalakīrti-sūtra*.

Titles of Buddhist texts are often long, and short versions have been well established in academic writing about Buddhism. I use the full title when a source is first mentioned, and thereafter use the short title, for example *Lotus Sutra*.

Medical terms translated from the Chinese are introduced and then used with capital letters to mark them as technical terms, for example "five agents" appears as "Five Agents." The key terms *ki* and *qi* for 氣 (気) remain untranslated as they have complex histories and meanings. I preferred the use of traditional Chinese characters in this book, depending on the context, but in modern titles the characters appear as the publishers used them so they may appear in simplified form. Characters are only inserted after the first mention of a term or name. An index at the end of the book serves as a reference for all relevant terms and names.

A few words about the Japanese writing system as it differs considerably from European writing systems: Texts in Buddhism and medicine, but also other fields, were written using Chinese ideographic characters and two syllabic scripts called *katakana* 片仮名 and *hiragana* 平仮名. The *kana* 仮名 syllabaries derive either from parts of Chinese characters or from cursive-style Chinese characters. The syllabaries were (and are to this day) used to phonetically render how Japanese thought the Chinese characters were pronounced and how Japanese said in their language what was coded in the text. This way of rendering text and reading it functions similarly to a translation. The texts explored in this book are often in a combination of Chinese characters, *kana* and additional marks that helped Japanese read. Interestingly, Buddhist texts, for example, were usually not translated from Chinese into Japanese in the premodern period although it would have been possible, so the writing (and reading) system described above – challenging to those who are used to a single phonetic alphabet – remained dominant well into the early modern period.

To pronounce romanized Japanese, articulate the vowels like in Italian and elongate the vowels marked with macrons, for example *ā* is pronounced as the first vowel in "father," not like the first vowel in "rubber." Consonants are pronounced similarly to in English but double consonants, for example in "Hokke-ji," are said with a glottal stop.

Chinese rendered in the pinyin system of romanization reflects the phonology of standard Chinese and is pronounced according to the following guidelines: The consonant *b* is pronounced like an English *p* but unaspirated as in "spy." The consonant *p* is aspirated as in "pie." Similarly, *d* is unaspirated as in "sty" and *t* aspirated as in "tie;" *g* as in "sky" and *k* as in "key." The consonant *z* should be pronounced as *ts* like in "cats" but softer. Further particulars are:

c like *ts* in "cats" but aspirated;
x like *sh* but softer;
j like *ch* but unaspirated and softer;
q like *ch* but aspirated and softer;
sh like *sh* but articulated with a retroflex;
zh like *ch* as in "chat" but unaspirated and articulated with a retroflex;
ch like *ch* as in "chat" but aspirated and articulated with a retroflex.

The vowel sounds romanized as *i, u, ü, e, a* and combinations such as *ia, ua, uo*, etc. vary according to their phonetic environment. For example, disregarding the tones, *qi* is pronounced with an articulated *i* as in "cheese" but the *zi* in *wujing zi* is pronounced like a soft *ts* without any "i" sound.

The pronunciation of romanized Sanskrit has the following particulars: Elongated vowels are marked with a macron but the diphthongs *e*, *ai*, *o* and *au* are always long; *ṛ* with a diacritical mark (not *r*) belongs to the vowels and is pronounced similarly to *ri* as in "rim." Consonants are articulated more or less as in English but note: *ṅ* like *ng* as in "lung," *c* like *ch* as in "child," *ñ* makes the *n* into a nasal sound and *ś* like *sh* as in "ship." A similar sound is *ṣ* but here it is articulated with a retroflex. Other retroflexes are *ṭ* and *ḍ*. Note also the *ḥ*, pronounced clearly like an *h* as in "house." The *ṃ* replaces either a nasal sound or is pronounced as an *m*, such as in Ratnasaṃbhava. Aspirated consonants have an *h* added, for example *dh* as in Dharma or Buddha.

The stress of the often long Sanskrit words roughly follow three rules: Stress is on the first long syllable counting from the end of the word; syllables with a long vowel or a short vowel before two consonants are considered long; the final syllable of a word is never stressed even if it is a long syllable. Examples are: ma<u>n</u>ḍala, Avalokite<u>ś</u>vara, <u>*dhā*</u>*raṇī*, <u>Śā</u>kyamuni, Vai<u>ro</u>cana.

All translations are mine unless otherwise noted.

For a chronological overview of the cultural history of Japanese Buddhism, I recommend reading Deal and Ruppert (2015).

Introduction

> *Listen carefully, daughter of a good family. The Tathāgata, Arhat, Fully-enlightened One [the Buddha] has taught the four supports, relying on which a bhikṣuṇī [nun] goes forth and takes full ordination. Can you maintain these bhikṣuṇī practices for the rest of your life? If so, answer "I can." [...] It is by relying on putrid medicine that one goes forth and takes full ordination. [...] If you receive additional offerings, such as clarified butter, oil, fresh butter, honey, or raw sugar, you may accept them.*
>
> From the *Four-Part Vinaya, Collection of Rules for the Nuns*, trans. Bodhi Translation Committee (2015, 23–24)

It may seem difficult to think of East Asian Buddhism as being linked to the realm of medicine since the domain of religious healing is usually thought to be restricted to prayers for divine intervention and faith healing. In conventional medical circles, faith healing is often seen to be an obstacle to the development of proper and effective medicine. How could prayers and rituals arising purely from a religious belief in divine intervention and designed to evoke a divine presence possibly be effective in treating disease and impairment? Enlightenment thought emphasized the distinction between the "religious" and the "scientific." Premodern textual sources, for example from Ancient Egypt, Tibet and East Asia, however, combine religious and medical instructions and practices in an organic way using objects such as *materia medica* substances or talismanic texts.

What is recognized today as belonging to two different systems – religion and science – has rarely been regarded as separate. Since the realm of healing was and continues to be highly contested in many societies because of the associated guaranteed access to power and privilege, it is essential to look at processes of inclusion (like initiation into a lineage of healers) and exclusion (like accusations of quackery or wizardry) in order to see how and why social actors construct orthodoxy and heterodoxy in healing methods – in other words, in order to grasp the emic "boundary work." The outcome of research in emic terminologies will contribute to a redefinition of categories such as "religion," "faith-based healing" and "medicine" for the comparative study of religions. Processes of knowledge transfer and methods of medical and religious practices aimed at safeguarding coveted knowledge are among the major foci of this book. When state interference or social pressures dictate the abolition of certain practices deemed "superstitious," "backward" and "harmful," the potency of a certain substance or talismanic text is questioned. This leads to a categorical change, and medicinal objects which were once considered potent start to be regarded as useless, ridiculous or dangerous. Such categorical changes will be explored in selected case studies of early and medieval Japan using primary sources to uncover past debates about medical and ritual orthodox and heterodox practices to complement ongoing debates in academia on religion and medicine.

When Buddhism – with its new belief systems, rituals and philosophy – entered East Asia, Indian and Central Asian ideas of healing and medicine were transferred with it and became part of the local culture and society. Scholarly studies have reached diverse conclusions regarding how these ideas were transferred and the extent to which they were adapted. This is due to basic theoretical and methodological problems.

The first problem is defining illness and disease, health and well-being, and religion and science. A study of these culturally determined concepts in the complex history of East Asia with its different cultures and religious traditions, therefore, brings with it a discussion of the terminology and research categories. Various textual and visual sources in regard to Buddhist medical activities in Japan that encompass both fields of medicine and ritual – often because the authors of the sources combine medical and ritual instruction – will be examined, and problems of adequate terminology will also be addressed.

When analyzing sources that draw on reference material from modern scholarship, the use of terms such as "science," "faith healing" or "miracle healing," "medicine," "scientific medicine," "ritual" and "magic" in describing central themes in the original sources seems inevitable. Faced with the dilemma of being forced to work with terminology developed during a long and complex process in Western scholarship to describe and interpret non-Western phenomena, there is a danger of not being able to perceive important themes and indigenous concepts as well as prevalent categories. Throughout history, and around the globe, humans have striven to lead a long and healthy life. But what constitutes health can be so vastly diverse that individuals from different cultures – even from the same culture – and different time periods would not even perceive the efforts of the others as having some benefit. Regarding medicine as a set of ideas and knowledge produced and maintained as a social and cultural system, the sources will be explored without judging whether the efforts are indeed helpful or actually effective. Where "science" is viewed as reliable and rationally explainable knowledge (*scientia*) and contrasted with "religion," anything connected to religion or magic is deemed unreliable and irrational. Not regarding it as the scholar's business to question what is true or to deny the existence of cat demons, for example, a distanced stance of methodological agnosticism is taken. This also means, however, refraining from articulating enthusiastic statements on expressions of twelfth-century Japanese medical knowledge that seem akin to modern evidence-based biomedicine and thus could be termed "proto-scientific." In short, this book is not about what medicine does to human beings and their bodies in modern scientific terms, but how human beings imagine and practice medicine in their historical social and cultural setting.

The underlying assumption in terming a medical system "magical" from the point of view of modern science or that of institutional religion is that it is essentially ineffective, even harmful. "Medicine," in contrast, is empirical and evidence-based, and every healing system before the advent of this scientific medicine is deemed a type of healing art. "Medicine" here is understood to mean ideas, practices, and institutions relating to health, illness, well-being and feelings of *dis*-ease in line with the approach taken in medical anthropology. The effectiveness of a remedy or therapeutic treatment cannot and should not be taken as a yardstick in the exploration of these ideas. Aiming solely at couching premodern remedies or therapeutic treatments in the nomenclature of modern biomedicine might result in statements of a normative nature, either in the shape of a recommendation or a warning. The chapters in this book instead look at various primary sources in order to establish how contemporary social actors related a remedy or therapeutic treatment to their understanding of medicine and religion.

Regarding Buddhist medicine as "magical medicine" because of the use of spells, incantations and charms, risks the perception of there being a primitive–advanced dichotomy, with Buddhist medicine being identified with the primitive and pre-scientific. If magic is defined as a set of ideas and practices that aims to invoke powerful entities to bring about a desired change, then Buddhist healing could be termed magical, although in the esoteric Buddhist worldview, a divine response is not necessarily seen as being automatic and available instantly upon request. Additionally, the universal Buddha is not seen as being forced or manipulated as popular definitions of magic imply.[1] The terms found in the sources, such as 呪 (*ju, noroi*), "utter a spell, conjure up, curse," 護符 (*gofu*), the use of "charms and talismans," and 占 (*uranai*), "divination," indicate further that these practices are akin to what in European history was understood to be magic, which has existed side by side with science in European culture.

---

1 See e. g. Malinowski's approach in his influential study "Magic, science and religion ([1925] 1955). For a refutation of Malinowski's thesis, see Thomas ([1971] 1980, 647–648). See also Harrison's account and discussion of the boundary making between "religion" and "science" in European intellectual history (2006).

Scope of the Book

When studying the early history of Japanese Buddhism, research on the Chinese sources often tends to become the main focus. The same appears to happen in the study of the history of medicine in Japan: The influence of Chinese paradigms and practices seems so overpowering that Japanese medical history emerges as a mere extension of Chinese medicine, possibly in a degenerated form due to the many pitfalls of cultural and literary translations. A book on Buddhism and medicine in Japan, therefore, may easily be a treatise on Chinese Buddhism and medicine with some asides on its adaptations in Japanese culture and society. This book seeks to examine adaptation processes and the particular characteristics of religious and medical knowledge transfer focusing on the perspective of Japanese institutional players and interest groups. Chinese sources and aspects of cross-cultural translation of Buddhist and medical paradigms from the Indic world did play an eminent role in this process and, naturally, form a prominent part of this study. The main focus, however, is on religious, cultural and scientific dynamics in Japan and outlining the narrative and institutional history of Buddhism in the country. The timeframe chosen reflects the history of Buddhism in Japan from its official inception in the sixth century CE and follows developments until what is usually referred to as the early modern period in Japan beginning with the seventeenth century when the house of military rulers from the Tokugawa family took control of the Japanese empire and changed the governmental seat from Kyoto to Edo (today's Tokyo). Various policies instigated by the Tokugawa shogun affected the realms of both religion and medical science. Foreign Christian missionaries and Japanese converts were banned, executed or imprisoned, ending a period of official engagement with knowledge about European Christian culture and scientific developments. Trade with European nations was restricted to a small group of Dutchmen – that in fact included other nationals – who, being predominantly of Calvinist leanings, were preferred to traders from Catholic nations by the shogunal government. The government also tried to address the perceived need to prevent colonization by European powers and avoid losing control over the hard-won union of provincial domains by introducing strict bureaucratization of what had previously been comparatively independent religious organizations and clerical landholdings. Some decades into the Tokugawa (or Edo) period (1600–1868), a growing network of academies enabled learning to take place outside of Buddhist temples. The seventeenth century witnessed the beginning of Neo-Confucian engagement with thinking about society, nature and the world of spirits. The activities of the learned resulted in new science communities that also included scholar-physicians. In most histories of Japan, 1600 is seen as the logical temporal boundary between the medieval and the modern worlds because of paradigmatic changes at the beginning of the Tokugawa period.[2] Traditional periodization is problematic however, because developments in the late nineteenth century with the radical adoption of a new medical system largely modeled on German medicine can cloud judgment of the earlier periods which may appear to be backward.

In this book, a survey of different sources – medical texts, Buddhist sutras, Chinese *materia medica* literature, narratives and legends – allows an assessment of knowledge about healing the physical body that was produced, circulated and negotiated during a time period spanning roughly from 500 to 1600. In the case studies, significant paradigm changes are outlined and contextualized. New ideas, as will be indicated throughout the five chapters on instances of Buddhism and medicine in Japan, were constantly developed and combined with old paradigms to create a plurality of forms. This development is not indicative of continuous progress towards one homogenous and superior form of religion or one universal form of medicine. The overall narrative of this book thus constitutes a history of religion and medicine in Japan. It provides an alternative to most historical writing, in which the master narrative insists on the idea of steady progress.[3]

The basic approach in the main part of the book is topical and comprises chapters on treating sight-related diseases, women's health, plant-based *materia medica* and medicinal gardens. There is also a chapter on equine medicine, bringing in veterinary knowledge in addition to ideas and practices from human medicine, botany and pharmacognosy. Additionally, the main part of the book occasionally follows a micro-historical approach and presents research on the history of specific Buddhist temples and individuals. These case studies serve as empirical examples of the complex developments in the field of Buddhist medicine. Buddhist medicine refers here to a set of ideas and practices about healing the physical bodies of humans and animals with the aim of providing a path to salvation and thus eradicating all ills in the world. In East Asia, Buddhist traditions have incorporated various references to healing in their textual corpus, as well as ritual activities that originated in India. Because of the beginnings of Buddhism in India, "Buddhist" combined with "medicine" often indicates, especially in the Chinese context, that a particular medical therapy or idea originates in the complex Indian medical tradition referred to as *āyurveda*, the "knowledge of [prolonging] life." It is particularly interesting that traces

---

2 I adapt, to some extent, Bowring and his seminal study of religions in Japan that follows this rationale (Bowring 2005).
3 See Bartholomew (1989) on the formation of science or Bowers (1970) on the history of Western medicine in Japan.

of āyurvedic elements can be found in medical compendia and other sources from Japan, an island empire where Indian Brahmanical doctors seem not to have ever set foot and thus could never have provided any direct training of physicians in Indian healing techniques, although there is clear evidence that Buddhist monks from India did visit Japan in early times.[4] Indian medicine in Japan remains relatively understudied. This book seeks to make a contribution to the subject.

Medicine and Religion in Japan

To assess the field of the study of medicine and religion in Japan, the works of various disciplines and studies need to be taken into account: history of medicine, philological studies of medical sources, cultural history of medicine, folk medicine, Buddhist folklore studies, biographical studies of historical figures, history of Buddhism, Buddhist studies, religious studies and, finally, works on Buddhism and medicine. Comparative studies in medicine and religion referring to Japan have also shaped the field.

Earlier studies in the history of medicine, usually conducted by scholars trained in biomedicine, often subscribe to an evolutionary model of the development of medicine from "demonic medicine" – practiced by people who still maintained a magico-holistic worldview – to modern Western biomedicine. This view hinders the interpretation of sources that treat both ritual and medical knowledge not as two separate categories but as one field of knowledge. It also disregards domestic cultural development in a given time period and, moreover, makes claims that can or should be questioned. Another problem is an often essentialist view of "Buddhism" as a religion that preaches disengagement from the world.

Works on the history of medicine from the perspective of modern science tend to take the position that European models and practices are superior to in-

---

[4] The best-known instance of an Indian who spent time in Japan was the Buddhist monk Bodhisena (704–760). Bodhisena came from his travels in China to Nara, Japan in 735 and is known to have officiated at the "eye-opening ceremony" of the great Buddha statue during the inauguration festivities of Tōdaiji Temple 東大寺, Nara in 752 (Rosenfield 1986, 22). The foundation legends of Japanese Buddhist temples as well as legends pertaining to particular Buddhist deities make references to Indian monks which may be fictitious, however, or quote from well-known Indian epic literature such as the *Mahābhārata* (Triplett 2001, 20; Triplett 2018, 83).

digenous ones and cast the latter aside as magic or superstition.[5] Physician and East Asian studies specialist Erhard Rosner's history of medicine in Japan, published by Brill in 1989 as part of a multi-volume "Handbook of Oriental Studies," is an interdisciplinary work bridging medicine and cultural history. Despite being just 135 pages long, including various glossaries, the handbook is valuable because it provides annotated bibliographies of works in Japanese, English, German and other languages. Rosner addresses the historiography of medicine in Japan as a question of *cultural* historiography and concentrates on the autonomous developments (*Eigenständigkeit*, Rosner 1989, 3) of Japanese medical history. He points out that most medical historians have focused on the Chinese core of the Sino-Japanese tradition that evolved in several waves from the Asuka period (538–710) to the early modern period, neglecting the specifics of Japanese medicine (Rosner 1989, 1). Moreover, as the period of active reception of "Western" medicine during the nineteenth century is seen in many studies as representative of Japan's path to modernity, the evolution of Western-style medicine has been treated extensively. This is particularly the case in Japan itself where scholars began to research the history of medicine in Japan as early as the nineteenth century (Rosner 1989, 2). Rosner's handbook does not focus on religion but treats it as one factor among others. A second, more recently published German-language handbook on the history of traditional Japanese medicine also focuses on cultural developments and the accomplishments of individual physicians (Michel-Zaitsu 2017). A French-language volume on the history of medicine in Japan, edited by Pierre Huard et al., was published in 1974. Mieko Macé's monograph (2013) on doctors and medicine in Japan outlines the history of medicine in Japan from ancient times onward, with a focus on the Edo period, her field of expertise.

The twentieth-century scholars Fujikawa Yū 富士川游 (1865–1940) and Hattori Toshirō 服部敏良 (also: Toshiyoshi, 1906–1992) address the topic of religion in their now classic volumes of the history of medicine in Japan. Fujikawa's work includes his 1934 (revised edition 1978) summary of Japanese medical history in English which is a translation from his German book published by the Japanese Imperial Ministry of Education in 1911 (reprinted 1976). Fujikawa, who studied medicine in Jena, Germany, from 1889 to 1890, also wrote on Buddhist thought, as well as education and social matters. During the Meiji period (1868–1912),

---

[5] The above-mentioned study by Bowers (1970) emphasizes the superiority of European medicine, as does the quasi-official five-volume series on the history of medicine in premodern Japan, edited by the Japan Academy (Nihon gakushiin 1955–1964). The short volume by Tatsukawa (1979) on disease and healing in early modern Japan also includes references to an increasing disenchantment with the world.

medical science and practice taught by German scholars was especially influential in the formation of modern biomedicine in Japan. Throughout his life, Fujikawa collected medical sources from the diverse Japanese tradition to preserve them after the radical shift to European medicine. He was knowledgeable about Japanese medical and intellectual history but saw premodern Japanese medicine as a phase that needed to be concluded so that Japan could successfully modernize. The doctor and historian of medicine Hattori Toshirō shared this outlook to some extent. His history of medicine appeared in several volumes from the 1940s to the 70s. It covers the Nara period (710–794) to the Edo period (1945, 1955, 1964, 1971, 1978). Hattori highlighted the Indian and Chinese influences on the development of early Japanese medicine. In a special volume ([1968] 1982), he explored early Indian Buddhist sources to outline what he called "Śākyamuni's medicine" (*Shaka no igaku* 釈迦の医学). To date, his work has not been translated into any European language. A German translation, published in 1999, of Ishihara Akira's 石原明 (1924–1980) seminal book of 1959 relays important intellectual developments in the field of Japanese medicine. Although Ishihara narrates a story of steady progress, it is interesting that he is not partial to modern biomedicine. His lifelong work on East Asian medicine in a period of official neglect and even scorn led to the foundation of the Japanese Society for Oriental Medicine (Nihon tōyō igakkai 日本東洋医学会) that ultimately contributed to obtaining acceptance of what emerged as modern Sino-Japanese medicine (*kanpō* 漢方, Chinese-style therapies)[6]. Historian of medicine, Sakai Shizu published a comprehensive Japanese-language standard work on the history of medical healing in Japan (1982) but her work has also not been translated into any European language.[7] Sōda Hajime's 宗田一 (1921–1996) work is a standard reference for studying the history of *materia medica* in Japan (1981, 1993) but he also published a comprehensive and richly illustrated volume on the cultural history of medical healing in Japan ([1989] 2017).

Those interested in the history of Japanese medicine in the English language, therefore, still have to rely to a large extent on Fujikawa's work, which was published in the early twentieth century. However, Japan is mentioned in one of the chapters (Otsuka 1976) in the ground-breaking, but highly specialized, collected volume entitled *Asian Medical Systems: A Comparative Study*, edited by Charles Leslie (1976).

---

6 On the emergence of "Kampō" medicine, see Oberländer (1995), Shin (2016) and Michel-Zaitsu (2017, esp. 263–330).
7 Another relevant volume is an account of illness and medicine in history edited by Yamada and Kuriyama (1997). The volume includes contributions on medicine in China, Japan and Tibet and encourages a comparative perspective.

Text editions of major medical sources include the complete edition and translation into modern Japanese (1993–2012) of the thirty-volume tenth-century compilation of medical texts primarily from Sui and Tang-period China (sixth to tenth centuries), the *Essentials of Medicine* (*Ishinpō* 医心方, 982–984). The editor Maki Sachiko, a historian and literary author, also provides short introductions to the numerous sections of this compilation. Her introductions express an image of premodern medicine as proto-science and depict premodern Japanese as primitive, albeit in a well-meaning way. This somewhat evolutionist way of relating the history of medicine as the history of an increasing progression towards perfection is shared by other authors in the field.

The numerous studies on the Dutch School (*rangaku* 蘭学) of science, technology and medicine of the Edo period emphasize the school's impact on Japanese medicine but do not sufficiently explain the nature of the eclectic medical practices developed during that time period (e.g. Beukers et al. 1991). Studies on traditional Chinese-style medicine (*kanpō*) as practiced in Japan, in contrast, praise the virtues of traditional medicine, not as an alternative but sometimes as superior to Western models (e.g. Kosoto 1999). Seminal works on the history of medieval and early modern Japanese doctors and their medical sources include publications by historian Yakazu Dōmei 矢数道明 (1905–2002), a towering figure in research on traditional Chinese-style medicine in Japan. Social, scientific and anthropological studies with a focus on early modern or contemporary phenomena are less interested in this compartmentalization but often lack the historical perspective.[8]

Studies from a Buddhist perspective are doctrinal and about important Buddhist concepts, but usually omit the significant historical development around the nineteenth and twentieth centuries. Such works also tend to propagate Buddhist teachings, which makes them less helpful as historical sources. Some works on Japanese Buddhist medicine reveal apologetic tendencies when the author is both a physician and a Buddhist teacher such as in the case of Kawada Yōichi.[9] Such studies in Buddhist ethics focus on the ideals of "active compassion" (*jihi* 慈悲), caring for suffering beings and the social dimension of medical

---

[8] See e.g. Jannetta on epidemics in early modern Japan (1987), the works on contemporary Japan by medical anthropologist Margaret Lock (1980; Norbeck and Lock 1987), the anthropologist Emiko Ohnuki-Tierney (1984) and the volumes on health care by Margaret Powell and Masahira Anesaki (1990) and sociologist Sonoda Kyōichi (1988, 2010).

[9] See e.g. Kawada (1976, 2013) and the works by the physician Obinata Daijō 大日方大乗 (1877–1970) who travelled to Sri Lanka and visited ancient Buddhist sites in India before he entered the Sōtō Zen Buddhist order at the age of sixty (Nakanishi 2005). Obinata taught and published widely on Buddhism, hygiene, health and care in his later life (e.g. 1958, 1962, 1965 and 1966).

practice in Buddhism from a normative standpoint. Exceptions are Fukunaga Katsumi's *Bukkyō igaku jiten* (Dictionary of Buddhist medicine, 1990), which focuses almost exclusively on Indian Buddhism, and the work by the historian Nihonyanagi Kenji who investigates the use of ritual substances in Japanese Buddhist tradition (1994, 1996, 1997a).

Other Japanese works look at healing and therapies from ethnographical and folkloristic perspectives, which often focus on *materia medica* and the production of healing remedies in Japanese culture (e. g. Miura 1980). Studies on early ideas of healing and medicine base their findings on Buddhist legends (*setsuwa* 説話), especially those that report miracle healings, and examples from Heian-period (794–1185) court literature. Unique sources are the picture scrolls (*emakimono* 絵巻物) which sometimes display drastic images of the sick. Legends are equally fascinating to those scholars who research early descriptions of physical disorders and their treatment in the context of religious ideas and rituals. Views on impairment and disability[10] have also been researched, using Buddhist legends as the main sources. Looking at religious sources such as the myths and legends in search of early "scientific" models of medicine and the art of healing, researchers have carefully sifted through religious texts in order to find disease names and names of medicine ingredients.

In an anthology of short essays relating to sickness, Maki Sachiko, for example, invites her readers to understand the concerns of those living in ancient Japan (2000). Apart from the edition of the *Essentials of Medicine* (*Ishinpō*), Maki also published, in 1985, an edition of the Heian-period medical compilation *Classified Prescriptions of the Daidō Period* (*Daidō ruijuhō* 大同類聚方, 808) which reveals inter-religious struggles among the ruling elites of the era.

In 2013, Shinmura published a volume dedicated solely to the history of medical therapeutics (*iryō* 医療) in Japanese Buddhism from its inception until the twentieth century. The historian specializes in ancient and medieval Japanese medicine and has introduced his research in several book-length publications (1985, 2006). His volume on Buddhist medicine first presents thoughts on life-threatening disease and suffering in Japanese Buddhism, followed by

---

10 Current works in disability studies insist on distinguishing between impairment and disability and work with the following definitions: "Impairment is the functional limitation within the individual caused by physical, mental or sensory impairment"; "[d]isability is the loss or limitation of opportunities to take part in the normal life of the community on an equal level with others due to physical and social barriers" (Goodley [2011] 2017, 9). See also Waldschmidt (2017) who advocates an approach to impairment and disability that assumes that "impairments and disabilities [structure] culture(s) and at the same time are structured and lived through culture" (Waldschmidt 2017, 20). This approach informs later chapters in the present volume.

chapters on theories of the origin of disease and therapies, the interplay (*kōsaku* 交錯) of healing by prayer (*kiryō* 祈療) and healing by medical means, care and birth in the Pure Land (*ōjō* 往生), caring for the ruler, epidemics and popular cults of itinerant ascetics, imagery of illness found in illustrated scrolls, views on sickness by influential monks of the Kamakura period (1185–1333); monastic pharmaceutics, monastic doctors and the medical thinking of two famous Zen monks. All aspects are considered in the context of their historical evolution in chronological order, ending with the Meiji period. From the Meiji period onward, Buddhist priests had the role of providing the humanitarian background and the fundraising facilities for establishing hospitals whereas the medical care of these hospitals was in the hands of medical experts. Shinmura closes his historical survey by stating that the division (*bunka* 分化) between medicine and Buddhism accelerated the modernization of Japan (2013, 289).

Shinmura's recounting of medical views by famous monks who are still deeply revered by many of his audience to this day as founders of Buddhist schools, follows rather traditional lines of historiography. However, as a specialist of the literary and pictorial heritage of early and medieval Japan, he not only relates the ideas held by individuals regarded as important but also provides a cultural history of Buddhism and medicine using a plethora of different sources in an illuminating way. The volume is rather concise but is a mine of information for those who want to study the topic in more detail and perhaps unpack some of the issues addressed by Shinmura, such as images giving vivid impressions of day-to-day Buddhist medical care in Japan, or the prevailing activities of yin-yang diviners and female mediums (*miko* 神子) and their rejection by Buddhist monks such as Rennyo 蓮如 (1415–1499) (2013, 191).

"Buddhist Medicine" as a Field

The use of the term *Bukkyō igaku* 仏教医学, literally "Buddhist medicine," by many modern Japanese authors including Fukunaga (1991) as mentioned above, suggests that there is a specific kind of medicine that is Buddhist as opposed to another kind of medicine. Since the term is not historical, we can surmise that the denotation of a medical system or certain ideas and practices as "Buddhist" is a conscious choice in order to contrast it with Western biomedicine. Using the term "Buddhist medicine" when looking at historical phenomena is not wrong when we mean to explore medical ideas and practices in the Buddhist monastic or communal framework. However, as with the term "Christian medicine," meaning the health care provided by Christian missionaries in many parts of the world, the term "Buddhist medicine" can be associated with imperialism, or at least there is a danger of this being the case. We will see in the chapters below that Chinese-style medicine was introduced to Japan at approximately the same time as Buddhism. This included medical lore from India, where Buddhism has its roots. As such, in Japanese publications on the *history* of Japan, "Buddhist medicine" primarily means non-Chinese-style medicine. In this book, both Buddhism and medicine are examined in their complex relationship, not only as "Buddhist medicine" in the narrower sense, but also as a cultural and social phenomenon, which could be termed "Buddhistic"[11].

Important works on sources in the Indian language Pāli include Sylvain Mazars' 2008 volume on Buddhism and traditional Indian medicine which contains mainly Indian and Pāli Buddhist sources with occasional reference to those of Chinese pilgrim monks who traveled to India and reported on the medical practices they observed. Kenneth Zysk's 1991 study addresses the role of Buddhist monastic medicine in ancient India and beyond. As Indian medicine was primarily developed in Buddhist monasteries, it can be considered the work of renunciant ascetics rather than that of Brahmans as was previously thought to be the case. In the sources available to him, Zysk observes a shift from "magico-religious to empirico-rational medicine," not least brought about by changes in the role of the physician and what he calls "heterodox" (non-Brahmanic) ascetics. These ascetics, i.e. *śramaṇas*, included Jains and Buddhists who not only engaged in healing, a pursuit regarded as ritually polluting, but also in philosophy and the rational observation of nature. For example, in an important passage of a Pāli text, the Buddha as the All-knowing corrects the claim that suffering was caused solely by previous acts by explaining that humankind's suffering has eight causes: (1–4) the three "humors" (*tridoṣa*) and their combination, (5) change of the seasons, (6) stress of unusual activities, (7) external agency and (8) previous acts. Zysk points out that this ennumeration of the eight causes of disease and suffering is central to classic Indian medical (āyurvedic) etiology (1991, 30), thereby illustrating the, as he terms it, empirical as opposed to magical, nature of medicine in Indian Buddhism.

Jñanrañjan Haldar, who published a short volume on references to medicine and hygiene in Pāli literature in 1992, also emphasizes the rational nature of health care in Buddhist India. His argument does not discuss the changing role of the physician but he comes to a similar conclusion to Zysk. As Haldar is concerned with outlining the emergence of public health, his interest lies in

---

[11] "Buddhistic" refers to cultural expressions that are associated with regions in which Buddhists are or were culturally dominant, rather than being specifically associated with the religion in the narrower sense.

governmental engagement for the people's health: When the ancient government started to support Buddhism, which advocated welfare and health care because of its stance of love and compassion, a wider concern for sanitation and hygiene developed (1992, 18–19). Haldar's presentation of the historical case is guided by an interest in evidences of civilization in progress even critiquing governments of the modern world: The famous account of the travels of the Chinese monk Yijing 義淨 (635–713)[12] to India shows, according to Haldar, that the level of public health maintenance in early India exceeded attempts by modern governments (1992, 53).[13]

In studies on the history of medicine in China, Indian-style medicine appears primarily as "Buddhist medicine." Indian (Buddhist) medical doctrines before the codification of āyurvedic texts must have varied much more widely than previously thought. Historian Pierce Salguero (2014) shows that the process of the "translation" of Indian medical texts and concepts was not only highly dynamic but also a major concern especially during the Tang period (618–907) in China, the period when the exchange of ideas, concepts and materials included the domains of the Korean peninsula, and the Japanese archipelago.

The theme of Buddhism and medicine in general was introduced to Western academia by the sinologist and Buddhologist Paul Demiéville (1894–1979). In his seminal 1937 article on "byō" 病, "sickness" in the French-language Buddhist encyclopedia Hōbōgirin, Demiéville outlines early activities of the imperial family with respect to mainstream Buddhist healing rituals. These activities included dedications of statues of a Buddha who is popularly called the Medicine Buddha,[14] and other Buddhist deities with prayer inscriptions for healing the illness of a family member. They also included recitations of chapters of specific sutras and compassionate works such as caring for lepers and establishing dispensaries. All were well documented in eulogies for the hegemonic rulers in early textual and material sources (cf. Demiéville 1937, 244–245, Demiéville/Tatz 1985, 52–53). This foundational contribution to the understanding of Buddhism, sickness and healing spans more than forty pages, and more than sixty in the reprint (1994). It was turned into a small booklet of just over a hundred pages in its English translation by Mark Tatz (1985). Paul Demiéville's encyclopedia entry clearly outlines the different Buddhist concepts in regard to sickness, illnesses, healing

---

[12] For a translation of Yijing's chapters on health care, see Kleine (2017).
[13] See also Kitagawa who provides a useful overview on Buddhist medical history with a focus on ancient Indian culture (1989).
[14] The "Medicine Buddha" is the Buddha Bhaiṣajyaguru meaning "Master of Medicines," referred to in Japan as Yakushi Nyorai 薬師如来.

and medicine but is quite brief on the historical implications and concrete policies of devotees, monastics and laypeople in Japan.

Buddhism and medicine in medieval China is discussed in a three-volume work edited by Catherine Despeux (2010a) in French that studies manuscripts in Chinese taken from the ancient trade centers in Central Asia such as Dunhuang and Turfan. The extensive volumes explore different topics that emerged after studying over four hundred medical texts from various collections in Europe and Asia. Medicine accounts for one percent of the manuscripts found in the Central Asian cave temples and more than half of the texts on medicine consist of medical writing in Buddhist literature. This portion may seem small but considering that most of these texts are the only extant ones from the eleventh century or before the caves were sealed, these manuscripts provide unique insights into the ideas and practices of medicine in conjunction with Buddhism. Among the texts is a version of the *Sutra on the Use of Medicinal Herbs for Healing Illness by the Thousand-eyes, Thousand-hands Avalokiteśvara* and another text praising the power of the Buddhist deity Avalokiteśvara as well as one copy of the *Sutra on Relieving Sores*.[15] Since these were all popular in Japan in the same period, the three volumes edited by Despeux are an important source for this study.[16]

Considering the number of book-length publications there is, overall, a surprising lack of English-language scholarship regarding medicinal practices in Mahāyāna and East Asian Buddhism. The scholarship that does exist consists of specialized studies on particular texts or individual figures. An often-cited work is Raoul Birnbaum's (1979) now classic study of texts and ritual practices connected to central Buddhist healing deities: The Medicine Buddha and two bodhisattvas, or Buddhas-to-be, who, as their names "King of Healing" and "Supreme Healer" indicate, also care for those who suffer from sickness.[17] The spe-

---

15 Sutras (Sk. *sūtra*, "thread," meaning "guideline"), for which the Chinese character 經 (Jp. *kyō*) for "scripture," "classic," etymologically also meaning "thread," is used, count as the original words of the Buddha and are thus authorized teachings. The three sutras mentioned are found in the Japanese Taishō-era (1868–1912) edition of Buddhist texts in Chinese as T(aishō shinshū daizōkyō no.) 1059, T 1060 and T 1325 respectively. The edition also contains numerous volumes with images, and the entire collection is found online available via the SAT Daizōkyō Text Database (21dzk.l.u-tokyo.ac.jp/SAT) and the CBETA Chinese Electronic Tripitaka Collection (cbeta.org). For the three sutras, see passage below starting on p. 44.
16 See also the volume on Dunhuang medical manuscript edited by Lo and Cullen (2005).
17 The two bodhisattvas are referred to in Japan as Yakuō bosatsu 藥王菩薩 and Yakujō bosatsu 藥上菩薩. They appear as two brothers in important Buddhist texts and seem to have enjoyed veneration in a variety of rituals. One of the most popular texts is a sutra dedicated solely to contemplation on the two bodhisattvas, the *Sutra on the Visualization of the Two Bodhisattvas,*

cialist in early medieval China and East Asian religious history Michel Strickmann (1942–1994) explored Buddhist and Daoist ideas and practices in the context of demonology and epidemics, spells, ensigillation, spirit possession and exorcism. His study, containing numerous references to Japan, was edited by Bernhard Faure and appeared posthumously in 2002 under the title *Chinese Medical Medicine*.

An anthology of multi-authored short translations into English of relevant texts from premodern Asia, including Japan, edited by Salguero (2017a) is expected to stimulate the field of study in the years to come. Andrew Edmund Goble's book-length study (2011) explores the various factors that influenced the way the Japanese acquired and adapted Chinese medical knowledge in the Kamakura period. It focuses on the influential Buddhist priest and physician, Kajiwara Shōzen 梶原性全 (or Jōkan 浄観, 1265–1337), who published two seminal works on medicine. Japanese scholars in the Kamakura period benefited especially from the flourishing trade and cultural-religious and scientific exchange with the mainland. Printed texts from Song-dynasty (960–1279) China supported scholars and medical practitioners such as Kajiwara Shōzen in developing their specific notions of treatments, therapies and formulae for their patients. The study of Japanese medicine is closely connected to China not only because many sources from China were adapted by Japanese physicians, scholars and clerics, but also because numerous classical Chinese texts have survived (in fragments) in Japanese compilations as will be shown below.

Chinese-style medicine as practiced in Japan has been contrasted with Buddhist healing because Chinese medical texts are viewed as being secular or at least non-religious and not ultimately aimed at leading humanity to a final goal of being relieved of suffering altogether. A closer look at the sources, however, reveals that this categorization oversimplifies the matter, as will be shown in the chapters below. Still, early Buddhist legends on karmic retribution were clearly used in proselytizing: Acute as well as chronic diseases would be healed miraculously by adhering to pious practice and worship of the bodhisattva Avalokiteśvara, usually referred to in Japan as Kannon,[18] and other Buddhist deities. Miraculous cures could be expected for all whose past deeds have resulted in physical suffering and pain if they followed the Buddhist teachings, the Dharma. Those born with bodies viewed in the sources to be clearly deficient – such as

---

King of Healing and Supreme Healer (*Kan Yakuō Yakujō nibosatsu-kyō* 観薬王薬上二菩薩経, T 1161), English translation by Birnbaum (1979, 115–148).

18 Depending on the text, Avalokiteśvara, probably meaning "the Lord who perceives the cries of the suffering beings," is rendered in Sino-Japanese as Kanjizai 観自在, Kanzeon 観世音 or Kannon 観音.

female bodies – could still attain buddhahood, thus showing the superiority of the Dharma. To have the power to ensure or bestow a fulfilling and successful life cycle gives, of course, great authority in a society. It is no wonder that the knowledge connected to this power was guarded and contested throughout the history of Japan (as elsewhere).

Outline of the Book

Tackling questions of continuity and change in regard to Japan requires careful consideration of Japanese polemic discourses on healing. As every medical system is a hybrid and those that pass on knowledge share a contested space, it will be necessary to reconsider categorical boundaries such as magic, science and religion by interpreting polemic discourses of the past. This will provide us with a clearer understanding of premodern Japanese worldviews, which can then be studied further.

The aim of this study is to provide a contribution to the comparative study of religions. Therefore, critical terms such as "medicine," "religion," "science," "magic," "reason," "knowledge," "ritual," "Buddhism," "healing" and "salvation" are discussed in the context of the history of ideas instigated by European thinkers to form the initial two chapters of this volume and are further mentioned in the context of Japan and East Asia throughout the book. Chapter 1 elaborates on the view of premodern European and non-European medicine and briefly sketches the evolution of the critical terms "religion," "science" and "magic" that we have to operate with in academic writing in English today. Modern perspectives on premodern medical thinking are by no means uniform. Neither is the image of Buddhism as one of the world's major religions. Chapter 2 examines the modern gaze on Asian Buddhism to familiarize the reader with some basic problems and pitfalls in the academic study of Buddhist traditions. This book does not seek to tell the complete story of Buddhism and medicine in Japan. Instead, it focuses on key aspects that must be explored in order to gain a comprehensive understanding of East Asian Buddhism and medicine. To this end, the alleged beginnings of the history of Buddhist healing rituals and medicine in Japan are addressed and Chinese systems of Buddhist and medical knowledge introduced, both with a certain focus on the esoteric Buddhist teachings that constitute the background to most of the ideas and practices. Esoteric, or tantric, Buddhism is a form of Buddhism based on a particular body of texts and stresses initiation into "secret" teachings and ritual practices to benefit the suffering beings. Cosmological ideas and views of the body from the Buddhist, Daoist and other indigenous traditions find mention in the case studies as do specific treatments and cures. Besides elaboration of the ritual and material dimension of religion, the narrative dimension is addressed with stories of miracle cures and Buddhist legends. Sources that contain religious combined with medical and pharmaceutical knowledge are highlighted and special cults of principal Buddhist deities are discussed in the context of these sources.

The exploration begins with a case study of the healing of sight-related diseases in Chapters 3 and 4. The eyes are an extremely sensitive and an especially valued human organ. In Buddhism, eyes also have a deep symbolic association with seeing the truth, and tales of the miraculous healing of blindness abound in collections of Buddhist tales in all of East Asia. To propagate and promote belief in the efficacy of the principal deity of a Buddhist temple has not only spiritual motives. A constant stream of pilgrims who seek to obtain the special benefit from their visit is the foundation of a healthy economy. The promotion of benefits was not always exclusively in the hands of the temple leaders. At least since the medieval period, the fame of particular blessings for the visually impaired attracted groups of semi-religious entertainers who also wanted to participate in the activity of promoting a particular Buddhist deity's miraculous powers and, in doing so, earn a living. The wide non-elitist spread of incantation texts was, as will be shown in Chapter 3, strongly connected with the development of the culture of blind itinerant ritualists and minstrels in medieval and early modern Japan. Chapter 4 explores medical sources that praise the surgical treatment of cataracts.

Chapter 5 introduces the topic of reproduction and birth, two "total social facts" (*faits sociaux totaux*, Marcel Mauss 1923/24, 179) and therefore good examples for the comparative study of culturally specific ideas and practices connected to the reproductive female body. Married female members of the Japanese aristocracy who were lay Buddhists often made considerable donations and acted as patrons and founders of temples. While married aristocratic women followed the ideal of bearing children, female Buddhist novices and ordained women, often belonging to the aristocracy themselves, were to abstain from sexual activity and reproduction according to the ordination rules. Infertility in the first group was viewed with disdain, while in the second group, not bearing children was the utmost expression of leading a virtuous life. Both groups were concerned with keeping their physical bodies healthy: the first in order to become mothers, the second in order to live as nuns. Focusing on the early medieval period, Chapter 5 examines various sources to illuminate the ways in which women were cared for and the kind of views and ideas that informed this care. Special attention is paid to relevant chapters of a tenth-century compilation of medicine, the aforementioned *Essentials of Medicine* (*Ishinpō*). The investigation of other sources such as Buddhist legends and doctrinal texts suggests that women were recommended to seek the transformation of their female bodies into male bodies in order to reach ultimate healing in terms of salvation. In lay circles, however, the Buddhist divinities and other powerful deities were worshipped to ensure this-worldly healing in terms of successful procreation and continuation of the family line.

A significant portion of religious and medical knowledge production and circulation is connected to *materia medica* as ingredients for medicines and as substances used in rituals. Chapter 6 focuses on the use of plant-based medicines and the harvesting and cultivation of medicinal herbs in Japan. It explores the contribution that female Buddhist patrons made to medical and pharmaceutical culture. While Buddhists in Japan were well aware of the origin of their religion in India and knew about the vows to keep the "four supports" for leading the liberated life of a renunciant, Buddhist activities in Japan included trading and producing rare and valuable *materia medica*. A monk or nun would officially vow to rely on wearing discarded rags, on alms food, on dwelling under a tree and, lastly, on putrid medicine – often interpreted as consisting of fermented bovine urine or discarded medicine (May 1967). Vowing to rely on the Four Supports (Jp. *shie* 四依) was to ensure that one would lead an austere life of non-attachment in order to focus on the Dharma without distraction.[19] However, as the short quote from an ordination text at the beginning of this introduction shows, the Buddha is said to have allowed the Five Medicines (Jp. *goyaku* 五薬), here, clarified butter, oil, fresh butter, honey and raw sugar – to keep the community of monks and nuns in good health. Unlike putrid urine, the five are all appealing types of food. The ordination texts contain numerous passages explaining which kinds of foodstuffs were permissible for healing and nourishment in different circumstances, expanding on the Five Medicines. While the extant ordination texts provide a unique window onto ancient Indian *materia medica* and health care,[20] Chapter 6 provides an insight into the rich pharmaceutical culture that developed around Buddhist institutions in Japan. The chapter explores various sources on the use of plant-based medicines, among them an enigmatic thirteenth-century manuscript scroll.

Chapter 7 looks at the same manuscript scroll in the context of veterinarian medicine in Japan. Ritual healing and medical therapies were not limited to humans but also included domestic animals such as the horse. The chapter also examines various other manuscripts on equine medicine from early modern Japan. These sources can be considered as media that connect common and se-

---

19 Cf. Yamagiwa (2001) who analyzes passages with the Four Supports in the vinaya texts.
20 For more on medicines in an Indian Buddhist text with ordination rules, see Fiordalis (2017).

cret knowledge of healing. The chapter establishes that charismatic Buddhist monks and monastic institutions were interested in the care of domestic animals. It also finds that individuals in the Japanese military who were trained in equine medicine were surprisingly knowledgeable about ritual and magical techniques.

The final chapter summarizes the discussion from the first two chapters and outlines the findings of the topical survey.

1 Buddhism, Medicine and Magic: The Boundary Problem

If religion and medicine are deemed to be two discrete social domains then "Buddhism" may be regarded as a religion, formed in India by Siddhartha Gautama ("the Buddha"), that is defined by the engagement of various social actors with a set of ideas and practices. Buddhism as a religion proposes a path to end suffering and expresses a concern with sickness as suffering in a variety of ways, while the Buddha is regarded as the Supreme Physician.

Buddhism has diversified considerably in terms of its doctrinal, ritual, institutional, social and material expressions. The diverse traditions of Buddhism in Asia all go back to a common root in northern India.[21] They grew from a religious order of the disciples of a master, Siddhartha Gautama, who probably lived around 448–368 BCE and was revered as the Buddha Śākyamuni. Like many other ascetics of the fifth to fourth century BCE, Siddhartha Gautama chose a lifestyle of homelessness and sexual abstinence. The reason for the wide range of teachings, exercises and rituals within Buddhism can be traced to his encouragements to continually reflect on his ideas and teachings and formulate them anew or differently. The monastic rules of the order, however, were supposed to remain unchanged and regulate community life within the order itself and with the surrounding laypeople who provided the religious with food and all other objects regarded as necessary for their livelihood, including medicines. While the traditionally itinerant lifestyle of Buddhist monastics was largely abandoned, the lives of Buddhist monks and nuns were, and are still, shaped by the rituals of an itinerant lifestyle.

It is assumed that sedentary monastic communities, especially for the elderly or infirm, existed already in ancient times in India. The history of Buddhism has been molded by the establishment of magnificent religious structures and monastery grounds, funded for the most part by laypeople from the elite. At the same time, the tradition of solitary seclusion in the wilderness has always played a role, for example when monasteries in urban settlements were razed in times of war or persecution and when the religious order was in danger of being eradicated.

Early collections of the monastic rules and codes (*vinaya*) have stayed legally binding since the fourth century BCE and even form the foundation for ordination in the present-day orders of the branch of Buddhism called the "Great Ve-

---

[21] The following passages have been in part adapted from Triplett (2016).

hicle" (Mahāyāna). The Mahāyāna branch of Buddhism gradually emerged about four hundred years after the passing of the Buddha and by the sixth century CE, Mahāyāna texts expressed views using self-assertive, if not polemic, language when referring to traditions that uphold the older ideals of monastics who strive to live the virtuous life of a "noble one" (Sk. *arhat*). The new ideal was a practitioner who used different skills to guide all living beings to liberation. The bodhisattva as a future buddha takes center stage in Buddhist devotional practice. Texts from the early Buddhist traditions were brought to Japan via Chinese translations of sources mostly in Sanskrit and served as reference literature for the Buddhist communities, the sangha. While the vinaya rules prohibit monks and nuns from supporting their lives with healing skills or selling medicinal drugs, the Mahāyāna texts praise the bodhisattva as a physician and healer of all beings. The Buddha and the bodhisattvas are presented in these texts as applying medical therapies and medicines.

The study of medicine (Sk. *cikitsā-vidyā*) as one of the Five Fields of Learning (Sk. *pañca-vidyā*) was part of the curriculum at the great monastery of Nālandā, a Mahāyāna Buddhist institution of higher learning, much like a university, in ancient India. Non-Buddhist learning was supposed to provide the monks and nuns with skills to defend the Dharma and, in the case of medicine and the arts and crafts (Sk. *śilpakarma-sthāna-vidyā*), enable them to help others.[22] The institution, which trained generations of Buddhists from all over the Buddhist world, flourished from about the fifth century until it was destroyed by troops of the Muslim Mamluk dynasty around 1200. However, medicinal knowledge was by no means limited to adherents of Mahāyāna Buddhist thought and practices. The vinayas that form the earliest stratum of authoritative texts provide a wealth of references on medical issues including hygiene concerns. Since the Dharmagupta vinaya, the so-called *Four-Part Vinaya*,[23] became the principal source of authority in early Japan, monastic rules regarding health and care of the sick are of importance for the study of Japanese Buddhism and medicine although the strict adherence to ordination and the precepts is a contested issue in the history of Japanese Buddhism. While the tradition of full monastic ordination was introduced in Japan by the Chinese monk Jianzhen 鑑真 (Jp. Ganjin, 688 – 763) and passed on to Japanese vinaya masters, the monk Saichō 最澄 (767 –

---

[22] See Dutt's classic study on the cultural impact of the Buddhist centers of learning on Indian culture, especially the chapter "From Faith to Knowledge"; on the *vidyā* in the context of Indian Buddhist learning, see Dutt ([1961] 1988, 323).
[23] *Four-Part Vinaya* is the translation of the Chinese title of the vinaya: *Shifen-lü* (Jp. *Shibun-ritsu*) 四分律, T 1428, trans. Buddhayaśas (408 – 413) and Zhu Fonian 竺佛念 (412 – 413). At least five more Sanskrit vinayas were translated into Chinese in the medieval period.

822) abandoned it by introducing separate ordination rules, in fact establishing the Tendai 天台 school modeled on a leading Buddhist school Saichō encountered during his stay in China. He replaced the *Four-Part Vinaya* ordination with a procedure based on precepts for lay Buddhists in order to more adequately reflect Mahāyāna principles. The revised procedure eventually culminated in the idea of a "unified precept" transcending all dualistic distinctions and *confirming* one's salvation or buddhahood (*jōbutsu* 成仏) (Bodiford 2005, 185–187) instead of declaring it a goal in a future life. This revision had wide implications in Buddhist Japan not least because the boundaries between lay and monastic communities were redefined.

Buddhism spread through the activities of laypeople, such as merchant families travelling along the Silk Road, and monastics. The first written editions of the monastic rules, teachings as guidelines (Sk. *sūtra*) and philosophical treatises (Sk. *abidharma*) are believed to be from the first century BCE. By the beginning of the Common Era, Buddhism had developed into a mass movement. The establishment of institutions such as monasteries and hermitages, devout laypeople's households and Buddhist kingdoms all took place at different times and in different regions of South, Central, Southeast and East Asia.

Buddhism has been marked by both growth and decline in different regions and at different times. In India, where Buddhism has its roots, it largely disappeared in the thirteenth century. Or, more accurately, the Buddha was regarded as one of many manifestations of the Hindu god Viṣṇu.[24] Java was briefly ruled by a Buddhist royal family who built one of the largest, still extant Buddhist monuments, the Borobudur Temple, in the eighth or ninth century. This temple was only discovered and made world famous in the nineteenth century as it had been lost in the jungle following a volcanic eruption and a shift in power in the late tenth or early eleventh century. In Tibet, Buddhism was short-lived at first. After it was officially adopted as the state religion in the eighth century, Buddhists were persecuted there a century later. Then, in the late tenth and early eleventh century, Indian monks disseminated the Buddha's teachings in the country during a period of revival of Buddhism.

Within Buddhism, knowledge has been passed on by different means. In addition to oral transmission and teaching within their own order, monks and nuns, and sometimes also pious laypeople, were encouraged to visit different

---

24 Buddhism only regained a notable footing in India in the twentieth century as a result of a number of movements. These included Dr. Bhimrao Ramji Ambedkar's (1891–1956) political activism for the dalits (so-called untouchables) and the development of Reform Buddhism; Buddhist migrants arriving in India from Tibet after the exodus in 1959; and countries such as Burma and Japan establishing temples in India in order to facilitate missionary activities.

masters from other orders and receive teachings from them, which mostly comprised certain texts or text cycles. Although many modern introductions to Buddhism talk of "schools" or "sects," signifying specific lineages of master and disciple, a comprehensive education and the study of several traditions in one's lifetime was regarded as the ideal.

There have been two broad approaches to dealing with the great range of teachings and formulations of the correct Buddhist path. In some cases, the Buddhist teachings were systematized, for example certain teachings were sorted into broad schemata, devised by individual monastics who tended to take an inclusivist approach. At the other extreme, Buddhists selected a single practice and teaching from those that were offered and rejected all others, indulging in exclusivism. The latter approach often involved accusations of heresy by both state and religious authorities. Authorities tend to clamp down on teachings that they see as non-conformist and that they fear threaten the social order by inciting unrest or rebellion.[25]

Another noteworthy factor is the acceptance of local deities in Buddhism as protectors of the new religion. Concepts like ancestor veneration in China also became an integral part of the ritual system of Buddhism. In general, the creative coalescence with aspects of a region's predominant religious, philosophical and aesthetic movements is characteristic of Asian Buddhism.

The traditions developed very differently and it is no wonder that until the eighteenth century, it had not occurred to European scholars that they were dealing with a single religion – which by virtue of Buddhism's sheer diversity and the self-conception of Buddhists could still be argued. Today, a strictly celibate Burmese monk and a typically married Japanese Buddhist priest could regard each other as members of the same religion, especially when both are wearing monastic robes, however, their lifestyles and expectations are very different. Regardless, they would both count themselves as a part of the Buddha Śākyamuni's "family."

To this day, the translation of texts from Indian or other Asian languages remains a great concern both for the intentional spreading (mission) of Buddhism and for modern academic research. It is often difficult to separate these two objectives. For instance, we have the case where hundreds of years ago a term like *bodhi* (awakening) had to be translated into Old Turkish or Chinese or Tibetan:

---

25 A compelling example is the reform movement the monk Hōnen 法然 (1133–1212) inspired in Japan. Hōnen preached the single practice of saying the name of Buddha Amitābha. He and some of his followers were exiled, others sentenced to death. Eventually the authorities pardoned the monk, and his movement later became recognized. For an indepth study on Hōnen and the question of Buddhist heresy, see Kleine (1996).

Should one work with a phonetic reproduction? Does one carry over the meaning into one's own language? Or find equivalents and orient one's self by prevalent philosophical concepts? These and similar problems were solved in various ways by the translation teams of the ancient Buddhist institutions as well as by individuals. This development has by no means come to a halt and is, as will be more evident in the remaining chapters, one of the major concerns of this book.

1.1 Mysteries of "Buddhism" and "Medicine" in Premodern Japan

After considering "Buddhism" and its presence in Asia, the social domain of "medicine" will be briefly outlined and followed by an example from the Japanese tradition to show the boundary problem. "Medicine" is shaped by social actors who are concerned with health, well-being, illness and disease, all of which are culturally specific. The current standardization of diseases and diagnoses by the World Health Organization is not only concerned with healing the physical bodies of humans and animals but also includes mental disorders. Social inclusion is also an important factor to consider in guaranteeing health and well-being. "Medicine" is usually understood to be the science of the healthy or sick organism, its diseases and the prevention and healing of those diseases. The organism may be human, animal or plant, and medicine is a set of ideas and practices produced and maintained as a social and cultural system.

Both religion, in this case Buddhism, and medicine are two different social domains or fields but share common ground in that similar, or even identical, ideas and practices may be found in both domains. Practices have persistently been performed in both domains over a long period of time. The question is whether this persistence and constancy derive from the common ground or "overlap." An overlap is an area where boundaries are normally regarded as clearly defined. In the statement that in undifferentiated societies the medicine man and the priest were one and the same person, boundaries appear blurred or even non-existent. To approach the subject of specifying the relationship between Buddhism and medicine in the history of Japan, we need to look at sources that may be associated with the perception of boundaries and an area of overlap.

Let us consider the following detail from a sixteenth-century Japanese manuscript entitled *Secret Transmission about the Final Mystery of the Eye* (*Meigan gokui hiden* 明眼極意秘伝). The labeled diagram in fig. 1 shows important theoretical aspects regarding the human eye.

The title above the diagram of the human eye reads "Diagram of the Correspondences to the Five Spheres." The outer "sphere" or ring is labeled "upper

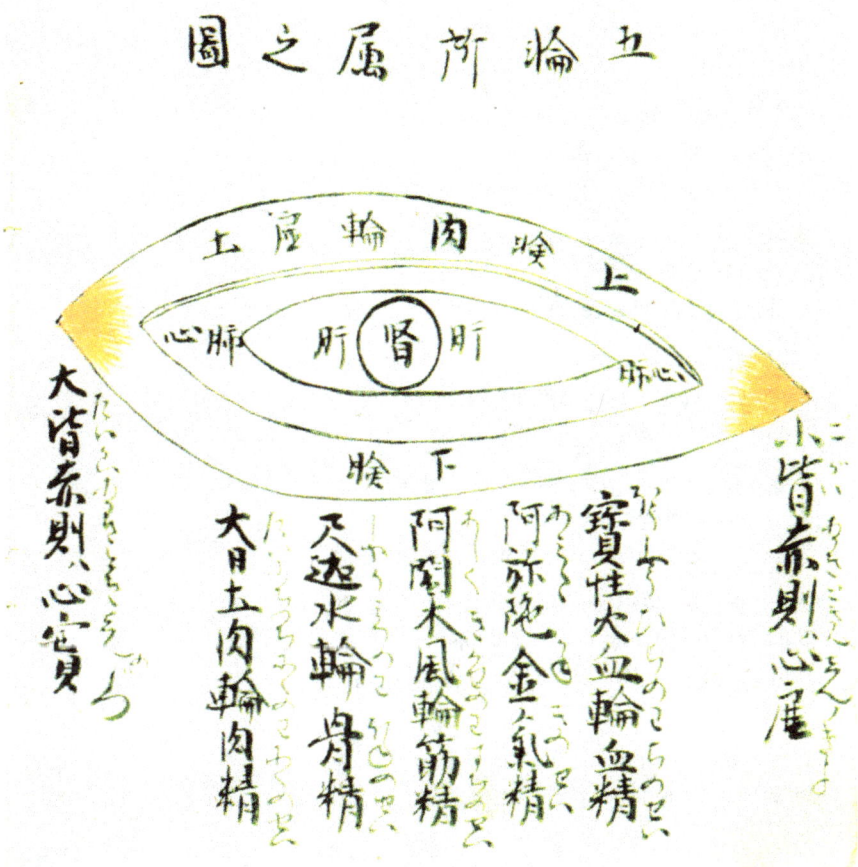

Fig. 1. Buddhistic eye theory, colored illustration from a manuscript on ophthalmology, *Secret Transmission about the Final Mystery of the Eye* (*Meigan gokui hiden*), 1575, Okusawa Collection. Source: Mishima et al. (2004, 100, fig. 6–7).

lid, flesh sphere, belongs to earth" and "lower lid." The next sphere is marked "heart, lung" and "lung, heart" respectively and finally "liver" on each side of what is recognizable of the iris or pupil. In the innermost sphere, we find the character for "kidneys." There are also seven lines of characters, one labeling the outer corner of the eye (canthus), another the inner canthus and five labels directly below the drawing of the eye. The writing is in Chinese characters with syllables in Japanese script on the right side of the characters denoting how they are read, which is a common way of rendering "Chinese" texts:

小眥赤則心虛 （こざいあかきごきんハしんのきよ）
Kozai akaki gokin wa shin no kyo
Redness of the outer canthus means depletion of the heart.

寶性大血輪血精 （ほうしやうたいちのわちのせい）
Hōshō taichi no wa chi no sei
Hōshō, large blood sphere, blood essence

阿弥陀金氣精 （あみたかねきのせい）
Amida kane ki no sei
Amida, metal, *ki* essence

阿閦木風輪筋精 （あしくきかぜのわすちのせい）
Ashuku ki kaze no wa suji no sei
Ashuku, wood and wind spheres, essence of the muscles/tendons

尺迦水輪骨精 （しやかみづのわほねのせい）
Shaka mizu no wa hone no sei
Shaka, water sphere, essence of the bones

大日土肉輪肉精 （たいにちちにくのわにくのせい）
Dainichi chi niku no wa niku no sei
Dainichi, earth, flesh sphere, flesh essence

大眥赤則心實 （たいさいあかきのっとろハこころのじつ）
Taizai akaki nottoro wa kokoro no jitsu
Redness of the inner canthus means repletion of the heart.

The reference to the meaning of the canthus' redness – depletion and repletion of the heart – is connected to a basic principle in Chinese-style medicine. In general, "depletion" and "repletion" refer to *qi* 氣, 気 (Jp. *ki*), which permeates the matter that composes everything that exists in the cosmos. It energizes every process including the processes in the human body. There is no single system of Chinese-style medicine, and traditions have changed over millennia and centuries. However, all known traditions refer to the idea that depletion in the circulation of *qi* leads to illness and shortening of life, and repletion to health and the extension of life.

The five lines in the middle mention five Buddhas, Hōshō (Ratnasaṃbhava), Amida (Amitābha), Ashuku (Akṣobhya), Shaka (Śākyamuni) and Dainichi (Mahāvairocana), four of whom correspond, according to the diagram, to the "five spheres" of the human eye such as upper and lower lid, the white of the eye or the pupil. Amitābha does not link to any sphere whereas Akṣobhya corresponds to two spheres. Standard sets of Five Buddhas (Jp. *gobutsu* 五仏, Sk.

pañca-buddha) are also found in the esoteric Buddhist tradition in Japan. The monk Kūkai 空海 (773–835) who is often referred to piously as Kōbō Daishi 弘法大師, spent some time in China and is accredited with introducing to Japan the practice of two *maṇḍala* (circular diagrams of deities' abodes, hereafter mandala) which include sets of the Five Buddhas. This practice became the defining characteristic of the Japanese Shingon esoteric Buddhist[26] tradition and Kūkai is seen as the school's founder. The two mandalas, the Diamond-World Mandala and the Womb-World Mandala,[27] both include four Buddhas who occupy the four cardinal directions, with the Buddha Mahāvairocana in the center of each of the diagrams. The Diamond-World Mandala boasts Ratnasaṃbhava, Amitābha, Akṣobhya and Amoghasiddhi (Fukūjōju 不空成就) whereas the four directions of the Womb-World Mandala are presided over by Hōdō 宝幢 (Ratnaketu), Kaifugeō 開敷華王 (Saṃkusumitarāja), Amitābha and Tenkuraion 天鼓雷音 (Divya-dundubhi-mega-nirghoṣa). The five Buddhas mentioned in the *Secret Transmission about the Final Mystery of the Eye* differ from both sets. The group mentioned in the text is closest to the Diamond-World Mandala set. The fact that Amoghasiddhi is replaced with Śākyamuni points to yet another important set of five Buddhas, the Five Wisdom Buddhas[28] of the Diamond World who represent the five wisdom qualities of the universal Buddha mind. In this set, either Amoghasiddhi or Śākyamuni appears, depending on the ritual text. It is important to remember that the mention of five Buddhas is a clear indication of a close affiliation with esoteric Buddhist practice.

In all, five spheres are listed as blood, wood, wind, water and flesh and as corresponding to the Buddhas. In addition, the Buddhas link to the following "essences" (*sei*, Ch. *jing* 精): blood, *ki* (Ch. *qi*), muscles, sinews or tendons (筋), bones and flesh. The labels in the drawing of the eye denote a correspondence to four of the five principal viscera (Ch. *zang* 臟) heart, liver, spleen, lungs and kidneys. The spleen is missing from the list of the five Zang Viscera in the Japanese source. While the viscera mentioned refer to solid organs they, together

---

26 Shingon esoteric Buddhist teachings in Japanese is *Shingon mikkyō* 真言密教 meaning "True words [= mantras] secret [Buddhist] teachings." Esoteric Buddhist scriptures and ritual implements were already popular decades before Kūkai's and Saichō's activities. For an account of esoteric Buddhism in eighth-century Japan, see Beghi (2011), Abe (1999); for healing rituals, see Winfield (2005). For an overview on Japanese esoteric Buddhism and the problems relating to the study of its many gods, see Faure (2016a, 1–19).
27 The Diamond-World Mandala (Sk. *Vajradhātu maṇḍala*) represents the wisdom of the Buddha Vairocana in its indestructible, invincible form whereas the Womb-World Mandala (Sk. *Garbhadhātu maṇḍala*) represents the source or matrix of such wisdom.
28 These are the five Buddhas as embodiments of five distinct types of cognition (*gochi nyorai* 五智如來).

with six hollow viscera (Ch. *fu* 腑) – the stomach, small and large intestines, gall bladder and urinary bladder and the so-called triple burner – form a paradigm of functionalities working in a variety of ways that go beyond the mere morphology and anatomy of the human body. Together they form the set of Zang and Fu Viscera. Chinese-style medicine also works with the cosmological concept of "five agents" (Ch. *wuxing* 五行), often referred to as the "five phases" or, somewhat misleadingly, as the "five elements." The Five Agents is a conceptual model used to explain observable processes. It describes a dynamic system of generating and overcoming that permeates the cosmos including the human or animal body. Metal, Wood, Water, Fire and Earth are the names of the agents that support or hinder each other, here referring to the interaction of human organs.

Four of the Five Agents – Metal, Wood, Water and Earth – appear in the diagram, however Wood is mentioned as a sphere and Fire is not listed at all. The diagram presents the somewhat unorthodox lists of correspondences in a highly abbreviated way. Both style and content of the five lines leads to the assumption that the students of the secret record were provided with phrases that were easy to remember – a common occurrence in such sources – and that they were deeply familiar with esoteric Buddhist thought.

To sum up, the Japanese diagram from the sixteenth-century text clearly combines Buddhist cosmological concepts with ideas and principles of Chinese-style medicine. Can we therefore categorize the source as Buddhist in nature or does it belong to the system of medicine? Does the term "Buddhist medicine" capture the meaning of the manuscript best because two systems are combined but medical concepts are the main focus of a source that seems to have been passed on within the framework of Buddhism? Also: Given its rather metaphysical appearance, how should we categorize Chinese-style medicine as presented in this example? A thorough contextualization and comparison with other similar sources would be a first step to approaching the problem of categorization.[29] By way of introduction to the problem at hand, it is instructive to compare the diagram to one from the Chinese tradition that circulated widely in Japan and can be said to be the model for the "Buddhistic" diagram described above. The model diagram is found in the fifteenth-century ophthalmological classic *Essential Subtleties on the Silver Sea* (Ch. *Yinhai jinwei* 銀海精微) – "silver sea" meaning the human eye (see fig. 2). It lists the five spheres with the following corresponding Agents – here referred to as "phases" by the translators – in a systematic and stringent manner:

---

[29] Further investigations on this ophthalmological source will follow in Chapter 4.

The inner and the outer canthi constitute the blood-sphere; it belongs to the heart [and the phase of] fire.
The black part of the eye constitutes the wind-sphere; it belongs to the liver [and the phase of] wood.
The pupil constitutes the water-sphere; it belongs to the kidney [and the phase of] water.
The white part of the eye constitutes the qi-sphere; it belongs to the lung [and the phase of] metal.
The upper and the lower lids constitute the flesh-sphere; they belong to the spleen [and the phase of] earth. (trans. Kovacs and Unschuld 1998, 133)[30]

The theory of the eye is firmly placed within the framework of Chinese-style medicine, without any reference to Buddhist teachings. The question that concerns us here is whether the theoretical model of correspondences of visible parts of the human eye to Five Agents (or phases) and to the Zang Viscera can be termed "scientific" in the sense of "non-religious" as opposed to the Japanese record, which posits the Agents and Viscera in direct relation with the Five Buddhas. Although medicine in premodern China is by no means coherent, the Chinese-style correlative system is, overall, a closed system that strictly operates with the processual causality of depletion and repletion. It may, however, not be "scientific" when considered from the modern gaze which regards "science" as something that must be proven by experiment. In addition, the reference to cosmologically active forces such as the Five Agents must appear more "religious" than "scientific" unless one wants to categorize them as something akin to natural laws. Even then, because the Five Agents are akin and not identical to natural laws, the Chinese correlative system may be termed "pseudo-scientific" or "proto-scientific" at most. In addition to the Chinese case, we must also consider the situation of Indian science, medicine and religion because principles of Indian thought were appropriated and reworked in China before they reached Japan via Buddhism.

Compared to the "Buddhistic" source from Japan, the passage of the *Essential Subtleties* is so systematic that it might as well be rendered as a table. Kovacs and Unschuld notice irregularities in the representation, however, when comparing it to another, much older ophthalmological work from India that in turn provided a model for the Chinese theory of the human eye. The final chapter (*uttaratantra*) of the *Compendium of Suśruta* (*Suśruta saṃhitā*) was composed in India between about 250 and 500 CE and brought to China. In translation, we read the passage on the theory of the human eye:

---

30 The *Essential Subtleties* also contains a short version of the Five Spheres correspondences for memorizing purposes, clearly pointing out the didactic character of the source.

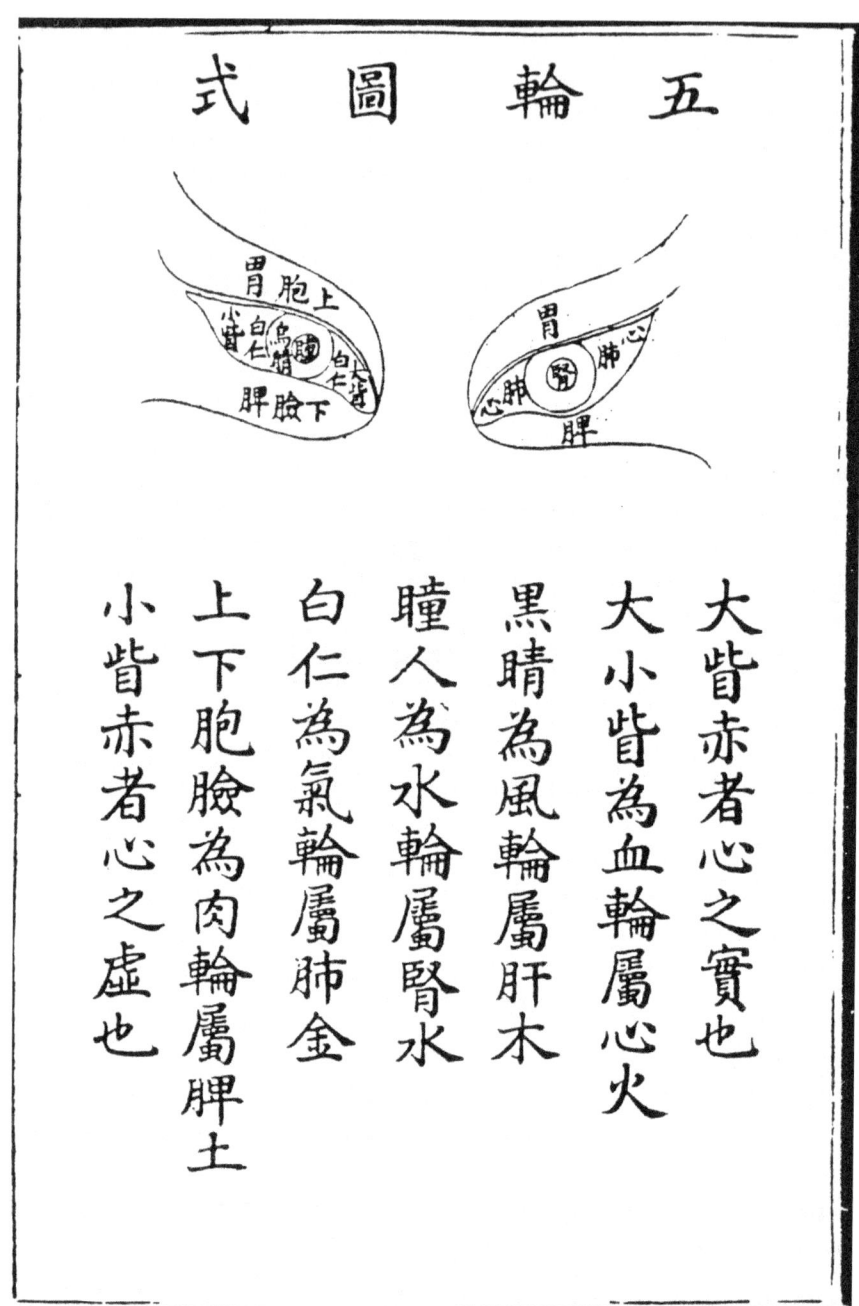

Fig. 2. "Diagram of the Five Spheres," from *Essential Subtleties on the Silver Sea* (*Yinhai jingwei*), compiled 14th/15th century in China; early modern print. Source: Kovacs and Unschuld (1998, 134).

The eye-ball is almost round in shape and resembles the teat of a cow. It is made up of all the (five) elements of which the universe is built up. The element of the 'solid' earth (Bhu) contributes to the formation of its muscles, the element of 'heat' (Agni or Tejas) is in the blood (that courses in its veins and arteries), 'the gaseous element' (Vayu) contributes to the formation of the black part (Iris, etc.) in which the pupil is situated, the fluid element (Jala) preponderates in the lucid (white) part. (Vitreous body) and the void (ethereal) Space (Akasha) is there to form lachrymal or the other ducts or sacs (Ashrumarga) through which the secretions are discharged. [...]

The Mandalas or sub-divisions or circles of the eye-ball, the Sandhis or Joints (parts where these sub-divisions meet with one another) and the Patalas (layers or coats) of the eye are respectively five, six and six in number. (trans. Bhishagratna [1907] 1916, 3:3–5)[31]

Without going deeper into the theory as such, we can clearly recognize that the five circles ("Mandalas") of the eyeball are referenced in the Japanese and Chinese sources described above. The *Compendium of Suśruta* (*Suśruta saṃhitā*) also mentions five elements that constitute the universe: earth, heat (fire), gas (wind), fluid (water) and space, all found in the eyeball of a human. When external or internal factors disturb the Five Elements, the development of symptoms and an outbreak of disease follow. Again, the reference to the notion of a macrocosm corresponding to a microcosm is "scientific" from an emic perspective but broadly speaking "non-scientific" from a position outside the system many centuries later.

The correspondence of the lower eyelid to the element earth and the great cosmic Buddha Mahāvairocana, the "Grand Resplendent One," must seem very strange indeed to most modern readers. The basic hermeneutical problem is that if we apply categories developed in a culture separated from the time when the *Secret Transmission about the Final Mystery of the Eye* was compiled in Japan, the source will – by the force of the European history of ideas – appear to be "religious," "superstitious" or plain nonsense. The question is whether a direct comparison with other premodern cultures is warranted and will yield a typological classification based on emic categories formed during a certain time period. Necessarily, this approach presupposes that premodern cultures display common features compared to modern cultures, and that they share similar attitudes, concepts and practices just by being located temporally in the past.[32]

---

31 *Suśruta saṃhitā*, Volume 6: *Uttara-tantra*, Chapter I – Diseases of the eye and its appendages, trans. Bhishagratna ([1907] 1916), vol. 3. For an annotated summary of the *Uttara-tantra*'s chapters on the eye, see Meulenbeld (1999, 1 A:300–308).
32 Thinkers reflecting on Shmuel Eisenstadt's Axial Age theory, not endorsed in the present book, arrange ancient cultures by their perceived level of ability to reflect on self-reflection

In a search for a possible blueprint of how to study ancient and medieval medicine in Japan, it is important to look at how compilations of medical texts from an "ancient civilization" have been approached by European scholars in the modern period. An interpretation of the famous compilation known as the *Corpus Hippocraticum* by an early English philologist, William Henry Samuel Jones (1876–1963) will be introduced because it shows prevalent debates informed by modern views on premodern medicine in an exemplary way. Jones was a fellow of St Catherine's College, Cambridge and is perhaps best known for his theory that malaria was responsible for the decline of both the Greek and the Roman empires.[33] A quote from the introduction to his Greek-English edition of the *Corpus Hippocraticum* will serve as a basis for learning about views on ancient Greek ideas about the human body, disease and the cosmos.[34] Of special interest is the terminology used by the English scholar to describe ancient polemical debates on the correct way of healing and practicing medicine.

1.2 Modern Views on Premodern Medicine

The term "medicine" derives from the Latin *ars medicina*, the "art of healing." A person who practices this art is the *medicus*, the physician or healer. The notion of healing as an *ars* (gr. *techné*) is significant in this context: The *medicus* requires not only special skills, techniques and specific knowledge but these must be combined with a particular gift or talent to render his skill an art. Looking at the history of medicine in regions strongly influenced by ideas and practices developed in the ancient Mediterranean world, it is important to examine the idea of the source of this gift or talent. The most influential work in this regard is the *Corpus Hippocraticum*. It is interesting to compare this compilation with works of Chinese and Japanese medicine not because of what is said about diseases and healing but because of the character of the compilation itself.

---

among other factors, such that, for example, ancient Greece and ancient China are counted as expressions of cultures of the Axial Age. Interestingly, Eisenstadt saw Japan as an exception; see esp. Eisenstadt (1996); see also Sonoda and Eisenstadt (1998).

33 See Jones and Withington (1909), and an earlier study on ancient Greece and Rome (Jones et al. 1907).

34 It is an attractive topic to compare systems of medicine, i.e. views of the body, disease, the role of the physician etc., in ancient Greece and China, and there are several English-language books that have engaged in such study: The historian of medicine Shigehisa Kuriyama has published a comparative study of Greek and Chinese medicine (Kuriyama 1998). Historians Geoffrey Lloyd and Nathan Sivin jointly wrote on early Greek and Chinese science comparing the two (2002); on medicine, see also Lloyd (1996).

Apparently, physicians or others involved in healing felt the need to compile vast treatises, comment on them and thereby enlarge the corpus over the years. The *Corpus* is best known in its sixteenth-century form, when it was printed and widely circulated in Europe. When it had lost its value as a fount of medical knowledge in the nineteenth century with the advent of modern medicine and its drastically different paradigms, Grecian and Latin scholars started editing and translating the seventy texts of the collection. We can now browse the *Corpus* online in various bilingual editions and discover the history of the medical ideas of the ancient Greeks. These ideas were also important to the physicians of the Roman Empire and those of Renaissance Europe.

We can also discover the nature of what I call the modern gaze on this complex collection of writings that were, for the most part, written in the fifth century BCE. The texts were written over a period of a hundred or even three hundred years and were repeatedly copied and translated into other languages. In his "General Introduction" to the Greek-English edition of the *Corpus*, William H. S. Jones acknowledges the knowledge of the ancient authors on typical courses of disease and their various ideas about treatment. He continues, saying:

> Beyond this he [the Greek] knew, and could know, nothing, and was compelled to fill up the blanks in his knowledge by having recourses to conjecture and hypothesis. In doing so he was obeying a human instinct which assures us that progress requires the use of stop-gaps where complete and accurate knowledge is unattainable, and that a working hypothesis, although wrong, is better than no hypothesis at all. System, an organized scheme, is of greater value than chaos. Yet however healthy such an instinct may be, it has added considerably to the difficulties of the historian in his attempts so to reconstruct the past as to make it intelligible to modern readers.
>
> Primitive man regards everything he cannot explain as the work of a god. To him the abnormal, the unusual, is divine. The uncharted region of mysterious phenomena is the peculiar realm of supernatural forces. 'It is the work of heaven' is a sufficient answer when the human intelligence can give no satisfactory explanation. (Jones [1923] 1945, ix–x).

Jones then shows that the Greeks generally viewed all phenomena as being equally divine and equally natural because they observed that there are rationally explainable causes of disease despite the fact that all phenomena do, at the same time, contain a mysterious and unexplained element. Jones regards the development of Greek philosophy as hindering the truly scientific progress of medicine because Greek philosophers sought, for the most part, to find the universality of all phenomena, which seemed to have led to a strictly monistic approach. In Jones' words: "[T]he desire to find this uniformity led to guesswork and to neglect of fact in the attempt to frame a comprehensive theory" (Jones 1945, xi). Basically, Jones is concerned only with those parts of the *Corpus* which "show signs of a great mind" since those parts have, in his opinion, a lasting value to doctors and scientists. He himself seems to greatly admire the treatises he selected as particularly meaningful and as "truly scientific, in the modern and strictest sense of the word." The treatises are scientific because they are devoid of religion, speculative philosophy and superstition. Those all neglect building a hypothesis on the basis of observable facts, and, by their very nature as belief systems, resist proof or revision by empirical tests and experiments (Jones 1945, xiv–xv; 6–7).

The *Corpus* itself contains two works that polemically attack positions that insist on a divine origin of disease: *On Sacred Disease* and *Ancient Medicine*. However, the *Corpus* overall is an extremely eclectic collection including numerous works that Jones characterizes as philosophic or as containing superstitious elements.[35] In early Greek medical writing, the concept of "religion" meaning pervasive divinity was not seen to be the opposite of "science" but the category of "magic." The Hippocratic text *Ancient Medicine* referred to above does not mention the Greek word for "magic" (*magea*) but the second polemical text of the *Corpus* entitled *On Sacred Disease* condemns those who use the explanation that the cause of cerebral seizures (epilepsy) is divine and can thus be treated with "magical" arts. The argument in a further passage from *On Sacred Disease* is that those who claim to possess special, magical powers have false and harmful views. The gods work in wonderful ways and could not possibly cause impurities in humans such as diseases because the gods are inherently pure and are concerned with purity and with protecting humanity. A truly religious person, however, looks to natural causes and human treatments of diseases including epilepsy. Interestingly, the author of the text does not deny the power of magical arts but merely denies them being divine. This text was well known in early modern Europe and was commented on variously during the phase of intense study of the Hippocratic texts in the nineteenth and early twentieth centuries (cf. Jones 1945, 129–135).

Schiefsky comments extensively on the Hippocratic *Ancient Medicine* in his 2005 study and points out that the author – whether or not he was the historical Hippocrates – and his opponent share more common ground than other modern commentators such as Geoffrey Lloyd[36] have supposed. What the author of *Ancient Medicine* expresses is not skepticism towards the study of the stars as such, i. e. the "knowability of 'things in the sky and under the earth', but the more restricted view that theories on such subjects are not empirically verifiable"

---

[35] The collection also varies greatly in terms of style. The only two common denominators are the use of the Ionic dialect and the connection to "medicine" in all parts of the *Corpus*.
[36] On theories on the identity of the attacked in this key text, see e.g. Lloyd (1991, 51–53).

(Schiefsky 2005, 119). The point of the argument is that medicine *is* empirically verifiable and careful observations must be the starting point to obtaining medical knowledge. The effect of magic was not denied in the Greek text but it is regarded as an *inappropriate* means in the art of medicine.

The modern gaze – represented by William S. H. Jones in 1923 in the example above – regards the evolution of human knowledge as directional from the primitive man, via the early civilized man, to the modern man. Jones does not speak of a development infused with meaning. However, evolution is depicted as progressing from one step to the next, a view much discussed in the early twentieth century of course. This evolution is a process of the gradual unlocking of the human potential, culminating in the victory of the *ratio* as evidenced in modern accomplishments such as the victory over some terrible diseases, which could be realized by turning medical discoveries into effective treatments of these diseases. The final aim of this evolution is attainment of accuracy and completeness of scientific knowledge. Whether Jones truly envisions such a perfected state or whether the "Faustian" striving to reach it is human destiny remains unclear. A certain teleological view shines through in his statement that when scientific knowledge is unattainable, humans tend to fill the "stop-gaps," sometimes with non-scientific, i.e. magical, superstitious, religious or philosophical explanations. This image suggests that there is a state of completeness in knowledge without any gaps which amounts to the same as omniscience or reaching a state of something like "total knowledge." It is akin to the successful and completed search for the universal law or primordial principle (*logos*), the *Weltgesetz*. Knowledge of such a law itself does not say anything about its application, however. Still, the person who has access to the universal law and is empowered to apply it may exert considerable power. He or she would be the ideal typical universal ruler. We will return to this below in the context of the idea of knowledge and power in Buddhist nations.

Although Jones' image seems to be in line with Plato's metaphysical ideal of perfect knowledge as espoused in *Ideas*, Jones clearly supports the approach of studying phenomena and "facts," just as the writer of *Ancient Medicine* in the Hippocratic *Corpus* prefers to reach an approximation of truth which is the opposite of philosophical "postulates" (*hypotheses*)[37] or improvable axioms (Jones 1945, 8). "Total knowledge," as outlined above, therefore, does not equal perfect knowledge.

Another interesting point in Jones' introduction to his translation is his idea of the human instinct. Humans tend to, instinctively, and therefore by nature,

---

[37] These are not hypotheses in the modern sense but unfounded speculations.

explain the world as if guided by an inner force. Civilization and progress tame humans so that the explanation increasingly found by observing facts and experiments reflects the "actual" processes and laws of nature and life. In the true positivistic fashion of his day, Jones strives with his translation of the Hippocratic *Corpus* to reconstruct the past in a scientific way so as to provide the modern reader with an accurate picture of the ancient medical beliefs and practices. He also intends to give access to several proto-scientific treatises that he greatly admires because of their particular value or pioneering quality for the evolution of modern biomedicine. His reconstruction, therefore, is actually a sorting process of the *Corpus* that he regards as a thoroughgoing "medley" (Jones 1945, xxviii) as it probably was the remains of the ancient library of the medical school in Cos, into scientific parts and elements of what could be called quackery.

As a philologist, Jones criticizes those editors and translators who focused too much on the medical content of the Hippocratic texts for neglecting to resolve the textual difficulties (Jones 1945, § 13, lxv–lxix). He himself attempts to reconstruct the past in order to understand older medical systems as well as brilliant individual minds. Medical annotations are not his main focus but he does point out how carefully the ancient Greeks observed important symptoms that seemed to have been passed over for many centuries in Northern Europe until the eighteenth century and the advent of modern medicine. He points to an accurate description of the so-called Cheyne-Stokes respiration in the Hippocratic description of a mumps epidemic (Jones 1945, lx–lxi). Selected parts of the *Corpus* are thus admired and praised because they speak of astonishing feats in the discovery of scientific truths by the ancient people, e.g. the ancient Greeks already knew that a particular respiration pattern indicates a specific disease. Jones has a tendency to explain certain observations of the ancient Greeks as being the result of natural observation in the absence of real knowledge. For example, he comments on the complex theory or theories of the humors:

> The doctrine of the humors probably had its origin in superficial deductions from obvious facts of physiology, but it was strongly colored by philosophic speculation, in particular by the doctrine of opposites. [...] Even the most superficial observer must notice (a) that the animal body requires air, fluid, and solid food; (b) that too great heat and cold are fatal to life, and that very many diseases are attended by fever; (c) that fluid is a necessary factor in digestion; [...] (d) that blood is in a peculiar way connected with life and health. (Jones 1945, xlvi)

A tendency to decide the origin of errors made by ancient people, in this case, the construction of a medical system based on "humors," is also part of the modern gaze.

A final point of interest in Jones' deliberations is his treatment of history in terms of a series of "great men." He searches the available sources for expressions of these alleged or actual geniuses. These expressions, when found and canonized, will eventually amount to total knowledge. This view naturally excludes other voices. Herbert Spencer's writings on history and social evolution had a revisionary effect on the idea of great men as sole movers in history: Society and social factors form these great men, so research has to focus on social factors. Karl Marx with his focus on the struggle of the classes as the prime dynamic force for historical development, and the *Année Sociologique* school in France shifted the center of attention to social forces, away from the individual. For our discussion, it is important to note, however, that the great man theory has deeply informed history writing despite Spencer's and others' work around the turn of the nineteenth century and the first decades after.

Since the extraordinary feats of a great man need a backdrop so as to make him shine more brilliantly, the activities and character of a lesser man are used as a motif in writing in primary and secondary sources. A good example is *Ancient Medicine* with its polemic stance against the trend to postulate "hypotheses." The ancient author mentions Empedocles (ca. 495–435 BCE) who wrote on natural science (*physis*). The ancient author claims that "[All] that philosophers or physicians have said or written on natural science no more pertains to medicine than to painting" (trans. Jones 1945, 53). Empedocles then receives a not very flattering description from Jones:

> Empedocles, who flourished somewhat earlier than Philolaus, was a 'medicine-man' rather than a physician, though he is called by Galen the founder of the Italian school of medicine.[...] The medical side of his teaching was partly magic and quackery. (Jones 1945, xii)

Jones' ideas tie in nicely with the colonial politics of the time of his writings although he himself does not seem to be prejudiced. The colonial gaze regarded non-European nations and ethnic groups as being in need of civilization so that they, too, could enjoy the benefits of, for example, progress in scientific medicine. The modern gaze cannot but perceive healing and ritual activity as either science or "merely" faith-based, and faith or belief systems equally dichotomously as either religion or magic. Medical healing is either scientific or quackery. As these concepts have a long history in modern Western thought, they form a powerful intellectual legacy within the comparative study of religions, not only in the study of ancient Greek medicine but also in the study of non-European societies in the age of colonialism.

While in Japanese history, lineages of exalted men are significant to the self-understanding of both Buddhist and medical traditions, the sources can also tell us about the wider networks of social actors in religion and medicine as fields of social interaction, and much of this book will be devoted to other voices beside or among those belonging – or ascribed – to charismatic monastic physicians and other "great men."

1.3 Terms and Concepts for a Survey of Buddhism and Medicine

Intellectual debates about the validity of these categories are clearly embedded in the social, economic and political circumstances of their time. In other words, because of the historicity of analytical categories, methods and theories can be said to be fleeting and highly unreliable tools. Is it then at all possible to make objective statements, as Max Weber claims it is, using methods developed in a given context? How do we deal with the three terms or concepts that appear in interpretations of premodern, non-European healing systems: magic, religion and science?

A direct comparison of "magic" and "science" is misleading as "magic" will always be regarded as "false science" given its different perception of similarity and the erroneous idea of manipulation by homeopathic transmission, as the classicist and social anthropologist James George Frazer (1854–1938)[38] suggests.[39] The result will, in principal, be similar to Edward Evan Evans-Pritchard's (1902–1973) assessment of the Zande healing system.[40] Current interest in "tradi-

---

38 The second edition (1900) and subsequent editions of Frazer's multi-volume work *The Golden Bough* has the subtitle "A Study in Magic and Religion." Trained in classical studies and archaeology, Frazer goes to great pains to divide magical practices found in textual sources into various subcategories. For example, according to Frazer, magicians work with "homeopathic or imitative magic" (sympathetic magic) when they follow the principle of similarity. Frazer's evolutionary scheme puts magic at the beginning, followed by religion, with overlapping states of "fusion or confusion" of the two, and culminating in science. He considers magic to be mistaken which is problematic because his view of truth is, of course, part of his own frame of reference, which is informed by particular linguistic, social and cultural propositions.
39 See below p. 124.
40 In his influential *Witchcraft, Oracles and Magic Among the Azande* (1937) that Evans-Pritchard wrote ten years after his twenty-month stay among the Azande, a Southern Sudanese ethnic group, he consciously tries to describe "the facts in such a way that the interpretations emerge as part of the description" ([1937] 1950, 5) thereby highlighting the role of the researcher and active participant observer. To Evans-Pritchard, the researcher's rationality and the rationality of the Azande are comparative. However, the relativity is not absolute; the two systems can be principally graded as superior or inferior when proper evidence is found, and he found the Zande (singular of Azande) healing system wanting.

tional" or magic healing systems aims at selecting the "drugs" from the "medicines" – *materia medica* that have a verifiable therapeutic value. Ancient collections of Chinese-style medicine are, for example, examined for useful formulae to produce new and effective medicines. A famous example is the anti-malarial artemisinin (*qinghaosu* 青蒿素) discovered by Tu Youyou 屠呦呦 who received the Lasker Award in 2011 and the Nobel Prize in 2015 for her discovery.

The healing system of ancient literary cultures such as the Egyptian's has been studied for over a century, and one of the results of *earlier* Egyptological studies is the separate cataloging of text passages into the categories of "medicine" in terms of modern medical science and "magic" although these passages always appear or are combined in one single text.[41] We will encounter the boundary problem with regard to "magic" and "science" in medical texts in Japan briefly outlined at the beginning of this chapter in more detail in the following chapters.

How do we identify a healing system as "magical"? Do we actually need to differentiate between magical and scientific elements in the sources we study? According to Stanley Jeyaraja Tamibah who worked on Buddhist rituals and wrote an influential theoretical work on magic, science, religion and the scope of rationality (1990), we are able to differentiate clearly: If we find the use of persuasive analogies in our text or interview script we have a case of "magic." The efficacy of rituals including "magical" (healing) may lie in the performativity of the ritual itself. As Tambiah has pointed out, the fulfillment of the expectations of the ritualists and those for whom the ritual is performed is the adequate performance of the ritual, not particularly the achievement of the objective, for example a long-expected downpour. According to this view, it is inadequate to judge a ritual as empirically false or ineffective.

As to European history, Brian Vickers, a specialist of English literature and history, emphasizes that occult practices and science should be regarded as two different thought systems, or "mentalities" (1984). This allows for a correction of the erroneous or misleading view that magical and hermetical ideas were transformed by Renaissance personalities such as John Dee (1527–1608/9) into experimental science put forth by the scholar of Renaissance thought, Frances Yates and others (Vickers 1984, 6–7). There was also nothing particularly new in Renaissance magic, as Yates claims, since the Arabic and Hellenistic sources used had existed for many centuries before. Moreover, magic practiced as science in

---

[41] For a brief discussion and further relevant literature on the topic in ancient Egypt and Mesopotamia, see Töpfer (2014, 318n1); see also Zucconi (2007).

the context of the *prisca theologia*⁴² ideology was strongly contested by both the Catholic Church and the Protestants. It is a contestation of the beginnings of Christianity. Christian (religious) science, was ultimately victorious, not magic science or magic religion, Vickers claims. According to historian Keith Thomas, however, religion in Europe outlived its magical competitors and triumphed over magic, as he wrote in his study on popular beliefs in sixteenth- and seventeenth-century England ([1971] 1980). According to Thomas, it was *religion* that replaced magic – religion that recognized the authenticity of mechanical philosophy. Thomas fails to consider that the occult arts and the scientific natural philosophies coexisted and influenced each other for a long time during the period in question. He wants to see a clear-cut shift of paradigms, which do not seem to present themselves.

The study of paradigms – seen as universal frameworks – may be a way to tackle the problem of boundaries in global history. Nakayama Shigeru (1928–2014) applied the influential theoretical work of Thomas Kuhn (1922–1996) to Japanese history and developed original ideas based on Kuhn's assumption of a scientific revolution following a substantial paradigm shift (1975).⁴³ However, Nakayama's model did not go uncontested as the study of the history of chemistry in Japan by historian Togo Tsukahara (1993) shows. Tsukahara criticized Nakayama's approach in that "paradigms" as extremely broad conceptual frameworks cannot encompass local developments and are not adequate for the analysis of the intercultural encounters of the Western and Japanese sciences (1993, 10). The two scholars' discussion refers to the encounters in Japan beginning in the late sixteenth century, and since this period is at the very end of the timeline investigated in this book, it will only be alluded to here. The question of intercultural encounters and the incorporation of conceptual frameworks from one culture into another is highly informative for the topic of this book, however, since both Buddhism and Chinese-style medicine entered Japan and, as will be outlined in the following chapter, later became powerful "incorporation regimes" in premodern Japan.

---

42 *Prisca theologia* is a concept of the Renaissance thinker Marcilio Ficino (1433–1499) who claimed that such a theology was revealed in ancient times. It is contained in all religions although it has lost its priscine form.

43 For example, see his study of academic and scientific traditions in China, Japan and the West (Nakayama 1984), a translation of his 1974 Japanese-language work on the history of science. In 2013, a year before he died, Nakayama published a major volume on paradigms and the scientific revolution ending with digitalization and globalization. Nakayama and Kuhn knew each other personally, see Nakayama's recollections (2007).

Religion, science and magic as terms or concepts seem particularly unusable in light of the debates in the history of European intellectual history.[44] The question is whether we can perceive and make use of a system of terms in the study of premodern Japanese religions and health-related methods that resemble the binary (religion, medicine) or trinary (religion, medicine, magic) developed in Europe. And whether the application of such terms and concepts to the analysis of Japanese primary sources will actually yield an acceptable and satisfactory outcome.

In his substantial overview on "sickness" (*Byō*) in Buddhism in the *Hōbōgirin* encyclopedia, Demiéville introduces a trinary, a threefold classification of healing practices. He argues however that these three categories comprise overlapping fields, as, in his view, all of Buddhism is therapeutics. The three categories are: (1) "religious therapeutics" by which he means activities such as good works, (2) "magical therapeutics" such as the uttering of mantras and incantations and (3) "medical therapeutics proper" that include dietetics, pharmacy and surgery (1937, 227–228, Demiéville/Tatz 1985, 6). Demiéville states that this classification is taken from the Buddhist tradition itself.[45] He presents excerpts from the primary sources later in his article – these sources being his "faits" (facts). For instance, according to a passage in the *Udānavarga*,[46] the Buddha lists three kinds of therapeutics: (1) medications for treating "hot" and "cold" diseases caused by the four elements; (2) recitation of Buddhist texts

---

44 For those who are not familiar with the complex controversies and debates about magic and the various ways in which magic has been defined, the following two volumes are a good starting point: Although published nearly four decades ago, sociologist Hans G. Kippenberg's introduction to an anthology of important modern intellectual texts about magic in German translation (Kippenberg and Luchesi 1978) is still a useful overview on the controversy about understanding non-European thinking (Kippenberg 1978). Another anthology *Defining Magic: A Reader* contains an insightful introduction and a wider range of works. In it, study-of-religions scholars Bernd-Christian Otto and Michael Stausberg introduce and present historical sources from Plato to Theosophist Helena Blavatsky, foundational works of the academic debate on magic, and texts representing later debates in the twentieth and twenty-first centuries (Otto and Stausberg 2013).
45 "Quant aux pratiques médicales, elles se laissent répartir sous trois chefs, d'après une classification bouddhique qui répond bien aux faits" (Demiéville 1937, 227). Tatz translates this passage using a somewhat misleading formulation: "Healing practices may be distributed under three headings, following an eminently suitable buddhist [sic!] classification" (1985, 6).
46 He mentions the *Udānavarga*. However, the *Udānavarga* corresponds most closely to the *Sutra of the Appearance of Light* (*Shutsuyō-kyō* 出曜經) T 212 and not to T 211.11.579 a–b, the text referenced by Demiéville (1937, 257). The Chinese text T 211 is now in volume 4 (575b–609b) and is similar to the *Udānavarga*. It has the Chinese title *Faju piyu jing* 法句譬喻經 (*Sutra of Dharma Phrases and Parables*).

and spells to treat diseases caused by demons; (3) the worship of saints and deities, compassionate works and the destruction of the aggregates by insight (Demiéville 1937, 257; Demiéville/Tatz 1985, 82). He then continues to list examples of "religious," "magical" and "properly medical" treatments in Buddhist texts and traditions.

It is worth noting that in his article, Demiéville works with the three modern critical terms having deduced them from emic categories found in Buddhist texts. There is little doubt, however, that his readership would have been surprised by the fact that religion, magic and medicine (as science) formed one single system in ancient and medieval Buddhism with none of the conflicts that supposedly existed in the context of the European history of religion and medicine. Although Demiéville does not go into detail, he does address this issue, for instance, on the acceptance of magic in organized religion in China he writes:

> Ces deux textes avaient été condamnés par les autorités ch[inoises] [...], mais à titre d'apocryphes et non pas en tant que Charmes[47] médicaux; la magie curative était parfaitement admise par l'Eglise ch[inoise] et jamais elle ne fut, en tant que magie, exclue des collections canoniques. (Demiéville 1937, 260)

Demiéville addresses another instance of the relationship between magic, medicine and religion in the context of the early Japanese establishment of authoritative legal codes. The eighth-century legal code of the Taihō 大宝 era (701–704) and the later Yōrō 養老 era (717–724) legal code intended to regulate all aspects of society in the Japanese empire including the communities of monks and nuns. Whereas there were clear definitions of what constituted impermissible magical cures, monks and nuns were allowed to make particular curative spells and charms (Demiéville 1937, 260).[48] Here, it is supposed that the readers of Demiéville's article did not expect to find such a detailed differentiation of impermissible and permissible magical healing practices in ancient Japan.

Despite its relative age, the *Hōbōgirin* article in many ways remains unsurpassed in modern academia. Works by Japanese, French and German researchers are quoted by Demiéville, alongside the occasional annotation by Jean Filliozat (1906–1982), the physician and historian of ancient Indian medicine, so crucial for the understanding of passages in Buddhist texts and medical ideas and practices in China and Japan. Since the publication of *Byō* in 1937, relevant sources such as texts, Buddhist statuary, works of art and architecture have either been

---

[47] Capitalized nouns indicate the encyclopedia's project to create a French Buddhist set of technical terms.
[48] See also below p. 66.

discovered or examined in more detail. However, taking the position from within Buddhism and working with categories that appear to match European critical terms so neatly but *concurrently* admitting that they form one coherent system with its own orthodoxies and heterodoxies is extraordinary indeed. Most histories of medicine in Japan (and elsewhere) tend to outline a steady progression from magic to scientific medicine, neither paying much attention to emic categorical ideas and epistemologies used for making distinctions nor to the complex history of the critical terms magic, religion and science themselves. Demiéville does express judgmental views, however. For example, he openly expresses his disdain for the way the Chinese translated Indian terms pertaining to medicine and medical care.[49]

As the case of the Japanese secret record on the human eye at the beginning of the chapter shows, the boundaries of what we hold as two different social domains, "religion," here represented by "Buddhism," and "medicine," seem ambiguous. To those who circulated the record in premodern Japan, the concept of medical activity in a Buddhist framework may have been entirely obvious. A closer look at the social spheres of those who produced and circulated the knowledge, and those who benefited from it (or were excluded from its benefit) will reveal emic differentiations and conceptual frameworks used to distinguish between various approaches, that, summarized into types, will serve future comparative studies. In the next chapter, the survey continues with an outline of the historiography of Buddhism and medicine in premodern Japan to give context to the case studies that follow.

---

[49] See for instance Demiéville (1937, 245), Demiéville/Tatz (1985, 54); for a critical assessment of the article *Byō*, see Salguero (2015).

2 Operating with Buddhism

Buddhist practice is famously depicted in principal Buddhist texts as a method of healing the fundamental suffering of sentient beings caught in *saṃsāra*, the cycle of birth and death. The Buddha is presented as a supreme healer or "physician" and his Four Noble Truths are structured in accordance with ancient Indian medicinal practice: He (1) identifies the symptoms of suffering, (2) reveals the causes of suffering, (3) states that there is a way to heal the disease, and finally, (4) prescribes a therapy. In current medical terms, the Buddhist path follows the four medical principles of (1) diagnosis, (2) etiology, (3) recovery and (4) therapeutics (Kleine and Triplett 2012, 1–2).[50][51] To be healed in a metaphysical sense means to escape *saṃsāra* and attain ultimate salvation.

Buddhist canonical literature contains numerous references to diseases and medical treatments, also in connection to eligibility for receiving ordination as a monk or nun.[52] In addition to these passages in the scriptures, we also find related themes in Buddhist legends. Some sutras and especially tantric texts provide – in addition to the liturgy – detailed instructions for the preparation and administration of medicine within the context of rituals. In numerous Buddhist sutras, therefore, ritual instruction goes hand in hand with medical instruction.[53] This connection can be fairly weak as is the case in the *Sutra on Relieving Sores*.[54] This sutra has been widely known in East Asia since its translation from the Sanskrit by Yijing in Tang-dynasty China, in the late seventh century. It is very short and consists of a dialogue between the Buddha and his disciple Ānanda. A large retinue of monks is suffering from terrible sores, and Ānanda asks how these can be healed. The Buddha preaches that listening to the sutra will not only completely heal the sores but enable the monks and other practitioners to gain super-knowledge and supernatural powers. He then lists the kinds of sore that the sutra, which includes two mantras, will heal:

> [W]ind sores, heat sores, depression sores, triple sores, blood sores, abdominal sores, nasal sores, dental sores, tongue sores, eye sores, ear sores, head sores, limb sores, back sores,

---

50 An example of this can be found in the *Sutra on the Medical Simile as Told by the Buddha* (*Bussetsu iyu-kyō* 佛説醫喻經, T 219), trans. Dānapāla (d. 1017) in the late tenth century.
51 The following passages follow Kleine and Triplett (2012) and Triplett (2012) in part.
52 See below p. 71.
53 For an exhaustive list of Chinese Buddhist texts from the Taishō edition that refer to healing and medicine, see Salguero (2014, 195–201).
54 *Ryōji byō-kyō* 療痔病經, Sk. *Arśapraśamana-sūtra*, T 1325.

anus sores, and sores that grow on joints all over the body, all such festering boils would dry up, fall off, perish, and undoubtedly be cured. (T 1325.490c05–490c08)

In the *Sutra on Relieving Sores*, the only medical knowledge is this relatively unspecific list of sores and is therefore negligible; the ritual instruction is to utter the sutra itself, including two mantras, following a pattern widely found in Buddhist Mahāyāna sutras. The healing of a bodily ailment is one of the many worldly benefits that can be obtained through the sincere observance of specific Buddhist rituals. Other texts are much more explicit and reveal specific medical knowledge. They also include ritual instruction and detailed guidelines for the preparation and administration of medicine. Sources such as these appear to have had a significant impact on the development and circulation of medical knowledge in Japan. Many Buddhist texts found their way to Japan during the sixth and subsequent centuries. The question is whether they were thought to merely describe practices from far-off India and China, or whether the content of the texts was held to be *pre*scriptive, guiding the readers to a concrete application. In other words, were the Buddhist texts actually used in medical contexts?

According to systems theory, espoused by Niklas Luhmann among others, the system of medicine in functionally differentiated societies is solely concerned with healing humans and animals from physical and mental ailments whereas the system of religion focuses on a form of ultimate healing. Luhmann claims that it is quite different to think from illness (*Krankheit*) to health (*Gesundheit*) than to think from suffering (*Leid*) to salvation (*Heil*) (Luhmann 1982, 193). To cope with contingencies in life, religion as a system proposes solutions that other systems do not offer or do not offer in the same way. If we suppose that premodern societies were as yet functionally undifferentiated, functions such as healing the physical body could be presented by one and the same figure such as a "medicine man." In premodern Japan, Buddhist priests treated illness with incantations, spells and talismans which can be regarded as clearly belonging to the system of religion, according to Luhmann. Since priests also administered medicinal drugs – considered to be part of the system of medicine – premodern Japanese society appears to have been functionally undifferentiated. The Buddhist monk or nun would be a medicine man or witch. Another conclusion would be that the Buddhist priests operated in the system of religion when casting spells to heal someone and switched to the secular sphere of medicine when using medical therapies. From the point of view of Buddhism, interestingly, spells etc. against "demons"[55] belong to the secular sphere. The diseases caused by such demons are hindrances to Buddhist practice in this world and can only be treated with particular techniques that require prior training. Such techniques are considered to be equivalent to administering medicines, which also constitutes an engagement with secular matters and is aimed at obtaining this-worldly benefits. Practices aiming at attaining buddhahood and dealing with the absolute level of truth, in contrast, are of the non-worldly sphere. Consequently, Buddhist texts in the esoteric tradition are divided into those containing "mixed" practices dealing with relative, i.e. worldly (Jp. *seken* 世間, Sk. *laukika*) matters and those regarded to be "pure," which are concerned with the highest, i.e. non-worldly (Jp. *shusse* 出世, Sk. *lokōttara*) goals.[56]

Given the competition from "secular" physicians in early and medieval Japan, giving up the power to heal cannot have been easy. However, it seems to have been relinquished at the end of the medieval period apparently without much resistance. One reason may have been the perception that Buddhist engagement in healing the physical body was essentially worldly. "[...] Buddhism, as perceived in elite discourses, located its exclusive competence in the domain of *lokōttara* [the non-worldly]" (Kleine and Triplett 2012, 4). The factors leading to the relinquishment of certain functions of Buddhist medicine to the secular sphere – a clear change in paradigms – require further discussion. It is unclear why Buddhist priests continued to provide healing services with spells, incantations and talismans throughout the Edo period. If these were regarded as worldly, then they would have also been passed on to the system of medicine, which

---

55 In China, a spirit returning from the world of the dead that causes disease and misfortune is called a *gui* 鬼, a figure that was conflated with the *oni* (using the same character 鬼), an evil-bringer of an ambivalent nature, in the Japanese *imaginaire*. With the advent of Buddhism in China, noxious spirits and wrathful deities that played a significant role in religions and medical systems in India and other areas found their way into healing practices in China. They are also significant in Japan. "Demons" is used here as an established umbrella term for this heterogeneous group of beings. On healing and "demonology" in esoteric Buddhism, see McBride (2011). See also below p. 151, 186 and 191.

56 Scholars usually categorize texts into "mixed" (*zōbu* 雑部) and "pure" (*junsei* 純正) esoteric practices (*mikkyō* 密教), shortened to *zōmitsu* and *junmitsu* respectively. The "mixed" category mainly comprises *dhāraṇī*, which are aimed at attaining worldly benefits. The "pure" category contains sutras based on the *Mahāvairocana-sūtra* and the *Vajraśekhara-sūtra* and are thus aimed at attaining buddhahood. However, as Reis-Habito shows, the influential *Dhāraṇī of the Bodhisattva With a Thousand Hands and Eyes* (T 1060) fits into both categories (1993, 101); see also below p. 79. In the Nara period, eighty percent of the Buddhist texts that scholars classify as "mixed" were already known in Japan. However, they were primarily used exoterically, i.e. without the prescribed initiation into the practices, before Kūkai introduced esoteric Buddhism as a separate paradigm (Beghi 2011, 665, quoting Abe 1999, 159–184).

seems not to have happened. It can be assumed that the practices were not seen as worldly by all.

Buddhist clerics also continued to practice medicine and surgery well into the nineteenth century, and only the top-down restructuring of the medical education and licensing system in the late nineteenth century led to the strict allocation of Buddhists to the sphere of religion (*shūkyō* 宗教). It would be unreasonable to see Japanese society as functionally undifferentiated until the Meiji period. By any standard, Japanese society must be said to have been differentiated into spheres with clearly allocated functions from ancient times. At the same time as Buddhism was incorporated into Japanese society, Chinese-style learning and bureaucracy started to organize knowledge production in all areas including medicine and science.

2.1 Operating with "Buddhism" in Modern Academic and Popular Accounts

Nineteenth and twentieth-century academic discussions in the West about societies influenced by Chinese "civilizational" expressions have similarities with discussions in China itself, i.e. they are rather unfavorable on the subject of Buddhism and far more favorable regarding scientific achievements. Paul Unschuld, a well-known specialist on the history of Chinese medicine, states that only the purely religious elements of the Indian art of healing became an important part of medical care in China whereas the underlying ideas of the Indian system were too strange and ultimately incompatible with the corresponding Chinese ideas (1985a, 152–153). According to Unschuld, some worldviews support a particular medical system because the level of individual health corresponds to central social values. In contrast, Buddhists did not care which methods and which medical system healed the human body as long as it was successful; the relief from suffering was the central point, not the proclamation of healing methods and therapies of a particular medical system.

This assessment has been criticized by Pierce Salguero in his work on Chinese Buddhist medicine of the second to the eighth centuries. Salguero shows that the decline of Buddhist medicine in China was less connected with the incompatibility of the (Indian) medical content with Chinese medical practices. Rather, Buddhist exegetes became increasingly concerned with various types of formal equivalence of Indian and Chinese texts in Tang China. Since these texts are extremely technical, the resulting treatises were understood only by a highly specialized group of practitioners, according to Salguero (2014, 119). Therefore, the actual content and the instructions for therapies and treatments became increasingly less accessible. Moreover, as Salguero points out, whereas geopolitical changes led to a sharp decrease in the introduction of Indian medical ideas and practices, Buddhist institutions such as hospitals and charities were closed, or their administration and control moved to governmental offices, culminating in the severe persecution of Buddhism starting in 843 CE. Consequently, the decline in Buddhist medicinal practices had apparently nothing to do with a lack of acceptance of Indian medical models in China, but instead related to changing modes of translation and religio-political power struggles for important resources such as landholdings. The lasting impact of Buddhist medicine in China may not have been the result of Chinese Buddhists being too tolerant concerning the choice of a healing system in line with central social values, as Unschuld claims. Instead, it was caused by the fear of a Buddhist state based on "foreign" ideas because, as Salguero shows, Buddhist "translators were aware that their choices had far-reaching political and social implications" (2014, 66).

The view that Buddhism is a hinderance to medicine in China – medicine here being understood as "science" – was also shared by the biochemist and historian of Chinese medicine Joseph Needham (1900–1995).[57] However, since Buddhism and medicine were simultaneously incorporated into Japanese society and culture, a complex and interwoven relationship emerged over a period of more than a millennium. The translation of Indian texts was also not an issue since the texts entered Japan in Chinese. Japanese authors such as Shinmura and Hattori, who have written comprehensive accounts on Buddhism and medicine in Japan, see the philosophical and also practical contributions of monastic and lay Buddhists in the world of medicine in a favorable light. Writing for an audience familiar with the tradition of Buddhism, as Shinmura and Hattori did, is very different from writing for an audience to whom Buddhism is an unknown religion. Operating with Japanese Buddhism as a broad social and cultural phenomenon is an achievement of nearly a century of writing on it in European languages.

The image of Asian Buddhism was formed by Christian and Buddhist missionaries, scholars and artists in the nineteenth and the early twentieth centuries. It still resonates in popular depictions of Buddhism and "the Buddha" in the West. This period was an epoch of lively exchange between various individuals who were interested in Buddhism. Some of these individuals knew and highly valued each other, while others regarded each other with hostility and dis-

---

57 Needham founded the series *Science and Civilisation in China*, to which he contributed numerous volumes. Needham challenged the view that considered the "defining boundaries of science as Western" (Hart 1999, 95–96) and emphasized scientific achievements in the history of China.

approval. Networks of exchange activities between Europe, the USA, India and Japan and other places in Asia have been investigated in recent decades as part of entangled histories.[58] This history writing provides new insights into the struggles of participation in the colonial project, and highlights political, religious and cultural engagement in an increasingly connected world. While early and contemporary research on Buddhism is predominantly text focused, images and archaeological evidence of Buddhist traditions across all of Asia have played an important role in both scientific and political, as well as religious discourses since the emergence of the networks. The history of "Western" writing on Buddhism is particularly well studied.[59] As such, it is sufficient to sketch out the most pertinent images of (Japanese) Buddhism for the purpose of this book.

The academic opus with the largest impact was, without doubt, initially the monumental although incomplete *Introduction à l'histoire du Buddhisme indien* by orientalist Eugène Burnouf (1801–1852), released in 1844. Burnouf writes in his comment on the translations and commentaries of individual texts:

> The authority on which the monk of the Śākya race supported his teaching was entirely personal; it was formed of two elements, one real and the other ideal. The first was the consistency and the saintliness of his conduct, of which chastity, patience and charity formed the principal features. The second was the claim he made to be buddha [sic!], that is to say, enlightened, and as such to possess superhuman science and power. With his power, he performed miracles; with his science, he perceived, in a form clear and complete, the past and the future. (Burnouf 1884, 153, trans. Buffetrille and Lopez 2010, 24; 180–181)[60]

Burnouf's goal was to prove that there once had to have been an historical figure, an Indian man, who was to be considered the founder of Buddhism and accredited with omniscience (*science*) and miracle-performing power (*puissance*). It is striking to see that introductions to Buddhism in European languages even today operate with the *science* part of the Buddha's achievements rather

---

58 Recent studies include contributions to a special issue of the journal *Zeitschrift für Religionswissenschaft* on Buddhism in Nazi Germany (2017), Triplett 2016, Vandenreydt (2011), Robson (2011), Tweed (2005), Borup (2004) and Offermanns (2002). The following passage has been adapted from Triplett (2016, 387–389).
59 See footnote above.
60 The original passage reads: "L'autorité sur laquelle le Religieux de la race de Çākya appuyait son enseignement était toute personnelle; elle se formait de deux éléments, l'un réel et l'autre idéal. Le premier était la régularité et la sainteté de sa conduite, dont la chasteté, la patience et la charité formaient les traits principaux. Le second était la prétention qu'il avait d'être Buddha, c'est-à-dire éclairé, et, comme tel, de posséder une science et une puissance surhumaines. Avec sa puissance, il opérait des miracles; avec sa science, il se représentait, sous une forme claire et complète, le passé et l'avenir."

than with the *puissance* part. While Burnouf expresses his highest regard for the Buddha's teachings, he is more than disappointed with the tantric texts of Nepalese esoteric Buddhism that he investigated as part of his *Introduction:*

> The founder of Buddhism is even expressly depicted in them as the institutor of the ritual and magical prayers of the tantras. The mixture of these two orders of ideas, which in their expression and their object are almost the opposite of one another, is so intimate in the tantras that if one did not possess other specimens of Nepalese Buddhism, one would form an idea of this belief far distant from that given by the texts of which I have spoken thus far. [...] It is not my intention to long dwell on this part of the Nepalese collection, which I am inclined to regard as the most modern of all, and whose importance for the history of human superstitions does not compensate for its mediocrity and vapidity. It is certainly not without interest to see Buddhism, which in its first organization had so little of what makes a religion, end in the most puerile practices and the most exaggerated superstitions. But this deplorable spectacle has quite quickly wearied the curiosity and humiliated the intelligence. (Burnouf 1884, 468; 470, trans. Buffetrille and Lopez 2010, 482–483)

The image of esoteric Buddhism remained negative in the wake of Burnouf's writings although he does refer to Csoma de Kőrös[61] who appreciated the tantric texts as beautiful (Burnouf 2010, 483). The popularization of Buddhism, but not esoteric Buddhism, as an attractive religion primarily goes back to enthusiasts and spiritual seekers such as British journalist Sir Edwin Arnold (1832–1904) and the Japanese Buddhist philosopher and writer Suzuki Daisetsu 鈴木大拙 (1870–1966).

While Burnouf's dense academic study was slightly pushed aside shortly after its release because of the rapid growth of new translations of Buddhist texts, the poetic book *Light of Asia* by Edwin Arnold started conquering Europe and America. It also gained traction in India. In his time, Arnold influenced the image of the Buddha unlike any other writer. His poem, which runs to nearly two hundred pages, was first published in 1879 and is still in print today.[62] The title *Light of Asia* is a reference to the Buddha, who shines like a light over Asia, and the Asian world as a cradle of spirituality and wisdom. After the academically rejected but nevertheless bestselling *Light of Asia*, Arnold published a poem in 1891 about Christ which he entitled *Light of the World*. This book, however,

---

[61] Alexander (Sándor) Csoma de Kőrös (1784?–1842), originally from Hungary, travelled to Ladakh and later lived in various parts of India. He studied numerous languages including Tibetan. He published several works in English on the Tibetan language and religion.

[62] The Kindle edition from Amazon is free of charge. The text has also been freely accessible online for some time, e.g. on the website urbandharma.org (last accessed 13 Nov. 2018) which hosts information and texts for Buddhists in America. This shows its importance as an edifying source even in the present.

was not nearly as successful. In his later life, Edwin Arnold dedicated himself almost completely to Buddhism and, not least through his Buddha poem, promoted a revitalization of Buddhism in India where the tradition had, as mentioned before, ceased to exist as an autonomous religion by the thirteenth century. Together with the Singhalese lay Buddhist Anagarika Dharmapala (1864–1933), he founded the Maha Bodhi Society of India, which supported the preservation of ancient Buddhist sanctuaries in India. Arnold also studied the Buddhist tradition in Japan where the journalist and poet moved later in life. It is important to remember that Arnold not only poetically eternalized the Buddha alongside Christ, and painted a positive picture of Buddhism throughout, but that he was also an activist.

Another important figure in the popularization of Buddhism, especially of Japanese Buddhism, as an attractive religion was Suzuki Daisetsu. In contrast to Arnold, Suzuki was an intellectual and writer socialized as a Buddhist. New models of a reformed Buddhism emerged in the context of the political changes in Japan at the end of the nineteenth century. Partaking in this movement for a "modern" Japanese Buddhism, Suzuki published widely in both English and Japanese. He lived in the United States for many years as well as being active in Japan, and traveled extensively throughout his long life giving lectures in various parts of the world. In his writings about "Zen" experience, the lay Buddhist Suzuki outlined the history of Zen Buddhism according to the orthodox tradition but, at the same time, he adapted insights of contemporary European thought on the history of religion and of the then popular phenomenology of religion. When we deeply connect to the Buddha, he writes, "the history of religion thus becomes the history of our own spiritual unfolding" (Suzuki [1927] 1949, 49). He also employed vocabulary used in writings in the field of psychoanalysis of the time to depict traditional Zen Buddhist teachings as modern. The great variety of Buddhist teachings and practices are, he writes, expressions of man's search for the truth. Suzuki emphasizes that we should not be attached to the cultural form of religion and praises the possibility to access the original spirit of each great religion including Buddhism in the here and now. For Buddhism, this is the experience of enlightenment or awakening for which he popularized the Japanese expression *satori*.[63] Through his English-language books and essays, he shaped the image of Japanese Buddhism as essentially an individual search facilitated by sitting meditation and contemplation.

---

[63] *Satori* 悟 literally means "comprehending," "seeing," "understanding." Here, it describes a state of seeing the true reality of the world or "the intuitive looking into the nature of things" (Suzuki 1949, 230).

His position, which is primarily ahistorical and essentializing, is clearly informed by his eagerness to propound an attractive image of Japanese Buddhism. This image, not least epitomized in Suzuki's "Zen," cannot be used in the present study since the study seeks to further overcome essentialist and rectifying viewpoints. (Japanese) Buddhism is seen here as a social and cultural phenomenon that changed over time and of which the modernizing reform by Suzuki Daisetsu and others is but one development. It is therefore important to briefly outline both the historiography and the history of Buddhism and medicine in order to situate the case studies that follow.

2.2 Incorporation of Buddhism and Chinese-style Medicine into Japanese Society

Since the official introduction of Buddhism to Japan in the sixth century CE, Japanese religious history has been shaped by movements combining traditions usually associated with Shinto and Buddhism. Buddhist traditions and organizations were introduced from Korea and China and also later emerged in Japan. As Buddhist texts were first written in India and then translated into Chinese, ancient Indian medicine came to the attention of ruling families in Japan. Chinese-style ceremonies were also introduced and provided pervasive structures in the Japanese court and indeed the entire realm. With the introduction of sources of Chinese-style medicine, indigenous models of medicine started to change. What exactly the old Japanese medicine consisted of is hard to determine in light of the scarcity of sources. Today, research on ancient Japanese medicine concentrates on analyses of the earliest written sources, including studying medical issues in the imperial chronicles, early Japanese poetic songs and the local gazetteers (*fudoki* 風土記) (cf. Hattori 1945, 245–262). Most historians claim that before the reception of continental ideas, affliction with disease was thought to originate from a divine curse. According to this view, healing before the Nara period, i.e. before the eighth century, consisted in prayers. From the Nara period onwards, prayers were combined with dietary regimens and drug treatment (Hattori 1945, 1). The codification of medical, pharmaceutical and calendrical practices led to the establishment of new institutions of training and the standardization, at least in theory, of knowledge. While the 701 version of an initial Japanese Chinese-style legal code has been lost, the revised version survives as the code of the Yōrō era.[64] The *Yōrō Code* (*Yōrō-ryō* 養老令, 718) serves as a rich textual source for imagining Nara-period medical and religious institutions and features dominantly in pioneering studies of the history of medicine in Japan.

The use of "foreign" regulations, *materia medica* and formulae was by no means unopposed in the decades following the Nara period. By the end of the Nara period, the Nakatomi 中臣 family – from which the, by then all-powerful, Fujiwara 藤原 family originated – had gained dominance with the imperial family over the Inbe (Imube) 斎部 family. With the support of the Inbe, Emperor[65] Heijō 平城 (or Heizei, r. 806–809) engaged in a – short-lived – reform that, significantly, included the practice of medicine. Heijō wanted to create a new canon of autochthonous healing arts. In an official ceremony, a hundred-volume medical compilation entitled *Classified Prescriptions of the Daidō Period* (808),[66] which was to serve as the foundation for a radically new regulatory system for medicine and ritual, was dedicated to Heijō.[67] Many of the formulae in *Classified Prescriptions* are said to have been conveyed to the physicians and healers of Japan by Japanese divine ancestors. Apparently, officials had collected local prescriptions in the various provinces of the Japanese empire for the compilation, often using Chinese characters to phonetically transcribe the local Japanese plant names. Heijō's reformed medical legal code states that the use of medicines from Korea or China is harmful, and insists on only using plant material grown in Japan. The code prescribes certain purification rites to the court physician such as abstention from sexual intercourse before treating the emperor. If the emperor was ill, the physician was not allowed to participate in Buddhist ceremonies and had to avoid Buddhist monks and nuns. The purchase of *materia medica* from abroad was strictly forbidden and *Classified Prescriptions* was to be used as the standard reference work before engaging in medical treatment (Karow 1953, 161–162). As there was no antecedent "Japanese" medical compila-

---

64 For a complete translation of the *Yōrō Code* (as preserved in the *Ryō no gige* 令義解, 833) into German, see Dettmer (2009–2015) 4 vols, also Dettmer (1972).
65 Emperor or empress is a translation of the title *tennō* 天皇, literally meaning "heavenly ruler." In the soures Heijō is therefore referred to as Heijō Tennō.
66 For a detailed critical study of the compilation and its reception by the Japanese nativist school of *kokugaku* (National Learning) see Karow (1953) and Karow and Weller (1954). See also Rosner (1989, 24–25).
67 The dedication survives (see Karow 1953, 160–161) but the compilation itself only exists in a later reconstruction created not long after the original manuscript was either destroyed by the Nakatomi or accidentally burned in a fire in 875. An edition was published by Maki (1985).

tion to serve as an example for *Classified Prescriptions*, it largely followed Chinese models.[68]

Overall, the history of early Japan is portrayed as having been shaped by a dominant civilizational influence from the continent. However, official acceptance and support of newly introduced or emerging religions, as well as cultural and technological ideas and practices, depended on different factors inherent in the incorporating political system. Events such as strife among the powerful families, warfare, epidemics or natural catastrophes often led to changes in the hegemonic discourse in the imperial court or military government, for example regarding the composition, style, structure and configuration of the state religious cult. The hegemonic discourse also determined the distribution of religious teachings and practices in the provinces of the empire, resulting in a complex pattern of local variation.

One incorporation process that led to the hegemonic structures of one religious tradition prevailing over another is the incorporation of Buddhism into Japanese culture and the stylization of the emperor as a universal (Buddhist) ruler in the eighth century.[69] The focus here is not on the history of the assimilation, adaptation or other dynamics of Buddhism in Japan *per se* but rather on the institutional framework. Within this institutional framework, various actors reproduced, circulated and created medical or religious ideas and practices that had been incorporated from a different framework.

The work of sociologist Yasemin Soysal (1994) is helpful here. Her "collective cognitive maps" for the justification of state policies on the incorporation of contemporary migrant traditions provides an interpretative approach for the incorporation of introduced religious traditions and historical developments. It will be applied here, in an experimental way, to premodern, non-European history.[70] Although not directly related to religion, Yasemin Soysal's concept of "incorporation regimes" allows us to understand developments of religious plurality and heterogeneity as processes of discursive negotiation. Instead of perceiving individuals or groups as subjects of "integration" into a religious or secular mainstream consensus, it enables us to analyze the discursive forms and structures *behind* these negotiation processes. The incorporation regimes – when looked

---

[68] See Karow's comparative study of the classification and structure of the text published in several parts between 1953 and 1959.
[69] For political history in ancient Japan and the emergence of kingship, see Piggott (1997).
[70] Portions of this section were first introduced at the annual conference of the European Association of the Study of Religions (EASR) in Liverpool in 2013 on "Religion, Migration, Mutation." I would like to express my gratitude to the organizers of the panel on "Incorporating Religions – A Comparative View."

at from a macro-level – are patterns of discourse and policy, and, according to Soysal, incorporation takes place *independently* of the integration of individuals or the perception of such integration (1994, 31). Collective organizational patterns emerge that form "collective cognitive maps" that permit social entities to justify recourse allocation, etc. (1994, 44). Soysal's concept allows us to shift our attention from "religious groups" to the structural ramifications of the host country, its legal system and other structural and discursive conditions, which are – at the same time – subject to re-interpretation and mutation. Unlike Soysal's original approach, it seems appropriate to discuss the concept as a more general means of interpretation in the context of historical topics. In the following, developments in the context of the incorporation of such systems as Chinese Buddhism and the Chinese medical system in Japan are highlighted.

In ancient Japan, the leaders of the various local regimes were chief priests who were devoted to the gods of the land, the *kami* 神. This religious system is referred to as *shintō* (or *jindō*) 神道, the "way of the gods." At the beginning of the movement towards a centralized government in Japan, the struggle for hegemonic rule of one lineage (*uji* 氏) over the others was reflected in the hierarchy of the protective lineage deities in the official pantheon: The victorious lineage leaders were direct descendants of the Sun Goddess, presented as the most powerful of all deities. The basic organizational configuration in ancient Japan can therefore clearly be said to be of the "fragmental type" since the family or lineage (Soysal: "primordial" group) represented the main social unit. Even as the successful leaders became involved in the controlling and promoting of imported Buddhism, they seemed to realize that the primary source of their spiritual authority lay in their hereditary roles as high priests of native *kami* worship (Sonoda 1988, 389). This administrative structure involving the ruling elite, the various lineages and the *kami* shrines made up the collective cognitive map at the time and shaped the way Buddhism was incorporated. However, this map, or matrix, eventually changed with Shōmu Tennō 聖武天皇 (r. 724–749).

Shōmu Tennō, usually referred to as Emperor Shōmu in English-language literature, was, among other rulers, instrumental in the incorporation phase of Buddhism in Japan. Starting in the late fifth century CE, continental influence on Japan became more and more dominant after initial exchanges of a more sporadic nature. Immigrants from the Korean kingdoms provided political and military expertise. They also introduced technological and medical knowledge and skills, as well as new ideas about rulership, and religious ideas and practices. The most widespread religious creed, Buddhism, was officially introduced during the sixth century and became well established during the seventh. During the seventh and eighth centuries, immigrants brought literacy and text production to Japan. The ruling elite of the Yamato – the emergent regime in central

Japan – wrote using Chinese characters (Totman 2000, 41). As regards political ideology, there were major developments in both the sixth century and the seventh century up until 671. The most notable of these developments was the use of Buddhism for the legitimation of political authority. The king of Baekje (Jp. Kudara) 百濟 sought military aid from a Japanese ruler, Kinmei 欽明 (r. 539–571), against Silla 新羅 around 530. Both Baekje and Silla were rival kingdoms on the Korean peninsula. To encourage the Japanese ruler to send troops, the king of Baekje presented Kinmei with Buddha images in gold and copper, several flags and umbrellas for cultic use and numerous volumes of Buddhist texts. An accompanying message said that the Buddhist doctrine was superior to all other doctrines – it could create religious merit and retribution without measure and led to the highest wisdom; every prayer was fulfilled. It was transmitted from distant India to Han China, and everyone had received it with reverence, attesting to its superiority and efficacy. Even the Duke of Zhou, the wisest ruler of all times, and Confucius could not comprehend it fully. This was high praise indeed, and the Japanese elite was duly impressed. Rulers valued the religion and used it as a political tool. However, members of the ruling elite and, later, commoners also cherished Buddhism as providing a powerful means of curing illness and warding off other forms of affliction (Totman 2000, 57–58).

As the religion blossomed in Japan with the support of the powerful Soga 蘇我 family, Suiko 推古 (r. 592–628), established offices to exert control over the fledgling religious community, employing immigrant Buddhist priests with advanced expertise in doctrinal matters. Suiko conducted a religious census in the year 623. The result of forty-six Buddhist temples, 816 priests and 569 nuns indicates that Buddhism had become entrenched in the system (Totman 2000, 58). The health and well-being of members of the ruling families – whether in this world or the beyond – seemed to have been a major concern behind the establishment of Buddhist temples and the commissioning of statuary, as the well-known inscription on the back of the aureole of a statue of Buddha Śākyamuni (Shaka 釈迦) dated 623 indicates[71]: Prince Kamitsumiya 上宮 (ca. 573–622) and his consort had fallen ill and they and all the officials at court had vowed to make a statue of Śākyamuni the size of the prince to alleviate his illness. However, as the inscription further relates, both the prince and his consort died and the statue was therefore dedicated to their and the prince's mother's awakening

---

[71] For a short section on Buddhist mission and the role of medicine in Japan that mentions this episode see Demiéville (1937, 244–245; Demiéville/Tatz 1985, 52–53); for an edition and translation of the inscription into French see Maitre (1925, 408–411), for an English translation see Lurie (2011, 216–217).

(or enlightenment) after birth in the Pure Land.⁷² The prince mentioned in the inscription was a member of the Soga family and none other than the prince regent revered later as the saintly founding patron of Buddhism in Japan, Shōtoku Taishi 聖徳太子 (cf. Como 2008, 4; 165). Religion and medicine connect in this ritual and material practice in two ways: The commission of the statue – actually a group of Śākyamuni and two attendants – can be regarded as healing and ensuring longevity by meritous acts, whereas the inscription expresses also the idea of the transfer of the merit to revered ancestors on their way to salvation after corporeal death.

Kōtoku 孝徳, who ruled from 645 to 654 after the reign of the Soga family was cut short by a coup, decreed an order for the proper instruction of monks and nuns and the appropriate maintenance of the temples established by members of the elite families, many of them of Korean origin. By controlling the temples, Kōtoku was in the position to exert considerable authority over the chiefs (Totman 2000, 58). Tenmu 天武, the monarch who first took the title of *tennō*, and ruled some decades later from 673 to his death in 686, promoted Buddhism and Buddhist ceremonies at his court and also set out restrictions on the killing and eating of animals as a way to obtain merit and show piety (Totman 2000, 72)⁷³. He instigated the reading of the *Sutra of Golden Light* (*Konkōmyō-kyō* 金光明經)⁷⁴ for the protection of the state on a grand scale. Tenmu not only lavished his attention on Buddhism but also supported Chinese-style court ceremonies and those dedicated to the local and lineage deities, the *kami*. Ise Shrine (Ise jingū 伊勢神宮) and its principal deity, the Sun Goddess Amaterasu ōmikami 天照大神, who was – and is to this day by some – regarded as the divine ancestor of the imperial monarch, remained the center of state ritual. In addition, Tenmu followed the continental tradition of sponsoring the construction of Buddhist sanctuaries for the benefit of members of the ruling family. For the well-being of his consort, later ruling Empress Jitō 持統 (r. 690 – 697), Tenmu commissioned the construction of a temple dedicated to Medicine Master and King of Lapis Lazuli Light (Bhaiṣajyaguru-vaiḍūrya-prabhā-rāja), the Medicine Buddha, in 680.⁷⁵ The magnificent temple, the Yakushiji 薬師寺, graced Tenmu's capital city of Fujiwara-kyō 藤原京 although he did not live to see its completion. His consort Jitō, however, for whose health the temple was commissioned in the

---

72 For more on the prince, his wife and his mother, see p. 111.
73 For the reign of Tenmu, see Ooms (2009); see also Ooms (2015, 41–42).
74 Different versions were used in Japan; the full title of the sutra translated by Yijing is *Konkōmyō saishōō-kyō* 金光明最勝王經 (Sk. *Suvarṇaprabhāsottama-sūtra*), T 665.
75 For an overview of the Yakushi cult in early Japan with a focus on Buddhist material culture, in particular on statues, see Suzuki (2012).

first place, completed the structure. Nearly a decade later, it was moved to the new capital of Heijō-kyō 平城京, at present-day Nara 奈良. This clearly shows that the first Buddhists and Buddhist institutions in Japan served to ensure the health and well-being of the ruling imperial family.

After the year 672 CE, with a change in the ruling family branch, a central state took shape after a long process of political consolidation. A system of penal and civil codes was established, which was heavily based on Chinese precedents, as was mentioned above. The new capital city served as the center of a bureaucratic network linking the provinces and all their resources to the ruling elite. The main written source from this system, the *Record of Japan* (*Nihon shoki* 日本書紀), was compiled in 720 CE to legitimize the establishment of the system (Totman 2000, 60). The source can be read as the current discourse of the ruling elite at the time and therefore provides us with insights into patterns of incorporation of, for example, migrants from Korea and China, the incorporation of Buddhism and the justification for making Buddhism the state religion with a heavenly ruler – the *tennō* – at its center, and the rationalization behind frequently moving and building new capital cities that can be seen as expressions of a particular world order and cosmology according to Chinese ideas (Totman 2000, 70).

2.3 Historiographies of Buddhism, Medicine and Healing Rituals

The process of incorporation was completed by Shōmu Tennō. His most ambitious plan was the building of a new capital northeast of Heijō-kyō (Nara), but he had to return to Nara after wildfires and earthquakes finally forced him to abandon his great scheme.[76] After his return to Nara, however, Shōmu threw himself into another building project: The creation of a Buddhist temple complex of unprecedented dimensions that would serve not only as a center of the capital but also of his entire empire, if not the universe. He managed to bring this project to fruition. The result was a temple complex of magnificent style called Tōdaiji 東

---

[76] By the time Shōmu became "heavenly ruler" (*tennō*) after his aunt Genshō 元正 (r. 715–724) abdicated in his favor, the capital city of Heijō-kyō was a flourishing urban center. The capital was built by Shōmu's grandmother, Genmei Tennō 元明天皇 (r. 707–715). Shōmu Tennō was, like his predecessors, a devout Buddhist. When natural disasters hit during his reign, he considered them to have been caused by his own failures as ruler. Shōmu tried to counteract and pacify the lands by fervently promoting Buddhism but also supporting initiatives related to the *kami* (cf. Totman 2000, 63–64).

大寺.⁷⁷ In 747, Tōdaiji became the supreme center of Buddhist learning in Japan and served as the place of ordination for all those applying to become licensed monks and nuns. The monastics staffed the various sub-temples in the provinces. The temple network therefore has a clearly defined center, radiating out to all corners of the realm (Totman 2000, 75–76).

Shōmu chose Vairocana Buddha, the central figure of the newly introduced *Flower Ornament Sutra*,⁷⁸ as the main Buddha image. This sutra is regarded as revealing the interaction of cosmic and mundane planes of consciousness, i.e. the interconnectedness and interpenetration of spiritual and secular power. The scripture is believed to be the condensed expression of universal truths and their phenomenal representations in the ordinary world. Shōmu's design of his enormous Buddha hall can be said to be a full representation of the *Flower Ornament Sutra* in three-dimensional form. It is very probable that Shōmu was somewhat intrigued by the figure of Buddha Vairocana because of the name, meaning "Resplendent One," an Indian name for the sun. This Buddha is also equated to or identified with the Sun Goddess who – as mentioned above – is an important Japanese deity and regarded as the ancestor of the *tennō*. Shōmu Tennō's new temple system became an instrument for the interconnectedness of the political and spiritual realms (Totman 2000, 74) following the idea of the *Flower Ornament Sutra*. In addition, he ordered the provincial monasteries and nunneries to serve as protectors of the state by promoting the copying and reciting of the *Sutra of Golden Light*, most prominently the highly regarded chapters on the *Four Deva Kings* and on *Medicine*,⁷⁹ among other Buddhist sutras. Nuns in particular had the task of reading the *Lotus Sutra* (*Hokekyō* or *Hokkekyō* 法華經)⁸⁰ for the social good of the realm and its imperial subjects.

The project completed the association of government and Buddhism that the Soga family had begun promoting after Buddhism was first introduced by Korean emissaries and immigrants about two hundred years before. The result was the establishment of a full-fledged state religion. The idea of a universal Buddhist

---

77 Even in its present smaller reconstruction, Tōdaiji is one of the most famous historical architectural complexes in the world due to its sheer size.
78 *Kegon-kyō* 華嚴經 (Sk. *Avatamsaka-sūtra*). Various translations exist: T 278, T 279 and T 293.
79 Pioneering research on this sutra was done by the German indologist Johannes Nobel (1887–1960). Nobel not only provided the Sanskrit text of the sutra in a 1937 publication but he also published a full translation of the sutra into German in [1944] 1958. Nobel analyzed the chapter on medicine (1951) in a version translated by Yijing. Translations of the Chinese version of this sutra's chapter into English are provided by Salguero (2013).
80 The full title of this sutra is *The Lotus Flower of the Wonderful Dharma* (*Myōhō rengekyō* 妙法蓮華經, Sk. *Saddharma-puṇḍarīka-sūtra*). The version translated by Kumārajīva (344–413), T 262, is the most popular in Japan.

ruler is an ancient Indian idea. However, as power began to centralize in Japan, Chinese Confucianism provided the idea of a natural hierarchy composed of a monarch and the subjects. In this system, a person's role in society was associated with familial relationships. The monarch was like a parent to the subjects, and consequently, the subjects were like his or her children. Being semi-divine, however, the rulers could not be impeached if their rule was regarded as unjust. Before the entrenchment of Buddhism, the *kami* shrine institutions with their hereditary systems and the Chinese-style decorum and hierarchical social organization that followed Confucian ideas were the basic cognitive and organizational map.

Summarising, Buddhism, as a translocal institution, provided a universal model of human existence, a new cosmology, and was regarded as a supremely powerful religion that would (especially) benefit the ruler of a nation. The Buddhist organizations were combined with the prevalent religious system to the effect that Japan as a national project was seen as an idealized Buddhist "nation." This became, after Shōmu Tennō, the dominant collective cognitive map. In Soysal's terms: Buddhism became, in fact, an incorporation regime of its own. A similar view is reflected by the classical study of Matsunaga (1969) on what she called the philosophy of assimilation of Buddhism in Japan. However, since Buddhism and Shinto could be "separated" in some form a millennium later, we cannot speak of a totally homogeneous religious amalgam under the label of Buddhism. In the late nineteenth century, Shinto shrines and Shinto-style ceremonies were given precedence and the government in the Meiji period tried to "clarify," and later separate, religious institutions and have them divided into fixed categories of "Shinto" and "Buddhism." Whereas religious institutions in Japan generally venerated both *kami* and Buddhas in a way that saw both religious traditions as different from each other, this policy sought to separate or: "x-corporate" (author's term) Buddhism from officialdom and to establish a form of Shinto as state ritual. Both the discourse and the policy were thus quite the opposite of what Shōmu Tennō and his government had promulgated. Meiji-period policies, overall, led to the dissolution of century-old organizational forms of religious institutions. This process of x-corporation ultimately led to the compulsory allocation of religious groups to one of four categories – Buddhism, Shinto, Christianity or "other" – according to the legal regulations based on the (post-war) constitution guaranteeing religious pluralism and freedom. Similarly, medicine was subject to a new state licensing system that excluded the practice of traditional forms in favor of Western-style medicine.

Chinese medicine and its incorporation into the medical system of early Japan went along similar lines and have to been seen in close connection with the incorporation process of Buddhism and Chinese-style ceremonies and deco-

2.3 Historiographies of Buddhism, Medicine and Healing Rituals — 61

rum. The institutional framework created by incorporating legal codes, establishing offices, introducing certification guidelines and other bureaucratic measures has been studied in detail by scholars such as the historian of medicine Hattori Toshirō. One potent motivation to accept Buddhism was its image as powerful in healing all ills as outlined above. Hattori discusses Buddhist texts that he sees as having had a significant impact on medical ideas and practices in the first chapter of his pioneering study and, interestingly, mentions Chinese-style medicine only in a later chapter on medical theory. In his study, Hattori outlines major classical Chinese sources such as *materia medica* literature and formulae compilations, as well as the principles of medicine in China and their place in Japan.[81] Hattori's work (1945) vividly depicts the multicultural and multireligious cooperation, as well as the dynamism of the Nara period. He discusses influences and effects of Buddhism on the development of medicine (*igaku* 医学) by examining elite views of the Buddhist teachings in the Nara period, and the impact of Indian medicine transmitted via Buddhist texts translated into Chinese. He selects three principal sutras and three influential vinaya texts: the *Sutra of Golden Light*, the *Lotus Sutra* and the *Vimalakīrti-sūtra*[82]; the *Four-Part Vinaya*, the Mahāsāṃghika vinaya[83] and, finally, the Sarvāstivāda vinaya text *Ten Recitations Vinaya*[84]. The choice of the texts is well founded because they represent canonized knowledge on medical matters and healing in Buddhism following the systematization attempts of texts from a wide range of sutras and commentaries composed on the continent not long before the compilation reached the Japanese shore. Therefore, they are significant for the understanding of early Japanese medical and religious culture in the context outlined above.[85] Moreover, Hattori highlights the activities of several individual "nurse monks" (*kanbyōsō* 看病僧) – Buddhist priests who took care of members of the imperial family when they fell ill and "monastic physicians" (*sōi* 僧医)[86]. Included in the portrayal of "nurse monks" are Genbō 玄昉 (d. 746) who studied for twenty years in China and

---

[81] The historian compiled numerous studies on medicine in Japan, divided into periods. He started with a volume on Nara-period medicine, published in 1945, followed by three volumes on succeeding periods up until the Edo period, as well as a volume on Buddhist medicine, published in 1968 as briefly mentioned above.
[82] *Vimalakīrtinirdeśa-sūtra* (*Yuimakitsu shosetsu-kyō* 維摩詰所説經) (*Vimalakīrti Sutra*), T 475, trans. Kumārajīva.
[83] This text is referred to in Sino-Japanese as (*Maka*)*Sōgi-ritsu* (摩訶)僧祇律, T 1425.
[84] *Jūju-ritsu* 十誦律, T 1435.
[85] For the problem of canonization and the need for studying each translation of a sutra or commentary in light of its historical context, see Salguero (2015).
[86] This is a term used by modern scholars. On monks as healers in premodern Japan, see Kleine (2012).

brought back numerous Buddhist texts to Japan, Rōben 良辯 (良弁, also Ryōben, 689–774) who established the clergy at Tōdaiji, Hōei 法栄 (dates unknown) who was active in curing Shōmu Tennō's illness, Dōkyō 道鏡 (d. 772) who entered Tōdaiji under Rōben and was highly favored by Shōmu's successor after healing her from an illness when she reigned under the name of Kōken 孝謙 (r. 749–758), and other "nurse monks" who were among Rōben's group that recited sutras for the *tennō*'s recovery such as Jikun 慈訓 (Jikin, 691?–777) and Ankan 安寛 (dates unknown).

Among the monastic physicians, Beop-jang 法藏 (Hōzō, dates unknown), a monk from Baekje, is mentioned who is credited with sending a powerful medicinal plant from Baekje[87] to Japan for the recovery of Tenmu Tennō, and the eleventh abbot of Hōryūji, Hōren 法蓮 (dates unknown) who was versed in the medical arts (*ijutsu* 醫術).[88] The most illustrious priest in accounts of the history of medicine in Japan is Jianzhen (Jp. Ganjin), a vinaya master from China. He imported not only numerous Buddhists texts and ritual objects but also *materia medica* from China. According to tradition, he identified medical substances by their smell after he went blind due to an illness.

Overall, Hattori relates passages from the Buddhist writings and other textual sources interpolating them with brief comments on the understanding of the origin of disease, therapy and keeping the Buddhist precepts in Tang-period China, as well as the appropriation of Buddhist medicine in Japan. Of particular interest is the section in which Hattori addresses influences from other cultures on the development of Japanese medicine. Apart from influences from Indian and Chinese medicine, both Confucianism (*jukyō* 儒教) and Christianity (*kirishitankyō* 基督教) had an impact – Confucianism because of its idea that a virtuous ruler brings well-being to the ruled and Christianity because of the record of a man travelling from Silla named "Ri Mitsuei" 孝密翳 (dates unknown), allegedly a Nestorian Christian missionary who was active at the Japanese imperial dispensary (1945, 71–74).[89]

Maruyama Yumiko (1998) has described the ancient Japanese codification of all matters related to medicine and compared it with the Chinese legal codes. Maruyama is a specialist in comparative textual study and the importation, production and circulation of Chinese texts in Japan. In contrast to Hattori, with his strong emphasis on Buddhist medicine, she focuses exclusively on medicine as developed in China. Although it is not immediately obvious or explicit, the topic

---

87 See Miyata (2012, 167–168); for some reason, Hattori writes "Silla".
88 See below p. 102.
89 According to Sugiyama (1994) and others, Ri Mitsuei was one of the Persian visitors to the Japanese court.

of religion does feature prominently in her work. Legal and ritual codes regulated the time and condition of drug intake, for instance. As such, it can be affirmed that calendricity relates to medical therapies and cosmologically correct behavior. The calendrical structuring of the year into seasonal sections accompanied by the performance of rites can certainly be said to belong to the realm of religion. Michael Como, a specialist in ancient Japanese religions, urges us to scan sources for conceptions of ordinary household religiosity in sections that are not labeled as "religious" or do not appear to be explicitly devoted to religion (2015, 30) in more conventional ways.[90] Along the same lines, the scarcity of sources must not necessarily indicate a lack of influence, as historian Nana Miyata emphasizes in her monograph on entanglement history and strategies for adapting Chinese cultural techniques and concepts in ancient Japan (2012, 224).[91]

These discussions lead to the problem of Daoism in Japan. Incorporation of continental forms of religion excluded formally institutionalized Daoism, which seems to have been a conscious decision on the part of the Yamato rulers, probably to prevent power struggles as witnessed in China at the time.[92] Because of the lack of Daoist institutions in Japan, the worship of deities from the Daoist pantheon arrived, in Como's words, as "stowaways" in Japan and added to religious plurality (2015, 26). Epidemic diseases transmitted from the continent hit those living on the Japanese isles hard and, as Como surmises, aided and abetted the acceptance and spread of the teachings of the Buddha as the supreme healer of all ills more effectively than official Buddhist missionaries (2015, 26).

It does not seem that pre-Buddhist medicine in Japan prevailed or ever enjoyed a significant renaissance in later centuries. An exception is the eighteenth-century attempt to divorce Japanese from Chinese ideas in the wake of nativist endeavors. Ancient sources such as the *Nihon shoki* (*Record of Japan*) and especially the *Chronicle of Ancient Matters* (*Kojiki* 古事記, 712), once written to legitimize the hegemonic rule by the Yamato lineage and the institution of the *tennō*, became an object of much interest. In the *Nihon shoki*, two *kami*, Ōnamuchi no kami 大己貴神 and Sukunabikona no kami 少名毘古那神, introduced regulations and medical therapies to ensure the health of men and animals in their realm. This mythical foundation of medicine is reminiscent of the Chinese founding figure of medicine, the mythical emperor Shennong 神農, the Divine Husbandman or Farmer, who also had an important function in Japan (cf. Rosner

---

90 For a comprehensive study on immigrant religion in ancient Japan, see Como (2010).
91 See also Miyata's chapter 4 on Daoism in Japan (2012, 179–267).
92 Cf. Ooms (2009, esp. Chap. 6 on Daoism, 2015, 49; referencing Shinkawa [1999]).

1989, 9). In the nativist schools that included a group of physicians engaged in revitalizing "ancient Japanese medicine" (*koidō* 古医道) or "Japanese-style medicine" (*wahō igaku* 和方医学), the two Japanese *kami* came to play a central role and the Chinese Shennong had to leave the stage. To speak of a renaissance of Japanese pre-Buddhist, pre-Chinese-style medicine is overstated, however.[93] The incorporation and development of Buddhism and Chinese-style medicine as an "incorporation regime" was so complete that we cannot conceive of any particular or seperate *kami*-related medical tradition.

2.4 Licit and Illicit Talismanic Cures, Rituals and Incantations

Whereas most of the sources mentioned above have been extensively studied from early on in Japan and elsewhere in various academic disciplines such as art history, literature and history, little attention has been paid to material sources such as talismans or amulets. This oversight is the consequence of two discursive practices: (1) an evolutionist history of medicine that narrates the progress of medicinal practices from "primitive" magical medical practices to modern medicine; (2) Buddhist historiography with its focus on doctrines and commentary works of important monastic thinkers and the pressure to depict the history of Buddhism as an evolving system of philosophy and faith relevant to late nineteenth-century, or modern, society.

Unsurprisingly, talismanic cures and material sources do not fit this academic program. Just as in European academia, here too, practices deemed "superstitious" or "popular" – as they deviated from officially sanctioned religious practices – were banished to the realm of folklore studies. However, Japanese folklore studies was dominated by nativist views that marginalized the Chinese and Buddhist dimensions. The historian Gorai Shigeru 五来重 (1908–1993) who studied Buddhist folk practices and can be considered the founder of Buddhist folklore studies (*Bukkyō minzokugaku* 仏教民俗学) challenged approaches of a nativist nature. Gorai Shigeru endeavored to look at "popular Buddhism" of different time periods in Japan and wrote extensively on different themes and issues that he subsumed under the heading of popular Buddhism: Shinto-Buddhist combinatory practices as well as performative, artistic and narrative aspects of

---

[93] A debate about the authenticity of the "nativist" *Daidō ruijuhō* ensued but because the most influential branch of nativism ultimately saw the work as a forgery – which it is decidedly not – it had no role in the reformulation of "ancient Japanese medicine" as envisioned by its representatives; see Karow (1953, 156).

rituals.⁹⁴ He also made efforts to systematize the emerging field of Buddhist folklore studies, which in turn constituted a marked and conscious departure from the more traditional Japanese folklore studies with its strong focus on beliefs and practices in regard to the Japanese *kami*, or the allegedly autochthonic, pre- or non-Buddhist deities. His students continue this line of investigation, predominantly but not exclusively, with a focus on modern Japan, among them Toyoshima Osamu on folk practices in Kumano (1990) and Anne-Marie Bouchy on Japanese mountain asceticism and related topics (1992). The subjects of healing and medicine in Japanese Buddhism feature prominently in Buddhist folklore studies as the volume dedicated to different facets of devotional practices directed to the Medicine Buddha (Yakushi Nyorai 薬師如来), edited by Gorai (1986), shows.

In rituals of the esoteric Buddhist tradition prevalent in early Japan, there is a certain moment when the universal power of the deity and the power of those who conduct the ritual merge. This moment in the ritual is referred to in Japan as *kaji* 加持 (Sk. *adhiṣṭhāna*) which translates as "assistance." Because the practitioner's power merges with that of the cosmic Buddha, we often find the English translation as "empowerment."⁹⁵ The effect of the ritual is thought to be highly beneficial and is often equated with healing and protection from disease. According to Pamela Winfield, the monk Kūkai introduced a new "hands-on healing technique" to Japan where it was combined with, or supplemented, existing methods of treatment. She distinguishes between the esoteric Buddhist doctrine of *kaji*, or the "mutual empowerment between the self and Buddha that characterizes tantric deity yoga," and the bestowment of *kaji* "when a trained master concentrates and extends Buddha's universal energy to a receptive subject for healing purposes" (Winfield 2005, 108). Because the students of Kūkai's Shingon school could gain official acceptance due to the Bureau of Medicine, the Ten'yakuryō 典薬寮, allowing "incantation masters"⁹⁶ to practice alongside doctors (*kusushi* 医師) from 718, these Buddhist incantationists could practice their art of *kaji* healing, filling this "niche" (Winfield 2005, 117). For example, Shinzei (Shinsei) 真済 (800–860), one of the ten disciples of Kūkai, was reported to have conducted rituals (*shuhō* 修法) for preserving the health of his patron Em-

---

94 He was a prolific writer; his collected works were published in 2007–2009.
95 In esoteric Buddhism the practice consists of visualizing and experiencing unification with a central deity. All deities including the Buddhas are part of one cosmic or universal Buddha. This universal Buddha is thought to be identical with one's mind. The practice aims at realizing that there is no separation between oneself and the power of this cosmic Buddha (non-dualism).
96 These engage in *zugon* or *jugon* 呪言, "incantations," "spells," which is often translated as "exorcism" or "sorcery."

peror Montoku 文徳 (r. 850–858), though in vain. Does this mean, however, that Buddhist monastics were barred – as incantation experts – from "proper" medical practice such as the administration of medicines or pharmaceutical activities? The establishment of care facilities (hospitals) and apothecaries in the Buddhist temples of Nara suggests that this was not the case. Rather than this particular niche, concurrently occupied by Kūkai's disciples, an existing group of (Daoistic) incantation masters was granted a place in the official ranking system, thus placing them under tight governmental control. This situation continued until 780 CE when incantation practices were discouraged as they were considered "unorthodox," leading ultimately to the dissolution of the rank of official master of incantations (Rosner 1989, 17).

In *kaji* rituals, objects are turned into medicine or curative talismans. These objects have only rarely been discussed in scholarship, and it is only recently that scholars of Japanese religions such as Lucia Dolce, Benedetta Lomi and others have started to research material sources and images in the study of Buddhist history and medicine.

An example from such research is a talisman made from an ox bezoar (*bezoar bovis*) to ensure safe delivery in childbirth, known as "bezoar assistance" (*gokō kaji* or *gokō keji* 牛黄加持) (Triplett 2010a, 161). The bezoar is also used in an ointment for the birthing woman (Lomi 2017). Another example is a talismanic medicine created in relation to the Heian-period "Ritual of the Six-syllable Sutra" (*rokujikyōhō* 六字経法), analyzed by Lomi (2014). During a fire offering ceremony, three effigies were manipulated. The effigies were generally made of paper but could also be molded into small dolls by mixing flour, different poisons and water. The ritual constituted an exorcism by very carefully burning this set of three effigies referred to as the "three foxes" (*sanko* 三狐) although they had the shapes of a kite, a hog and a woman.[97] The ceremonial master had to pay attention not to empower the dangerous "foxes" by the flames of the ceremonial fire but to subjugate or rather transform them into curative powers. The ash was used to make medicine for the donor of the ceremony. The medicine was supposed to be taken orally, sometimes being formed into a pill and then administered (Lomi 2014, 291). The tradition of magic cures in Japanese Buddhism makes use of techniques from Chinese Daoism. The religious tradition of Daoism survived as ritual technology as briefly outlined above. The later version of the legal code, the *Yōrō Code*, reiterated the earlier prohibitions for Buddhist monastics in the *Administrative Laws for Monks and Nuns* (*Sōni-ryō* 僧尼令). They were not to engage in divining and reading omens, meddling in

---

[97] Cf. image in Lomi (2014, 273).

state and military affairs or misleading, killing or having sexual relations with others – thus regulating monastic life in direct accordance with the vinaya rules. However, in the later code, they are also forbidden to cure sickness using Daoist techniques, as is apparent in a later commentary, the *Collected Interpretations of the Administrative Laws* (*Ryō no shūge* 令集解, ca. 860–870) that in turn quotes from yet another commentary:[98]

> Monks and nuns who engage in oracles and prophesying or cure illnesses by relying on the Small Way (by which magic amulets and the like are meant) or magical techniques[99] shall be returned to the lay status. However, this shall in most cases not apply to the use of curing spells that are in accordance with Buddhism. (*Ryō no shūge, Sōni-ryō*)

We can therefore surmise that monks and nuns[100] must have engaged in curing sickness with exorcism spells and amulets identified with "techniques of the Way" (*dōjutsu* 道術). However, as the example of the "Ritual of the Six-syllable Sutra" from the Heian period shows, popularity of Buddho-Daoist exorcisms remained high. Exorcisms were practiced widely although a state office of exorcism no longer existed.[101] Purification through fire or by burning effigies was also practiced in other religious traditions in Japan such as mountain asceticism which has always profoundly engaged in healing.

As with the study of Daoistic healing and ritual practices in Japan, the therapeutic activities of those not belonging to the learned and licensed elite presents obstacles for academic research due to the relative scarcity of texts. However, we do find testimonies of miracle healings in the early Buddhist legends that provide some insights into the activities of individuals outside of the official temple hierarchy and the ruling elite. For example, an episode from the *Records of Gratitude to the Numinous* (*Kanreiroku* 感霊録), a ninth-century collection of Buddhist legends, tells of a miraculous eye-healing ritual at a particular temple near Nara that is even today renowned as a pilgrimage temple for those afflicted with sight-related diseases or blindness. The passage relates that a blind nov-

---

98 Demiéville (1937, 260); Ooms (2015, 52); see also Miyata (2012, esp. 184–224).
99 *Mujutsu* or *fujutsu* 巫術.
100 The question of Buddhist women as practitioners of medicine is yet to be explicitly addressed. Points to be considered are: The *Taihō* and *Yōrō Codes* allowed men and women to practice medicine, although occupations were gendered. Since women were not prohibited from chanting *kaji* prayers or using them for healing, nuns must have conducted healing rituals and medical applications. For more on the topic, see Chapter 5.
101 For numerous examples of such exorcist practices in China and Japan, see Strickmann (2002).

ice[102] named Chōnin 長仁 (dates unknown), who grew up as a beggar, came to the temple and uttered an incantation (*jinju* 神呪) uninterruptedly for many years with the wish to have his sight restored by the bodhisattva Avalokiteśvara, the principal deity of the temple. His piety to the bodhisattva was immense and he became wholly devoted to him. In the end, Chōnin regained his eyesight and, according to the text, became a widely recognized *hakase* 博士, which can be translated as "yin-yang diviner." The legend ends by stating that he served the community as a healer for many years until his death.[103] While the story follows a rather conventional pattern, it is interesting to note that the ascetic Buddhist adept engages in curing illness, apparently using techniques recognized as belonging to the expertise of a "Daoistic" healer or diviner. By the ninth century, this may not have been seen as condemnable anymore but rather as a praiseworthy pursuit in a Buddhist.

In a similar fashion to the attempt to keep Buddhist monastics from using "Daoistic" exorcism spells in the Nara period, some forms of esoteric Buddhist ritual and thought were deemed heterodox and "evil" (*jagi* 邪義) by inner-Buddhist authorities in the late medieval period. Interestingly, this categorization may have prevented modern scholars from taking the study of materials from these "heterodox" traditions seriously or finding them worthy of consideration, as Lucia Dolce points out in her survey of the *Secret Treatise on the Repository of Quintuple Wisdom* (*Gochizō hishō* 五智蔵秘抄, 1261) (2016), hereafter *Secret Treatise*. The concern of this treatise is not so much healing a namable disease but theorizing on embryology – the generation of a perfect body – and guiding adepts through the stages corresponding to the stages on the path to awakening. The process of gestation is imagined as physical procreation during sexual intercourse (with the help of corresponding images in the treatise), followed by pregnancy and birth from the mother's womb. In the treatise, we find the fetal and spiritual development correlated and described in detail. As such, this discourse can be categorized as "medical" in the sense that it is concerned with ideas of a healthy gestation and birth, and "religious" because of its concern with overcoming dualist views and reaching ultimate and full awakening. In her study, Dolce outlines the embryological discourses as found in several early (Indian) Buddhist sources (2016, 264–269) stating that the Japanese works such as the *Secret*

---

102 *Shido no shami* 私度の沙彌, literally "self-ordained novice." They were men and women who neither belonged to a Buddhist institution nor counted as officially ordained.
103 See Triplett (2010a, 155–163), including a translation of the passage into German; Triplett (2012, 74–76) with full English translation; see also Triplett (2010b, 487–489). For editions and analyses of the compilation, see Nagai (1966), Kawase (1958) and Tsuji (1981). The passage is quoted fully below p. 104.

Treatise reflect Chinese correlative cosmological paradigms and body concepts as well as Chinese medical and Daoist embryogenetic discourses (Dolce 2016, 269–270). The focus on the later reception of works such as the *Secret Treatise* as heterodox, even heretical, clouds, in her view, the question of historical connections of Japanese with continental esoteric Buddhism at the time of their circulation and production (Dolce 2016, 287).

The *Secret Treatise* and related works are excellent examples of the general discussion about the dynamics of both religion and medicine in an extensive geographical region as well as of (re)considering particular material sources in a given culture besides their relevance for a survey of the relationship between Buddhism and medicine. It is important to note for the remainder of the book that esoteric Buddhism remained the prevalent cultural paradigm throughout the medieval period after the incorporation phase and subsequent changes by Kūkai and others.

This overview of the popular and academic literature on the complex relationship between Buddhism and medicine shows that the debate is far from closed. Indeed, the differences between the Chinese and Japanese cases underline the need for a continued discussion on the evolving relationship between "Buddhist medicine" and other medical and religious systems. In the following chapters, four case studies will provide new answers to these questions.

3 The Eye I: An Organ as a Site of Empowerment and Healing

The eye is perhaps held in higher regard than any other part of the body. Throughout history, the visually impaired have found different ways to live with the sighted. In many contexts, the blind have depended on the sighted and in some cultures, the sighted have relied on the blind. Until the late nineteenth century, when the Meiji reforms changed the lives of many, the blind, both men and women, had a fairly secure prospect of working as singers and musicians, masseurs, acupuncturists and shamanic mediums. Blind minstrels shaped Japanese culture as artists, healers and religious experts. Visually impaired storytellers and performers were responsible for the creation and transmission of the best-known and admired pieces of performance and literary art, such as the stirring *The Tale of the Heike* (*Heike monogatari* 平家物語), an epic account of two rival houses.[104] Studies have been published on the different activities of blind minstrels, semi-monastic entertainers and healers in the fields of history of literature, ethnomusicology, social history and folklore studies,[105] but little research has been conducted in the field of the history of medicine. Medico-historical studies concentrate on institutional history and the milestones in the evolution of modern medicine in Japan.[106]

---

104 For pioneering English-language studies on blind minstrels and the emergence of epic literature in Japan, see Ruch (1977, 1990). For a study on Buddhism and the performing arts with chapters on blind entertainers, see, e.g. Suzuki ([1993] 2016) and the volumes by Fukuda et al. (1999) on shamanic mediums and blind priests and their oral literature.
105 Nakayama Tarō's comprehensive *Nihon mōjinshi* (History of the blind in Japan), published in 1934, was followed by a second volume in 1936, *Zoku Nihon mōjinshi* (Continued history of the blind in Japan). Katō Yasuaki's *Nihon mōjin shakaishi kenkyū* (Studies in the social history of Japan's blind) (1974) reconstructs, as the title states, the social history of the blind. Ingrid Fritsch in her study on blind musicians (1996) explores the musicians' professional guilds. The scholarly contributions of Hirose Kōjirō concentrate on the organizations and welfare systems of the blind and visually impaired from medieval times to the present; he addresses the topic of blind monks in the medieval period in Hirose (1994a, 1994b); see further works by Hirose on p. 108n219. In a recent study on early modern and present-day female visually impaired musicians in Japan, Groemer briefly outlines their historical roots (2016, 24–26).
106 Blindness and ophthalmologic issues in the modern era are discussed in the monumental seven-volume *Nihon ganka no rekishi* (History of ophthalmology in Japan), published in 1997 by the Japanese Ophthalmological Society Centennial Commemoration Compilation Committee (Nihon ganka gakkai hyakushūnen kinen hensan iinkai). Early Japanese-language works on the history of ophthalmology in Japan include Fujikawa ([1899] 1980) and Ogawa ([1904]

This chapter will discuss specific examples from Buddhist authoritative writing, such as sutras and their commentaries, in order to highlight the symbolic involvement of the eye. The narrative continues in Chapter 4 and introduces Japanese Buddhist monastics' intense engagement in supporting the visually impaired. Sources such as miracle healing legends, which were established and passed on in early Buddhist Japan to attract the suffering to remote sanctuaries, are also discussed in Chapter 4.

3.1 The Eye in Buddhist Texts

Both "blindness," symbolizing the state of delusion in the Buddhist sense, and "healing from blindness" by the Buddha as the Master of Medicines are interlinking motifs in popular tales in the Buddhist world, both past and present. The vivid imagery of the ancient Jātaka tales about the Buddha's former births, and pictorial representations of them found in Central Asia, exerted a strong influence on East Asian Buddhism, including the early forms of Buddhism in Japan. The most important mural in the largest monastery-style cave found in Dunhuang along the Silk Road depicts the story of "The Forest of Recovered Eyesight."[107] The mural is about six meters in length. It shows various scenes in which five rough-looking men, representing five hundred robbers, are defeated by soldiers in battle, struck with blindness and banished to a wild forest. The next scenes show that the robbers meet the Buddha in the forest and start following his teachings. The former criminals repent their evil deeds and finally regain their eyesight, taking up monastic orders. The message of the Buddhist tale is that even an evil person can reach awakening after repenting. The eye, or rather eyesight, may have only a symbolic value here but it is important to note that according to the vinaya, only the sighted can enjoy ordination into monastic life and thus have access to liberation. In the ordination rules, blindness, deafness and other impairments are regarded as factors that preclude an aspirant from joining the monastic community.

Other early Indian Buddhist texts that have been influential in Asia and found their way to Japan refer to the "eye" as a symbol of spiritual advancement in a differentiated way. For example, in the *Discourse on the Stages of Concentra-*

1971). For a standard work in English on the history of ophthalmology in Japan from ancient times to the present, see Mishima et al. (2004).
107 Mogao Cave 285 (Western Wei, 534–556 CE). For a description in English and images of the cave, see Dunhuang Research Academy on http://public.dha.ac.cn (last accessed 16 Feb. 2017).

tion Practice (*Yōgācārabhūmi-śāstra*)[108], a fourth-century encyclopedic work by Maitreya,[109] we find references to a set of several different types of eye. The *Yōgācārabhūmi-śāstra* relates eleven eye types[110] to different stages of spiritual attainment, the stages being the main subject of the discourse. The physical organ of the eye and the ability to perceive are linked in specific ways in Indian thought. The visual sense perception is one of the five aggregates (Sk. *skandha*) that result in the arising of the sense of self (Sk. *svabhāva*, Jp. *jishō* 自性) which Buddhist practice seeks to dissolve. The nature of the eye, its ability to perceive and its role in the formation of the sense of self thus come under close scrutiny in Buddhism in general.

In the Yōgācāra Buddhist tradition, with its emphasis on the development of the consciousness and the mind-only concept, exploration of the sense organs, such as the eye, ear and nose is central. By gradually obtaining increasingly higher stages of insight, the "eye" (*gen* 眼) changes from type one as the most fundamental type of eye to type eleven, the highest type. The eye in the final stage can see into the past, present and future. It is able to see inner and outer objects and so forth. The adept obtains the divine eye or "Buddha eye" (*butsugen* 佛眼), a popular Indian trope for someone who has obtained omniscience. The "Buddha eye" is a mark of the highest attainment.

References to the eyes of the Buddha as one of the traditional thirty-two marks of the Buddha's distinctive bodily characteristics found their way into many texts, and sculptors and painters attempted to portray these features in their works of art. Famously, the Buddha in his perfected form appears to have eyes of the greatest beauty in both color and shape. His eyes are of a deep blue with eyelashes like a bull. A tuft of shining white hair (Sk. *ūrṇākeśa*, Jp. *byakugō* 白毫) between his eyes is an additional mark of his awakened state. The tuft is thought to emit a beam of light by which the Buddha is able to show unenlightened beings a vision. Sculptors in the Central or East Asian tradition represent the hair tuft with an inlaid crystal between the eyes of the Buddha statue that reflects light.

---

108 *Yuga shiji ron* 瑜伽師地論, T 1579.30.279–882, trans. Xuanzang 玄奘 (602–664) between 646 and 648.
109 The putative author of the *Yogācārabhūmi-śāstra* lived ca. 270–350 CE. The Tibetan tradition attributes the text to Asaṅga, a fourth-century monk, who is said to be the older brother of Vasubandhu, another influential Buddhist thinker.
110 See list of the types of eye and various subcategories: T 1579.30.289c24–292b29; cf. section on ophthalmology in Fukunaga Katsumi's dictionary of Buddhist medicine (Fukunaga 1990, 262–263). Fukunaga Katsumi collated passages from Buddhist texts to form a compendium of a "medical" nature; for a critical appraisal, see Salguero (2015, 50–51).

While the Buddha, as the greatest being, has perfect sense organs including the eye as the result, or rather the expression, of ultimate insight, a damaged eye or ear and afflictions such as blindness or deafness appear in Buddhist texts as the result of unwholesome deeds and attachment to the illusory sense of self. The deplorable existence of those afflicted is described in great detail. One such example occurs in a well-known treatise on the vast literature related to the "Perfection of Wisdom" (*Mahāprajñāpāramitā*). The treatise (*śāstra*), entitled *Mahāprajñāpāramitā-śāstra*[111], is ascribed to a famous Buddhist thinker, the second- or third-century South Indian monk Nāgārjuna who became a legendary figure. In all probability, the treatise is of Chinese origin, although Nāgārjuna's authorship remains undisputed in the Buddhist tradition. Whoever the author or compiler was, the Indian character of the text is striking in the passage on the ailments inflicted upon those who have committed unwholesome deeds in the past. As is the case in other texts, afflictions of the ear and other organs follow the passages on the eye, ultimately forming a popular trope. The *Mahāprajñāpāramitā-śāstra* mentions ninety-six kinds of diseases of the eye that may afflict someone as a consequence of deeds in past lives.[112] Only the Buddha and adherence to his doctrine can heal the afflicted from those terrible torments. The final chapter of the *Compendium of Suśruta* (*Suśruta saṃhitā*), an Indian medical compendium without any overt Buddhist character briefly mentioned above, extensively describes diseases of the eye, their origin and the proper treatment of the afflictions. The chapter mentions seventy-six kinds of eye diseases (Bhishagratna 1916, 3:5). However, the compendium was formed over a long period between about 250 and 500 CE, so the number of these diseases may have varied across time. Whether a list of ninety-six or seventy-six – the emphasis is on the high number of different afflictions. The vivid description in the Buddhist texts serves as a dark background against the shining ability of the Buddha to heal all ills. The more detail, the more convincing the argument that only the Buddha can help and lead all beings to ultimate liberation.

3.2 Eye-Opening Ceremonies

In India and in regions where social actors shared Indian religious ideas and practices, statues of deities are animated by an "eye-opening" ceremony. After

---

[111] *Dai chido-ron* 大智度論, T 1509, trans. Kumārajīva; French translation by Lamotte (1944–1980).
[112] T 1509.25.118c3–4 and 309b13–14.

the ceremony, the statues, now regarded as physical appearances of a deity (*mūrti*), can start exchanging glances (*darśana*) with the venerator – a cherished moment.[113] When the statues or paintings are fashioned, the eyes are left blank so the pupils can later be dotted in during the ceremony. This ceremony is also practiced in the Buddhist context. In addition to the eye-opening ceremony, called *kaigan kuyō* 開眼供養 in Japan, statues are filled with sacred texts, miniature statues and relics. In Buddhist traditions, paintings of venerated figures can show dedication texts, handprints of important teachers, mantras and other traces of empowerment on the back. In Japanese Buddhism, material objects related to ancestor veneration, such as memorial tablets kept on a Buddhist house altar at a private home, are also consecrated with an eye-opening ceremony.[114] The production of Buddhist images is an important practice because it is thought to be meritorious to a high degree in most Buddhist traditions.[115] If a consecration such as the eye-opening ceremony is the beginning of the "life"[116] of an object, the deconsecration ceremony introduces its "death" or at least a temporary disruption of its life. A proper deconsecration ceremony, called an "expulsion ceremony" (*hakken-shiki* 撥遣式)[117] in Japanese, is offered today in Buddhist temples for those who wish to repair sacred objects, remove them to another location or decommission them from use altogether. Interestingly, however, there is no mention of a "closing of eyes."

---

113 See Eck ([1981] 1985); see also Gell in his chapter 7.7 on "Darhsan: Witnessing as Agency" (1998, 116–121).
114 See Tambiah for reflections on Buddhist eye-opening ceremonies in contemporary Thailand and Sri Lanka (1984, 254–257).
115 See Sharf (1996) introducing the *Scripture on the Production of Buddha Images* which praises those who produce Buddha images and enumerate their merits. This short sutra does not provide instruction on how to produce the images.
116 On the view that the statues and other consecrated objects in Japan are alive, see, e.g. Faure (1996, 243–254), the contributions in Sharf and Sharf (2001) and Horton's monograph (2007). A tenth-century wooden statue of "the living" Śākyamuni, one of the principle objects of worship at Seiryōji Temple 清涼寺 near Kyoto, is reputedly an exact copy of the Buddha's portrait carved from life. It even contained replicas of human entrails. A Japanese monk brought the statue back with him in 987 from his voyage to China. When researchers opened the closed cavity in the back of the sacred statue in the 1950s, they found objects such as offerings of precious objects, texts and relics. According to the documentation found in the cache, nuns and other women in China had made the replica of internal organs from silk and then donated them to be placed inside the sacred statue (cf. Henderson and Hurvitz 1956, esp. 22–25).
117 Also written 發遣 or simplified 发遣, also read *hokken*. Literally meaning "abandonment." In esoteric Buddhism, this term is used when the Buddhas are returned to their abode after manifesting them in visualization practice in one's mind. This ceremony in relation to material images is mentioned briefly in Rambelli and Reinders (2012, 20); see also Triplett (2017c).

Ritual eye-opening also forms part of empowerment ceremonies in esoteric Buddhism. Here, the recipients are not statues or images but human initiands. The ceremonial master waves a metal implement in front of the initiand's eyes and states that now the Buddha, as the King of Physicians, has lifted the film clouding his or her vision. Demiéville describes this ritual as part of a consecration or "unction" ceremony (Sk. *abhiṣeka*, Jp. *kanjō* 灌頂) in which certain Buddhist precepts and teachings are typically conferred (1937, 261; Demiéville/Tatz 1985, 90). Both the terms used by the ceremonial master and the metal implement mentioned in texts suggest that the ceremony symbolically represents a medical healing procedure. Demiéville therefore relates the ceremonial eye-opening closely to cataract surgery as practiced originally in the Indian tradition. A passage from an esoteric Buddhist sutra illustrates the ceremonial use of the metal implement – a golden stylet, spatula or needle. The sutra in question became a fundamental scripture in Japanese esoteric Buddhism. It is usually simply referred to as the *Mahāvairocana-sūtra*[118] because of the central place of Buddha Mahāvairocana, the "Grand Resplendent One," in the esoteric tradition of Buddhism. In this text, the Buddha Mahāvairocana speaks and outlines essential ceremonies and ritual techniques such as the creation of the mandala related to the sutra – a gateway to realizing insight. Asked by his interlocutor Vajrapāṇi how the ceremonial master should conduct the initiation, the Buddha replies:

> At the time of the consecration he {the ceremonial master} should install [the initiand] on the wondrous lotus [in the center]
> And make offerings with unguents, flowers, lamps, and *argha* {miscellaneous offerings, especially water};
> He shades him from above with banners, pennants, and parasols and offers up enchanting music
> And the extensive and wonderful words of auspicious *gāthās* {verses}.
> After having made offerings in this manner and brought joy [to the initiand],
> He himself anoints [the initiand's] head in the presence of the Tathāgatas {buddhas}.
> He should again make him offerings of exquisite unguents and flowers,
> After which he should take a golden stylet {*konbei*金箆} and, standing in front of him,
> Exhort him and make him rejoice by uttering this *gāthā*:
> "Son of the Buddha, the buddhas have removed your film of ignorance,

---

118 *Dai Birushana jōbutsu jinben kaji-kyō* 大毘盧遮那成佛神變加持經, T 848. The text belongs to the tantras, a particular type of texts in the Esoteric Buddhist tradition, and is therefore usually referred to as the *Mahāvairocana-abhisaṃbodhi-tantra*, the "Tantra of Mahāvairocana's Manifest Enlightenment." Sanskrit versions are found only in fragments.

> Just as the world's king of physicians skillfully uses a golden stylet {*konchū* 金篦} [to remove the world's blindness]."[119]

The sutra text was probably composed in mid-seventh century India during the emergence of tantric practices in Buddhist circles and translated into Chinese by the Indian pandit Śubhakarasiṃha (637–735) with the assistance of the scholar monk Yixing 一行 (683–727) in 724. As it was subsequently brought to Japan by Kūkai, we can assume that the ritual initiation described in this important text was not only known but also practiced from early on in Japan. The "golden stylets" used as Buddhist ritual implements are described in some detail in Yixing's extensive commentary on the sutra.[120] Referring to the original Sanskrit verses in transliteration comments on the passage above, Yixing provides the dimensions and an indication of both the form and use of the implements. He states that they are shaped like elongated vajras, important ritual tools that symbolize the diamond-like indestructibility of one's innate awakened mind.[121] Yixing, who is known for his knowledge of astronomy, offers technical details that are reminiscent of the surgical procedure of cataract couching: The vajra-like instrument about the length of a hand has two rounded points that are to be covered with wholesome substances before being inserted into the eye. Indeed, the ritual seems inspired by the medical procedure of couching for cataracts as known and practiced in India, and may well be, as Demiéville claims, a symbolic representation (1937, 261). In my view, the passage provides a window on the sharing of knowledge in premodern Asia.

Other Buddhist commentators had some difficulty comprehending the reference to the couching, especially when the original Sanskrit text was not explicit. Demiéville draws our attention to a 1935 academic study of a palm-leaf manuscript with Sanskrit verses used in a tantric master consecration as outlined above. The Sanskrit verses were interpolated with a commentary in Old Javanese (1937, 3: Suppl. IV, fn. p. 261, a9), a language belonging to the Austronesian lan-

---

[119] T 848.18.12a; quote from the translation by Rolf W. Giebel (2005, 49–50), additions by the translator are in square brackets, those by the present author are in curly brackets. Cf. Yamamoto for an earlier full translation of the Chinese text into English. Yamamoto translates the passage as: "Next he will take a golden spatula and stay in front of his disciple. Let him rejoice by consoling with the following gāthā: 'O son of the Buddha, the Buddha will remove the membrane of ignorance for you just as a medical doctor makes good use of a golden spatula. [...]'" (1990, 34).
[120] *Dai Birushana jōbutsu-kyō sho* 大毘盧遮那成佛經疏, T 1796.39.669c, composed by Yixing between 721 and 747.
[121] Demiéville's article shows line drawings of three such implements (1937, 261, fig. 79; 1985, 90) from the 1932–33 edition of the *Mikkyō daijiten*, a major Japanese reference work on esoteric Buddhism. See also Fukunaga (1990, 267).

guage family. This manuscript, among other sources, shows that the practice of ritual initiation in the esoteric Buddhist tradition was not limited to East Asia but appears to have been also popular in insular Southeast Asia with the Buddhist empire of Śrīvijaya on the island of Sumatra as an important center. The region was by no means isolated, rather the opposite: Exchanges between China and India were not exceptional.[122] The Old Javanese master-consecration text entitled *Sang Hyang Kamahāyānan Mantrānaya* probably dates from the tenth century and was presumably compiled from earlier versions from the eighth century when there was frequent contact with monastic travellers from other parts of the Buddhist world. The *Sang Hyang Kamahāyānan Mantrānaya* contains several Sanskrit verses, including verse 16, that may have been directly quoted from the (now lost) Sanskrit *Mahāvairocana-sūtra* and other texts used specifically in the esoteric Buddhist context (Ishii 1992, 225).[123] The Sanskrit verse that is of interest to the present topic addresses the prospect that the Buddhas will eradicate the veil of non-realization the same way as the great physicians eradicate the cataract of the eye.[124] According to Wulff, the Javanese commentator was someone with a practical and not too philosophical mind (1935, 13–14). The commentator paraphrases the verse that when one's eyes are dull and impure, the doctor treats the eyes with an ointment so that they are healed. As a result, the sight becomes pure and fine because of the waning of the attack of a fungus or dirt or other irritants, the text reads. It is not exaggerated to assume that the commentator transposed the idea of eye healing with a *śalākā* ("spatula," "rod") to indigenous Javanese therapies with salves or poultices against various kinds of afflictions of the eye caused by external irritants. The reference to a spatula in the shape of a vajra is absent from the text – and perhaps was even absent from the initiation ceremony itself, so the concrete reference to Indian surgical methods was lost to the unknown commentator. The general meaning of the Sanskrit verse in the context of the Buddhist path to awakening, however, remained obvious to them.

The passage in the *Mahāvairocana-sūtra*, and in Yixing's commentary quoted above, elaborates on the meaning of the obscuration of the eye as being blind

---

122 Cf. Golzio (2010, 96, referencing Ishii 1992, 225–236); see also Heirman et al. (2018).
123 See also the table in Ishii (1992, 233–234) and Kandahjaya (2016, tables on p. 70 and 72).
124 The line of verse 16 reads *śalākair vaidyarājendraiḥ yathālokasya taimiram* with Wulff's translation "so wie die grossen ärzte [sic!] mit ihren sonden [sic!] den star [sic!] des auges [sic!] (ausmerzen)" (1935, 24; see also note on page 53–54). Wulff's use of the word *Sonde* meaning "tube" is interesting. Indeed, the couching instruments used in Europe were small tubes and not solid needles. I thank the anatomist Michael Schultz for this valuable information and explaining the procedure in vivid detail to me.

to the true nature of one's mind, and the removal of the obscuration by the Buddha by means of the golden "stylet" – or however the implement was termed in the texts – as awakening to the world of insight. These are powerful metaphors. The vajra wand has a symbolic role since its rounded points cannot truly puncture the eye membrane of the initiant in the ritual. Another important sutra requires the ritual master to rub the initiant's eyes with a wand to be covered with wholesome substances. This sutra is, along with the *Mahāvairocana-sūtra*, one of the two central scriptures of the Shingon school of esoteric Buddhism in Japan. Usually, it is referred to as the *Sutra of the Entering into the Vajra (World)* (*Vajraśekhara-sūtra*)[125] as it expounds teachings and ritual practices of entering into the Diamond-World Mandala. Here, the text explicitly guides the ceremonial master to use the vajra wand as in the method of eye healing.[126] And as a great number of ointments, fragrances, wholesome liquids and plants are to be offered in the initiation ritual, the medicine to be smeared on the wand or "stylet" may well be thought to be of a similar kind. We can thus speak of a clearly symbolic application of the golden "stylet" in the ritual. The metaphorical use of cataract surgery is by no means limited to the sutra texts introduced above. There are many more instances, and one further example will be discussed below in the context of Indian methods of healing sight-related illnesses practiced in Japan.

3.3 Medicinal Treatment of Sight-Related Diseases

Some sutras combine ritual with concrete medical instructions to heal the physical body much less metaphorically. This is obvious in the following example pertaining to the healing of a particular sight-related illness, a passage from

---

125 *Kongōchō yuga chū ryakujutsu nenju-kyō* 金剛頂瑜伽中略出念誦經, T 866 (*Sutra for Recitation Abridged from the* Vajraśekhara Yoga), composed and translated by the Indian monk Vajrabodhi (671–741). According to tradition, Vajrabodhi arrived in China in 720 and, having lost the massive original Sanskrit text on his journey from India, wrote about it from memory and using extant translations. The composition concerns the *Tattvasaṃgraha*, short for the Sanskrit title of *Sarva-tathāgata-tattva-saṃgrahaṃ nāma mahāyāna-sūtram* (*The Revered Sutra of the Great Vehicle, the Compendium of Principles of All Tathāgatas*). See Ishii (1992) who compares the tenth-century Old Javanese consecration text *Sang Hyang Kamahāyānan Mantrānaya* with T 866. Vajrabodhi famously visited Śrīvijaya on his journey to China in 718.
126 *Vajraśekhara-sūtra*, T 866.18.252a17–18: "The master should use a small golden pounder on the disciple, as in eye healing, and rub it on each of his or her two eyes" 師應執小金杵子如治眼法拭其兩目. The term 金杵 may be, as the footnote in the Taishō edition reveals, short for "golden indestructible" (金剛, Jp. *kongō*), the term for vajra.

one of the versions of the *Dhāraṇī of the Bodhisattva With a Thousand Hands and Eyes*.[127] The "Bodhisattva With a Thousand Hands and Eyes" refers to the Thousand-arms, Thousand-eyes Avalokiteśvara, a central figure in East Asian Buddhist worship. There are thirteen versions of this *dhāraṇī*, all of them translated into Chinese during the Tang dynasty. *Dhāraṇī* (*darani* 陀羅尼, or *ju* 呪) consist of long rows of Sanskrit syllables that usually do not form a sentence. Instead, the sound of the syllables "holds" the healing power of the deities. The version of the *Dhāraṇī of the Bodhisattva With a Thousand Hands and Eyes* translated by Bhagavaddharma around 650 CE can be said to be the most authoritative text among this group, and could even be considered the "most important of all the esoteric scriptures in China" (Yü 2001, 59). The text was brought to Japan in the eighth century and exerted considerable influence on practice and doctrinal debate.

The *dhāraṇī sūtra* is structured as follows: The text appears as if it is spoken by the Buddha in the palace of the bodhisattva Avalokiteśvara located on the island of Potalaka, the bodhisattva's realm. Suddenly, there is a great illumination. When asked the cause, the Buddha announces that Avalokiteśvara is now going to reveal a *dhāraṇī*. Avalokiteśvara then takes center stage and explains the origin and the powerful efficacy of the *dhāraṇī*. He urges everyone to follow him in making ten vows of compassion. The keeping of the *dhāraṇī* will result in fifteen types of good birth and the avoidance of fifteen types of unfortunate death. After enumerating them, he reveals the *dhāraṇī* consisting of 84 phrases. Instructions on constructing a sacred space are also provided in detail. The text explains further, as is typical for such sutras, that the correct keeping of the *dhāraṇī* leads to spiritual and worldly benefits. The sutra also offers numerous guidelines for handling certain materials to perform supernatural deeds, and it lists several recipes to deal with various problems, including gaining good physical health. For example:

> If one suffers from diseases of the eye, such as having a blind pupil (blindness) or darkened eyes (cataracts), or when the white of the eye is covered or red or has a lusterless membrane, take from the three fruits *harītakī*, *amalā*, and *vibhītaka* one piece each and pulver-

---

127 *Senju sengen darani-kyō* 千手千眼陀羅尼經, T 1060; the full title of the sutra is: 千手千眼觀世音菩薩廣大圓滿無礙大悲心陀羅尼經 which can be rendered as "Dhāraṇī of the Bodhisattva With a Thousand Hands and Eyes Who Regards the World's Sounds and Feels Vast, Complete, Unimpeded Great Compassion." The text in the Taishō edition includes a preface by the Emperor of China dated 1411. The sutra is fully translated into German by Reis-Habito (1993) in chapter III of her study, and into English by Giddings (2017). For a translation of a similar passage from a related sutra, see Unschuld (1985a, 315–316). See also below p. 105.

ize them finely in a mortar. While doing this, one has to pay strict attention to purity and avoid the presence of women who have just given birth, dogs and pigs.[128] One then calls out the name of the Buddha and covers the eye with a mixture of white honey and mother's milk. The milk that one uses on the person must be the milk of a boy's mother. Milk from a girl's mother has no effect. When the medicine is ready, recite the *dhāraṇī* 1008 times in front of a statue of the Thousand-eyed. After the medicine has covered the eye for seven full days in a dark room protected from the wind, the eye comes back to life. The blind pupil and the previously covered white of the eye will shine with a marvelous luster.[129]

We can clearly see from this example that medicine, healing practice and ritual form an interlinking system. The sutra presents a good example for a Buddhist text with references to Indian medicine as evidence of Indo-Sinitic scientific exchange. The three fruits *harītakī*, *amalā*, and *vibhītaka* are mentioned with their Sanskrit names and are all from plants grown in India.[130] Not only was the knowledge about these medicinal fruits transferred to Japan but portions of these plants were found in the Shōsōin 正倉院 treasure house in Nara, as part of a bequest from Empress Kōmyō 光明 (659–760)[131] to Tōdaiji Temple. We know that there were originally large quantities of these substances that were nearly used up in medical treatments, rituals and ordinary consumption by the tenth century.[132]

3.3.1 Buddhism and Cataract Surgery in Japan

Contemporary historians of medicine are fascinated by the transfer of the Indian technique of cataractopiesis (couching for cataracts) and its reception and practice in Japan. Several texts attest to the ritual use of implements that can be interpreted as needles, stylets, or even barbs or combs for operations to restore sight effectively in Buddhist temples in ancient and medieval Japan. In addition to the symbolic reference to the golden needle as a means to obtain insight during initiatory eye-opening ceremonies, the motif of the Indian technique of cat-

---

[128] Parturient mothers here are seen as particularly unclean, similar to animals such as dogs and pigs. For concepts of impurity of women's reproductive bodies, see Chapter 5.
[129] T 1060; author's translation as quoted in Triplett (2010b, 490).
[130] More on the three fruits follows in Chapter 6.
[131] The nature of Empress Kōmyō's bequest and other engagements related to medicine will be elaborated further in Chapter 5.
[132] On medicinal substances of the Shōsōin, see Asahina (1955), Kunai-chō Shōsōin jimusho and Shibata (2000) and Torigoe (2005). For more on Shōsōin's medicinal plants, see Chapter 6.

aract couching is frequently used in various other kinds of Buddhist scriptures. For example, a collection of miscellaneous *dhāraṇī* praises the workings and the vows of the bodhisattvas in a series of vivid images:

> There are four kinds of wondrous deeds of the bodhisattvas, enlightened beings. Which are the four? The first is that I hope to live in a world without a Buddha. [There] I would be like sun and moon on Earth, [so that] I remove the darkness from that world. The second is: As if I would break the membrane of the eyes of the people with a golden stylet (*konbei* 金錍), [so that] they see the light. The third is that I will change into great medicine trees for all living beings. All diseases and sufferings of those who smell their scent will vanish. The fourth is that the sermons of the Buddhist teachings will continuously spread like the moistening [of the soil] by a rain of teachings. The sprouts [of the Buddhist thoughts] will grow and prosper. [All this] arises from the unsurpassed mind of the awakening. Therefore, the bodhisattvas, enlightened beings, take four great vows.[133]

Clearly, the image of a golden stylet (or needle) breaking the membrane in passages such as this also serves a metaphorical purpose and is not meant to be medically instructive. The question is whether Buddhist monastics in China and other parts of East Asia transferred knowledge of this highly effective Indian medical technique and used it to heal patients, or whether anyone practiced the surgery at all. Records indicate that Indian Buddhists in China taught the technique to Chinese Daoist healers in the Tang dynasty (Unschuld 1985b, 64; Deshpande 2003–2004, 248).[134] Overall, cataract couching seems not to have been practiced widely in China compared to other treatments. The treatment did become popular in Japan, however, and by the medieval period, it was the domain of both Japanese Buddhist monastics and secular physicians.

Since the main reference to the Indian technique of cataract couching is found in the aforementioned *Uttara-tantra* chapter in the Sanskrit *Compendium of Suśruta* (*Suśruta saṃhitā*),[135] the search for textual evidence must start with translations or references to that Indian ophthalmology work. Knowledge of this form of cataract surgery and other Indian treatments for eye disorders had reached Japan by the tenth century.[136] An ophthalmological chapter in the Japanese medical handbook *Essentials of Medicine*, hereafter referred to by its

---

133 *Darani zōshū* 陀羅尼雑集, T 1336.21.596b21–27. Other examples include a mention in the *Mahāparinirvāṇa-sūtra*, T 374.12.411c20–412b8.
134 For an outline of Indian cataract surgery in China, see Unschuld (1985a, 144–148).
135 The technique of couching a cataract is outlined in *Uttara-tantra*, chapter 17. For an extensive list of translations and studies of this passage and the technique in Graeco-Roman antiquity and in other cultures, see Meulenbeld (1999, 1B:413n283).
136 The modern term is *hakunaishō tejutsu* 白内障手術, "cataract surgery," the traditional Japanese term is *tsuika-jutsu* 墜下術, "fall technique."

Japanese title *Ishinpō*, compiled by court physician Tanba (no) Yasuyori 丹波康頼 (912–995) in 984, mentions the Indian technique, although not in much detail.[137] However, we do not know whether the procedure of cataract couching was conducted in Japan at Yasuyori's time or any time soon after. As the description of the golden needle treatment remains vague in the *Ishinpō*, it can be surmised that the technique was transmitted directly by doctors from China (Mishima et al. 2004, 65) or by other books that we have no record of.

The *Ishinpō* quotes from a source that Yasuyori just calls the *Ophthalmological Treatise*.[138] From the content, it can be surmised that this is the abbreviated title of *Nāgārjuna Bodhisattva's Ophthalmological Treatise* (Jp. *Ryūju bosatsu ganron*, Ch. *Longshu pusa yanlun* 龍樹菩薩眼論). Since Nāgārjuna allegedly compiled, and perhaps even authored, the *Uttara-tantra*, the link to the Indian tradition is obvious. However, by referring to Nāgārjuna as a bodhisattva, the eminent eye specialist appears to be firmly placed in the Buddhist world. Today, the identity of Nāgārjuna is the subject of debate.[139] The eye doctor Nāgārjuna is surmised to have lived in the fourth or fifth century CE. In East Asian texts on the other hand, the name Nāgārjuna – written Longmu 龍木 "dragon-wood" or, more commonly, Longshu 龍樹 "dragon-tree" – usually refers to the famous Buddhist philosopher who lived several centuries earlier in the second or third century CE. The frequent mention of the name Nāgārjuna in the context of ophthalmology (Deshpande 2003–2004, 244) suggests both the conflation of the Nāgārjunas as well as the influence of Indian medical ideas and texts in China and beyond.[140] Yamano shows convincingly that the veneration of "Nāgārjuna (Longmu) Medicine King" was a secondary introduction to Chinese medicine in China, a medical system especially sympathetic to Daoism. She points out that adherents of the Buddhist Yogācāra school who blended esoteric Buddhism with Daoist "shamanistic techniques" (*fujutsu* 巫術) exerted a strong influence on late Song-dynasty medicine, and as a result, Nāgārjuna became increasingly recognized as a supreme healer and author of the *Longmu yanlun* 龍樹眼論, an important East Asian ophthalmological text (Yamano 2011, 37–38).

---

137 For an in-depth study of the compendium's history, see Sugitatsu (1991). For thoughts on the *Ishinpō*'s place in the history of Japanese Buddhism and early medieval medical history in Japan, see Triplett (2012), also Triplett (2014, 338–343); both publications are incorporated and extended in this chapter. See also Khan (2016).
138 *Ganron* 眼論, literally: "Eye Treatise."
139 For the debate on the historicity of Nāgārjuna, see, e.g. Mabbett (1998) and Meulenbeld (1999, 1 A:363–368).
140 Deshpande surmises that the name first appears in a revision of the Sanskrit text in India (Deshpande 2003–2004, 257).

Before exploring the quote from *Nāgārjuna Bodhisattva's Ophthalmological Treatise* in the Japanese work *Ishinpō* in more detail, it may be interesting to note that the quoted text is by far not the only Buddhist – or rather Buddhistic – source cited in the tenth-century Japanese compilation. At first glance, it gives the impression that tenth-century Japanese medicine was predominantly based on Chinese classical sources. Usually the *Ishinpō* is looked at as a vehicle of transferring (non-religious) Chinese medical knowledge to Japan where it was firmly implanted and adapted. Altogether the *Ishinpō* is comprised of medical writings originating in China, Korea and, to some extent, India. The compiler, Tanba Yasuyori, purportedly of noble Chinese or Korean origin (Hsia et al. 1986, 10), selected passages mainly from pre-Tang period Chinese literature, compiled the thirty-fascicle *Ishinpō* and presented it to the Imperial Court when he was at an already advanced age. Yasuyori's work is still extant today albeit only in a few relatively late versions. Over the centuries, copies were only made occasionally. A complete Japanese translation and critical text edition of the entire thirty-fascicle work was completed by Maki Sachiko and published between 1993 and 2012, based on the nineteenth-century efforts of members of the government Institute of Medicine. Before that, selected fascicles were transmitted separately. Fascicle 28 on "Health Principles and Chamber Exercises" in particular was published multiply in China.[141]

Since elaborations on the sources from the *Ishinpō* follow further below, and because it is a complete rendition of all available knowledge on medical matters and healing in the Heian period, it seems justified to list the chapters of the compilation in their entirety:[142]

1. Disease Treatment, Pharmacology, Posology
2. Acupuncture and Moxibustion
3. Afflictions of the Nervous System (Wind Strokes)
4. Whiskers, Hair, Face, Nose, Body Odours
5. Eyes, Ears, Mouth, Tongue, Teeth
6. Internal Organs, Stomach, Heart, Kidneys, Liver, Lungs
7. Genitals, Piles, Intestinal Worms

---

141 The English translation by Hsia et al. (1986) contains this fascicle as well as fascicles 1, 2, 26 and 27. An English translation of fascicle 28 was published as "The Tao of Sex" by Ishihara and Levy (1968).
142 The translation of the table of contents follows Hsia et al. (1986).

8. Nutritional Deficiency, Diseases of the Extremities
9. Cough, Asthma, Dyspepsia, Nausea
10. Hernia, Jaundice, Swelling
11. Cholera and Dysentery
12. Constipation, Diabetes, Hematuria, Bedwetting
13. Consumption, Exhaustion, Bone and Lung Disease, Insomnia
14. Sudden Death, Remittent Fever, Typhoid Fever, Drowning, Freezing
15. Boils, Growths in Lungs and Intestines
16. Carbuncles, Vicious Swellings, Varicose Veins
17. Skin Diseases
18. Wounds, Burns, Metal Wounds, Arrow Wounds, Falling from Horses, Dog Bites, Horse Bites
19. Various Types of Tonics, Mineral Diet
20. Antidotes for Mineral-Dietary Poisoning
21. Women's Diseases
22. Continuation of Women's Diseases
23. Obstetrics
24. Conception, Prediction of Sex, Pregnancy Tests
25. Pediatrics
26. Geriatrics, Attaining Longevity
27. Geriatrics, Mental Hygiene, Breathing Exercises
28. Health Principles, Chamber Exercises
29. Dietary Adjustments
30. Materia Medica: Grain Cereals, Fruit, Meat, Vegetables.

The best-preserved copy is the so-called Nakarai-bon 半井本 (1532),[143] a Japanese national treasure that had rarely been seen until it was copied, printed and published by the Government Institute of Medicine in 1860. Even after publication it was kept in a closed archive until the Imperial Household Agency purchased it in 1982. In his article on a survey of quotations from previous medical works in the *Ishinpō* Ma Jixing (1985) counted about two hundred different sources and over ten thousand quotations in all. Of special interest is the list of explicitly Buddhist sources that Ma compiled and that Tada Iori (2010) has described in some detail. Passages from these Buddhist sources include the following:

Konkōmyō saishōō-kyō 金光明最勝王経, *Suvarṇa-prabhāsōttama-sūtra*, *Sutra of Golden Light*, T 663, Sui period: T 664, Tang period: T 665.

Daishū darani kyō shinju 大集陀羅尼經神呪, *Great Collection of Dhāraṇī Sutra Spells* (unidentified).

Senju sengen kanzeon bosatsu jibyō gōyaku-kyō 千手千眼觀世音菩薩治病合藥經, *Sutra on the Use of Medicinal Herbs for Healing by the Thousand-eyed, Thousand-hands Avalokiteśvara*, T 1059.

Ryōji byō-kyō 療痔病經, *Sutra on Relieving Sores*, T 1325.

Nankai kiki naihō den 南海寄歸內法傳, *A Record of Buddhist Practices Sent Home from the Southern Sea*, T 2125, by Yijing.

Some other passages in the *Ishinpō* refer to legendary or historical Buddhist authors and their works:

Giba myakuketsubyō-kyō 耆婆脈決病經, *Sutra on Jīvaka*[144] *['s Treatments on] Vascular Diseases* (unidentified).

Gibahō 耆婆方, *Treatments of Jīvaka* (unidentified).

Ryūjuhō 龍樹方, *Treatments of Nāgārjuna* (unidentified).

E'nichiji yakuhō 慧日寺藥方, *Temple Huirisi*[145] *Treatments on Medicinal Herbs* (unidentified).

---

143 For a digital rendition of the *Nakarai-bon*, see Tokyo National Museum (B-3178) on <http://emuseum.jp> (last accessed 13 Nov. 2018).
144 Jīvaka (Ch. Qipo, Jp. Kiba or Giba 耆婆) is a legendary Indian physician. He is said to have been Buddha's personal doctor and is hailed as the father of Buddhist medicine. For Jīvaka in Chinese medicine and surgery, see Salguero (2009).
145 Huirisi was a temple in Chang'an and center of the "Three Stages Teaching" (*sanjie jiao* 三階教) movement of the sixth to eighth centuries.

Shiragi hōshi mikkyō hō 新羅法師密教方, *Secret Treatments of Buddhist Masters from Silla* (unidentified).

Kyōshinhō 鑑真方, *Reflections on the True Treatments* (unidentified).

Sōshinpō[146] 僧深方, *Sengshen's Treatments* (unidentified).

Gosō-shi hō 吳爽師方, *Treatments of Master Wushuang* (unidentified).

Shaku Egi kanshoku kaizatsu ron 釈慧義寒食解雑論, *Various Theories on Cold Foods by Shi Huiyi*[147], T 2059.

Ganron 眼論, [*Nāgārjuna Bodhisattva's*] *Ophthalmological Treatise* (see 3.3.2 below).

Overall, the compilation is a rare opportunity to glance at Tang-period medicine and observe the tremendous effort to relate new knowledge from the continent to those engaged in medical healing in Japan. Many of the sources can only be known from Yasuyori's compendium and are otherwise lost, including a Tang-period medical work compiled by the Song or Southern Qi monastic Shi Sengshen (Jp. Shaku Sōshin) 釈僧深 (ca. 420–502)[148] Tada mentions not only *Sengshen's Treatments* but also the many quotes from the *Arcane Essentials of the Imperial Library* (*Waitai biyao*, Jp. *Gaidaihiyō* 外台秘要), compiled by Wang Tao 王燾 (ca. 670–755) in 752. This compilation is another Tang-period work that is now lost.[149] According to Ma, there are 206 direct quotes from the *Sengshen's Treatments* and 13 passages that quote the *Sengshen's Treatments* indirectly. Although there are many repetitions, there is the possibility that these fragments found in the *Ishinpō* make up a large portion of a work of medical Buddhist literature that is otherwise not accessible today.[150]

---

146 The reading of this title is unclear.
147 Huiyi was active at Qiyuansi Temple 祇洹寺, a monastery in Yangzhou that was the home of the translator Guṇavarman in the Song dynasty.
148 This monk lived therefore between approximately 420 and 502 CE, under the Southern Dynasties (Tada 2010, 412).
149 See also p. 88n158.
150 According to Fujiwara no Sukeyo's 藤原佐世 (847–897) catalogue of literary works kept in Japanese libraries of his time, *Sengshen's Treatments* (Jp. *Sōshinpō*) was clearly known and spread within Japan as a separate book. Interestingly, works from temple libraries were not included in the ninth-century catalogue (Rosner 1989, 23).

3.3.2 *Nāgārjuna Bodhisattva's Ophthalmological Treatise*

Another example of a Buddhistic medical text that exists today only in fragmentary form, is *Nāgārjuna Bodhisattva's Ophthalmological Treatise* from the Indian medical tradition, briefly mentioned above. The compiler of the *Ishinpō*, Tanba Yasuyori, quotes from the treatise in discussing the treatment of "clear-blindness" or cataracts.[151] Nearly identical sections are included in the influential Chinese formulary *Holy Prescriptions for Universal Relief in the Taiping Era* (*Taiping shenghui fang* 太平聖恵方), composed in 992. This compendium consisted of one hundred volumes and was widely circulated in East Asia. An early ophthalmological treatise attributed to Nāgārjuna may have been compiled in China in the eighth or ninth century but a complete translation of the Sanskrit *Uttara-tantra* on diseases of the eye, if it ever existed, has been lost. Deshpande shows that the addition of "bodhisattva" to the title was made as late as the fifteenth century by Jin Limeng 金礼蒙 who lived in the fourteenth to fifteenth centuries (Deshpande 2003–2004, 251).[152] Whereas the earlier text has vanished and survives only as rather short quotes in other texts, there are two more surviving texts attributed to Nāgārjuna.[153] The passage on cataracts in the tenth-century Japanese compendium *Ishinpō*[154] reads as follows:

---

[151] Ch. *qingmang* 清盲; Jp. *seimō*.
[152] See also Deshpande's earlier publications on Indic ophthalmology in China (1999, 2000).
[153] The first is a text titled *Nāgārjuna's Treatise* (Ch. *Longmu lun*) that is mentioned in the *Comprehensive Treatise on the Sage's Advice* (Ch. *Shengji zonglu* 聖濟總錄) and that could be the text included in the twelfth-century *Secretly Passed Down Nāgārjuna's Comprehensive Discourse on Ophthalmology* (Ch. *Michuan yanke longmu zong lun* 秘傳眼科龍木總論) (Kovacs and Unschuld 1998, 45) by the Daoist Baoguang 葆光道人 (dates unknown). The second is *Nāgārjuna Bodhisattva's Ophthalmological Treatise* in the compendium *A Collection of Various Medical Prescriptions* (Ch. *Yifang leiju* 醫方類聚), compiled by the above-mentioned Jin Limeng and first published in Korea in 1445. See chapter 4 in Mishima et al. (2004) on the possible route by which cataract couching was passed on. The chapter also gives an impression of a translation from the classical Chinese text into English. The text used in Mishima et. al is from an 1823 copy of a manuscript brought to Japan from Korea in the late sixteenth century; see Mishima et al. (2004, 88–89). For a discussion on the text's print history, see Yamano (2011). For a survey of Baoguang's ophthalmological compendium, which circulated in Japan, see Nakazumi et al. (1987a, 1987b).
[154] *Ishinpō* fascicle 5, section 14, translated by the author from the classical Chinese text quoted and commented upon by Tanba Yasuyori, edited by Maki (1996, 5:129–139). English translation published in Triplett (2017b, 545–547). I thank Dr. Wang Xiaojing for her valuable advice.

Treatments of the Eye Afflicted with Cataracts

From the *Treatise on the Origin of Diseases:*[155] When afflicted with cataract, the pupil of the eye does not actually show anything abnormal. The dark and the white [parts of the eye] are clearly separated; however, the afflicted cannot see anything. (Note: The Essence[156] and the *qi* of the Zang and Fu Viscera flow upwards to the eyes.) If the Viscera are weak and afflicted with Wind Illness,[157] if there is phlegm, one gets sick. If it is warm, then it will be red and painful. If it is not warm, an obstacle is formed within the eye. The reason for this is that blood and *qi* are insufficiently nourished by the Essence. Therefore, the outer form seems not abnormal, just one cannot see anything. This is what is called cataracts [literally, "clear blindness"].

From *[Nāgārjuna Bodhisattva's] Ophthalmological Treatise:* There does not appear to be any particular cause or reason for this affliction – and there is neither pain nor itching – but one slowly becomes blind. Over the years, there is an increasing loss of eyesight. Now, we can observe that the form of the eye itself does not appear abnormal, but there is an obstacle exactly in the middle of the eye inside the pupil. Therefore, the pupil appears unclear and is of a green-whitish color. One cannot differentiate people, things and other objects anymore. However, one can perceive the three lights [sunlight, moonlight, starlight]. One can differentiate day and night. This [describes] exactly the condition of the cataract.

To treat the disease, it is best operated on with a golden needle. With one needle treatment, one can suddenly see everything again. It is as if the clouds have vanished and the sun is seen. After the needle treatment, one should take pills of rhubarb. Not recommended in case of strong diarrhea. These diseases are all caused by weak, warm, and Wind Illness conditions.[158]

From the same source: Concerning the cause of the attack of cataract, there is an obstacle inside the eye that has the consistency of a sticky or creamy matter the size of an acorn that is floating in the eye or swimming in the water [in the eye]. This is what obstructs the pupil. Then we can find various treatments of the eye by applying powder, drugs, ointments, or decoctions, but all these treatments are in vain. Stupid doctors do not have any idea and claim that the disease is located outside of the eye. Some of them recommend these treat-

---

155 *Zhubing lun* 諸病論. Tanba uses a shortened title for *Treatise on the Origins and Symptoms of Diseases* (*Zhubing yuanhou lun* 諸病源候論), quoting from chapter 28, section 13, of the influential Sui-dynasty Chinese medical treatise compiled by Chao Yuanfang 巢元方 (550–630).
156 Ch. *jing*, usually translated as "essence," was thought to form the material basis of the physical body.
157 Ch. *fengbing*, Jp. *fūbyō* 風病. External disturbance by "wind" was thought to cause various illnesses.
158 A nearly identical quote is found in the Tang compendium *Arcane Essentials of the Imperial Library* (*Waitai biyao*), first published in 752 (cf. Kovacs and Unschuld 1998, 37–40). Wang Tao who compiled the *Arcane Essentials* quotes the (lost) *Indian Classic Discussing the Eye* (*Tianzhu jing lunyan* 天竺經論眼) by the Daoist Xie Long-shang 謝龍上 (dates unknown) who is said to have learned ophthalmology from Indian doctors. In addition to the introduction to the eye and eye afflictions in China in Kovacs and Unschuld (1998, 3–115), see Unschuld (1985a, 61–68) and (1985b).

ments and others operate by scraping [it] off. These are all false theories, empty discourses, subterfuges and absurd explanations because even if you apply one thousand such treatments, they do not heal one single time. Also, Bian Que,[159] who opened bones, and Hua Tuo,[160] who operated on the brain, both studied in a narrow way, so [even] they could only master a small field, and because of that, the cataract, alas, is not healed.

Recipes for Healing the Eye:[161] [This is] for the healing of the eye afflicted with cataract when one cannot see anything. Recipe for pigeon powder: [Take] one pigeon, fry it until it is done, as if for eating. [Take] half a *sheng*[162] of cassia seed, two *liang*[163] of wild ginger, and two *liang* of *Divaricate saposhnikovia*[164] root. Mix all these four ingredients, cut and seal them up, and let them dry for fifteen days. Melt and strain them. [This is] to be taken with alcohol with a small spoon, three times during the day, twice in the night.

The same source: [This is] for healing the eye afflicted with cataract when one has not been able to see for thirty years. [Take] one part of wild ginger, twelve pieces of dried glow worm,[165] one *sheng* of oilseed[166] and three pieces of carp gall. Melt all four ingredients. Strain the three ingredients: wild ginger, dried glow worm, and oilseed, and mix with the carp gall. If there is not enough [gall], substitute with mother's milk. [This is] to be taken three pills at a time [the size of] the fruit of the parasol tree.[167] After seven days, there is improvement. After fifteen days, it is healed.

Another recipe: [Take] one piece of pig gall. Fry only this one piece on a small fire until it lets you form pills. Roll pills [the size of] broomcorn millet [seeds]. Apply to the middle of the eye, as long as one takes a meal. Then it has an effect. This recipe is for the beginning when the obstacle is formed. Then it is best to use less. Refrain from applying too much.

Treatments of Jīvaka:[168] Treatment of those with cataract who cannot see anything, day or night. [Take] *Cortex fraxini*,[169] *Cimicifuga simplex*[170] and Baikal skullcap.[171] Boil equal parts of each in three liters of water. Take one and a half *sheng*, [soak] a cotton cloth, and put that directly into the eye.

---

159 The semi-mythological figure Bian Que 扁鵲 is said to have lived ca. 401–310 BCE. He is traditionally reckoned to be one of the greatest Chinese physicians.
160 Hua Tuo 華佗 (ca. 145–208) was a historical surgeon who is said to have used anesthesia.
161 Ch. *Zhiyan fang* 治眼方. This ophthalmological work is found as chapters 3 and 4 of the anonymous Yuan-dynasty work *Precious Treasure of Clear Eyes* (*Mingmu zhibao* 明目至寶).
162 *Sheng* 升: In the Tang period, the *sheng* unit of volume was approximately 300 ml.
163 *Liang* 両: One Tang period *liang* measured about 42 g.
164 Ch. *fangfeng* 防風 literally means "ward off the wind." Yasuyori gives the Japanese reading *hamasukana*.
165 Ch. *yinghuo* 螢火.
166 Ch. *wujing zi* 蕪菁子.
167 Ch. *wu* 梧.
168 Ch. *Qipo fang* 耆婆方. For Jīvaka's relationship to Bian Que and Hua Tuo, see Salguero (2009).
169 Ch. *qinpi* 秦皮.
170 Ch. *shengma* 升麻.
171 Ch. *huangqin* 黄芩.

Small Item Formulae:[172] [This is a] recipe for the eye, [when] nothing can be seen. Mix red carp gall and brain. Combine with real pearls. Take a cotton cloth, take [the mixture] and apply to the eye.

The second passage quoted from the *Ophthalmological Treatise* expresses disdain for "stupid doctors" and "false theories" which is an interesting case of insistence on one correct and effective treatment for cataracts with all other treatments ruled out. However, the chapter in the *Ishinpō* includes other treatments before and after the *Ophthalmological Treatise*. The composition of the tenth-century handbook, therefore, provides us with a fascinating insight into the position of knowledge attributed to Buddhists within an ancient medical debate on the right course of treatment. The statement that only the surgical method of couching is effective is unmistakably clear. The quote does not include, however, any precise instruction on how to conduct a cataractopiesis. A fairly detailed summary of the procedure is found in the fifteenth-century Chinese ophthalmological classic attributed (incorrectly) to the earlier famous Chinese doctor Sun Simiao 孫思邈 (580–682 CE). The classic also gained wide acceptance in late medieval Japan. The classic, entitled *Essential Subtleties on the Silver Sea* (*Yinhai jinwei*), mentions the method with the golden needle in connection with invocations to bodhisattva Avalokiteśvara (Ch. Guanyin).[173] Only in 1644 do we find much more detailed technical instructions concerning cataract surgery in a major Chinese ophthalmological work, the *Precious Manual of Ophthalmology* (*Shenshi yaohan* 審視瑤函)[174] by Fu Renyu 傅仁宇 (dates unknown), equally embedded in religious ritual instructions including the use of a talisman and incantations to Guanyin.[175] This is further evidence that firmly connects specialist knowledge of eye surgery from India with the practice of Buddhism and devotion to Avalokiteśvara in East Asia over the centuries.

Overall, the practice was neither largely integrated nor widely practiced in China. It seems to have remained in the hands of Brahmanical healers. The present-day medical doctor Chi-Chao Chan, however, claims that the practice of

---

172 Ch. *Xiaopin fang* 小品方. This medical work was authored by Chen Yanzhi 陳彥志 (dates unknown) most probably in the Liu Song dynasty (fifth century CE), and became a compulsory text for medical students in eighth-century Japan. By the end of the Northern Song dynasty (960–1127) however, the twelve-volume work seemed to have become lost in both China and Japan. It is frequently quoted in the *Ishinpō*.
173 For an English translation of the passage, see Kovacs and Unschuld (1998, 403–406).
174 The manual includes illustrations.
175 See Unschuld (1985b, 64–65), including translations of two short passages from the work. For an English translation of a passage presenting cataract surgery in a Buddhist context, see Unschuld (1985a, 147–148).

3.3 Medicinal Treatment of Sight-Related Diseases — 91

couching for cataracts with a golden needle found acceptance after Tang-period physicians combined the practice with the system of acupuncture (2010, 395).[176] In contrast, Kovacs and Unschuld assume a rather marginal role in the actual clinical application in China due to the decline of Buddhism "as a major intellectual force" (1998, 44) which must have hampered its spread in the view of the two scholars. They see another reason for the apparent lack of eye surgery in China in the incompatibility of the Indian and Chinese medical paradigms. In India the cause of the eye disease is seen as brain tissue "falling down" (corresponding to the idea in ancient Greek medicine, hence the term "cataract" in European languages) into the eye obstructing the sight, and the healing of this affliction is sought by directly treating the sight organ. In China, however, external or internal treatment with drugs was thought to remove functional disturbances, and since according to Chinese medical thought the liver corresponds with the eye, the "wind" disturbance of the eye was treated via the liver.

It is interesting to see that in Japan, the surgical practice of couching for cataracts became widespread. Regardless of whether cataractopiesis was commonplace or rare in China, the practice took hold in Japan and gained acceptance over the centuries as will be discussed in the following chapter.

---

[176] In her article, Chan gives a very general historical overview of the practice in China ending with a short report on the activity of her mother Winifred who served as an ophthalmologist in the re-emergence of traditional Chinese medicine in the People's Republic of China. Both her parents, known as Winifred Mao (1910–1988) and Eugene Chan (1899–1986), were eye doctors and co-founders of an eye hospital and ophthalmic center in China. See more on the history of ophthalmology in China from a medical history point of view in Fan (2005) and Kovacs and Unschuld (1998, 6–115).

4 The Eye II: Buddhist Healing and Living with Visual Impairment

The institutional structure of Buddhism excluded the impaired from monastic life. The visually impaired were no exception to this rule. Such practices of exclusion are not an encouraging framework for those who already depend on other people's support. And yet Japanese Buddhist temples were also sites of medical care for those suffering from sight-related diseases. This chapter outlines the history of monastic ophthalmology in Japan.

Early Buddhist legends put a strong emphasis on the idea of problems in a person's current life being karmic retribution for past moral failures and misdeeds. This seems to place responsibility for blindness and other impairments on the disabled individual and their immediate family. The legends were designed to encourage them to devote their lives to Buddhism by visiting temples and donating money and clothing to the monastic community. The tales invite the reader to believe in healing by divine intervention by powerful deities that can be contacted at Buddhist sanctuaries and pilgrimage sites. The resulting pilgrimage economy could be seen to be materially exploiting those who were deemed or regarded themselves as ill-fated and reaping profit from their situation. The symbolism of "blindness" as a state of delusion that is contrasted with the "opened eye" appears to have been especially unfortunate and stigmatizing. By at least the early medieval period, the visually impaired in Japan had developed their own culture (with regional variations). This culture was not restricted to the Japanese archipelago.[177] The subject of blind priests (mōsō 盲僧) and visually impaired entertainers will be addressed in the final part of this chapter.

4.1 Development of Monastic Ophthalmology in Japan

Physicians from China who immigrated to Japan are frequently mentioned in Japanese sources. One of them may have treated Fujiwara no Takaie 藤原隆家 (979–1044), the powerful regional governor of Kyushu (Mishima et al. 2004,

---

[177] Ers For example, the blind priests (mōsō 盲僧) in Kyushu trace their tradition to ancient Korea; Korean blind priests primarily engaged in divination. See Nagai (2002) for the social history of the blind priests in Japan and Korea in comparative perspective.

65), who suffered from a sight-related disease. So great was the reputation of the Chinese ophthamologists that Takaie requested the post of governor in order to seek help for his affliction from the resident Chinese doctors, according to *The Great Mirror* (*Ōkagami* 大鏡), the eleventh-century Fujiwara family annals.[178] The Chinese doctor's treatment of Takaie would indicate that immigrants from the mainland practiced cataract couching in Japan and introduced the technique to resident physicians from the eleventh century onwards. Takaie – who recovered from his affliction – purchased an important Chinese treatise on ophthalmological treatment, the *Zhiyan fang*, which is also mentioned frequently in the *Ishinpō* (Maki 1996, 5:135–137).[179] Takaie's emperor, Sanjō 三条 (r. 1011–1016), had been sympathetic to his request to be transferred to far-away Kyushu because the emperor himself suffered from a sight-related disease. Sanjō, however, was less fortunate than the governor and died at the young age of forty-two. It might well be that he turned blind after his court physicians administered a medicinal drug that caused severe side effects. The emperor's plight is related in a passage of *The Great Mirror* (*Ōkagami*), providing us with an insight into contemporary debates about illnesses, their causes and adequate treatments which, in Emperor Sanjō's case, proved to be ineffectual:

> It was a great tragedy that this Emperor was troubled by failing vision after his abdication. His eyes looked normal, and so it was hard to believe that he was blind. His eyeballs were as clear as anybody's. Furthermore, there were times when he saw quite well. [...] His Majesty tried all kinds of ineffectual cures for his eyes. It was a sad case. In an effort to combat the nervous disorder [*kaze* 風, Wind (Illness)] from which he suffered so dreadfully, the doctors advised him to pour cold water over his head in midwinter [...]. The icy deluge made him tremble violently and change color, and I have heard that the witnesses all felt great sympathy and distress. He was also taking medicine for his ailment – a potion called the elixir of immortality. Some people said, "Anyone who drinks the elixir of immortality is bound to develop that kind of eye trouble," but as a matter of fact the blindness was caused by the Spirit of a Chaplain [...] named Kanzan, who announced through a medium, "I sit on the former Emperor's head and cover his eyes with my wings, when I beat my wings he sees a little." The Emperor's main reason for abdicating was that he wanted to make a pilgrimage to the Enrakuji Central Hall. [...][180] He did so, but nothing came of it in spite of his great sacrifice. What a tragedy! Even though he might not have healed on the spot, surely there

---

178 Trans. McCullough (1980, 177). The same episode is found in the *Eiga monogatari* 栄華物語, *A Tale of Flowering Fortunes* (1028–1107), chap. 12, trans. McCullough and McCullough (1980, 2:430–431).
179 A short passage of the *Recipes for Healing the Eye* (*Zhiyan fang*) is translated above on p. 89.
180 The central hall of Enrakuji, a major temple complex on Mount Hiei overlooking the capital of Kyoto.

should have been some improvement. It was rumored that a goblin[181] from Mount Hiei was persecuting him. His Majesty also made a retreat to Uzumasa,[182] where he lodged under a coffered ceiling, in quarters extending from the sacred image to the eastern eavechamber. (*Ōkagami*, trans. McCullough 1980, 82–83)

In the period that followed, highly influential noblemen such as Kujō Kanezane 九条兼実 (1149–1207) and Fujiwara Sadaie 藤原定家 (or Teika, 1162–1241), noted in their diaries that they preferred consulting monks rather than the physicians at court, who were mainly members of the Tanba family. These diaries, Kanezane's *Record of Jade Leaves* (*Gyokuyō-ki* 玉葉記) and the poet Sadaie's *Record of the Full Moon* (*Meigekki* 明月記),[183] mention the names of the monks they consulted for medical treatment. Monastic physicians, who were often themselves members of the elite, profited from their erudition and seem to have eagerly consumed Chinese medical literature imported to Japan, often via Korea. The Kamakura period saw a rise in the popularity of the services and activities of monastic physicians outside the court as well. By the end of the Kamakura period, court-appointed physicians, monastic physicians and "secular" physicians who practiced medicine as a trade could all be found in Japan. By the sixteenth century, medical training in Buddhist institutions was the standard route to becoming a doctor: Male members of the most influential medical families from the secular social sphere customarily trained in medicine in Buddhist monasteries. One result of this development was that it was impossible to distinguish "secular" and "religious" doctors by appearance (Ishihara 1999, 56). Both had the tonsure and robes of a Buddhist monk. In addition to this, secular physicians were employed by the temples and their status was evaluated within the structure of the monastic hierarchy. Their pay was dictated by the rank they attained within this structure. It should be noted, however, that the secular physicians did not perform any religious functions.

Texts imported from Song China related to many different areas of medicine. The Japanese liked to purchase books imparting both traditional and newly developed medical knowledge, such as the above-mentioned *Taiping shenghui fang*. Another extensive compilation from the subsequent Mongolian Yuan dynasty (1279–1368), the two-hundred volume *Comprehensive Treatise on the Sage's Ad-*

---

181 "Goblin" here refers to *tengu* 天狗, nefarious supernatural creatures that were thought to bring disease and misfortune.
182 Uzumasa is an area of Kyoto; the passage probably refers to the practice of sleeping in a temple building, here Uzumasadera, close to the sacred image for healing. This "incubation ritual" was referred to as *komori* 籠り.
183 See below p. 145.

4.1 Development of Monastic Ophthalmology in Japan — 95

vice (*Shengji zonglu* 聖濟總錄, 1111–1117/8), reached Japan and was used by monk physicians such as Kajiwara Shōzen. Shōzen's work is especially noteworthy because he made new medical knowledge widely available in Japan as a compendium entitled *Book of the Simple Physician* (*Ton'ishō* 頓医抄, 1303/4), which is the first medical work written in Japanese. Interestingly, the surgical technique of cataract couching is not included in the *Book of the Simple Physician* (Mishima et al. 2004, 76) even though Shōzen does cite extensively from the *Taiping shenghui fang*, which has a chapter on eye surgery (Mishima et al. 2004, 87). Shōzen's second major work, the *Myriad Relief Formulae* (*Man'anhō* 万安方, 1315), was written in Chinese and references the newly published *Shengji zonglu*. Some parts of the *Shengji zonglu* were missing in the prints that were available to the Japanese. These were sloppily published, possibly due to the upheavals in China as a result of the Mongolian conquest.

This was also the case for the section on cataract couching (Mishima et al. 2004, 77; 87, quoting Ishihara 1956a and 1956b) which must have been included in the original *Shengji zonglu*. As such, Shōzen's second major work does not mention the surgical method either. Cataractopiesis does appear to have been conducted in the Kamakura period by both monk physicians and private practitioners (Mishima et al. 2004, 78).[184] The surgery may have been conducted frequently by private practitioners if we take an episode of the well-known twelfth-century *Scroll of Illness and Deformities* (*Yamai no sōshi* 病草紙) as an indication. In this illustrated scroll, various illnesses and impairments are depicted in a rather scornful way, and the episode on eye surgery is particularly cruel. The illustration shows a doctor sticking a knife-like implement into his patient's right eye while a woman holds a basin to catch the fluid spurting from the wound of the left eye, which has already been punctured. Curious onlookers in the background of the scene, the facial expression of the woman holding the basin and the overall tone of the accompanying text are enough to satisfy readers of the scroll seeking thrill and delight in another's misery. The comment states that, while the surgery itself was successful, the patient became totally blind, the surgeon obviously having been a quack.

Most of the delicate eye operations were conducted in Buddhist monastic institutions. Not long after Kajiwara Shōzen's death, ophthalmology, including eye surgery, was professionally organized by a group of monks at Majima 馬島 near Nagoya. This group eventually split into two schools, the Myōgen-in 明眼院 and

---

[184] For an image from a picture scroll depicting a private practitioner operating on a patient, see Mishima et al. (2004, 78, fig. 5–7). The caption for this image only mentions the library of Chinese and Japanese medical and pharmaceutical books and materials, Kyōu Shooku 杏雨書屋 (part of the Takeda Science Foundation). Neither the title nor the date of the scroll is mentioned.

the Daichibō 大智坊 schools, named after two temple buildings of the Iōzan Yakushiji 医王山薬師寺 in Majima. The two schools had numerous branches and styles. The Buddhist monk Seigan 清眼 (d. 1379) of Iōzan Yakushiji, whose name literally means "clear eye," is revered as the founder of the establishment. Iōzan Yakushiji and the entire temple compound eventually became a large hospital specializing in treating sight-related diseases. The monastic hospital was famed for its staff who professed special skills to heal eyes and successfully conducted cataract couching (Mishima et al. 2004, 85–91). Whereas the Myōgen-in eye doctors remained stationary at Myōgen-in in Majima, members of the Daichibō school left the original temple after losing a competition against the rival Myōgen-in physicians for the temple leadership in 1810 (Mishima et al. 2004, 90). They established hospitals all over Japan and brought ophthalmological care to other parts of the country.[185] The temple hospital remained in existence until 1874 when the performance of medical services by monastics was prohibited by the Meiji government.

Many of the activities of the monks who were involved in eye care remain unknown because knowledge was passed exclusively from master to disciple without the help of written records until the sixteenth century. There are no written records from this period but eventually the monastic eye specialists did note down what they saw as central to their work in the form of confidential or "secret" records (*hidensho* 秘伝書). These manuscripts helped students of ophthalmology and other medical fields to memorize important aspects of their healing art. They were not systematically constructed handbooks. Detailed drawings are a salient feature of some of the manuscripts.[186] The use of colored ink enhanced access to knowledge about the human eye[187] and its afflictions.[188]

---

[185] See Okuzawa (1997, 197–198) for the names of the principal ophthalmological schools (families, clans) in Japan. To differentiate themselves from others, sub-schools of the Majima school used different characters for their names such as: 麻嶋, 真嶋, see Okuzawa (1997, 199) on the varied spelling. Mishima et al. (2004, 133–140) introduces the most important schools of the 149 schools that Okuzawa has identified. Many have a monastic background. The Majima school, with its numerous sub-schools, remained the largest and most influential from the fourteenth century until the end of the Edo period and still produces practicing eye doctors today; for a history of Myōgen'in, see Ōharu chōshi henshū iinkai (1979). See Okuzawa's list of sixteenth- and seventeenth-century "secret" manuscripts (1997, table 1, p. 198 and table 2, p. 206–225). Mishima et al. provide tables in English of genealogies and manuscripts of the Majima lineage based on Okuzawa's work (2004, tables 6–1 to 6–4, p. 106–114).

[186] Chinese manuscripts also contain drawings but they are rather abstract compared to the Japanese ones (Okuzawa 1997, 200).

The sixteenth-century secret records from the Majima school in particular have a strong Buddhist character (Okuzawa 1997, 199) – perhaps because these medical practitioners were monastics and based at Buddhist institutions. In addition to the use of the Chinese system of yin and yang and the eight trigrams often used in divination as well as the theory of the "five rings and eight boundaries" (*gorin hakkaku* 五輪八廓) which can be termed "medical," the manuscripts contain ideas such as the teaching of the Five Viscera in conjunction with the Five Buddhas (*gozō gobutsu* 五臟五仏) as evidenced, for example, by the diagram of the eye in the Japanese manuscript described above in Chapter 2 (see fig. 1).[189] The manuscripts also point to the veneration of the Twelve Gods (Jūnishin 十二神)[190] who serve the Medicine Buddha.

The hagiographic writings on the founder of the Majima school of ophthalmology, Seigan, hints at his being familiar with the medical teachings attributed to Longshu (Nāgārjuna). For example, a secret record written by a monk from the Majima lineage in 1601, which is part of Okuzawa's private collection, relates that their illustrious founder went to China and was taught by bodhisattva Nāgārjuna himself. Another record, written in 1610, states that the bodhisattva transmitted his knowledge directly to Majima Seigan (Mishima et al. 2004, 86–87). Disregarding the story that Seigan himself went to China to study, these passages suggest that Seigan might have received his knowledge via *Nāgārjuna Bodhisattva's Ophthalmological Treatise*. It is possible that Seigan did know the *Treatise* as the work was introduced to Japan in the early ninth century, as was the nearly identical passage in the *Taiping shenghui fang*. Seigan may have been very familiar with their content (Mishima et al. 2004, 86–87). In summary, early seventeenth-century writers of the secret records assume that the teaching of Nāgārjuna played a great role in their lineage and that Nāgārjuna, as bodhisattva Dragon Wood, was celebrated as a Chinese sage and physician. His name was assumed to be a genuine Chinese Buddhist name, and there was probably no knowledge of the Sanskrit origin of it. The Indian heritage had been all but forgotten, at least by the seventeenth century.

Moreover, it may also be possible that Seigan received special training in the Indian technique of eye surgery from a Chinese specialist. While frequent ex-

---

187 For example, bitot spots in child night blindness were depicted. As Mishima et al. (2004, 96) points out, this condition was described two hundred years before it was described in Europe.
188 See, for example, Mishima et al. (2004, fig. 6–4, 6–5 and 6–6).
189 See also Michel-Zaitsu (2017, 137, fig. 73).
190 These twelve fearful figures from the Indian tradition are associated with the twelve hours of the day, of which they are guardian spirits.

changes between China and Japan came to a halt in the Yuan dynasty, limited contact did allow the transfer of goods and knowledge. Furthermore, the last decade of Seigan's life coincided with the rule of the Ming dynasty (1368– 1644) when trade and visits by diplomats and Buddhist monastics opened up again. The secret records of Seigan's disciples and those of later seventeenth-century schools not only dealt with major Chinese publications such as the *Repeated Views from a Box of Precious Jade* (*Fanshi yaohan* 番視瑤函, 1644), with its influential depictions of cataract surgery, but also with books from Europe containing, among other things, the idea of a three-dimensional view of the eye. Until the end of the Edo period – that is, before the introduction of Western ophthalmology to Japan and subsequent changes in eye theory, categorization, and therapy – Japanese ophthalmologists treated sight-related diseases with a surgical method that ultimately derived from Indian medicine and that was transmitted and practiced mainly by Buddhist monastics.

Another example is the well-known physician Manase Dōsan 曲直瀬道三 (1507–1594), who was originally trained as a Zen monk but left the order later in his life. His medical textbook *Collection of Writings of the Keiteki [Academy]* (*Keiteiki-shū* 啓迪集, 1574) became a standard work in Japan.[191] Dōsan treated various high-ranking military men and enjoyed high esteem among members of the elite, especially during the latter part of his long life. Members of his school also practiced ophthalmology as a secret record from a European collection clearly shows (Mishima et al. 2004, 94–95). Overall, the monk physicians were highly trained, and developed and incorporated newly imported ophthalmological (and other medical) knowledge into their own system of healing and providing care. The various sub-schools of the specialized Majima school, however, kept their supremacy in the field of ophthalmology.

4.2 Monks as Doctors, Patients as Pilgrims

While Myōgen-in did provide patient care as a center for the treatment of sight-related diseases, the institution was also a fully functioning Buddhist temple with ritual services for the Medicine Buddha (Yakushi Nyorai). It would be

---

[191] For the medical career of Manase Dōsan and his disciples, see Yakazu (1982). A collected volume on various aspects of Manase Dōsan's life and work appeared in 2015, edited by the Takeda Science Foundation Kyōu Library (Takeda kagagaku shinkō zaidan Kyōu shooku henshū).

wrong to disregard the economic upside of this arrangement combining medical healing and spiritual care. The success was not limited to Myōgen-in and institutions connected to the Majima lineage. Other Yakushi temples offered care for physical afflictions of the eyes as well. The temple Iōzan Ichibataji 醫王山一畑寺, founded in 894 near the city of Izumo in what is now Shimane Prefecture, is perhaps the best-known instance of a pilgrimage site for those seeking eye healing.[192] Ichibataji was the seat of ophthalmologists of the Ichibata-ryū 一畑流 named after the popular name of the temple (Okuzawa 1997, 215, table 2, no. 46). Both Ichibataji and another rural temple, Tsubosakadera 壺阪寺 near Nara,[193] are pilgrimage sites that continue to offer eye healing to this day.[194] Such temples oversaw fairly large compounds with springs and wells and had powerful statues of Yakushi or Kannon. Pilgrims seeking treatment could rinse their eyes with the healing water or use special tea brewed with it for rinsing and consumption. Water, tea and other remedies were offered in exchange for a donation. Housing pilgrims, also for incubation rituals (*komori* 籠り), led to a further increase in income so it was possible to establish nursing rooms and then hospitals such as the Iōzan Yakushiji in Majima (Okuzawa 1997, 201–202). Others, such as Hōgonji 宝厳寺 on the island of Chikubushima in Lake Biwa have today lost their particular attraction for pilgrims with eye problems, although Hōgonji remains an important pilgrimage site as part of the Kannon pilgrimage circuit.[195] Hōgonji on Chikubushima must have held a great attraction for the blind in the sixteenth to eighteenth centuries, however, as we can surmise from the popularity of the late medieval and early modern narrative *Chikubushima* 竹生島 found in numerous versions (cf. Triplett 2004, 57–61). The narrative tells the story of a young girl who sells her body to pay for her father's memorial service only to be sacrificed to a monstrous, human-eating snake. In the end, the story continues, she is saved by her devotion to the *Lotus Sutra*. The girl finally returns home to her blind mother, restores her mother's sight with a magic jewel and manifests herself as the deity Chikubushima Benzaiten 竹生島弁財天, a

---

192 Since 1953, the temple has been registered as an independent religious corporation called Ichibata Yakushi kyōdan 一畑薬師教団 and belongs to the Rinzai school Myōshinji branch 臨済宗妙心寺派. On contemporary ritual activity at Ichibataji, see Triplett (2013).
193 Tsubosakadera is the popular name of this temple. Officially, it is called Minami hokkeji 南法華寺. The temple was founded in 703, only 150 years after the official introduction of Buddhism in Japan by a monk from one of the earliest Japanese Buddhist temples, the Moto-Gangōji 本元興寺.
194 For the history of Tsubosakadera and the role of narratives on famous episodes of eye healing, see Triplett (2010a).
195 For more on this pilgrimage circuit, see Triplett (2018).

form of the Indian goddess Sarasvatī. Chikubushima Benzaiten is combined with Ugajin 宇賀神, a theriomorphic male *kami* worshipped for a good harvest and revered as a syncretic deity. The statues dedicated to Hōgonji from at least the beginning of the sixteenth century show Uga-Benzaiten 宇賀弁財天, the six-armed, warrior-like, esoteric form of Benzaiten with a small *torii* 鳥居 shrine gate and Ugajin as a coiled snake with the head of a bearded man. Benzaiten's function is not directly connected to the harvest, she is venerated as the goddess of music and wealth. The combination with a snake deity makes sense in that Benzaiten herself can manifest as a (white) snake. Despite the remoteness of the island in the northern part of the lake – or perhaps because of its secluded location – pilgrims also came to worship Kannon at Hōgonji.[196]

The tiny Biwa Lake island of Chikubushima has been a sacred site since prehistoric times. After the arrival of Buddhism, this island sanctuary was thought to be an ideal site for the veneration of Benzaiten (Sarasvatī), a female deity associated with water who is usually enshrined on small islands in artificial lakes in Japanese temple compounds.[197] At the same time, Hōgonji was the seat of a school of ophthalmologists as evidenced by secret records from the Shinkyō-ryū 神教流 school of eye healing doctors at least during the Keichō 慶長 era (1596–1614) (Okusawa 1997, 210; table 2, no. 26, p. 211). Further research is necessary to determine whether these doctors maintained an office or hospital on the island or whether they cooperated with Hōgonji and Chikubushima because of the miracles of healing sight-related diseases associated with them.

The members of the Shinkyō-ryū held Chikubushima Benzaiten as the revealer of the healing arts of their school. She passed on the therapies and teachings in a dream during a period of prayer, presumably to the founder of the ophthalmological school. The name of the school fittingly means "school of divine teachings." In the early nineteenth century, Furusawa Gentai 古澤元泰 (ca. 1762–?), whose grandfather was the ninth head of the Shinkyō-ryū, retired from his position as medical officer of Ōshū province where Chikubushima is located, and moved to Edo. His name at birth was Minamoto Tokihide 源時英, so we know that he was born into an ancient, once powerful family. The fact that he used a pen name, Ben'an 梅庵, meaning "plum hermitage," adds to the assump-

---

196 After the forced separation of Buddhism and Shinto in the late nineteenth century, the "Shinto part" on Chikubushima offered services to Azaihime no Mikoto 浅井比売命, the Shinto manifestation of Benzaiten. However, a recent visit to the shrine revealed a new wooden statue of Benzaiten visible to visitors in the altar hall, indicating perhaps a return to a more syncretistic style of worship. For aspects of contemporary religious culture on the island, see Pye (1996).
197 See Ludvik (2007) on the transformation of the goddess Sarasvatī into a Buddhist deity; for Benzaiten of Chikubushima, see also Faure (2016b, 210–212).

tion that the Shinkyō-ryū school must have trained members of the ruling and educated elite in the late medieval period as well. Gentai was in contact with an eye doctor called Satō Keiun (or Kyōun) 佐藤慶雲 (dates unknown) in Kuki, which is to the north of Edo. His family is believed to have passed on his ophthalmological knowledge over many generations. However, according to Nakazumi et al. (1985, 228), Gentai formally passed on the secret Shinkyō-ryū knowledge of the diagnosis and treatment of sight-related illnesses to Satō Keiun as evidenced by the numerous Shinkyō-ryū manuscripts in Saitō's possession. Modern historians of science who report on the manuscripts use the term "passing on of secrets from father to son" (*isshi sōden* 一子相伝) (Nakazumi et al. 1985, 228). The needle treatment of cataracts and glaucoma as part of this secret transmission were held especially dear by members of the Shinkyō-ryū school because the two methods[198] were reported to have been revealed on the fifteenth day of the eighth month of the Keichō era year 2 (1597) by the deity. According to Nakazumi et al., however, the therapeutic methods were, similarly to the Majima school whose members propounded that their healing methods were prophesied by Yakushi Nyorai, actually based on Ming-dynasty Chinese medical texts (1985, 229). Interestingly, the divinely communicated texts were passed on orally within the family before Gentai, and only then committed to writing and given to an eye doctor far from Lake Biwa. It would also be of interest to learn how far the activities of these doctors go back in history and whether Gentai was seen as a traitor to or savior of the coveted ophthalmological knowledge. However, divorcing medical practice from the context of Buddhist temples was a general trend in the Edo period, so Gentai may have been acting in accord with other practitioners of the Shinkyō-ryū school. Although "Gentai" might be a Buddhist ordination name, we do not know exactly whether the earlier members of this school were formally ordained. The strong dedication to Benzaiten points to a medical family that was, however, firmly set in a Buddhist context, and the reference to medical knowledge as divine revelation from the popular Chikubushima Benzaiten must have given those with afflictions solace and a sense of reassurance before delicate operations.

It is not altogether clear who formed the (anonymous) Buddhist narratives praising and propagating the temples as pilgrimage sites in medieval times. Analyzing popular narratives such as *Chikubushima* in detail will shed light on the storytellers and those who may have formed these narratives. Exploring the tradition of glorifying devotional practice at a pilgrimage site, we will find that the

---

[198] For a description of the two methods, see one of the manuscripts introduced in Nakazumi et al. (1985, 228).

tradition reaches far back into the beginning of the incorporation of Buddhism in Japan and points to the activities of not (officially) ordained elite monks and nuns but religionists who were active outside of the newly established hierarchy in early Japan.

4.3 Miracle Healing of Blindness in Early Japanese Buddhist Records

Beside the two groups of officially licensed exorcists (or perhaps converging with them), Asuka and Nara-period "miracle working" ascetics (*shugenja* 修験者) or "holy men" (*hijiri* 聖), "self-ordained monks and nuns" (*shido no shami* 私度の沙彌) or just "novices" (*shami* 沙彌), similarly played a role in the circulation of medical knowledge understood to include the recitation of sutras and *dhāraṇī*. These "free" monks and nuns were instrumental in establishing Buddhist centers in Japan outside – or in combination with – the state Buddhist institutions in early Japan and continued to exert considerable social and cultural influence. Few Buddhist miracle healers are remembered today, such as Hōren, an eighth-century ascetic active on Kyushu, who is celebrated for his skill of healing. An eminent figure in local legends involving the god Hachiman 八幡 and the foundation of the Hiko mountain asceticism, Shugendō 修験道, Hōren may turn out to have been a historical person if we follow two entries in the imperial chronicle *Records of Japan, Continued* (*Shoku Nihongi* 続日本紀, 797):[199] One record of Taihō 大宝 era year 3 (703) mentions that the monk received land in Buzen in northeast Kyushu as a reward for his exorcistic healing arts (*ijutsu* 翳術).[200] The name Hōren appears again in an entry for Yōrō 養老 era year 5 (721) in the reign of Empress Genshō 元正 (r. 715–724). An imperial edict lists the following noteworthy activities and a reward:

> His mind-heart dwells in the branches of meditation, his practice is in the supportive beams of the Dharma, his excellent energy lies in the healing arts, he saves and heals the suffering of the people. Praise to this young man! Why not reward him! Let us bestow on him and his relatives up to the third degree the family name of Usa.

---

199 On Hōren and his activities, see Iinuma (2004, 26–30); also Hattori (1945, 66) in his chapter about monks providing care.
200 Most editions use the characters *ijutsu* 医術, "medical arts." However, as Nakano, a specialist for the religious history of Usa and its famous Hachiman Shrine indicates, the character 翳 is used. This character contains both elements for "medicine" and "shamanistic medium, diviner" indicating a background in Daoistic exorcism and healing (1985, 19).

4.3 Miracle Healing of Blindness in Early Japanese Buddhist Records

Whereas Hōren must have come to the attention of Empress Genshō for there to be some evidence in the official chronicles of praiseworthy religious and healing engagement in the Nara period, textual sources of early healing ascetics active in the early Buddhist network are rather scarce. In examining documents such as collections of Buddhist tales, we learn more about strategies of propagation than about historical developments of early Japanese Buddhism. Buddhist tales reveal prevailing concerns of the common people, often by presenting the perspective of an eyewitness and testimonials to elucidate miracles of healing or other remarkable events. The compilers of the tales intended to show that the "foreign" and "strange" Buddhist entities from India and China respond efficiently and promptly to devotional acts by the Japanese on their native soil too, and not only to acts in far-away lands. Often the tales are combined with a moral indicating its clearly normative character, as we can see in the *Miraculous Stories from Japan* (*Nihon ryōiki* 日本霊異記), the best known and earliest collection of Buddhist tales (*setsuwa* 説話) in Japan, compiled by Kyōkai (or Keikai 景戒) (dates unknown) in the ninth century.[201]

An episode about a healing ritual from another ninth-century *setsuwa* collection, the *Records of Gratitude to the Numinous in Japan* (*Nihon kanreiroku* 日本感霊録), *Kanreiroku* for short, can serve as an example for these important sources because it addresses the history of a pilgrimage site for the blind, Tsubosakadera. It is a collection that is, in my view, equally as important in regard to its role in Japanese Buddhist history as the *Miraculous Stories from Japan* (*Nihon ryōiki*).[202] Unfortunately, the *Kanreiroku* is very fragmented in comparison to the *Nihon ryōiki*, which has survived the centuries fairly well. The *Kanreiroku* fragments are also found in relatively late copies, of which some are rather heavily damaged, thereby making research of this important collection even more problematic. The episode quoted in a chronicle[203] written in 1211 survives as a fifteenth-century copy.[204] The original chronicler, Jōkei 貞慶 (1155–1213), may

---

[201] For a detailed analysis of a tale from this collection, see below p. 117.
[202] Stories of exemplary devotion to Yakushi and Kannon to restore eye-sight are found in *Nihon ryōiki* vol. 3, nos 11 and 12, see translation into English by Nakamura (1973, 236–238). In 3.11 the statue leaks a pink and sticky mass from its breast. After consuming the gum-like liquid – a miraculous medicine – the blind widow could see again.
[203] The chronicle has the title History of the Minami Hokkeji Temple (Minami hokkeji korōden 南法華寺古老伝). The episode is cited as being number 15 of the *setsuwa* collection; possibly this was originally in the first fascicle of the ninth-century collection.
[204] The original is kept in the temple archive and a facsimile can be found in the Nara Prefectural Library. For an edition of the chronicle, see Nagai (1985). The copy, dated 1496, has the title *History of the Tsubosakadera* (*Tsubosakadera korōden* 壺坂古老伝). For a brief treatment of the

have transcribed his master's words. Jōkei's master was Kakken 覚憲 (1131–1213), his Fujiwara uncle, who had been in charge of the consecration (eye-opening) ceremony of the Great Buddha at Tōdaiji and had retired to Tsubosakadera in his old age. The chronicle was compiled just after a devastating fire destroyed Tsubosakadera, killing many, so it may be surmised that it had been Kakken's wish to record its history and the miracles surrounding the site before passing away. In reference to the miraculous Eleven-faced, Thousand-armed Avalokiteśvara (Kannon) the chronicler quotes an episode from the ninth-century *Kanreiroku*:[205]

> A blind, self-ordained novice named Chōnin[206] used to be a beggar boy <...>. It is unclear whether he had had a home or a family. Approaching his tenth year, he became suddenly blind in both eyes <...>, without any apparent reason, and could see absolutely nothing anymore. Therefore Chōnin went to the Thousand-armed [Senju, i.e. Kanjizai or Kannon] of the temple Tsubosakasan some time during the Kōnin era [810–823] and intoned the incantations[207] to the Thousand-armed full of devotion and praised his name with "Hail bodhisattva Kanjizai, the Great Compassionate One who makes blind eyes see with the Hand of the Jewel of the Sun Essence"[208]. He continued in this way, day and night, through all six periods of the day, without becoming tired or weary. People invented a new name for him and started calling him "Senju shami," the novice devoted to the Thousand-armed. Many years passed but he persevered and did not give up. In the end he regained his eyesight. As a result of this he later proclaimed yin-yang [oracles] and all ordained and non-ordained came to rely on him <...>. He did not lack any of the necessary things, nor was he stricken with poverty <...This I was directly told by [Chōnin] himself>.
>
> Praise: [Kanjizai] replied to the sincere devotion of the novice, so that he saw the white light of the sun in the end <...>. If you ask for the miraculous medicine, your wish will become true. Therefore, we transmit the extraordinary sound of the miraculous benefit into far regions and for ten thousand generations. As it were, the secret power of his blessings[209] radiate into the ten directions. Truly he is the great consoler of ordinary men. He is also the Great Medicine King[210] over [all] roots of disease.[211] (*Tsubosakadera korōden* 4オ–5オ)[212]

episode, see Triplett (2010b, 487). A more thorough discussion of the foundation narratives of Tsubosakadera is found in Triplett (2010a).
205 The original text contains glosses by the chronicler (or the copyist). I omit the content of the glosses – with one exception – in my translation and indicate the glosses with <...>.
206 The name of this novice, Chōnin 長仁, is apparently found only in this document.
207 *Jinju*, a synonym for *darani* 陀羅尼 (Sk. *dhāraṇī*).
208 *Nōmaku nisshō mani ju myō gen an Daihi[shō]ja Kanjizai bosatsu* 曩謨日精摩尼手明眼暗大悲者観自在菩薩.
209 Power of blessings, *rei'i* 霊威, could be translated literally as "show of numinous authority."
210 Great Medicine King (Dai'iō 大医王, Sk. *Vaidyarāja*) is an epithet of a Buddha or bodhisattva, in this case of Kanjizai. This means that the Buddhist deity does not only heal physical illness but also eradicates its (karmic) causes.

The gloss in the text ("This I was directly told by Chōnin himself") clearly emphasises the testimonial character of the story. As readers, we are supposed to witness a miraculous eye healing by the power of the bodhisattva Kanjizai (Kannon) and are told that the healed novice became a recognized healer himself in the Sino-Japanese yin-yang tradition. Chōnin appears to have been a self-ordained novice, possibly an orphan and forced to beg for food. He is described as having belonged to the lowest social caste, and then rising from "rags to riches" by his devotion and the beneficial resonance of the Thousand-armed Kannon. He uninterruptedly intoned the *dhāraṇī* – the short episode even mentions the actual words – for many years at the temple. He was known to the people as a devotee of the principal deity of the temple and they may have provided him with food and clothes. Chōnin is a typical representation of someone becoming a religious expert not necessarily of his own choice or following the decision of his family (as with aristocratic boys or girls) but through his unfortunate social circumstances partially caused by physical impairment. The incantation Chōnin recited is from the *Senju sengen darani-kyō*[213] and is directly linked with one of the many benefits of Avalokiteśvara: The healing of physical (and spiritual) ills with spells thought to be extremely powerful and available to all, not only to fully ordained monastics.

Later in the medieval period, Buddhist legends for the most part described the terrible suffering of the principal characters who, in the end, achieve the ultimate end and are revered as powerful deities. As to the eye healing temple, Tsubosakadera, a medieval Buddhist legend tells the story of a pious girl, Matsura Sayohime 松浦さよひめ, a story that is nearly identical with the plot of the tale *Chikubushima* mentioned above. In fact, it can be said that the two stories are related. In the versions that include Tsubosakadera, the giant serpent in the end manifests as Tsubosaka Kannon 壺阪観音, whereas the girl Sayohime becomes the deity Benzaiten of Chikubushima. The two pilgrimage centers for eye healing, therefore, are connected in this tale.[214] In medieval times, more tales praising the principal object of worship of Tsubosakadera were formed that remained highly popular even well into the early modern period. The authors of these tales are unknown, and we are more or less left with interpreting self-referential elements in the narratives to attempt to establish who created them originally. Many plots belong to the genre of sermon literature (*sekkyō* 説

---

[211] Root, or cause, of disease (*byōen* 病縁).
[212] For a translation of this episode into German, see Triplett (2010a, 158–159).
[213] T 1060, see above p. 79.
[214] Since medieval times, the two temples have been connected on the famous Saigoku pilgrimage circuit to thirty-three temples featuring Kannon as the main object of worship.

教) performed by itinerant story-tellers who were depicted in contemporary picture scrolls and other materials and sources. The pictorial and textual sources point to professionals who themselves had visual impairments and by studying these sources, we can uncover the lives and concerns of those who performed the narratives.

4.4 Musicians, Ritualists, Healers: The Professional Lives of the Visually Impaired

Benzaiten, as the goddess of music and sound, was the protective deity of blind musicians in medieval, early modern and (in some regions) modern Japan. It can therefore be surmised that the Buddhist narrative of Matsura Sayohime and the serpent girl who ultimately manifests as Chikubushima Benzaiten and Tsubosaka Kannon may have been partially shaped by blind minstrels. In particular, Tsubosaka Kannon was revered as an eye-healing deity as mentioned above.

The following passage from a seventeenth-century version of (Matsura) Sayohime,[215] which is found in all longer versions of this popular tale, allows us to learn more about the group that was closely involved in the formation of the narrative. On the long journey to northern Japan where the virgin girl would be offered alive to be devoured by the monster in a human sacrifice ritual, Sayohime and the man who purchased her for this purpose reach Yamashina near Kyoto. The girl Sayohime reflects on famous local legends and events, in this case on the deity of Mount Ōsaka:

> In Yamashina she hurried shakily through Shi-no-miyakawara, then to Mount Ōsaka where the parting as well as the coming meet. "One says that the god (*myōjin* 明神) of Ōsaka once was the Lord Semimaru, the noble son of the emperor of the Engi era [901–922]. Because he was blind in both eyes, he lost his rank [as imperial prince] and is [now] known as the god of the mountain barrier station."

The short episode about the blind prince Semimaru 蝉丸 is an important part of the foundation legend of the so-called blind priests, men with a visual impairment who were clad in monastic robes and led an itinerant lifestyle providing Buddhist services mainly to farmers. They primarily engaged in the recitation of particular sutras with lute accompaniment and were supported by influential

---

215 The passage is from *Sayohime*, a three-volume illustrated manuscript in book form, undated, belonging to the Voretzsch Collection of the Frankfurt Museum of Applied Arts; vol. 2, 6 recto and 6 verso. See German translation, transcription and edition in Triplett (2004, 88); for an introduction in Japanese and a full transcription, see Triplett (2017a).

temples and shrines in northern Kyushu. They also recited tales after conducting ceremonies for local families. Additionally, members of the fourteenth- and fifteenth-century guilds (*tōdōza* 当道座, literally "my way" guild) of "lute-playing priests" (*biwa hōshi* 琵琶法師) who go back to the epic singers who formed the tales of the war between the Heike and Genji in the thirteenth century, saw Semimaru as their legendary ancestor (Triplett 2004, 213–214).[216] The lute-playing priests likened Semimaru to a bodhisattva called "Wonderful Sound," Myōon 妙音, who is often considered to be one and the same entity as Benzaiten, the deity of music frequently depicted with a lute.[217] Only male blind musicians praised Semimaru. We can therefore assume that this group of medieval entertainers may have been instrumental in the formation of the Sayohime-Benzaiten legend. In northern Honshū, in Isawa, Matsura Sayohime has been worshiped, particulary in connection with Yakushi, since the seventeenth century. The Yakushi hall of a temple connected to the mountain ascetic school of the Haguroha 羽黒派 used to be a center for the treatment of lung and eye ailments. It is thought that the legend was brought to the temple by groups of visually impaired entertainers (*zatō* 座頭) who belonged to the professional guild of lute players.

Another group of blind professionals may also have participated in forming the narrative under consideration: Itinerant female musicians with sight-related impairments (*goze* 瞽女, literally "blind women") who were organized more locally but also in hierarchical structures like the guild. By the seventeenth century, they had a relatively high social position compared with the male members of the guild and the religious blind priests.[218] The musical activities of the female blind and visually impaired musicians go back to about the fifteenth century. Since the medieval legend of Sayohime contains details about pregnancy and the hardships of female life, as well as a passage from the *Lotus Sutra* praising the real possibility for women to reach the state of awakening, it can be surmised that groups of female musicians, and the (often visually impaired) female mediums who worked with mountain ascetics in healing sessions, shaped the content and religious outlook of the narrative (Triplett 2004, 217).

When organized groups of visually impaired men who worked as ritualists, storytellers and entertainers were established, they obtained a social standing, support and income. Access to the professional guild could only be gained by those regarded as visually impaired. In fact, they had a monopoly on certain

---

216 For a study of Semimaru as both a historical and legendary figure, see Matisoff (1978).
217 See Fritsch (1996) for a book-length study on visually impaired musicians and their reverence for Myōon-Benzaiten (esp. 1996, 26).
218 See Fritsch (1996, 198); see also Matisoff (1978, 123). For the early modern history of *goze* as well as fieldwork on *goze*, see Groemer (2016).

melodies and entertainment arts and even tried to prevent the ritualist blind, the *mōsō*, from engaging in the profession. In other words, blindness meant some sort of hallmark of excellence when it came to the art of musical and storytelling entertainment. The model seems to have been a great success, as the ongoing rivalry between blind priests and the guild shows. By the early Edo period, the conflict between the rival factions of priests and guild entertainers was decided in a lawsuit in favor of the guild. After this, the *mōsō* had to limit their activities to Buddhist ceremonies.[219] The blind priests ultimately became part of a temple in Kyoto, and in 1871, the Meiji government dissolved all professional guilds including the *tōdōza*, effectively abolishing the blind entertainers' monopoly. *Mōsō* groups also exist today in Kyushu, albeit as priests of the Tendai school.[220]

While the *mōsō* did engage in healing rituals, there are also historical records of blind acupuncturists, masseurs and doctors. After the demise of exclusivist participation in the entertainment sector and other spheres of activity in the nineteenth century, foundations such as the Kyoto Buddha Eye Association (Kyōto butsugen kyōkai 京都仏眼協会) were established. The association was originally founded in 1921 to offer training in therapeutic techniques such as acupuncture and massage to the visually impaired.[221]

***

According to the historian of medicine Okuzawa Yasumasa, the scientific nature of Japanese medicine is of Chinese origin and rather philosophical, but since the medieval ophthalmological manuscripts were produced by monks to teach novices, the content is suffused with religious Buddhist thought and teachings. Indeed, Buddhist terminology is found rarely in medical writing of Chinese origin. To Okuzawa, "the borderline between religion and medicine is blurred in the Ma-

---

[219] There is extensive Japanese research on Edo-period blind entertainers and the various groups of men and women (with and without visual impairment) who practiced performative art, often in combination with religious rituals. There is also extensive research on how these groups developed later. See, for example, the history of northern Japanese blind monks (*bosama* 盲僧) and female mediums (*itako* 巫女): Ogata (2003); on the disabled in Japan from the perspective of anthropology of religion, see Hirose (1997); from the perspective of a visually impaired individual: Hirose (1999); on blind monks and their Earth God (Chijin 地神) rituals and texts in early modern Japan, see, e.g. Nishioka (2000) and Yamane (1999); for studies in English, see Groemer (2001).
[220] See Nagai (2002, 97–105).
[221] I thank Rev. Deguchi Kyōtarō for this information. For the establishment of welfare institutions for the blind, see also Mishima et al. (2004, 327–330).

jima ophthalmological school" (1997, 200). He juxtaposes the religious leanings of the Majima school with the comparatively early (in the history of medicine) regard for empirical principles in the clinical practice of the Majima monks. Here, couching for cataracts is mentioned as an important and exceptional example, which clearly indicates that Okuzawa, as a historian of medicine, sees religion as a complicating and hindering factor on the path to modern medicine. During the Meiji period, a clear division between Buddhism and ophthalmology was established in modern Japan. When the division was formally instituted, many conformed. The last abbot of Myōgen-in, for instance, left his monastic order and started to perform eye medicine after obtaining a license in Western ophthalmology (Tanihara 2013, 980).

When analyzing the medieval and early modern secret documents used by the medical families, it is tempting to regard them as documenting a gradual and progressive evolution towards modern European-style medicine. In other words, looking through the lens of the modern division between Buddhism and medicine, the boundary between early and medieval practice of eye medicine and Buddhism must appear to be blurred or as not yet "properly" divided. However, such an evolutionist view may easily overlook the dynamism and the plurality of voices in the medieval and early modern periods. In early and medieval Japan, there were boundaries between various elite groups – court physicians and monastic doctors – that practiced highly coveted knowledge. Group affiliation was determined by birth, secret initiation, or both. There are also boundaries between those who conformed with the official institutionalized facilities and those who did or could access these facilities and formed other groups and sub-groups such as the *zatō* guild entertainers. In turn, these non-elite sub-groups also worked with the notion of secrecy and instigated initiatory structures clearly modeled on those of the monastic elites. Esoteric Buddhist healing was an intricate part of Japanese culture more or less throughout the entire period under consideration, and secrecy and access to power and empowerment was of the highest concern.

In his widely-quoted eighth-century medical work, Wang Tao writes as the voice of the Daoist Xie, who learned ophthalmology from Brahmanical doctors:

> Now I have heard, between heaven and earth, nothing has a greater value than Man, and as far as the human body is concerned, nothing is treasured as much as the eye. It provides the most wonderful link for communication with the gods, and if we speak of the six sense organs the eye occupies the most important position! Hence prescriptions to cure the eye [from affliction] cannot be regarded lightly. (*Waitai biyao*)[222]

---

[222] Adapted from the translation of Kovacs and Unschuld (1998, 38).

Since the human eye is the object and at the same the subject of empowerment in Japanese Buddhist culture as incorporated from China, Korea and India, the source material in Japanese is especially rich. Quite naturally perhaps, the eye is of great concern to humans. What body part could be considered more important? The next chapter will explore human reproduction and concern for the female reproductive body in early and medieval Japanese society.

5 Women: Care of the Reproductive Female Body

[Umayado, Prince Stable Door,][223] was the second son of Tachibana no Toyohi tennō.[224] His mother the Empress was called Anahobe no Hashihito no Himeko.[225] When the Empress was near the time of delivery, she took a tour of the inner Palace grounds, looking at the posts of various officials. When she came to the horse station, she suddenly gave birth painlessly at the door of the stables.

From the *Nihon shoki*, Suiko 1.4.10, trans. Como (2007, 406)

The eight-century *Record of Japan* (*Nihon shoki*) appears to provide a factual account of this imperial birth, stating that it occurred suddenly and painlessly during an inspection of the palace grounds. The pregnant empress visited the horse station when she went into precipitate labor and bore a healthy boy. While the prince's birth was unusual, it cannot be described as miraculous. The account serves to explain the prince's unusual name Umayado 厩戸, Stable Door. The nature of the birth also suggests that the safe delivery was the result of positive karma: The prince was born outside, without any of the usual elaborate preparations and without the accompaniment of midwives, Buddhist ritualists, exorcists, yin-yang diviners and other specialists who were normally employed to ensure the safe delivery and postnatal care of an aristocratic mother and child.[226] The baby boy became none other than the crown prince Shōtoku Taishi, who, even during his lifetime, was depicted as an ideal ruler.[227] The reference to the horse in his birth story indicates royalty as the horse is one of the symbols

---

223 Umayado 厩戸 (574–622), also known under several other names including Kamitsumiya 上宮 (see above, p. 56), became crown prince after marrying his cousin, the daughter of his paternal aunt, the reigning monarch Suiko (554–628). Shōtoku Taishi, as the prince became known more than a century after his death, was one of the main proponents of implementing Chinese forms of government and etiquette as well as Buddhism in Yamato (Japan).

224 Tachibana no Toyohi 橘豊日 (518–587) was known as Yōmei 用明. He reigned from 585 until his death two years later. The title *tennō*, "heavenly ruler" was actually only introduced a hundred years later, so the use of the title in the chronicle is anachronistic.

225 Anahobe no Hashihito no Himeko 穴穂部間人皇女 (d. 621/622) was Yōmei's consort and younger half-sister as she, like Yōmei, was a child of emperor Kinmei. Suiko, who later became her sister-in-law, was also a child of the emperor.

226 For a translation of a Japanese historical record of an imperial birth involving these specialists, see Andreeva (2017a); see also Andreeva (2014, 358–359). Bowring translated a detailed account of the birth of an imperial child from the diary of court lady Murasaki Shikibu 紫式部 (ca. 973–1025) (1982, 51).

227 For the history of the devotional cult centering on Shōtoku, see, for instance, Como (2008) and Walley (2015). See also above p. 56.

(Sk. *aśvaratna*) of a Buddhist king. However, the emphasis in the episode is on the suddenness and painlessness of the birth, a perfect way of bringing a child into the world.

The desire to procreate successfully, and have a safe delivery and a healthy child is expressed in many Buddhist sources. There are numerous records of perinatal rituals dedicated to the well-being of the mother-to-be and the infant. In the twelfth century in particular, Shingon ritualists who were often ordained imperial princes, frequently conducted rites centering on Mahāmāyūrī, the "Great Peahen," to protect pregnant empresses which was akin to protecting the state itself.[228] In China and Japan, this female bodhisattva is rendered as a fierce *vidyārāja* (*myōō* 明王, "enlightened king"),[229] a powerful being that commands extraordinary knowledge to protect the state and the Dharma. According to the vinaya of the Mūlasarvāstivādins, the *dhāraṇī* of Mahāmāyūrī was connected to the removal of poison. An episode in this vinaya underlines the Buddha's superiority in curing illness (in this instance, poisoning): A secular doctor, wanting to test the Buddha's power, gives something perverse to a monk who has been bitten by a snake. The Buddha is not deceived, heals the sick monk and takes the opportunity to give a sermon on the origin of the healing spell.[230]

The Mahāmāyūrī vidyārājñī (Jp. Kujaku myōō 孔雀明王), often translated as Peacock Wisdom Queen, who appeared in later Mahāyāna sutras, was not only thought to cure all illnesses. The ritual for Mahāmāyūrī was also considered to bestow rain and happiness on the kingdom to which a healthy progeny belonged.[231]

Buddhist rituals also involved empowering *materia medica* used in Chinese-style medicine. Bezoars, milk and water were empowered in order to ease delivery as well as to increase or cause fertility in women:[232] "If a woman is without children, write [the Pure Avalokiteśvara] *dhāraṇī* on a leaf made of birch bark

---

[228] For an introduction to the Mahāmāyūrī cult in China and Japan, see de Visser (1980); in Tang China, see Des Jardins (2011).
[229] In East Asia, this female deity is rendered as a male figure.
[230] See Granoff (2011, 20–21).
[231] Through Kūkai and several of his disciples, the ritual outlined in the *Sutra of the Buddha Mother Great Peacock Wisdom King* (*Butsumo daikujaku myōō-kyō* 佛母大孔雀明王經), T 982, became popular in Japan but declined in popularity in the thirteenth century (see de Visser 1980, 207–209). The spells also derive from the *Peacock King Dhāraṇī Sutra* (*Kujakuō jukyō* 孔雀王呪經) of which several versions exist ranging from T 984, trans. Saṃghabhara (fl. fifth century), to T 988, trans. Kumārajīva. For a full translation of T 982 into French, see Des Jardins (2011, 201–263).
[232] Male reproduction, fertility and virility will not be discussed in this chapter. Most fertility cults in Japan are connected to the *kami*; see below p. 187.

using the cow bezoar. By wearing it in her sash, she will soon become pregnant,"²³³ wrote the scholar-monk Kakuzen 覺禪 (1143–?) in his extensive collection of notes on Buddhist rituals. In a recent publication, historian of East Asian Buddhism Benedetta Lomi introduced empowerment rituals for substances used to ensure safe childbirth and fertility that were commented on by Kakuzen and other monks in the Shingon Buddhist tradition, showing the importance of such ritual activity (Lomi 2017).

The ruling families are known to have hosted elaborate Buddhist ceremonies for aristocratic women who were about to bear heirs. As Anna Andreeva, historian of Japanese Buddhism, discovered, childbirth in Heian Japan involved ritualists and exorcists but rarely physicians (2014, 376).²³⁴ This chapter does not focus on birth and fertility practices. Instead, it explores views and practices regarding the reproductive aspect of the female body within the framework of medicine and Buddhism in more general terms.

5.1 The Female Body as an Obstacle to Becoming a Buddha?

While "worldly" women focused – or, at least, were socially obliged to focus – on procreation and maintaining power and the family lineage through their children, those who took refuge in "homelessness" (*shukke* 出家) vowed to abstain from both reproductive and non-reproductive sexual activities. In Buddhism, desire and lust were traditionally regarded as the main factor tying beings to the painful circle of births (Sk. *saṃsāra*).²³⁵ Views on female bodies thus diverged considerably with some women wanting to fulfill the ideal of motherhood and others wanting to realize a virtuous life by adhering to the precepts of celibacy.

Early Buddhist scriptures usually describe the female body in a negative light, stating that the female body is handicapped by its reproductive physiology, i.e. by menstruation, pregnancy and delivery.²³⁶ This view is frequently repeated throughout subsequent Buddhist scripture, in texts from different centuries and from different Asian cultures and societies, including Japan. This raises a key question: Is this view an intrinsically Buddhist idea? Or does it reflect a pre-existing cultural prejudice against female bodies, already prevalent in the areas

---

233 Translated by Lomi (2017, 354).
234 See also Andreeva's other works on women, Buddhism and medicine (2017a, 2017b and 2018). For birth rituals in Japanese history, see Göhlert (2014) and Suzuki (2014).
235 Faure (1998) addresses Buddhist approaches to sexuality.
236 Some of the following has been adapted from Triplett (2014).

where the Buddhist teachings were adapted: The view that female bodies are deficient and that humans in these female bodies are unable to obtain enlightenment and the perfect body of a Buddha.

The karmic burden specific to the female sex is laid out in numerous authoritative Buddhist texts. For example, Buddhist scriptures mention the Five Hindrances and Three Subordinations (*goshō sanju* 五障三從)[237]: A set of karmic (and societal) obstacles to women realizing buddhahood in their female bodies. According to conventional Buddhist teaching, a sentient being can be born into one of six different realms (*rokudō* 六道): three unfortunate realms and three fortunate realms. In the unfortunate realms, beings suffer as sub-human beings, i. e. animals (*chikushō* 畜生, Sk. *tiryag-yoni*), or as ever-hungry and thirsty ghosts (*gaki* 餓鬼, Sk. *preta*) or are tortured in cold or hot hells (*jigoku* 地獄, Sk. *naraka*). The fortunate realms are the world of humans (*ningen* 人間, Sk. *manuṣya*), the heavens of gods (*ten* 天, Sk. *deva*) and the realm of feuding jealous warriors ([*a*]*shura* [阿]修羅, Sk. *asura*). Beings in all six realms suffer in ways specific to their bodies and their environment. In the case of the human realm, the pains of reproduction and menstruation, along with the struggles associated with an inferior social status, are regarded as forms of suffering for those in female bodies. In each realm, bodhisattvas are present, however, to assist the suffering beings and make sure that they are eventually liberated from suffering, meaning that they are not being born in *saṃsāra* anymore.

The idea that women cannot attain buddhahood in their present bodies has been the subject of academic studies, including those on the Buddhist narrative passage from the *Lotus Sutra* on the young snake-shaped divine princess (Sk. *nāginī*), a female non-human being, who transforms into a male, an enlightened being, and finally obtains buddhahood, all in an instant.[238] This well-known motif from the *Lotus Sutra* – an influential and culturally important Buddhist scripture – dominated the ideas about women's enlightenment for centuries, as can be seen from its inclusion in popular narratives in medieval and early modern Japan (Triplett 2004, 109–110). However, not all Buddhist writings refer to this motif. There are other ideas that have inspired lively discourse on the nature of women and the possibility of attaining buddhahood in their female

---

237 The Five Hindrances for women stipulate that they cannot be born a god in the Brāhma heaven, a god in the Indra heaven, a Māra king, a wheel-turning king or a Buddha. The Three Subordinations are that women are subordinate to their fathers, husbands and sons.
238 See for example Levering (1982), Nishiguchi (1998), Nattier (2009), Faure (2003, 91–118), Ueki (2013) and Abé (2015); see also Groner (1989).

bodies.²³⁹ One frequently quoted obstacle to women attaining buddhahood is that the body of a Buddha is male since one of its characteristic features is a sheathed penis – a symbol of the complete overcoming of sexual activity and thus detachment from worldly desires. The Zen Buddhist thinker, Dōgen Kigen 道元希玄 (1200–1253), who founded the Sōtō Zen 曹洞禅 tradition in Japan, wrote repeatedly that the path to enlightenment was open to both men and women, and that from the point of view of the absolute truth – the basic tenet of East Asian Buddhism is the exposition of a relative (mundane) and an absolute truth – categories such as male and female were meaningless. This abstract exposition was known and accepted, at least within Zen Buddhism. However, at the mundane level, people struggled with the idea that women might be sinful because of their reproductive and therefore potentially "impure" bodies and thus might be barred from ultimate healing and salvation without ritual counter-measures, such as sutra recitation and copying.

In this light, it is easy to see why an apocryphal sutra dedicated solely to the transformation of the female body into a male body was so popular. The *Sutra of the Buddha's Sermon on Transforming the Female Body* (*Bussetsu tennyoshin-kyō* 佛説轉女身經), T 564²⁴⁰, translated by Dharmamitra (356–442), ascribes the origin of the particular suffering of women to one hundred worms that live in the female body. These worms are the reason for women being in a state of defilement. The worms can be interpreted as the cause of a diseased body. The sutra thus suggests that the female body is not essentially defiled but is instead afflicted with disease-causing agents. If the worms were removed, the female body would be freed from these originators of suffering and therefore "healed." However, it seems that only female bodies are afflicted with these worms. The sutra therefore depicts women as vulnerable and weak. In the *Sutra of Transforming the Female Body*, the Buddha expounds other social and corporeal reasons why a woman "must give rise to the thought of abhorrence and getting rid of her female body":

> [T]he female body resembles that of a maidservant and cannot obtain self-sovereignty for she is constantly troubled by sons, daughters, clothing, food and drink, and other necessi-

---

239 See Paul (1979), Kajiyama (1982) and the collected volume edited by Ruch (2002); see also Katsuura (2003) on early and medieval Japan and the monograph by Ambros (2015) that provides an overview on the history of women in Japanese religions; see also Ambros (2016). For an in-depth discussion of problematic passages referring to the karmic burden and "sinful" nature of women in canonized Buddhist writings in Japan, see Heidegger (1995; 2006, 53–66). For women in Indian Buddhism, see Wilson (1996) and Ohnuma (2000, 2001); see also Schuster (1981) and Mrozik (2007).
240 For a detailed analysis and contextualization of this text in China, see Balkwill (2016).

ties related to family matters. They must remove dung and defilement, nasal discharges, saliva, and other impure things. A female will go through nine months of pregnancy, during which she will suffer numerous pains. When she gives birth to a child, she suffers great pains to the brink of death. (*Sutra of Transforming the Female Body*, trans. Balkwill 2016, 142)

The owner of the female body in the above passage is a woman who cares for the children herself. She thus shares a social background with the majority of Chinese at the time. In the passage immediately following the above, the sutra states that the life of a court woman must also give rise to the thought of a sex change:

Furthermore, as for a woman who is born inside the imperial palace, she necessarily belongs to another person. Throughout her life, she is like a maidservant who must serve and follow a great family, also like a disciple who must venerate and serve his master. She is beaten by different kinds of swords and staves, rocks and tiles, and is defiled by every evil word. These kind of sufferings deprive her of self-sovereignty. (*Sutra of Transforming the Female Body*, trans. Balkwill 2016, 142)

The Buddha in this sutra describes how the life of a woman – whether of low or high birth – is like one resembling descriptions of Buddhist hells where the beings suffer from claustrophobic anguish: "Furthermore, the female body is constantly being tethered and restricted, like a snake or a rat that is in a deep hole, from which they cannot come out at their will" (trans. Balkwill 2016, 142). According to the sutra, recitation of the sutra will result in the transformation of the female body.

A second sutra, composed in China in the late twelfth century, deals with negative views of the female body, particularly because of women's reproductive functions. Although it is a late apocryphal work, it may be surmised that the basic thoughts existed earlier in East Asian Buddhism. This sutra, *The Buddha's Correct Sutra on the Bowl of Blood* (*Bussetsu daizō shōkyō ketsubon-kyō* 仏説大蔵真経血盆経), also became popular in Japan. It is popularly referred to as the "menstruation sutra"[241] and is based on the understanding that women are in danger of being born in a bowl or pond filled with blood, symbolizing the blood shed in menstruation and parturition. Reciting and keeping the sutra as a talisman can prevent this terrible fate.

In addition to passages from the scriptures, themes of corporeality and monasticism are also addressed in Japanese Buddhist legends. Early collections of these legends (*setsuwa*) relate moralistic stories of vice and virtue and connect

---

[241] See, for example, the study on the "menstruation sutra" belief in Japan by Takemi (1983) and Kōdate (2004).

5.1 The Female Body as an Obstacle to Becoming a Buddha? —— 117

familiar as well as imported narratives with a Buddhist message. The oldest and fairly complete extant collection of Buddhist legends in Japan, the aforementioned *Miraculous Stories from Japan* (*Nihon ryōiki*), compiled in the early ninth century, is of special interest in relation to the topic of bodies thought to be deficient. The story about a girl born from a flesh ball, for example, contains a description of unusual physical features:

> [A woman in the Higo province of Japan was reported to have given birth to a flesh ball (*shishimura* 肉團) that looked like an egg. Not considering this a good omen, she and her husband stored the flesh ball in a cave.] After seven days they returned to the cave and discovered that a girl had been born of the flesh ball, breaking through its covering. The parents took her home, and her mother nursed her. There was no one in the province who did not wonder at this. After eight months had passed, she suddenly grew very large, but her head and neck were joined without a chin, in a form different from the other people, and she was three and a half feet high. Endowed with wisdom, she was by nature brilliant. Before she was seven, she recited the *Hoke-kyō* [the *Lotus Sutra*] and the *Eighty-volume Kegon-gyō* [the *Flower Ornament Sutra*] [...] She was reserved and never boasted. Eventually she decided to renounce the world, shaved her head, and wore a surplice. Prompted by her faith, she practiced good, and enlightened people. She had such a good voice that it could lead her audience to become merciful. In her deformed body there was no vagina but only an opening for urine. Foolish laymen mocked her, calling her Saru hijiri [...], False Sage. (*Nihon ryōiki* III.19, trans. Nakamura 1973, 246–248)

The story ends in the triumph of the shunned female "cripple." The legend describes what could be seen as perhaps typical kinds of discrimination:

> [A certain man from the local gentry held a retreat with the famous] Dharma Master Kaimyō to lecture on the *Eighty-volume Kengon kyō* [sic] The nun was seated in the audience, never missing a lecture. Seeing her, the lecturer said accusingly, "Who is that nun unscrupulously seated among the monks?" [...] In reply she said, "Buddha promulgated the right teaching out of his great compassion for all sentient beings. Why do you restrain me in particular?" Then she asked a question by quoting a verse from the scripture, and the lecturer could not interpret it. In amazement, all the famous wise men questioned and examined her, but she never failed. [...] In that way they learned that she was an incarnation of Buddha, and named her Bodhisattva Sari [Sari Bosatsu 舍利菩薩]. Clergy and laymen revered her and made her their master. (*Nihon ryōiki* III.19, trans. Nakamura 1973, 247–248)

The nun is clearly a woman but lacks the female sexual organ so she can be interpreted as being in a stage between female and male. Nakamura interprets this story as indicating a feminizing shift from male-centered discourse in India to a more female-centered discourse in Japan. Noting that Indian stories only mention boys being born from flesh-balls and that there are no examples of female bodhisattvas in India, Nakamura asserts that the girl's lack of physical sex characteristics can be interpreted as a stage in the process of transitioning from the idea of a male bodhisattva in Indian Buddhism to a female bodhisattva in tantric (esoteric) Buddhism which was prevalent in Japan (Nakamura 1973, 72). A more plausible explanation is that the text refers to the early Buddhist idea of a separate "monastic gender:" Whereas female monastics discard their femininity and reproductive functions and turn into beings akin to males, men realize an ideal gender imagined as male minus the sexual drive and desire to reproduce.[242]

The body of the enlightened nun Sari Bosatsu is described in detail as being severely deformed. She is discriminated against by laymen as a female monastic who does not actually break the rules by sitting among monks at the official religious instruction. She also faces discrimination as a person with "abnormal" physical features and is continuously mocked as a fraud by those who, in reality, likely envy her for her success. This story is similar to the story of the *nāginī* princess who turns into a bodhisattva in the *Lotus Sutra*. While the *Lotus Sutra* emphasizes the speed of the transformation, the fact that a non-human, very young female is able to transform is supposed to be awe-inspiring. Sari Bosatsu, despite her outer appearance as a "deformed" female, amazes "all the famous wise men" with her insight into the Dharma. Still, both the *nāginī* and Sari Bosatsu, are not regular women but dharmic beings that are depicted as especially physically "abnormal" for the purposes of dramatic plot development.

Earlier interpreters of the *Nihon ryōiki* legends, such as Nakamura, see women and femininity as *symbols*. In her introduction, Nakamura writes that the compiler, the monk Kyōkai, did not accept the Chinese and Indian view of women as socially and spiritually inferior because "the women in the *Nihon ryōiki* convey a quite different impression." According to Nakamura, Kyōkai insists on the equality of all before the Dharma (Nakamura 1973, 76). Nakamura argues that in ancient Japan, women had a particular importance as symbols of cosmic power, a role that was exemplified in their procreative function. She contends that Buddhism added a further layer of symbolism regarding women: that of women as symbols of selfless love.[243]

Whether women were actually regarded as symbols of cosmic power in ancient Japan is not entirely clear. Neither is whether this translated into women having equal social status. Nakamura's argument that women were symbols of cosmic power is linked to corporeality; her argument that women were symbols

---

[242] On the idea of a monastic gender (*Sanghageschlecht*), see the study by Grünhagen (2013). Dumas gives an overview of interpretations in modern scholarship and her own reading of this famous episode from the *Nihon ryōiki* in the context of images of "abject femininity" (2013, 259 – 260).

[243] For a different assessment of the body in early Japanese cosmogony, see Ambros (2015, 22 – 39). See also Wittkamp (2018).

of selfless love, while adding an ethical dimension, is still tied to the physical dimension (women's roles as mothers).

The argument in the Buddhist narrative about Sari Bosatsu is that *even* if a human is a woman, buddhahood can be obtained. That makes the specific teaching appear greater because even deficient or afflicted, impure and sinful humans, i.e. women, can become buddhas, born in the paradisiacal Pure Land, albeit in a male body. They are promised that they will ultimately shed their female body and thus end suffering.

As we can see, although Buddhist sutras and teachings provide ways of overcoming the affliction of being born in a woman's body, the female body is still essentially seen as an affliction. Healing therefore would mean not only the healing of a human body, but also of a female body. Ultimate healing of the female body, though, according to the views encapsulated in the sutras mentioned above, is healing them of their femaleness altogether.

The unknown author (or authors) of a popular Heian-period apocryphal sutra, in contrast, painted an affirmative picture of being female. The *Sutra on Transforming Women into Buddhas* (*Bussetsu tennyo jōbutsu-kyō* 仏説転女成仏経) countered contemporary conceptualizations of a woman's chances of achieving awakening in her own body – as outlined above – in a number of ways.[244] According to the sutra, women have both the potential and the means to conduct Buddhist practices and lead a virtuous life, whether they are lay or monastic women. The sutra also contests that women do not need to undergo a sex change and become male in order to become buddhas. The main message of the text is that because all the buddhas of the past, present and future are born of female bodies, i.e. wombs, every woman is a mother of the buddhas. Women's bodies from which the buddhas emerge are to be regarded as "matrices for good deeds" (Blair 2016, 264). The image of an inherent potentiality in women is invoked by using the word *zō* 蔵, which has the basic meaning of "storage place" and is used as a translation of Sanskrit *garbha* in the sutra. *Garbha* derives from the root "to conceive" and has a variety of meanings, among them matrix, womb and embryo.

Buddhist embryology as such, however, was used to describe the path to awakening using the image of the unborn child's gestation in the womb.[245]

---

244 Translations into English include those by Meeks (2010, 303–304) and, with interspersed comments and interpretations, Blair (2016, 274–278). For a transcription of the sutra of which only two manuscripts exist today, see Nishiguchi (2014, 259–260) who published pioneering works on this text.

245 For more on this topic in regard to China and Japan, see the collected volume edited by Andreeva and Steavu (2016); see also Andreeva on reproductive imagery in premodern Japan

Texts created for the propagation of an ascetic lifestyle such as the *Sutra on Entering the Womb* (Sk. *Garbhāvakrānti-sūtra*) relate the suffering of the unborn in their mother's womb to the "female body's inner loathsomeness" (Langenberg 2017, 3). This text preaches relinquishing sexual desire in order to ultimately cease being born into the cycle of suffering. As Buddhist-studies scholar Robert Kritzer (2014) and others point out, the description of the suffering fetus was taken from Sanskrit compilations, such as the *Compendium of Suśruta*, that are regarded as having a clear medical nature. While the descriptions of the suffering fetus in the Sanskrit medical compendium were followed by a section on medical remedies and treatments for the alleviation of physical suffering, the Buddhist sutra pursues a radically different agenda: It leaves out the medicinal part completely. The message now is that the only healing – in terms of salvation – is to become a celibate monk or nun. While not part of the Mahāyāna literature, this sutra was known in medieval Japan. As Andreeva shows, the *Encyclopedia of Childbirth* (*Sanshō ruijūshō* 産生類聚抄, ca. 1318) quotes a passage strongly reminiscent of a fourth- or fifth-century Chinese translation of the *Sutra on Entering the Womb*.[246] The exceedingly negative image of the female body and human birth is also reflected in the birth stories of the Buddha: Instead of going through the "foul" parturient canal, the Buddha sprang from the side of his mother.[247]

The choice of *zō* for the Buddhist technical term *garbha* ("womb") in the apocryphal *Sutra on Transforming Women into Buddhas* "amplifies its claims that women engage in soteriologically effective reproduction" (Blair 2016, 276). The short sutra states that reproduction – generally regarded as evidence of women's impurity and moral deficiency – is *not* a hindrance to transformation. The sutra asserts that a woman's corporeal transformation (*tennyoshin* 轉女身) is not a sex change as an intermediate step toward awakening but that "woman" transforms (*tennyo* 転女) into the perfect body of the Buddha. As Nishiguchi Junko (2014) and others have shown, the *Sutra on Transforming Women into Buddhas* played a not insignificant role in the lives of elite women and men. Sources on its popularity in wider society are rare, but a school of (male) preachers referred to the sutra in their sermons, so it can be assumed that it was not only

---

in the same volume (2016); for embryology in Tibet, see Garrett (2005, 2008); in ancient India, see Kritzer (2009); see also Huebotter (1932).

246 For a translation of this passage in the encyclopedia, taken from the *Sutra of Five Kings as Told by the Buddha* (Jp. *Bussetsu goōkyō* 佛説五王經, T 523), see Andreeva (2017a, 194–195).

247 For an analysis of the Buddha's birth stories in Japan from a feminist perspective, see Buck-Albulet (2016); see also Sunim (1999) for a modern critique of sexual transformation for enlightenment. Chen (2005) wrote on possible influences of Indian ideas about female-to-male sex change on Chinese gynecology.

aristocratic women who endorsed the idea of women transforming into buddhas (Blair 2016, 285).

The various ideas regarding the possibility and impossibility of attaining buddhahood in the female body were not without consequences for the lives of individuals in premodern Japanese society, monastic as well as worldly. Participation in the monastic enterprise differed considerably for men and women in aristocratic circles from the Heian period onward.[248] Ordained aristocratic women stopped officiating Buddhist ceremonies and led – or were expected to lead – a pious life within the confines of their residences. They enjoyed the medical care of physicians of the court whose expertise included the treatment of gynecological disorders. The physicians' care extended to elite women whether or not they were tonsured. Knowledge about how to care for the female body within the monastic framework, however, derived from the ancient vinayas, texts that were conceived in the ancient India. To what extent were these strict guidelines and treatments actually practiced in premodern Japan? Answering this question requires not only an evaluation of sources found within the fields of religion and medicine but also an assessment of the social role of women in Japanese Buddhism as care recipients and caregivers.

5.2 Care of the Reproductive Female Body

Buddhist canonical literature contains frequent references to female hygiene and medical treatments of women. In the Pāli scriptures and ordination texts, we find very specific descriptions of gynecological disorders that render female adepts unfit for ordination (Jyotirmitra 1985, 363). The Pāli texts include hygiene rules for female monastics to prevent conception, for example by accidentally touching the clothes of a male monk that are stained with semen, and describe regimens for menstruating women and the use of sanitary napkins for nuns. Abortive and contraceptive medicines are also mentioned. For example, in the catalogue of nascent Buddhist scriptures in China, *Compilation of Notes on the Translation of the Tripitaka* (*Shutsu sanzō kishū* 出三藏記集, T 2145) compiled by the Chinese monk Sengyou 僧祐 (445–518) around 515, we find fourth-century guidelines and precepts for nuns including guidelines on hygiene and medicinal treatment specific to women and based on early Buddhist prescriptions and

---

[248] For "vicissitudes in the ordination" of women in early medieval Japan, see Groner (2002). Further publications on this topic include Lori Meeks' study on the Hokkeji temples and the re-emergence of female monastic orders (2010).

ideas. With the introduction of the precepts to China, ideas on herbal treatments from the Indian tradition were introduced and translated in the first half of the fourth to the fifth centuries as well. Works such as these were brought to Japan not long after that and were studied by monastic men and women there. Over the subsequent centuries, people in Japan attempted to adopt the content of the vinaya texts and incorporate them into their own social situations. Gynecological and obstetric knowledge from the Indian context, however, remained marginal compared to treatments, medicines and formulae for the care of the female body introduced via Chinese-style medicine, for example those found in the tenth-century *Essentials of Medicine* (*Ishinpō*). However, the *Ishinpō* includes numerous references to Buddhist *dhāraṇī* and Daoist talismanic practices, too, as briefly outlined above and as the following analysis shows in more detail.

5.2.1 The *Essentials of Medicine* (*Ishinpō*) on Women's Health

The three fascicles 21, 22 and 23 of the *Ishinpō* relate to women's health in particular: "Women's Diseases," "Continuation of Women's Diseases" and "Obstetrics."[249] Fascicle 24 on "Conception, Prediction of Sex, Pregnancy Tests" also relates to women's physical issues. As Fascicles 21, 22 and 23 show, medication and treatments for women's bodies and sensibilities, which were regarded as different from men's, were considered carefully in China 1400 years ago. The following introduces some of the most salient issues of the three fascicles on women's health and provides a critical assessment of their interpretation in modern scholarship.

The main points in Item 1 of Fascicle 21 contain descriptions and treatments of polyps or tumors in breasts and the womb – leading concerns of modern medicine. The term "cancer" (*gan* 癌) for these pathological growths did not yet exist. The disease was termed *gan*, using the character 岩, in the Edo period (Maki 1997, 21:i). Nevertheless, it can be assumed from the explanations of the symptoms that the compiler of the work, Tanba Yasuyori, describes what we now call cancer. In cases where women suffer acute inflammation of the mammary glands, mastitis, after a first birth or before nursing, they are treated by fastening a plaster to the breast after a medicinal bath, fomentation or poulticing (*anpō* 罨法), the application of ointments and the administration of medicine taken internally as well as moxibustion.

---

[249] For a study of the culture of childbirth in China that makes frequent use of these sources, see Lee (2005). For gender in China's medical history, see Furth's seminal study (1999).

Fascicle 22 "Continuation of Women's Diseases" was transmitted separately from the other fascicles and, perhaps because of this, contains some oddities. Tanba Yasuyori originally compiled this text on women's diseases in 984 when he was 82 years old, for the recently abdicated Emperor En'yū 円融 (r. 969– 984) (Maki 1995, 22:i). The fascicle was circulated independently from the other fascicles for centuries and only rejoined the other texts in 1983 when it was purchased by the Japanese state from private owners, the Nakarai family. There are two theories for this unusual transmission. The first is that a disciple of Nakarai Zuisaku 半井瑞策 (1522–1596) from the Okamoto family obtained this fascicle in order to save his master's daughter from serious illness after childbirth, and that it was then transmitted to Okamoto Yūken 岡本由顕 (dates unknown). The other is that Okamoto borrowed the scroll from Nakarai Zuisaku but never returned it. These scenarios are unlikely, but in the end, the Okamoto family, one of the Kyoto medical clans, sold the scroll with Fascicle 22 as a separate work in the middle of the Edo period in a period of decline for the family fortunes of the Nishikikōji 錦小路 family who descend from the Tanba family.[250] It was then passed on further and finally obtained the status of a national treasure and was reunited with the other scrolls. In the version from 1854 (Ansei 安政 era year 1), Fascicle 22 renders parts of the drawings in red whereas all other drawings are monochrome. Other versions have red ink in their illustrations as well (Maki 1995, 22:iii). The fascicle contains a text that was referred to separately as the *Classic on Obstetrics* (*Sankyō*, Ch. *Chanjing* 産経), a Sui-dynasty text that is now lost in China.[251]

Fascicle 22 is divided into 37 items pertaining to the special treatment of pregnant women with acupuncture and moxibustion, care of the fetus, preventative care before the onset of birth, morning sickness, dropsy, frequent urination, fever, coughing, backache and other ailments that may afflict a pregnant woman. The last item, number 37, describes how to abort the fetus to save the mother's life (Maki 1995, 22:vi).

The most outstanding feature of this fascicle is the remarkable illustrations of women in different stages of pregnancy.[252] The drawings illustrate the monthly stages of pregnancy with the growing fetus inside the womb of an entirely unclad woman. Since pregnancy was divided into ten months in premodern East Asia, the text includes ten pictures in all. These are remarkable pictures of a growing fetus – something that is very rarely seen in sources on pregnancy

---

250 Considering that the Tanba family had historically been in fierce competition with the Nakarai, this purchase must have been a triumphant affair.
251 On the *Classic of Obstetrics* (*Chanjing*), see Lee (2012).
252 See e.g. the facsimile edition in NKZ (1935).

from early cultures. The hairstyle of the pregnant woman with two knots to the side of the face that resemble a Chinese woman with an ancient dance (*gigaku* 伎楽) mask was popular in the Sui dynasty. It is believed that Tanba Yasuyori had an artist insert the images from the *Classic on Obstetrics* into his compilation, copying an early version of that work. They remain the only evidence of the images in the lost Chinese text on birth (Maki 1995, 22:iii–iv).

According to Maki Sachiko, much of the modern advice for pregnant women is derived from this fascicle such as "one should not lift heavy objects in the early stage of pregnancy" or "one should not eat stimulating food" (Maki 1995, 22:v). The influence on medieval court culture was so great, she claims, that although the exact nature of the influence is difficult to determine "it is not an exaggeration to say that if you removed Chinese medicine, there would be no Japanese court culture" (Maki 1995, 22:v). Maki is eager to point out continuities and developments in the field of Asian medicine following an evolutionary model from a lower, primitive, to a higher, advanced level. This is especially evident in her passage on food taboos. Food taboos for pregnant women are also prevalent in modern *kanpō* (Chinese-style) medicine, and many of these taboos derive directly from the tenth-century text, as she can show.[253] Maki declares these to be "superstitious" (*meishinteki* 迷信的) for the most part, quoting Frazer with an unmarked passage to show that these food taboos are indeed connected to superstition (Maki 1995, 22:iii–iv). The original passage is from Frazer's *opus magnum* "The Golden Bough": "As might have been expected, the superstitions of the savage cluster thick about the subject of food; and he abstains from eating many animals and plants, wholesome enough in themselves, which for one reason or another he fancies would prove dangerous or fatal to the eater" (Frazer [1911] 1927, 291).[254]

As is well known, Frazer saw certain elements of behavior in modern, civilized societies that he interpreted as deriving from ancient, primitive ideas when the human mind – the mind of the "savage" – was still developing and trying to achieve an orientation in the natural environment. Frazer did not explain the *meaning* of the rituals and myths; he arranged what he found in a schema to point out a hypothetical temporal lineage of human mental conditions. Trained in classical studies and archaeology, he went to great pains to divide magical

---

[253] For works on perinatal avoidance (taboo), see e.g. Tonomura (2007). Katsuura (2007) addresses knowledge on avoidances found in early *materia medica* compendia.
[254] The passage refers to Frazer's chapter V (Tabooed Things), § 10 Foods tabooed.

practices found in textual sources[255] into various subcategories, including various subcategories of taboos.[256] Academic researchers still use these subcategories as if they were factual and not derived from Frazer's personal ideas on the "savage." This is particularly common in folklore studies in the "West"[257] but Japanese researchers have also used the subcategories, as we just saw. The question of whether or not food taboos for pregnant women were physically harmful, ineffective or helpful from a modern medical perspective cannot methodologically be part of a study on cultural and religious history. The sources' recommendations indicate the deep concerns of the writers. Fascicle 22 lists 82 kinds of medicinal remedies that must not be administered to pregnant women; it also lists a number of "magical" remedies for noble women that can be applied in the form of prayers and rituals (Maki 1995, 22:vi).

5.2.2 Religious Regulations and Spells in the *Essentials of Medicine* (*Ishinpō*)

Birth and death were the focus of the most rituals and regulations (taboos) in early East Asia.[258] Fascicle 23 on obstetrics, with its 50 items, is the best example of the thought and imagery connected to birth in early China that was later introduced to Japan. Many passages in this fascicle detail rituals and actions aiming to prevent spiritual pollution or to purify the polluted woman with the help of talismans and paying attention to the cosmic order. Special attention is paid to the site where the birth is to take place. The parturition chamber is ritually purified and certain auspicious deities are summoned to guard the cardinal directions against evil influences. The text mentions the deities of the twelve stems (*jūnishi* 十二支) of the Chinese cosmological system ordering space and time. In addition to these, the Eight Generals (Hasshōgun 八将軍) play a major role in keeping the birthing chamber pure and protected (Maki 1998, 23:ii). In Japan, the father of the Eight Generals, deities originally from Northern India, was identified with Gozu-ten'ō 牛頭天王, also called Mutō-shin 武塔神, who

---

255 Evans-Pritchard calls Frazer's method "scissors-and-paste method of compilation," see Evans-Pritchard ([1965] 1970, 9). Frazer is also ridiculed by cultural anthropologist Bronislaw Malinowski, see Malinowski (1926, 126).
256 Frazer lists tabooed acts, persons, things and words in Part II (Taboo and the Perils of the Soul) of his *Golden Bough*.
257 See, for example, Hand (1980, 171–172). A discussion of this is found in Georges and Jones (1995, 57n40).
258 For images of death and the afterlife in Japanese Buddhism, see the volume edited by Stone and Namba (2008).

we find in turn combined with the image of the Shinto god Susanoo-no-mikoto 須佐之男命 in the early modern period. The mother of these eight divine children[259] is the daughter of the dragon king Sagara 裟謁羅,[260] Toshitokujin 歳徳神, an important directional deity who is revered as the goddess of the New Year. It is evident that the original Chinese divinatory yin-yang and calendric systems with their pantheon of divinities were adapted to Japanese religious and cosmological ideas to ensure a safe birth of a healthy child.

Tanba Yasuyori also included many spells from ancient China in the *Ishinpō*. However, we learn from his expositions that the spells healed only when combined with medicinal herbs. For example, if a talismanic character, such as the character for fish 魚, is written with vermillion (*shu* 朱) on the afflicted part of the body or on paper, and the powder or ashes of the burned paper is then taken internally, it will have the desired effect. The vermillion used for paint was actually natural mercuric sulfide. Mercury was used in healing potions for boils and other afflictions until early modern times when its use was discontinued because of its toxicity (Maki 1997, 21:ii).

In China, protective talismans from Daoist sanctuaries played an important role in giving masters the secret powers to conduct an effective ritual (Maki 1998, 23:iv–v).[261] This idea was transferred to the Buddhist sutra texts. The healing power was moved to the brush by blowing on it. The *Ishinpō* includes talismanic texts in red and black characters originally by Tanba Yasuyori. For example, a passage from Item 9 on "Difficult Births: Prevention and Healing Methods" in Fascicle 23 instructs us to write an especially efficacious character with vermillion and swallow it for healing (Maki 1998, 23:86). Then, it says, the birthing process will start soon. The character is written on the afflicted part, possibly here the belly, or it could have been written on paper, which is then stuck on the belly, similar to in the ritual involving an ox bezoar referred to above. The paper can be easily removed and burned, and the ashes used for medicinal purposes.

The "spells" are diverse in nature. Some are blessing formulae (*iwai* 祝) such as the one in Section 10 of Item 9 that recommends the following to be uttered in a difficult birth situation:

---

259 See Maki (1998, 23:ii; ix) for an exhaustive list of all deities mentioned in Fascicle 23.
260 Alternatively written 裟竭羅 and read Shakatsura.
261 For an exposé on the Daoist traditions in China, including the use of talismans, see Kohn (2000).

The Heavenly sky above is blue, so blue, the Earth below is abundant with greenery, all for the subjects of the Emperor. Why do you not come out? Quickly come out, quickly come out, the Emperor is at the door. This is why N.N. must come out quickly, come out quickly.

Tanba Yasuyori frequently lists spells to ensure a safe birth from Buddhist sources, among them the popular *dhāraṇī*. For instance, he quotes *dhāraṇī* from a work called *Daishū darani-kyō shinju* 大集陀羅尼経神呪 which is probably, like other Buddhist spell collections in the *Ishinpō*, not of Indian origin but written in China (Maki 1998, 23:iii).[262] The *sowaka* (Sk. *swahā*) at the end of the spells indicates a Sanskrit *dhāraṇī* but since no Brāhmī syllables are given in the *Ishinpō*, it is impossible to establish the meaning of the *dhāraṇī*, or whether they are authentic or were invented in China[263], or even Japan.

The recurrent quoting of Buddhist sources, especially in the fascicle on obstetrics, and the inclusion of Buddhist spells may point to an influence of Buddhist thought on the *Ishinpō*. The eclectic – and, as mentioned above in the context of the treatment of cataracts, self-contradictory – nature of the compilation, however, would suggest that Tanba Yasuyori included *any* technique or method thought helpful in his compilation to provide a complete, encyclopedic manual for court physicians of his family.

5.3 Care by Buddhist Women and Female Spiritual Practice

Midwifery and perinatal care were, according to the survey of medieval Japanese sources conducted by Andreeva and others, mainly in the hands of women. The Tanba and Wake 和気 families may have included female physicians but if there are records of (secular) female doctors from the medieval era, they are yet to be discovered. Whether women were trained as physicians within the Buddhist framework is also not altogether clear. This would presuppose that women had access to that knowledge. To undergo medical training, they would have had to obtain permission from male monastics, who were superior to the female part of the sangha, to leave the temple precinct and provide medical treatment to lay society. While we have no records of formally trained female Buddhist monastic doctors, we do have evidence of the lives of scholar-nuns. As such, we can conclude that women with medical knowledge may have treated other

---

[262] See also Triplett (2012, 72).
[263] Maki tried to identify the *darani-kyō* in standard reference works but could not find them. For this reason, she rendered them in her edition as they were and without Japanese readings (1998, 23:iv).

women within the confines of the temple. One example of more public medical engagement is that both lay and monastic women provided treatments in bathhouses connected to convents in the Nara period. In this period, nuns enjoyed a rather high social status, and they were, compared to later times, relatively independent in their decisions and actions. As outlined in Chapter 1, the incorporation of ordination rules into Japanese society resulted in a blurring of the boundaries between lay and monastic worlds.

It was also customary well into the late medieval period that members of the elite, first of the nobility, later of the samurai class, built splendid residences and converted them into Buddhist temples upon retiring there as monks and nuns. Other, more rural temples were founded by patrons from various social backgrounds and by ascetics. Much of female spiritual practice centered on ensuring enlightenment (*bodai* 菩提) of the aristocratic women's male relatives or spouses in the beyond. During the phase of state formation, however, nuns were entrusted with conducting rituals and praying for the protection of the Yamato state and the imperial family. In this period, there was a dual temple system with monasteries (*kokubun[sō]ji* 国分[僧]寺) in the provinces headed by Shōmu's and the empress' Tōdaiji Temple, and nunneries (*kokubun niji* 国分尼寺) headed by the empress' Hokkeji 法華寺 temple. As mentioned in Chapter 2, the state-ordained monks and nuns were ordered to copy and recite the *Sutra of Golden Light*, especially the chapters on the *Four Heavenly Kings* and on *Medicine*.[264] Nuns also read the *Lotus Sutra* in this context.

The buildings that house Hokkeji temple in Nara were once the residence of Fujiwara no Fuhito 藤原不比等 (658/659–720), a courtier who is known to have composed the *Taihō Code* (*Taihō ritsuryō* 大宝律令), together with Tenmu Tennō's son Prince Osakabe 刑部親王 (d. 705) on the order of Monmu Tennō 文武天皇 (r. 697–707). Fujiwara no Fuhito also later, during the reign of Empress Genshō, oversaw the compilation of the *Yōrō Code*. One of his daughters was married to Monmu Tennō. Another, Asukabehime 安宿媛 (701–760), later known as Kōmyō, obtained the high status of queen consort (*kōgō* 皇后) to her husband, Shōmu Tennō, meaning she could have become regent upon her husband's death. This high rank went with a considerable stipend and a large retinue of staff, which explains how this devout Buddhist empress was able to establish large welfare institutions.[265] After her father's death, Kōmyō converted his residence, Himuro Palace 氷室御所, into a place of Buddhist worship. She called the institution "Temple for the Liberation from Transgressions through the

---

264 See above p. 57.
265 For more on this rank, see Naoki (1988, 248–249).

Lotus [Sutra]" (Hokke metsuzai no tera 法華滅罪之寺), Hokkeji for short. The temple housed a dispensary for free medicines (*seyakuin* 施薬院) and medical facilities called "field of compassion" (*hiden'in* 悲田院). The Buddhist idea of "fields of merit" (*fukuden* 福田, Sk. *puṇya-kṣetra*) informed the establishment of such institutions and the medical engagement of learned Buddhist monastics for centuries to come. The monastic physician Kitano Yūrin 北野有隣 (also 有林, d. 1410), for instance, who compiled the *Fields of Merit Formulae* (*Fukudenhō* 福田方, 1363), an important medical work, clearly connected medical healing to the Buddhist idea of "fields of merit." Yūrin writes in the foreword to his compilation that he wants "his formulae to save all from the eight kinds of suffering (*hakku* 八苦). Those who will apply these medicines will sow good seeds in the eight fields of merit (*hachi fukuden* 八福田)" (trans. adapted from Masamune 1936, 1).

Queen Consort Kōmyō also bequeathed *materia medica* to Tōdaiji Temple after Shōmu Tennō's death. These were housed in the Shōsōin repository and largely kept there for centuries as an offering to Vairocana Buddha and an imperial treasure, as will be further elaborated on in Chapter 6.

Kōmyō is celebrated for her personal treatment of "lepers" who were regarded as the most unfortunate among sufferers of disease. The word "lepers" was used as a general term to refer to those afflicted with unsightly and painful fatal diseases, of which leprosy (Hansen's disease) was the most feared. A legend designed to praise the empress' devotion and selflessness took shape in the late Heian and early Kamakura period (twelfth to thirteenth centuries). This involved an episode of washing the destitute at Hokkeji temple's bathhouse (*karafuro, yokushitsu* 浴室): The empress fulfilled her vow to wash 1000 monks and laity in the bathhouse. The last was a man afflicted with leprosy. She cleaned him and licked the pus from his boils. Suddenly, the man transformed into Buddha Akṣobhya and vanished. The bathhouse remained empty but filled with light and a beautiful scent.[266] The legend employs the motif of bathhouse donation, which is recommended as a most meritorious act in the well-known *Bathhouse Sutra* (*Unshitsu-kyō* 温室經, T 701), of which several editions exist.[267] Passages on the benefits of (monastic) bathing also appear in the vinayas and commentaries.

---

[266] For English translations of this legend, see Ury (2002, 194; translated from a fourteenth-century record), and Meeks (2010, 36–37; translated from a twelfth-century record). See also Moerman (2015) on bathing practices and medieval legends in Buddhist Japan.

[267] The full title of the sutra is *Sutra Spoken by the Buddha on Bathing the Sangha in the Bathhouse* (*Bussetsu unshitsu senyoku shusō-kyō* 温室洗浴眾僧經). The sutra is traditionally attributed to An Shigao 安世高 (fl. ca. 148–180) but it is now regarded as having been translated by Dharmarakṣa (ca. 233–311). For a translation into English, see Salguero (2017b).

Donating to bathhouses constituted an accepted act of donation in premodern Japan as the term "warm water merits" (*kudokuyu* 功徳湯) indicates.[268]

The message of the legend is also that moral purity always overcomes moral defilement. The "leper," symbolizing the vilest defilement possible in the world of humans, is a manifestation of a Buddha who possesses the highest moral purity. The empress was tested for her steadfastness when confronted with a repulsive body exuding an awful smell. The morbid body of the sick man is contrasted with the perfect body of a Buddha in the mundane world, but the moral of the story is that there is no difference between the two on the level of absolute truth. The motif of an exalted personality cleansing the lowest of the low and thus engaging in an act of moral purification that ends with a miracle frequently appears in Buddhist legends.[269]

The tradition of bathing and personal hygiene as espoused in the vinayas and sutras such as the *Bathhouse Sutra* met with acceptance in the populations of China and Central Asia. The tradition of bathhouse donation was especially welcomed in Korea and Japan with their ancient cultures of bathing in naturally occurring hot springs. The bathhouse at Hokkeji temple was a simple steam bath using fire-heated water with medicinal herbs. Warm-water baths[270] together with those fed by natural hot spring water were (and are to this day) the usual forms of spas in Japan. Therapeutic bathing in "divine waters" is attested to in the early gazetteers and appears to have taken the form of ritual purification in *kami* worship since ancient times. Water ablutions were among medicinal treatments and initiation rituals introduced from India via Korea and China. Important centers of natural hot springs also became sites of worship of the Medicine Buddha (Yakushi Nyorai). These included Arima hot springs, which are not far from Kyoto. It was thought that washing away "dirt" – understood as impurity or pollution of both body and mind – was beneficial both for one's present life and for the next. If dirt and impurity were allowed to remain, they would attract bad influences and have nefarious consequences (Despeux 2010b, 814).

The ordination rules provide detailed guidelines for bodily care including bathing for keeping healthy, clean (to earn the respect of lay society) and mentally pure. When a group of monks sought to reform existing ordination practices in the Kamakura period, they studied the ancient Indian vinaya texts in detail to

---

268 See Williams (2004) on meritorious bathing.
269 For example, a story in the twelfth-century *Collection of Stories That are Old Today* (*Konjaku monogatarishū* 今昔物語集), referred to by Moerman (2015, 76).
270 For a detailed description on bathing facilities in monastic compounds from the vinaya texts, see Heirman and Torck (2012, 31–32).

look for solutions to what they thought to be a dilemma. The charismatic Shingon monk Eison (or Eizon 叡尊, 1201–1290) and several others felt "impure" as they did not consider the contemporary ordination procedure to result in full ordination as intended by the Buddha.[271] It should be noted that a celibate life seemed to have been far from many monks' minds, and Eison himself was the son of a monk. Eison and his fellow activists tried to "purify" the sangha by instituting private ordination platforms, revitalizing the female monastic sangha and bestowing lay precepts on social outcasts such as lepers, "non-humans" or "non-persons" (*hinin* 非人) such as ex-convicts, and those working in professions thought to be polluting. The Shingon Ritsu (vinaya) reform movement (Shingon Risshū 真言律宗) which was eventually founded by Eison is also famous for establishing bathhouses and hospitals and repairing important Buddhist centers in Nara, such as Saidaiji 西大寺 and Hokkeji[272] as well as a temple built by Kōmyō in memory of her parents.

Eison and his followers worked to increase respect for women and openly supported the idea that women deserve gratitude because they are mothers (Groner 2005, 233). They encouraged salvation rituals that aimed to transform women's bodies into male bodies in order to ensure liberation from suffering. Monastics in the Ritsu tradition also worked to revive the female monastic order. They discouraged independent (secular) female patronage but granted "women greater institutional inclusion through the establishment of nuns' orders" (Meeks 2010, 117). These female orders were required to gain the approval of the relevant male order when making decisions. Contrary to the intentions of the male orders, ordained women felt empowered by the revival of the female orders and pursued their own interests, only nominally seeking approval from the male monastics. Some nuns in the Shingon Risshū promoted themselves as having oracular abilities like the shrine maidens or shamanesses (*miko* 巫女). As Meeks shows, they also engaged in the stewardship of Buddhist relics that could grant many benefits including female fertility (2010, 153–155). Nuns also raised their own funds. Shinnyo 真如 (1211–?) whose life is quite well documented (Groner 2005, 224), raised funds and rebuilt the derelict temple, Chūgūji 中宮寺. The temple was thought to have been the residence of Anahobe no Hashihito no Himeko converted into a temple by her son Shōtoku Taishi after her passing in 621. Shinnyo believed that it had once been a nunnery and instigated its revival.

---

[271] For book-length studies on Eison and other charismatic monks of the period, see the volume edited by Nakao and Imai (1983) and Wajima (1959).
[272] For a book-length study on the re-emergence of female monastic orders in premodern Japan with a focus on Hokkeji and the Shingon Risshū, see Meeks (2010).

The Shingon Risshū overcame the many objections raised against the full ordination of women by receiving divine messages in dreams or miracles. One episode involves a sex change during life: As a nun needs, according to the vinaya rules, another nun as a companion, and there were no additional nuns to accompany Shinnyo, one of the Ritsu *monks* suddenly changed his sex. The precepts had naturally been transformed to those of a nun – which differed in many ways significantly from a monk's precepts – and the ordination could be bestowed on other women, as well. Miraculously, the "nun" changed back to her original male sex after the event. To Groner, this episode is an "ironic variation on the more familiar theme of women changing into men to attain spiritual goals" (2005, 227). The episode can be interpreted with the Mahāyāna paradigm of skillful means: In order to re-establish the female monastic order and create the group of ten fully ordained nuns (*bhikṣuṇī*) required to do so, extraordinary means were necessary. Bodily transformation is one regular feature of a bodhisattva, so the monk, a certain Kyōen 教圓 (dates unknown) in some versions of the tale, manifests himself as a woman to engage in enlightened action. More importantly, because the story centers on the agency of the monk, it downplays Shinnyo's active role in the re-establishment of the female monastic order (Meeks 2010, 292).

***

Birth into the realm of humans has been depicted as fortunate because humans are the only beings who have the patience and intelligence to hear the Buddha's sermons and practice the Dharma. Some traditions see the world of humans as fundamentally defiled and impure, some regard it as a Pure Land. The central idea that specific features, the physique and disposition of one's body, are a consequence of actions in a former life informs much of the debates explored above. Impure thoughts result in receiving an "impure" body, and the female body is depicted as particularly polluted because of its reproductive functions. The births of "lepers" and blind people, as previously noted, were also regarded as unfortunate. The humanity of "non-persons" (*hinin*) is unquestioned although some, especially those working in the meat industry and leather production or as undertakers, were regarded as not belonging to normal society and thus are usually referred to in English as outcasts or "untouchables." Social differentiation corresponded directly to the epistemic concept of having a "fortunate" or an "unfortunate" birth and being endowed with "pure" or "impure" bodies and minds. In this light, female outcasts were probably the most socially disadvantaged in premodern Japanese society.

Sutras and narratives about special hells for women such as the Blood Pond Hell, or a hell for barren women who are tortured by having to dig holes with lamp wicks, strengthen the image of specific female suffering while also stating how women can achieve salvation and birth in the Pure Land. In mainstream Japanese Buddhist culture, this was seen to be achieved through praying for a female-to-male sex change, as well as prayers to particular Buddhist saviors. Some sources in medieval Japan took a different approach. They stated that a woman embodies the "embryo" of awakening both physically and mentally. "She" is the mother of the Buddhas, which has a much deeper significance than merely being the object of gratitude for being somebody's mother.

Compared to the cult of exemplary men, devotion to virtuous women of the past was a minor occurrence. However, Buddhist images for worship have been found that are widely held to bear a likeness to the model women who dedicated or founded the temples in which the images are located. One example is the Amitābha on a famous mandala tapestry housed at Chūgūji that is assumed to actually depict Anahobe no Hashihito no Himeko,[273] another is a Kannon statue at Hokkeji that is thought to have been modeled after Kōmyō from life.

Buddhist activity by both men and women in premodern Japan found expression in material culture on quite a large scale. This included establishing magnificent temples, endowing statues and other images, and sponsoring ceremonies with their rich array of ritual implements. The "merit economy" also involved donating health facilities including bathhouses to the sangha. As a vehicle for increasing their social capital, monastics and the laity contributed to presitigious building projects, the monastics organizing the projects and the laity providing monetary donations. The production and circulation of smaller material items indispensable for the daily routine in the establishments also increased. These included *materia medica*, often precious and in short supply such as bezoars or special herbs and fragrances used for the medicinal baths mentioned above.

Materia medica will be the topic of the following chapter, continuing the discussion of Nara-period female patrons such as Queen Consort Kōmyō. Chapter 6 will address central concerns of economy and specialized knowledge in the premodern Japanese world of medicine and Buddhist ritual.

---

273 See Meeks (2007) on interpretations of sources connected to the cult of Anahobe no Hashihito no Himeko. The mandala tapestry played a significant role in Shinnyo's revival of Chūgūji Temple. Meeks holds the empress to be a savior figure in her own right who "is even more available (and therefore more effective) than the highly regarded Amida [Amitābha] Buddha himself" (2007, 374). For a monograph covering the history of the tapestry, see Pradel (2016).

6 Plants: *Materia medica*, Medicinal Gardens and Panaceas

> [T]he Mysterious Heart of the Holy Hayagrīva of Matchless and Unthinkable Strength is explained [...]. One should chant his mantra over vegetables 100,000 times. [...]. One should burn 8000 twigs of a kind of sandalwood, both ends soaked in ghee. [...] Bad cold, fever, headache, pain in the feet, all the 404 sicknesses and the 10,000 pains, they will all be cured. And the 80,000 sicknesses that are caused by devils, they will all be cured without exception, and one will obtain all magic success.
>
> From a manual for the Horse-headed Kannon ritual,[274] adapt. van Gulik (1935, 90 – 92)

In order to follow Buddhist ritual manuals, originally from India, and offer a proper ritual service in Japan, ritualists were obliged to use various paraphernalia including plant-based substances ranging from ordinary vegetables to exotic sandalwood. While the unspecified "vegetables" mentioned in the above quote from a typical ritual manual were easy to obtain on Japanese soil, sandalwood (Sk. *candana*, Jp. *sendan* 栴檀) was a different matter altogether. It was regarded as most precious even in its native India and needed to be imported to Japan at high cost.

Esoteric Buddhist rituals involved the use of an extensive range of plant-based and other materials. Precise knowledge about these materials was indispensible to practitioners in the esoteric Buddhist tradition. Ritualists were expected to know the name and appearance of different plants and substances, their availability, preparation and administration.[275] One difficulty faced by the Japanese monks and nuns was that many of the plants had to be imported or introduced from India, the Himalayas and Southeast Asia, or even from the far-off Middle East.

Physicians in Japan shared this twofold problem of obtaining and circulating exact knowledge of the plants and their properties, and of procuring them in Japan. A further problem that both groups faced was ensuring that the coveted

---

[274] The ritual manual is usually referred to as the *Ritual Manual for the Supplication of the Horse-headed Kannon* (*Batō nenju giki* 馬頭念誦儀軌). Amoghavajra (705 – 774), a Buddhist monk of Indian-Sogdian descent who was active in China, is viewed as its translator, but stylistically the manual is likely to be a later work composed in Japan. Its full title is *Ritual and Offerings for the Great Fierce Vidyārāja, the Holy Hayagrīva* (*Shō Kayakakiribaku Dainuō jō Daishinken kuyō nenju giki hōbon* 聖賀野紇哩縛大威怒王立成大神驗供養念誦儀軌法品, T 1072 A. Van Gulik translated the complete text into English (1935, 85 – 94). Hayagrīva, the "Horse-headed One," is regarded as a form of Avalokiteśvara (Kannon) in this text; see below p. 186.

[275] For an outline of this topic, see Nihonyanagi (1997a). See also Shinmura (2013, 207 – 225).

knowledge remained within their lineages of transmission. Extensive lists of mostly plant-based *materia medica* from the Chinese tradition arrived in Japan and both court and monastic doctors worked to identify the plants listed among specimens of the local flora. Plants were gathered in the wild, cultivated in medicinal gardens or imported from abroad.[276] Trade within the Japanese empire also supplied dispensaries and places of healing. For example, traveling mountain ascetics (usually male) of the Shugendō tradition are known to have engaged in the domestic trade of pharmaceuticals.[277] Practitioners of a syncretistic, Shingon-based Shugendō engaged in obtaining superhuman powers (Sk. *siddhi*) to benefit the community. While they did not undergo formal medical training in a Buddhist institution, it is not unreasonable to suggest that they also administered medicinal herbs that they had collected in the mountains to the sick.

As the previous chapters of this book have shown, monastic physicians were both ritual and medical practitioners. As such, pharmaceutical and botanical knowledge was useful to them in their dual rôle. This chapter surveys selected sources containing such knowledge about plants. Although other materials such as animal products[278] as well as metals and minerals are among the wide range of *materia medica* used in rituals and medicine alike, plants remain the most conspicuous. Interestingly, the Sino-Japanese term for *materia medica*, *honzō* (Ch. *bencao*) 本草 literally means "basis herbs," indicating the prevalence of plant material in medicinal products.[279] The physicians' training included – and continued to include well into the nineteenth century – the study of *materia medica* and, thus, the study of plants constituted a large part of their training. Chinese-style compendia of these materials discuss plants largely for their medical use and how to unlock their potential for healing ailments that are described in the compendia. These compendia also provide medical formulae.

Of course, the power of plants goes beyond their use in restoring health (or even granting immortality in some traditions). Plants have the capacity to nourish, to satisfy a sense of beauty and to provide material for building and tools. They can also create hallucinations, interpreted as religious or spiritual visions, and they can kill. The potency of plants is the subject of studies in various academic fields but in the two initial parts of this chapter, it will be addressed spe-

---

276 For an early history of the pharmaceutical business and trade in Japan, see Ikeda (1929).
277 On mountain ascetics' healing services and trade in pharmaceuticals, see Nei (1976, 1980).
278 These included crude drugs derived from humans, such as mother's milk, hair and nails. For an outline of these "human drugs" in Chinese medicine, see Cooper and Sivin (1973). For the use of *mumia* (mummy) in drugs of the Edo period, see Kinski (2005).
279 The term can also simply be translated as "roots (*hon*) and herbs (*sō*)."

cifically in regard to Buddhism and medicine in premodern Japan. These first parts explore the tradition of medicinal gardens in Japan and introduce some evidence of the global trade in medicinal plants and drugs.

The sources explored in the third part reveal how the official state medical, imperial and Buddhist monastic networks were closely interwoven in the Heian period. Edward Drott (2010) argues that these networks were often centered in a Buddhist institution. Drott states that the examples he explored show that Buddhist priests in the Kamakura period attempted "to make use of authoritative and esoteric knowledge for the benefit of both the state – in the form of high-ranking imperial clerics and shogun – and, implicitly, the Buddhist community" (Drott 2010, 267). By providing healing rituals and prescriptions for longevity and well-being to the ruling class, elite Buddhists acted within the traditional ideological framework of an envisioned seamless cooperation between Buddhism and the state.[280] In the following, further examples from the field of medieval *honzō* studies, which included pharmacology, pharmacognosy and botany,[281] confirm this statement but also add insights into non-elite medical activities and their specific aims. The chapter closes with a section on cure-all medicines, or panaceas, that can be seen as an expression of both Buddhist ritual and medicinal knowledge.[282]

6.1 Medicinal Gardens

As shown in the previous chapters, the government of the early Japanese state started establishing new institutions after setting up the system of legal codes. How these eighth-century (and later) institutions were actually realized often remains a mystery, and it is particularly difficult to assess the nature of the medicinal gardens as traces of these early gardens are now largely lost. Textual records

---

[280] This passage and section 6.3 follow Triplett (2012) in part.
[281] In fact, *honzō* studies are often translated or understood by modern scholars as an early form of the natural sciences including pharmacology, pharmacognosy, zoology and botany. Recent studies in European languages on early and early modern science in East Asia, mainly China and Korea, include Métailié (2015) and Marcon (2015). For a classic study on the subject in Japanese, see Ueno ([1948] 1973).
[282] Section 6.4 below on potent plants and the production of Buddhist panaceas is based on research for the panel at the ninth International Congress on Traditional Asian Medicines (ICTAM) at the University of Kiel in 2017 on "Materiality, Efficacy, and the Politics of Potent Substances," organized by Barbara Gerke and Jan van der Valk, and the subsequent publication in *Himalaya* (Triplett 2019a) that has been adapted here for parts of this chapter.

6.1 Medicinal Gardens — 137

or maps directly pertaining to the gardens no longer exist. In his pioneering 1930 study of medicinal gardens (*yakuen* 薬園) in Japanese history, archaeologist Ueda Sanpei 上田三平 (1881–1950) notes the scarcity of written documents on such pre-Edo-period gardens.

In the seventeenth century, key sociopolitical and economic changes brought with them an increasing effort to identify plants indigenous to Japan and to compile purely Japanese herbals. At the same time, the arrival of botanical and pharmaceutical knowledge from Europe via Holland resulted in new combinations of knowledge systems. This period also saw the establishment of useful plant gardens throughout Japan by both the shogunate and the local rulers. Of the dozens of medicinal gardens in the Edo period, only two or three exist today (Ueda 1930, 2).[283]

In the sixth and seventh centuries, doctors from the kingdoms on the Korean peninsula, Silla and Baekje, introduced certain medicinal plants to Japan. Whether the magnificent Yakushiji temple built by Tenmu Tennō and dedicated to the Medicine Buddha included a garden for medicinal herbs, as some claim, is far from clear. As the early Buddhist temples in Japan had flower gardens, it is likely that useful plants including kitchen herbs and medicinal plants were grown there as well. For example, a South Garden is known to have existed at Gangōji Temple 元興寺 (Ueda 1930, 6). This temple is one of the earliest Buddhist institutions in Japan.

The *Taihō* and *Yōrō Codes* originally provided for the establishment of medicinal gardens primarily for the training of students of pharmacology or, rather, herbology[284]. There was a close connection between the practice of gathering medicinal herbs from the wild and the cultivation of plants in these gardens. Knowledge of germination and other aspects of the cultivation of herbs circulated long before the establishment of legal codes (Ueda 1930, 7) and the Japanese must have used plants for healing since ancient times. However, the Bureau of Medicine (Ten'yakuryō), in Nara, later Kyoto, managed all activities pertaining to the care of the medicinal garden(s) in a novel way. The legal codes and their commentaries mention sites where herbs were washed and dried for use in drugs, and a garden for growing tea. There was also a special farm where cows produced milk for medicinal purposes. We read in the *Yōrō Code* and its commentaries[285] that two Medicinal Garden Masters (*yakuen-shi* 薬園師) selected

---

283 A similar case is the pleasure gardens of the local rulers of the Edo period. Very few of the roughly one thousand gardens that existed in this period exist today (Shirahata 2016, x–xi).
284 The codes use the term "medicinal garden students" (*yakuen-shō* 薬園生).
285 The passage summarizes *Yōrō Code* Book 1, Part 2 (Dettmer 2010, 268–273) and Book 8, Part 24 (Dettmer 2010, 438–451).

six, later increased to ten, students. Under their supervision, the students not only studied the properties and names of the plants as well as their cultivation and preparation for medical use but also had to read *materia medica* manuals to accompany their practical training. The Medicinal Garden Masters were to take the students into the mountains and valleys to show them particular herbs and train them to move the plants into the garden for further cultivation and investigation. Of course, the selected few were to have ample assistance for these laborious pursuits, as the code decreed that 75 designated households had to send 37 men for gardening.

The central botanical garden(s) in or near the capital only provided some of the herbs used for medicinal purposes; the *Yōrō Code* decreed that the provincial offices had to send a portion of their crop and production of drugs to the capital. This centralized state distribution system followed the regular structure set up for all agricultural products and all other goods. An important motivation behind setting up the distribution system for medicinal herbs in particular was that demand could not be met when smallpox epidemics ravaged the land. The official gardens' supply had to be supplemented by deliveries from the provinces to treat all patients in the capital. Ueda states that epidemics in the early eighth century, specifically in 703, increased the need for medicinal plants dramatically. It was deemed necessary to establish medicinal gardens owing to the difficulties associated with importing plants or gathering plants from the wild. Queen Consort Kōmyō's central dispensary in Nara is known to have purchased herbs from all provinces to be handed out for free. It can be surmised that these must have come from gardens and not the wild because of the high demand for the free medicinal drugs (Ueda 1930, 7–8). It seems that the usefulness of gardens for the production of drugs in times of plague overshadowed their use in the training of students.

However, the existence of medicinal gardens in this early period is far from proven. The imperial chronicles that are usually a reliable source on events immediately preceding their publication may include references to the existence of such gardens. And indeed, *Records of Japan, Continued* (*Shoku Nihongi*) reports on the establishment of a medicinal garden north of Kōriyama 郡山 near the capital of Nara in 749 on the occasion of the enthronement ceremony of Princess Abe 阿部 (718–770), the daughter of Shōmu and Kōmyō, as Kōken Tennō 孝謙天皇. The garden was located to the south of the palace and hence called South Medicinal Plant Garden (Minami yakuen 南薬園). No traces are left of this garden today. It may have been the garden at Yakuon Hachiman shrine in Kōriyama

(Ueda 1930, 8). Yakuonji temple 薬園寺,[286] which is located next to the shrine, claims to have been erected in the middle of a medicinal garden that was originally established by Shōmu Tennō. The monk Gyōki 行基 (668–749) whose family had immigrated from Baekje to Japan and who is known for his charitable deeds is said to have founded this little temple as a hall of worship to the Medicine Buddha. Perhaps the garden was originally established by Shōmu and recreated for the enthronement ceremony of his daughter after his death.

Ninmyō Tennō 仁明天皇 (r. 833–850) decreed that a large medicinal garden should be built in Kyoto. The *Later Records of Japan, Continued* (*Shoku Nihon kōki* 続日本後紀, 869) state that it was established in the precinct of an existing "field of compassion" (*hiden'in*), a Buddhist term for a shelter that included a hospital.[287] We know the size and location of this garden but not exactly what was cultivated there (Ueda 1930, 9). Other Heian-period records state, in contrast, the kinds of plants to be cultivated for healing purposes but also for other uses, in great detail. The most important source is the *Procedures of the Engi Era* (*Engishiki* 延喜式, 927) that lists over fifty different medicinal herbs to be gathered from the wild or cultivated in the provinces. Over two hundred drugs are named. Although monastics produced knowledge about medicinal herbs, it seems that by the tenth century, medicinal gardens were no longer maintained in temple precincts. Whether the temples, which became increasingly influential landholders in the medieval period, controlled fields of medicinal herbs is not altogether clear. As most medicinal plants came from the wild, were produced on smaller plots or were imported from the continent, larger gardens seem to have no longer been a feature of either the Buddhist institutions or the central or local governments by the end of the medieval period.

One exception may perhaps be the garden of the Golden Pavilion in Kyoto.[288] The illustrious shogun Yoshimitsu 義満 (1358–1408) of the Ashikaga family 足利氏 rebuilt his residence in the north of Kyoto to retire there from his office at court. After he had taken the tonsure, his residence officially became a temple, the Rokuonji 鹿苑寺. He had the famous Golden Pavilion, actually a pagoda to house Buddhist relics, erected at this residence and had it surrounded by a large pleasure garden with both decorative and useful plants. The Ashikaga strived to collect rare plants for their prestigious building projects, and one of Yoshimitsu's successors, his grandson Yoshimasa 義政 (1436–1490), ordered the learned monk Kikei Shinzui 季瓊真蘂 (1401–1469) to supply his own new garden with

---

286 The temple's name is written with the characters for "medicinal garden" (pronounced here *yakuon*, not *yakuen*).
287 This particular shelter for the poor and sick was called Tōkōroin 東鴻臚院.
288 The site is commonly referred to as Golden Pavilion Temple (Kinkakuji 金閣寺).

a certain kind of camellia, for example. Shinzui who acted as a political advisor was also to have miniature rock features and various plants sent from other temples for Shogun Yoshimasa's ambitious building project (Ueda 1930, 11). Yoshimasa also wanted to build a retirement residence. The project was realized in the eastern part of Kyoto. It features a Kannon hall known as the Silver Pavilion.[289] The residence became the Zen temple Jishōji 慈照寺 belonging to the Shōkokuji 相国寺 network of Rinzai Zen temples as did Rakuonji, the temple with the Golden Pavilion.

In this period, the Japanese military rulers were in close contact with China and introduced new cultural techniques and recent writings on various aspects including medicine. It is significant that the Ashikaga family supported the establishment of Rinzai Zen Buddhism in Kyoto to make use of the learned monastics who had an excellent knowledge of Chinese matters. Also, rulers such as Yoshimitsu styled themselves as sage-like Buddhist kings in a period of rivalry between local rulers who vied for power and engaged in military combat. While the capital partially burned to the ground in such battles, the Ashikaga built beautiful gardens and temples and supported new forms of art and culture. But the shogun did not simply withdraw from the world into earthly paradises[290] built on their orders leaving the country to go up in flames. The era also saw the spread of general knowledge not least through publications by physicians trained in private academies.

The Muromachi period (1336–1573) saw the restoration of the Ashikaga Academy (Ashikaga gakkō 足利学校), a private academy located in the domain of the shogun in the city of Ashikaga, north of Edo. The academy, which was open to male students, taught subjects including *materia medica* studies and medicine. Manase Dōsan – briefly introduced in an earlier chapter – was among physicians trained at this academy. As a child he was educated in the Tendai tradition before being tonsured at the age of thirteen at one of the sub-temples belonging to Shōkokuji. Dōsan later laid the foundation for the practice of medicine in the early modern period following new inspirations from Chinese medicine. This was later known as the "Methods of the Later Period School" (Goseihō-ha 後世方派, or Gosei-ha 後世派). The name of the school refers to its use of post-Song medical works. Drugs were now increasingly categorized in line

---

[289] This site is commonly called Silver Pavilion Temple (Ginkakuji 銀閣寺).
[290] The garden as a representation of the paradisiacal Pure Land is a feature of the earliest temples in Japan. This particular style emulated the gardens of the aristocratic residences, the *shinden zukuri* 寝殿造り (Shirahata 2016, 28–29). Shirahata presents a history of such gardens and especially the later Edo-period gardens of local rulers in comparison to European baroque gardens.

with the system laid down in the ancient *Inner Canon of the Yellow Emperor* (*Huangdi neijing* 黃帝內經).[291] Theoretical considerations now played a more fundamental role than clinical experience. However, the physicians' common sense and pragmatism still ranked above the principles of the legendary Yellow Emperor and the ancient Chinese doctors, when required by a given situation. One remarkable feature of learning in this era is the rendering of Chinese-style medical knowledge into Japanese verse, amply effected by Dōsan and others, or setting the text to music, both for mnemonic purposes (Machi 2014, 173–174).

In the late medieval period, it appears that medicinal gardens associated with the private academies or other centers of learning such as Buddhist temples were no longer established. The revival of Chinese-style medicine by Manase Dōsan and others also meant an increase in demand for medicinals from China in order to be able to produce the complex drugs that became extremely popular. These drugs sometimes contained up to two hundred components. The temple gardens of the Ashikaga shogun contained some medicinal plants but their purpose was to provide an aesthetic experience designed to enhance the prestige and exemplify the power of these particular Buddhist institutions. Anti-Christian writings recount that Jesuit missionaries planted a large medicinal garden with herbs from Europe in the sixteenth century but its existence cannot be proved.[292] However, the making of a small garden with useful herbs including medicinal plants at a Jesuit missionary site in the south of Nagasaki and the laying out of a tobacco field belonging to the mission in the city's east can be gleaned from contemporary sources. These may have inspired the shogunate to re-establish the tradition of medicinal gardens (Reißenweber 1994, 27–28; 182).

Because of flourishing foreign trade, often via Nagasaki, the cherished *materia medica* reached Japan in great numbers from abroad. It was only in the Edo period that attempts to implement mercantilist policies and cultivate such costly plants as ginseng on Japanese soil were somewhat successful.[293]

---

291 The *Inner Canon of the Yellow Emperor* consists of two parts, the *Basic Questions* (*Suwen* 素問) on theories and diagnostics of Chinese medicine, and the *Numinous Pivot* (*Lingshu* 靈樞), a book on acupuncture. The work is the fundamental text for Chinese medicine. Compiled in the third to first centuries BCE, it subsequently went through several phases of editions. *Basic Questions*, the more frequently quoted part of the work, consists of a (fictive) dialogue between the mythical Yellow Emperor, or Thearch, and Qi Bo 岐伯, a wise doctor.
292 See Hattori (1971, 416–417); Leuchtenberger (2013, 16–17; 201–202, 202n6) and Triplett (2019b, 9).
293 For Edo-period medicinal gardens, see Ueda (1930) and Reißenweber (1994).

6.2 Global Trade in Medicinal Drugs: Evidence from the Shōsōin Repository

From the fifth century and throughout the early and medieval periods, trade with the wider Asian region provided physicians and households with the necessary materials for producing medicinals. The three myrobalan fruits *harītakī*, *amalā*, and *vibhītaka*, of which the panacea called *triphalā*, "three fruits," is made, frequently appear in Indian Buddhist sutras and āyurvedic texts.[294] In the Chinese sutras, the Sanskrit names of the berries are transcribed instead of translated, attesting to the plants' foreign origin.[295] Some vinayas include the Three Fruits among an often referred to set of the Five Medicines that monks and nuns are permitted to use. As such, the Three Fruits are of major importance for those who seek healing in the Buddhist tradition. Chebulic myrobalan, the Indian gooseberry, is especially renowned for its medicinal properties in the Buddhist world. It is no coincidence that the Medicine Buddha in Tibetan paintings holds a branch of this plant in his hands. The cherished fruits from the chebulic, emblic and beleric myrobalans are not native to Chinese or Japanese flora. These three fruits were imported from India and other places via China (or Korea) to Japan as evidenced by specimens kept in the Shōsōin repository belonging to Tōdaiji Temple in Nara.

While the present-day appearance of many of the extant plant specimens of the Shōsōin repository is rather disappointing, they are still a most spectacular find. Enormous quantities of the most expensive and attractive substances such as ginseng, cinnamon, rhubarb and licorice were initially stored in the repository but have largely been consumed. Others have now turned to dust or been eaten by insects. The one remaining *harītakī* berry (*kariroku* 訶梨勒) in the Shōsōin repository was once one of a thousand. It must have originally been picked somewhere in eighth-century Asia, shipped to Japan via China and then survived in the repository for over 1200 years. The drugs were part of a bequest from Kōmyō, the empress dowager, to Tōdaiji Temple and offered to Vairocana Buddha on the occasion of the memorial service for the emperor, her husband Shōmu, on June 21, 756. The 650 items in the bequest included sixty different kinds of medicinal substances of plant, animal and mineral origin. They were kept at the Tōdaiji repository as precious objects for the well-being of the sangha

---

[294] See above p. 79.
[295] *Harītakī* is transcribed as 訶梨勒 (Jp. *kariroku*), *amalā* as 菴摩勒 (Jp. *anmaroku*) and *vibhītaka* as 鞞醯勒 (Jp. *hikeiroku*). Their modern botanical and some of their common names in English are: *Terminalia chebula* (chebulic myrobalan), *Phyllanthus emblica* (emblic myrobalan, Indian gooseberry) and *Terminalia bellirica* (beleric or bastard myrobalan) respectively.

and to dispel all ills and heal all diseases according to the dedication in the original catalogue, the *Memorandum of Medicines* (*Shuju yakuchō* 種々薬帳, 756).[296]

In surveys of the medicinals held in the Shōsōin repository conducted in the 1940s[297] and in 1994–1995, the actual content of the repository was checked against the *Memorandum of Medicines* (Shibata 2000, 10). The *Memorandum* carefully lists the sixty medicinal substances and their quantities. We know that many were nearly or wholly used up in medical treatments, rituals and ordinary consumption by the tenth century. Today, only 38 of the 60 medicinals remain.[298] Those conducting the surveys also found twenty items of potential medicinal use not listed in the *Memorandum of Medicines*. These substances were mainly used as the base for producing incense for the Buddhist ceremonies at Tōdaiji but were also used for medicinal purposes. For example, some clove was preserved in a small wooden chest in the repository (Shibata 2000, 21). Clove was used in the eye-opening ceremony of Vairocana Buddha in 752, and the flower buds' essential oils – responsible for the aromatic scent and flavor of clove – were still detectable in the 1994–1995 survey through chemical analysis after over a thousand years in the wooden container.

The treasure of medicines, both prepared medicines and raw material (*shōyaku* 生薬), in the Shōsōin is closely tied to Buddhism. It exemplifies the devotion of Kōmyō, the pious Buddhist dowager. The medicines were to be regarded as an offering to the Great Buddha but the dedication in the *Memorandum*, signed by five officials for the empress dowager, encourages its use in healing. Given that so much of the medicines were consumed – probably by members of the close circle around the imperial family and Tōdaiji – during the first hundred years after the bequest was made, and that the treasure continued to be stored at the temple, surviving the two complete destructions of the main temple hall, her pious wish was fulfilled.

Some of the crude drugs are no longer used in contemporary *kanpō* (Chinese-style) medicine and thus give an insight into ancient medical activity in the framework of Buddhism and the fledgling state in Japan. Additionally, many of the labeled containers such as boxes and bags made from different ma-

---

[296] For a full list in English of the sixty medicinals listed in the *Memorandum*, see Shibata (2000, 23–24, table A and B); for a short introduction to the *Memorandum* including facsimile images of the scroll, see Yoneda (2000); see also Torigoe (2005).
[297] The first survey using modern technology took place in 1948–1949 when the repository was opened. At the time, the repository was under the administration of the Imperial Household Agency.
[298] The remaining 38 items are of plant (20), animal (5) and mineral (8) origin. They also include animal fossils (5).

terials survived, providing another fascinating source for studying the pharmaceutical practice of ancient and early medieval Japan. The Shōsōin originally contained many *materia medica* that were also listed in the standard *materia medica* compendia from Silla, Baekje and Tang China, which were available to students of medicine and pharmacology in Japan. Most scholars agree that the *Revised Materia Medica* (*Shinshū honzō* 新修本草) provided the basis for such knowledge although the earliest record of its use is from the year 731 (Dettmer 2010, 439n19).[299] The *Revised Materia Medica*, a Chinese work, was a revision of an even older compendium. This older work is ascribed to Shennong (Jp. Shinnō) 神農, the mythical Divine Husbandman who, according to tradition, taught humans the use of plant-based medicines. The book also appeared in ancient and medieval Japan as one of the references for physicians and scholars.[300]

Most medicinals in the Shōsōin came to Nara via China. The ginseng probably came directly from Korea. While the first modern survey of the *materia medica* relied on the data found in the *Revised Materia Medica* to establish the origin of the materials, the second survey, conducted in the 1990s, analyzed the substances to establish where, for example, the sandalwood originally grew. The results reveal that Shōsōin's black pepper was once harvested in western India, the Aleppo wasp galls[301] in northern Persia, the rhubarb in Tibet, the stick lac in northern India on the slopes of the Himalayas, the licorice on the shores of the Yellow River in China, the clove from Sulawesi (Indonesia) and the *harītakī* fruit in Thailand.[302]

To avoid relying on imported plant-based *materia medica*, Heian-period scholars attempted to identify plants in Japan or cultivate non-native herbs in Japan. The first compendium that provides Japanese names for non-native plants throughout is *Japanese Names for the Materia Medica* (*Honzō wamyō* 本草和名, 901–923) by the court physician Fukane Sukehito 深根輔仁 (dates unknown).[303]

---

299 For more on the *materia medica* literature available in the Nara period, see Yoneda (2000, 28–31).
300 This compendium has the title *Variorum of the Divine Husbandman's Classic of Materia Medica* (*Shennong bencaojing jizhu* 神農本草經集注). It was probably compiled in Han-dynasty China (206 BCE–220 CE). For more on the history of pharmaceutics in China, see Unschuld (1986); for a translation of the compendium into English, see for example Yang (2007). For the reception of Chinese compilations of *materia medica* in Japan, see the work of historian Mayanagi Makoto, for example Mayanagi (1993).
301 In the Nara period, these wasp galls (*mushokushi* 無食子) were used as an astringent in the treatment of diarrhea.
302 For a map with examples of where plants and other materials stored in the Shōsōin originate, see Kunaichō Shōsōin jimusho and Shibata (2000, 170).
303 For an introduction to this important pharmacopoeia, see Karow ([1948] 1978).

The *Essentials of Medicine* (*Ishinpō*) also lists *materia medica* with their Japanese names, as does another important Heian-period source, the above-mentioned *Procedures of the Engi Era* (*Engishiki*). Overall, these attempts aimed at, and to some extent resulted in, a standardization of medicinal plant names in Japan.[304] One important example of the cultivation of non-native plants in Japan is the tea plant, highly cherished for its medicinal and recreational value. Opinions differ as to when exactly tea was first grown in Japan but it probably first arrived from abroad in the early Heian period. While plants were cultivated in Japan, those living in the country remained dependent on overseas trade for obtaining the raw materials they needed to produce physic and even continued to import ready-made drugs. They also kept requiring exotic materials such as fragrant wood to properly conduct rituals and to create Buddhist statues, altars and other paraphernalia.

6.3 Japanese Compendia of Incense and Drugs

The work to standardize knowledge on plants and other *materia medica* that started in the Heian period may have stimulated competition between court physicians and monastic physicians in the medical care of aristocrats – or the production of knowledge may have been motivated by such competition in the first place. Rivalry between Buddhist temples as centers of learning also played an important role in this process. In the late Heian and Kamakura periods (twelfth and thirteenth centuries), monastic physicians are reported to have not only treated members of the elite but anyone who needed physical or spiritual healing (Drott 2010, 253). Episodes in contemporary diaries such as the *Record of the Full Moon* (*Meigekki*) by poet Fujiwara no Teika (Sadaie)[305] illustrate the competition between the two groups of medical doctors. In one passage analyzed by Edward Drott, court physician Sadamoto 貞基, a member of the powerful Wake family, struggled to heal Teika who was also treated by the – ultimately more successful – priest Shinjakubō 心寂房 for a skin condition (Drott 2010,

---

304 For a comprehensive history of the early study of *materia medica* in Japan, see Mori (1999). The newly structured *Compendium of Materia Medica* (*Bencao gangmu* (Jp. *Honzō kōmoku*) 本草綱目, 1596) by Li Shizhen 李時珍 (1518–1593) became the most influential compendium in early modern East Asia including Japan where it was introduced in 1607. An example of a Japanese herbal that was based on Li Shizhen's monumental work but introduced a different classification system is the *Japanese Materia Medica* (*Yamato honzō* 大和本草, 1708–1709) by the Neo-Confucian scholar Kaibara Ekken 貝原益軒 (or Ekiken, 1630–1714).
305 See above p. 94.

252–253). Both the Wake and the Tanba families vied for imperial support and tried to keep their writings secret, especially from each other. Nevertheless, secret knowledge was sometimes revealed as shown by the Buddhist treatise *Formulae for Longevity and Curing* (*Chōsei ryōyōhō* 長生療養方, 1184). Not only does this treatise include numerous passages from the *Ishinpō*, compiled and jealously guarded by the Tanba family for generations, but it also appears that Rengi 蓮基 (dates unknown), the author of the *Formulae for Longevity and Curing*, belonged to the Tanba family and was the younger brother of the head of the Bureau of Medicine. The extant version of the treatise was copied on the order of an imperial prince who served as abbot of Ninnaji 仁和寺, a Shingon temple established in 888 by imperial decree.

Nannaji remained a highly influential center of learning as a group of illustrated manuscripts authored by a twelfth-century Ninnaji monk Fujiwara Ken'i (or Kenni) 藤原兼意 (1072–ca. 1169) demonstrates. Buddhist monks there not only authored or painstakingly copied works on longevity medicine and rituals but also worked to preserve, study and pass on knowledge of pharmaceutical drugs and *materia medica*. At the time, Ninnaji, which enjoyed imperial support, was one of the most important centers of Shingon Buddhism in Japan. From 1101 onward, Fujiwara Ken'i spent most of his life on Kōyasan, the secluded mountain sanctuary and center of Shingon Buddhism. His father, Fujiwara Sadakane 藤原定兼 (dates unknown), was a vice minister at the Empress' court.[306] Ken'i is usually referred to as Ryō-ajari Ken'i 亮阿闍梨兼意 stressing that he was an enlightened master or *ajari*[307] in the Shingon hierarchy, with the addition of *ryō* which refers to his father's courtly office. Ken'i received his consecration (Sk. *abhiṣeka*) from Kan'i 寛意 (1062–1101) and in turn bestowed *abhiṣeka* on sixteen disciples. One of the disciples, Shinkaku 心覚 (1117–1180), is well known for his major work on esoteric ritual and iconography, *Assorted Notes on Individual Deities* (*Besson zakki* 別尊雑記, T *zuzō* 3007). The work contains fifty-seven beautifully illustrated fascicles that combine Tendai and Shingon doctrines. Shinkaku is worth mentioning here as he would later play an important role in the transmission of his master's works. Ken'i wrote important Buddhist commentaries, an instruction manual for creating mandala paintings and compendia on *materia medica* (Mori 1977, 4). The compendia derive from Chinese (and Sino-Korean) classical works. The relatively large number of copies of the compendia, created

---

[306] Mori (1977, 4) also mentions another biography that relates him to Fujiwara no Michinaga 藤原道長 (966–1028), the most powerful man in Japan of his time.

[307] This word is also read *azari* and transcribes Sk. *ācārya*, "preceptor." In Japanese esoteric Buddhism it denotes a monastic rank.

over a period of several hundred years, indicates that they were quite popular works.[308]

The compendia by Ken'i are called:

1. *Compendium of Essentials on Precious Substances* (*Hōyōshō* 宝要抄)
2. *Compendium of Essentials on Incense* (*Kōyōshō* 香要抄)
3. *Compendium of Drugs* (*Yakushushō* 薬種抄)
4. *Compendium of Varieties of Cereals* (*Kokuruishō* 穀類抄)

All four kinds of *materia medica* listed – precious substances, incense, drugs and cereals – were used in esoteric Buddhist rituals according to specific systems and teachings (cf. Shinmura 2013, 211–212), and they are widely mentioned in Buddhist canonical texts. The necessary ritual knowledge in Shingon also included the correct Sanskrit name for the plant or substance. Ken'i must have felt the need to compile these elaborate handbooks in order to provide the most cutting-edge knowledge available at the time. According to the early thirteenth-century collection of Buddhist legends, *Conversations About Ancient Matters* (*Kojidan* 古事談, 1212–1215),[309] Ken'i was famous for his erudition and knowledge of Sanskrit (Mori 1977, 13). Since it is difficult to determine the correct Sanskrit name from the Chinese sources, Ken'i often lists a variety of Sanskrit terms in Sino-Japanese transcription in his compendia. He provided pharmacopedic compendia that could be used not only by ritualists in the Buddhism but also by others outside this closely guarded circle. It is possible that this kind of pharmaceutical knowledge developed within the framework of ritual knowledge and became accessible to physicians at a later point.

In the early nineteenth century, members of the Taki family 多紀家, official physicians to the shogunate, began copying important medical manuscripts. Among them was the version of the *Compendium of Essentials on Incense* originally transmitted by Daigoji Temple 醍醐寺 in Kyoto and then stored in the Taki family's archives. Eventually, the Taki transferred the precious Daigoji scrolls to the Takeda 武田 family in Osaka. This family started a pharmaceutical company in 1781 that rapidly developed and became an international business, still dominating the market today. It is thus not surprising that the Takedas professed an

---

[308] Two compendia copies, both classified as important cultural properties are now housed in Tenri Library but were originally kept at Ishiyamadera 石山寺. A set of twelfth-century copies are kept in the Kyōu Library (Kyōu Shooku 杏雨書屋) of the Takeda Science Foundation in Osaka, see Mori (1999, 144–341).
[309] This collection was compiled by Minamoto Akikane 源顕兼 (1160–1215).

interest in these ancient pharmaceutical works. The scrolls are currently kept in the Kyōu Library (Kyōu Shooku 杏雨書屋) of the Takeda Science Foundation in Osaka.

Daigoji, as one of the Buddhist temples heavily supported by imperial and later shogunal representatives, may have been in some competition with Ninnaji, therefore the exchange of this usually well-guarded material may or may not have been completely voluntary. Mori surmises that Ken'i's disciple Shinkaku was in friendly contact with Shōgen 勝賢 (1138–1196), the 18th abbot of Daigoji. Shōgen was the son of Ken'i's relative and contemporary Fujiwara no Michinori 藤原通憲 (Shinzei 信西, 1106–1160)[310] and uncle to Jōgen 成賢 (1162–1232), the 25th abbot of Daigoji. It is very likely that Shinkaku gave versions of his master's work to Jōgen (Mori 1977, 6) at some point to study (and copy). The colophon by Shōgen of the *Compendium of Incense and Drugs* (*Kōyakushō* 香薬抄, 1165), an abbreviated compilation of two of Ken'i's compendia, provides good evidence of this process in that it mentions the circumstances of its genesis:[311]

On becoming abbot of Daigoji in 1160, Shōgen had to escape to Kōyasan from the turmoil caused by a sectarian conflict at Daigoji. Before his escape, he had received secret teachings about the Buddhist deities from Shinkaku and was sure to have had further dealings with him during his stay in the mountain sanctuary, resulting in the compilation work on the *Compendium of Incense and Drugs* in 1165. Moreover, the place where Shōgen resided was a hermitage erected by Kan'i, who was – as mentioned earlier – Ken'i's master. Since we know from the colophon Shinkaku compiled that the content of the *Compendium of Incense and Drugs* derives from Ken'i's two compendia on incense and drugs and that Shōgen copied passages at the hermitage on Kōyasan, it does not seem far-fetched to conclude that Shōgen took the opportunity to study the original four compendia with his gifted friend Shinkaku, who must have been given them by his master Ken'i (Mori 1977, 7). The rich and detailed drawings and list-like nature of the works would have been a major challenge for any copyist.

---

[310] He is not to be confused with the well-known disciple of Kūkai. This Shinzei 信西 was a Buddhist advisor to Emperor Go-Shirakawa 後白河天皇 but is mainly known for his later alliance with Taira no Kiyomori 平清盛 (1118–1181), a powerful general whose actions at court led to the war between his family and the Minamoto family 源氏 which ultimately resulted in the downfall of the Taira in 1185. Shinzei was captured after escaping from an attack on his house and then executed.

[311] It is found in the *Zoku gunsho ruijū* 続群書類従, a comprehensive edition of historical Japanese manuscripts and prints, started by Hanawa Hokiichi 塙保己一 (1756–1821) and continued by his students in the Meiji period; see the relevant quote from this extensive work in Mori (1977, 6).

Shinkaku with his artistic talent must have been the ideal person to study the compendia with. After Shōgen's return in 1178 from his nearly twenty-year long exile upon the death of his principal opponent Jōkai 乗海 (1116–1178), and his reinstatement as Daigoji abbot, he bestowed authority on his nephew Jōgen and passed his *Compendium of Incense and Drugs* to him as is evidenced by a second colophon entry mentioning this fact. At this time, Shōgen may very well have officially presented the four full-length compendia from 1156 to Jōgen as well. Shōgen was also the Buddhist teacher of Imperial Prince Shukaku (Shukaku Hōshinnō 守覚法親王) (1150–1202), a son of Emperor Go-Shirakawa and a Fujiwara mother. This prince was ordained when he was ten years old and later presided over Ninnaji as its imperial abbot (*monzeki* 門跡). His father Go-Shirakawa was the main supporter of Daigoji and maintained a close relationship to Shinzei, Shōgen's father, through the Fujiwara family connection.

In summary, we can see here a good example of an intricate, interwoven web of Buddhist and familial lineages, both through the male and female line, involving two nearly autonomous Shingon temples in the capital at that time. The time period in question included both the Hōgen (1156) and Heiji 平治 (1159) disturbances that preceded decades of civil instability and, eventually, great structural change in the religious setting during the ensuing Muromachi period.

As Ninnaji and Daigoji Temples owned or had owned numerous medical texts, they were important centers for learning and circulating medical and ritual knowledge in the Japanese medieval world. Drott (2010, 268) argues that since Ninnaji was an institution intimately connected to the imperial house, members of the (imperial) elite maintained a strong interest in medical and longevity practices conducted by the monks they supported, the relationship being beneficial for the (non-clerical) elite. From the Buddhist perspective, healing the bodies of worldly leaders and their families would ensure that the Dharma prospered in that land. Altogether, this seems to be a very elitist standpoint in that the powerful act to protect only their own health and interests "for the greater good." As a reaction to these elitist Buddhist activities focusing only on the welfare of a few and disregarding the majority of the people, several reformist, even radically anti-elitist, ideas emerged as is portrayed in many standard works on the new religious movements and groups of the Kamakura period. These ideas and the activities of certain charismatic individuals, such as Kajiwara Shōzen,[312] are interpreted as bringing about a massive change in the religious landscape in that they succeeded in popularizing Buddhism amongst the masses. Richard Payne and others have pointed out that this historical drama has more to do with

---

312 See p. 95.

the perspective and foundation mythology of representatives of Buddhist schools that trace their institution back to founding figures of that time period.[313] Still, Buddhist teachings and certain hitherto guarded practices were made accessible to a wider portion of the Japanese population in the late Heian and Kamakura periods.

6.4 Buddhist Panaceas Made from Potent Plants

Monastic and non-clerical physicians both continued to further their knowledge in the late medieval period. The last section of the present chapter illustrates the fascination with panaceas in Buddhist Japan and the notion of secret formulae that produce wondrous medicines to heal all ills of humans and animals alike. The Three Fruits briefly described above certainly counted among the panaceas with a definite Buddhist connection because they appear in the authoritative scriptures. As the availability of the ingredients of this tonic was extremely limited in Japan, the abundant wealth of *materia medica* and formulae transmitted within the framework of Buddhism provided a rich source for the production of alternative miracle-working medicines. What encouraged Buddhists to engage in concocting various complicated cure-alls while the Buddha famously advised the sangha to simply use "putrefied urine" (*chinkiyaku* 陳棄藥, *furanyaku* 腐爛藥) for healing? The answer is found in the enthusiastic adherence to Mahāyāna Buddhism, which clearly emphasizes that one should follow the passage in the vinayas permitting monks and nuns to administer the Five Medicines[314] and to engage in medical healing wherever possible. While the Five Medicines continued to play an important role in fire ceremonies (Sk. *homa*, Jp. *goma* 護摩) conducted in Japan,[315] Buddhists in East Asia primarily drew on Chinese-style medical tradition with its wealth of formulae for medicines that were thought to procure everlasting health, even grant immortality. The specifically Buddhist take on the production of such medicines that "nourish life" (Ch. *yangsheng*, Jp. *yōjō* 養生), a term often used in the context of Daoism, was to extend life so that one could practice the Dharma as long as possible and to ensure a good death and favorable birth in the next life. In fact, treatises that recommend particular practices at the end of life, and so belong to the genre of manuals for the dying and those who care for them, were frequently penned by Buddhist monastics in

---

313 See e. g. Payne (1998).
314 See epigraph in the Introduction.
315 Nihonyanagi explored the medical effects of the "Five Jewels, Five Drugs and Five Incenses" used in such esoteric Buddhist fire ceremonies (1996, 1997b).

Japan too.³¹⁶ Reflecting these ideas, infirmaries and hospices for monastics were called "Halls of Extending Life" (*enjudō* 延壽堂).

Manuals for terminal and palliative care and end-of-life rituals clearly differed from treatises on nourishing life although both must be seen as equally important for understanding the concerns of those living in premodern Japan. The *Formulae for Longevity and Curing* mentioned above is one example of such a treatise. The *Record on Drinking Tea for Nourishing Life* (*Kissayōjōki* 喫茶養生記, 1211) is another example. The text propagated the benefits of consuming green tea as a tonic and medicinal drug during a time commonly thought to be the period of the imminent decline of the Dharma (*mappō* 末法). Its author, the charismatic monk Myōan Eisai (or Yōsai 明菴栄西, 1141–1215), experienced the benefits personally during his stay in China.³¹⁷ Eisai is famous not only for having convinced the shogun's widow, the powerful Hōjō Masako 北条政子 (1156–1225), to establish the first Zen temple in Japan but also for promoting drinking green tea as a medicine and ingesting drugs made from mulberry, ginger and other plants to heal the various diseases often caused by demons. His treatise, overall, is firmly based in Japanese esoteric Buddhist thought.

Esai allegedly brought saplings and seeds of the tea plant from China for cultivation in Japan although tea from China remained a coveted luxury good. Tea became regarded not only as a medicinal but as a cure all remedy as well. To speak of tea as a Buddhist panacea would be exaggerating but the idea of nourishing life by drinking tea is clearly connected to Buddhist aspirations in this case. While Eisai addressed the ruling elite in Japan and as a consequence fostered the lucrative trade in tea and tea objects such as ceramics benefitting also the temples involved in the trade not least financially, other cure-alls could be produced on a more modest scale using local plants gathered in the wild. One important prerequisite was that the plants were ascribed certain potent properties. A thirteenth-century picture scroll of six meters in length shows that care for the most valuable of domestic animals, the horse, involved esoteric knowledge

---

316 The works of the charismatic Shingon Buddhist monk Kakuban 覺鑁 (1095–1134), also known as Kōgyō Daishi 興教大師, include *Secrets of the Crucial Moment of Death* (*Ichigo daigyō himitsushū* 期大要祕密集). This is one of the Buddhist works of the time outlining the practice of calling the name of Buddha Amitābha in the last hours of life (Sanford 2006, 166–167).
317 For a comprehensive treatment of Eisai's work in the context of *materia medica* knowledge in Japan, see Mori (1999, 342–533). For an introduction and a full translation of Eisai's *Record on Drinking Tea for Nourishing Life* into English, see Benn (2015; translation 2015, 145–171).

on how plants could be made into an effective remedy, as will be outlined in this last section of the present chapter.[318]

The scroll contains drawings of seventeen plants. In fact, these drawings are the oldest extant botanical drawings in Japan[319] – not counting the depiction of the lotus flower in Buddhist devotional images – and attracted attention from Japanese botanists in the first half of the twentieth century for this reason. The picture scroll itself is not titled, but because of its content, it is commonly called the *Scroll of Equine Medicine* (*Ba'i sōshi emaki* 馬医草紙絵巻). It is dated to 1267 and is held at the Tokyo National Museum.[320] The illustrated scroll was described and contextualized by zoologist and veterinarian Mitsu'i Takaosa 三井高孟 (1915–1980) in 1968[321] and incited some interest among botanists. It has only marginally attracted art historians due to the scroll's execution and style. This and the next chapter (in part) provide a full interpretation of the scroll from a Buddhologist and historian of religion's point of view. The scroll contains images of ten divine figures related to the healing of horses, followed by the seventeen pictures of plants and a short postscript. In the following, the botanical drawings will be explored first while the two parts with the divine figures and the postscript will be introduced and contextualized in the next chapter with its focus on equine medicine.

The botanical drawings are detailed and drawn true to life, so they could have functioned as a guide to identifying plants in the wild. Each plant image is accompanied by at least one plant name written in the upper left-hand corner above the image, as was customary for such compendia in the Chinese tradi-

---

318 This last section has been adapted from Triplett (2019a).
319 Bartlett and Shohara in their volume on the history of Japanese botany (1961) even describe the appearance of the scroll as a "premonition" of what they call the "natural history period of Japanese botany." They quote the Japanese botanist Shira'i Mitsutarō 白井光太郎 (1863–1932) ([1926] 2011) who considers this natural history period to have commenced with the Edo period because thought in this period was shaped by increasingly dominant rationalistic thinking in the Neo-Confucian tradition and the appropriation of scientific knowledge from Europe (1961, 19).
320 The source consists of a single scroll that has been designated as an important cultural property of Japan. The entire scroll can be browsed via the Japanese e-museum database at <www.emuseum.jp> (last accessed 28 Feb. 2018). The website provides explanatory texts in Japanese, English, French, Korean and Chinese. For a full presentation of the scroll, with a short introduction and captions in English, see Triplett et al. (2019), available at https://digitalcommons.macalester.edu/himalaya/vol39/iss1/5 (last accessed 25 Aug. 2019). Only very few copies of the scroll or fragments of similar pieces survive. One fragment is held at Tokyo National Museum (A-11961).
321 Mitsu'i (1994). This contribution goes back to a two-part article published in 1968. For an overview on research on this scroll and other materials related to equine medicine in Japan, see Matsuo (2005).

tion.³²² Many images from the *Scroll of Equine Medicine* have secondary and even tertiary plant names written below the picture. Those who created the scroll have also added the Japanese reading in *kana* (syllabic alphabet) next to the Chinese characters that make up the plant names. This was and is the common way in Japan to read Chinese or make texts which are thought to be obscure more comprehensible. Apart from the plant names, the scroll, including its short postscript, does not provide any information about the plants depicted.

It is usually thought that the plants in the scroll are medicinal herbs for healing horses and that this part is a regular if short Chinese-style herbal. But what if these images and their names were not intended to represent individual medicinal herbs at all? Finding explanations that appear plausible and rational to us today, when the intentions of the thirteenth-century creators of this source probably differed from our interests, is like providing the right answer to the wrong question.³²³

In order to determine the possible use or purpose of the seventeen plants in the scroll, it is essential to take a close look at the *names* of the plants. The table below lists the plant names in the order that they appear in the scroll. Transcriptions and literal translations of the plant names in English are added as far as the meaning of the Chinese characters or Japanese words used for the name could be determined. For convenience, the drawings are numbered.

Table 1. Names of plants in the *Scroll of Equine Medicine*

No.	Main plant name:	Additional names or annotations:
1	薬師草 ヤクシサウ *yakushi-sō* medicine Buddha plant	船裏 フナウラ ナリ *funaura nari* boat underside
2	法薬草 ホウヤクサウ *hōyaku-sō* Dharma medicine plant	完条草 シタヤキクサ, 朽 クタシ トモ云 *shishiyaki-kusa* end stream herb (?) *kutashi to mo iu* also called "rotten"

---

322 For a short overview of botanical illustration in China, see Haudricourt and Métailié (1994). The authors mainly focus on a comparison of Chinese and European botanical drawings from the seventeenth century onward. For a book-length study on traditional Chinese botany, see Métailié (2015).
323 It may even be a case of retro-botanizing, a practice aptly described and criticized by Mukharji (2014).

154 — 6 Plants: *Materia medica*, Medicinal Gardens and Panaceas

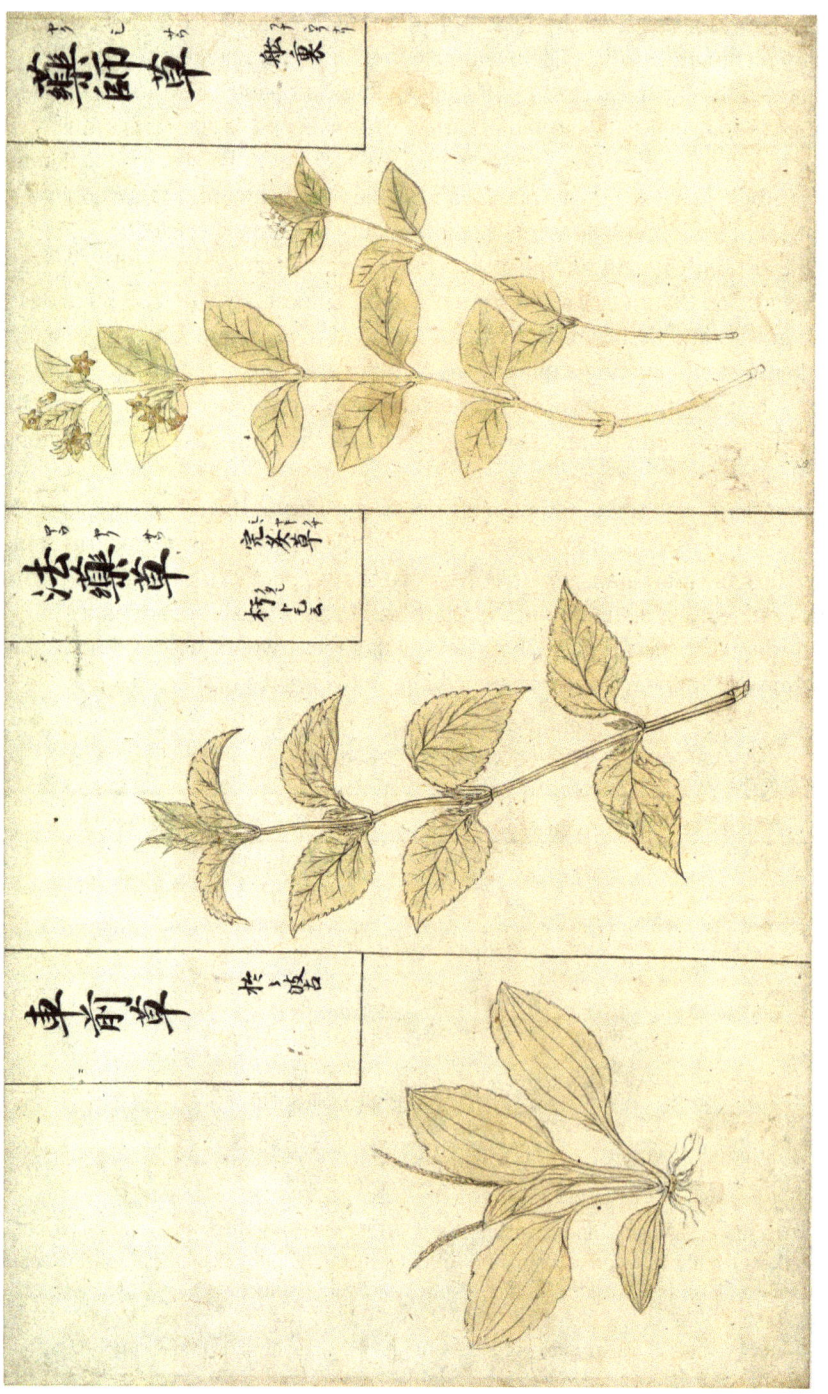

Fig. 3. *Scroll of Equine Medicine* (detail, the first three plants), ink and color on paper, 29.6 × 610.2 cm, Tokyo National Museum (sign. A-10479), ©Tokyo National Museum.

6.4 Buddhist Panaceas Made from Potent Plants — 155

Table 1. Names of plants in the *Scroll of Equine Medicine* (Continued)

No.	Main plant name:	Additional names or annotations:
3	車前草[324] *shazen-sō* in front of wheel plant	於々波古[325] *oohako* ōbako[326]
4	木草伝 モクソテン *mokusoten* wood herb sprawl (?)	茯苓 フクリヤウ *fukuryō* fu mushroom
5	阿度者崎 アトハサキ *atohazaki* atoha cape (?)[327]	梅寄生 ムメノホヤ *mume no hoya* living with the plum[328]
6	草王 クサノワウ *kusanoō* king of plants	狼芽 コマツナキ *komatsunagi* wolf sprout
7	衣草 コロモクサ *koromo-kusa* robe herb	唐苧 カラヲ *karao* Chinese ramie
8	仏前 ホトケノマヘ *hotoke-no-mae* in front of the Buddha	青木香 シヤウモカウ *shōmokō*[329] unripe wood scent
9	色々 イロ々 *iroiro* all sorts	毒散味 トクタミ *dokutami* poison spreading taste
10	長小草 チヤウセウサウ *chōshō-sō* long short plant	芭蕉綴毛 ハセウノツツリケ *bashō-no-tsuzurike* fibrous banana[330]

---

[324] No reading in *katakana* provided here.
[325] No reading in *katakana* provided here.
[326] The characters are used here for their phonetic value.
[327] The characters are probably used here for their phonetic value to write a place name ("Atoha").
[328] The name describes a parasitic plant using the plum tree as its host.
[329] The modern reading is *shōmokkō*.
[330] The characters literally mean "banana basting hair or fur."

Table 1. Names of plants in the *Scroll of Equine Medicine* (Continued)

No.	Main plant name:	Additional names or annotations:
11	狸尻巾 イタチノシリノコイ *itachi-no-shiri-no-koi* weasel's[331] buttock pouch or towel	犬尻 イヌノシリ *inu-no-shiri* dog's buttock
12	馬頭草 メツサウ *metsu-sō* horse's head plant	牛膝 キウシツ, キノクツチ *gyushitsu, inoguzuchi* ox's knee
13	甘草伝 カンサウテン *kanzōden* liquorice[332]	唐蓬 カラヨモギ *Kara yōmugi* Chinese artemisia
14	阿古免草 アコメクサ *akomegusa* akome herb (?)[333]	蛭筵 ヒルムシロ *hirumushiro* leech's straw mat
15	傳地草 テンチサウ *tenchi-sō* sprawling(?) earth plant	大犬蓼ヲタイヌタテ *ōinutade* big dog polygonum
16	天衣草 テンエサウ *ten'e-sō* celestial garment plant	蛇大鉢 ヘヒノタイハツ *hebi no taihatsu* snake big skull/pot
17	仏座 (ホトケ)ノサ *hotoke no za* the Buddha's seat	仙没香 センモツコウ *senbotsu-kō* hermit decline scent
		一名喜蘭草 *ichimei biran-sō* alias beautiful orchid plant

Shira'i ([1891] 1934) was the first modern botanist to identify the plants in the scroll. Several botanists have since examined the drawings, investigating the plants' historical names and attempting to establish their current names.[334] In the table below, the modern botanical names of the plants as identified by Mae-

---

[331] The first character is today used for the *tanuki* (Japanese raccoon dog).
[332] The characters literally mean "sweet plant."
[333] The meaning is unclear; the characters may have been used phonetically.
[334] Ueno (1973, 231); Kimura (1973, 130).

kawa (1975) are listed. Strictly speaking, the list contains sixteen plants and one fungus. The table below also includes the plants' common names in English, where available.

Table 2. Modern botanical names according to Maekawa (1975) of the plants in the *Scroll of Equine Medicine*

No.	Botanical name	Common name
1	*Vincetoxicum atratum*	swallowwort
2	*Isodon japonicus*, syn. *Rabdosia japonica*	isodon
3	*Plantago asiatica*	Chinese plantain
4	*Wolfiporia extensa*, syn. *Poria cocos*	Indian bread, tuckahoe
5	*Viscum album* subsp. *coloratum*	mistletoe
6	*Agrimonia pilosa* var. *japonica*	–
7	*Boehmeria nivea* var. *nipononivea*	Ramie
8	*Inula helenium*	horse-heal,[335] elfdock, elecampane
9	*Lysimachia japonica* Thunb. or *Lysimachia tanakae*	Japanese yellow loosestrife
10	*Musa basjoo* Sieb.: *Musa japonica* Thiéb. et Ketel. and *Musa basjoo* var. *formosana* (Warb.) S.S.Ying	Japanese fiber banana
11	*Carpesium abrotanoides* L. (?)	carpesium
12	*Achyranthes bidentata* var. *japonica*	ox knee
13	*Artemisia annua* or *Artemisia absinthium* (?)	mugwort, wormwood, sagewort
14	*Potamogeton distinctus*	roundleaf pondweed, bog pondweed
15	*Persicaria lapathifolia*	pale smartweed, curlytop knotweed, willow weed

---

[335] This common name indicates a use in equine medicine.

Table 2. Modern botanical names according to Maekawa (1975) of the plants in the *Scroll of Equine Medicine* (Continued)

No.	Botanical name	Common name
16	*Arisaema serratum*	cobra lily
17	*Ajuga decumbens*	bugleweed, ground pine

Some of these plants, including the only fungus listed, were, and are, widely used in Chinese-style human medicine. The best known by far is no. 13: *Artemisia* (mugwort). The dried and powdered leaves of the species *Artemisia princeps* – *mogusa* 艾 in Japanese – are burned in moxibustion therapy, a hallmark of Chinese-style medicine. Chinese horse classics found in Japan[336] not only recommend treatment with acupuncture, bloodletting and cupping but also moxa. *Artemisia* was apparently a pillar of both human and equine medicine. The plant may also have been used as horse fodder in Japan. Maekawa is not sure about the exact species depicted (1975, 26). Given that both *Artemisia* and *Persicaria lapathifolia* (pale smartweed, no. 15) are used in horse medicine in Europe today,[337] their beneficial effect on the animals may have been observed in premodern Japan.

The wood-decay fungus *Wolfiporia extensa* (Indian bread, no. 4) was another important ingredient in human medicines in regions where Chinese-style medicine was practiced. *Isodon japonicus* (no. 2) is equally known as a medicinal herb in the Chinese tradition in Japan but under another name. It is now called the "prolonging life herb" (*enmeisō* 延命草). Interestingly, the picture of *Viscum album* (mistletoe, no. 5) growing on a flowering plum branch differs from the other pictures in style. It looks as if another artist painted it. While all other plants are depicted in what we would today call a naturalistic style and are thus in correct proportion, in the image of the mistletoe, the parasitic plant is disproportionately smaller than the plum blossoms. However, the mistletoe is immediately recognizable. The use of mistletoe in premodern equine medicine and horse care along with most of the plants depicted in the scroll remains largely unclear.

---

[336] Most horse classics in Japan go back to the Tang-dynasty *Collection of Remedies for Blood Horses by Stable Grooms* (Ch. *Simu anjiji* 司牧安驥集) by Li Shi 李石 (786–847). See Chapter 7 on equine medicine below.

[337] I am grateful to Dr. Sabine Aboling (University of Veterinary Medicine Hannover) for this valuable information.

Establishing the exact identities of plants in Chinese-style compendia is especially complex. As Elisabeth Hsu outlines in her longitudinal study of the group of herbs with the designation *Artimisae annuae* in Chinese *materia medica* literature from ancient times to the sixteenth century, the name of the living plant is usually but not always the name of the medicinal drug. Additional obstacles to the study of plants in the areas where Chinese *materia medica* were used include the variation of names (synonyms) conditioned by local distribution and the specific preparation of the drug (2010, 87). The drugs consisted of multiple compounds and the exact composition of each drug was not entirely fixed. Botanical illustrations sometimes developed independently from the descriptive text in Chinese *materia medica* literature and as they are often crudely executed illustrations, they are largely unhelpful for the identification of a plant. A similar observation can be made regarding identification and naming practices for plants in Japan where the Chinese model was largely followed.

Returning to our seventeen Japanese plant drawings and looking closely at the primary names, the references to Buddhism and the horse are rather striking. When clustering these primary names into two groups, we find the following:

1) Plant names linked to Buddhism:

   No. 1   Medicine Buddha plant

   No. 2   Dharma medicine plant

   No. 8   In front of the Buddha

   No. 17   The Buddha's seat.

Two more primary names and one secondary plant name relate to Buddhism in an indirect way and can be added to this group:

   No. 7   Robe herb

   No. 16   Celestial garment plant

   No. 17   Hermit decline scent

The "robe" (no. 7) points to the Buddhist monastic robe while the term for celestial garment (no. 16) is used to describe the clothes of Buddhist deities.[338] The reference to a "hermit" in the plant name (no. 17) is also a clear reference to the religious sphere.

---

[338] This is an established Buddhist term for the garments of a bodhisattva, in pictures shown as a light cloth hanging down from both shoulders.

2) Plant names linked to the horse and other mammals:

The following primary names are linked to horses:

    No. 3   In front of wheel plant

    No. 12   Horse's head plant

Several primary and secondary names mention other larger mammals[339]:

    No. 6   Wolf sprout

    No. 11   Weasel's buttock pouch, dog's buttock

    No. 12   Ox's knee

    No. 15   Big dog polygonum

No. 8 "In front of the Buddha/Unripe[340] wood scent" may also have a connection to the horse: This medicinal plant in Japanese Chinese-style medicine is today also referred to as "horse's bell herb" (*umanosuzu-kusa* 馬の鈴草) because the leaves are shaped like a horse's head and the seeds like the bells hung on horses. However, this designation may not have existed in the medieval period.

    In summary, four to seven plant names are associated with Buddhism, and two to six of the plant names have a direct link to the horse or to a large mammal. Were the names given to the plants because they were thought to be important to equine health or were the plants selected for medicines because of their names? A sixteenth-century manuscript containing a strikingly familiar formula for producing a Buddhist panacea suggests it is more likely that the plants were selected because their names make reference to horses and Buddhism. Mitsu'i ([1968] 1994) describes the content of the sixteenth-century manuscript, which is a copy of the hippiatric manual, *Well-known Diseases of the Horse* (*Uma no yamai mishiru koto* 馬之病見知事, 1513) by a certain Raichū 頼忠 (dates unknown). The formula for the equine panacea detailed in the manual requires sixteen of the seventeen plants listed above. Only *koromo-kusa* (Chinese ramie, no. 7) is missing. As the manuscript is currently unavailable, we have to rely on Mitsu'i's analysis. He provides a table itemizing the plant names in the hippiatric manual and the *Equine Scroll of Medicine* (1994, 450). While the Chinese characters of the plant names vary only minimally, the Japanese reading of

---

[339] The leech and snake used in secondary names of two other plants may not be relevant here.

[340] It may be a coincidence but the first character of the secondary plant name, 青 (unripe, green, blue), can also mean "black horse."

the names varies considerably. Assuming that the difference derives partly from copying mistakes or from factoring in Japanese vernacular names from a certain region, the two sets of plants are identical. The passage in question indicates the quantity of the potent plants used for the formula. It also includes details on the preparation of the medicine and instructions for the Buddhist rituals required to empower the panacea. The medicine is called "Mount Tamura Dharma medicine" (*Tamurasan hōyaku* 田村山法薬) probably referring to a particular Buddhist temple.[341] The passage reads as follows:

> With Jōnen's[342] Mount Tamura Dharma medicine you can cure every disease without exception in animal husbandry. For treating a horse suffering from a cold disease, you heat it up in rice wine. For a horse that is suffering from fever, you treat it with the Dharma medicine in cold water and the horse will cool down. This Mount Tamura Dharma medicine is the best panacea (*hiyaku* 秘薬) when horses need to be treated with physic. In order to make some of this physic, choose the hour of the horse, just before the beginning of the hour of the sheep[343] on the fifth day of the fifth month and recite thirty-three chapters of the *Avalokiteśvara-sūtra* and the mantra of the Medicine Buddha one hundred and twenty times. After that, turn to the east and recite the name of the Medicine Buddha twelve times, look at the sky with your hands put together and pray by reciting three times: "Hail, Hundred Medicines[344] Medicine-king Dharma Medicine, residence of Ōnamuchi, you, hail the Source[345]." And then you can begin preparing [the medicine] starting with the Medicine Buddha plant. After that, dry it for thirty days in the shade. When it's dry, cover it with a lid. When pounding it all together you must do as you did before and recite the sutras and the names. You can also use it as a physic boiled in sifted rice wine lees. Jōnen-bō says: "There is no better medicine than that." And it is also said: "You should transmit to others that the secret panacea of the Abbot of Kokawa [temple][346] is a medicine that you can give to horses with both cold and hot disease." (translated from Mitsu'i 1994, 451)

Mitsu'i maintains that in the *Scroll of Equine Medicine*, the "Medicine-king Dharma Medicine" (*iōhōyaku* 医王法薬) is not the name of the Buddhist monk shown in the section of the scroll depicting ten divine figures (see below fig. 4) but simply the name of the panacea. In Mitsu'i's interpretation, the scroll is an instruction for producing the Buddhist miracle cure. It is more plausible, however, that the power of the physic resides in the Buddhist deities – Avalokiteśvara, the

---

341 Temple names in East Asia usually include a so-called mountain name. The identity of this temple is not clear. Tamurasan may also simply be a place name.
342 Jōnen, or further below Jōnen-bō, is the name of a monk.
343 This time designation covers the time period from 11 a.m. to 1 p.m. (horse) and 1 to 3 p.m. (sheep).
344 "Hundred medicines" means all the medicines there are.
345 In the ritual formula, the "Source" (*izumi* 泉) is directly addressed as a second person.
346 The Abbot of Kokawa was a famous Japanese horse doctor; see below p 182.

Medicine Buddha and Medicine-king Dharma Medicine – as well as in the Japanese god Ōnamuchi, the latter also shown in the scroll (see below fig. 5). The Buddhist monk shown in the scroll (fig. 4) can be regarded as the human form of a Buddha or bodhisattva, revered for his healing power.

The recipe of the 1513 hippiatric manual is for a wonderous Dharma medicine but it can be transmitted to everyone who needs help with curing their animals. Still, in order to follow the ritual instructions, the horse owner or healer has to be trained in Buddhist recitation. Ritual practice is required to turn the potent plants into an all-healing miracle cure.

***

It is unclear whether Buddhist panaceas only had a ritual or symbolic function, or whether they were seen as medical and healing to the physical body. The administration of an herbal remedy such as the "Mount Tamura Dharma Medicine" clearly points to the regular framework of Chinese-style medical practice. Its production, however, is intricately connected to the world of Buddhism and the hidden powers that only a ritual expert can access. This makes the medicine unique and effective, according to the tradition. The provision of panaceas, such as the "Mount Tamura Dharma Medicine," or the Sōtō Zen Buddhist "Poison-Dispelling Pill," described in detail by Duncan Ryūken Williams (2005, 86–102) remained a salient feature of temple economies well into the late Edo period. The "Mount Tamura Dharma Medicine" seems to have been solely concocted for animals. Interestingly, monastics encouraged pilgrims to purchase the cure-all medicines for human patients and to apply the panacea to their domestic animals in case of affliction as well. This shows a concern for suffering animals, a topic that will be addressed in the following chapter.

7 Horses and Equine Medicine

Announcement to passersby: one runaway dark bay stallion (has distinguishing marks: one eye is white, some white on forehead)

At the hour of the monkey on the 6th day of this month, the aforementioned horse ran away from the side of the pond in the flower garden of Yamashina temple.

If anyone sees and captures him, please come and report to the third chamber from the southern end of the middle cloister of Yamashina temple.

The 8th day of the 9th month.

From a ninth-century roadside public notice,[347] trans. Lurie (2011, 165)

Buddhist medical practice in Japan also covered animals, especially horses, which were considered the most precious and desirable domesticated animal. By the medieval period, equine medicine, primarily practiced by military staff in Japan, included both medical treatment of horses and Buddhist cosmological ideas and rituals. A class of officials was in charge of government-owned horses and cattle. These officials, *ba'i* or *uma no kusushi* 馬醫, belonged to the Bureau of Horses[348], and not to the Bureau of Medicine, according to the *Yōrō Code*. The first treatises on hippiatry and hippology that were studied in Japan came from the Chinese tradition.[349] These books were introduced as part of agricultural knowledge.[350] The Japanese had cared for horses, however, much earlier than they cared for books. A Central Asian horse breed was introduced via Korea at

---

[347] This notice was written on a wooden board (*mokkan* 木簡) of almost a meter in length and about 7 cm in width. It was found in Nara. Yamashina Temple was the local name for the famous and powerful Kōfukuji Temple of the Fujiwara family. The text can be found under no. 20 in the collection of such *mokkan* texts edited by Okimori and Satō (1994, 96–97; 11, fig. 20). *Mokkan* no. 21 has similar content (1994, 97). See also Lurie (2011, 165–166; 165n66).

[348] This institution, *Meryō* or *Uma no tsukasa* 馬寮, was divided into a left and a right division as all such governmental units were. Staff such as stable boys were affiliated to the Bureau of Horses as well. The Bureau of Horses was maintained until the end of Tokugawa period. An Office for Military Horses (*heibashi, hyōmashi* 兵馬司) also existed and was part of the Ministry of War.

[349] The following passages have been in part adapted from Triplett (2019a) and Triplett (2013–2014).

[350] This is evident from the *Catalogue of Extant Texts in the Country of Japan* (*Nihonkoku genzai shomokuroku* 日本國見在書目録, 891), compiled by Fujiwara no Sukeyo. For veterinary works in this period, see Manieri (2012).

https://doi.org/10.1515/9783110576214-011

the end of the fourth century CE[351] and became the focus of both veterinary care and religious attention in Japan. The introduction of equestrian culture to Japan is the subject of controversies that commenced in 1948 with archaeologist Egami Namio's 江上波夫 (1906–2002) famous theory that a group of horse riders from northeastern Asia crossed the Korean peninsula in the fourth century, entered Kyushu and finally made their way to central Japan to establish a kingdom which became the imperial house of Yamato.[352] While whether nomads of the Eurasian steppes conquered parts of Japan is still a contested issue, most researchers emphasize that there were intense and dynamic exchanges between the kingdoms on the Korean Peninsula and the Japanese archipelago in the fourth and fifth centuries.[353] Significant developments during this period can be gleaned from archaeological finds excavated from burial mounds. The practice of building these grave tumuli was discontinued with the introduction of Buddhism in the sixth century. While even the most elaborate of the typically keyhole-shaped burial mounds (*kofun* 古墳) from the fourth century did not contain any equestrian equipment, such equipment, made from iron and bronze, abounded as funerary objects in the fifth century. Equestrian equipment has also been found in the more modest graves from this period, a clear indication that horsemanship had become a widespread phenomenon by the fifth century. Since the equipment includes items used in mounted warfare or for driving horse-drawn chariots, it is clear that this technology introduced from the mainland must have played a significant role in the state-building of early Japan.

In every region of Japan with *kofun*, numerous pits have been found in the vicinity of moderate-sized burial mounds that contain the remains of horses and their tack. The fact that the great majority of the interred horses were not older than three years and thus in their prime, and that they were beheaded, leads

---

351 Horse bones found in prehistoric shell mounds in Japan initially led researchers to conclude that an earlier species of horse had been indigenous to Japan and hunted for food. However, chemical analysis identified these bones as belonging to the Central Asian breed introduced in the fourth century. The bones were deposited there in a later period when the shell mounds were reused as waste heaps (Shira'ishi 2016, 91).

352 The theory was published as part of a symposium on the origin of Japanese culture and the formation of the Japanese state in the *Japanese Journal of Ethnology* in 1948. It was part of revisionist historiographical thought after the war. For a discussion on the origin of the Japanese people involving Egami, see Ishida et al. (1958). See also a compact overview of the horse rider theory in Egami (1984). The theory is discussed anew in relation to equestrian culture in a volume published by the collective Kodaishi shinpojiumu "Hakken, kenshō Nihon no kodai" henshū iinkai et al. (2016). For discussions on the horse rider theory in English, see Farris (1998) and Como (2007, 394–396).

353 See, for example, Azuma (2016).

most archaeologists to agree that these horses were ritually sacrificed (Shira'ishi 2016, 93; 96), perhaps on the occasion of the funeral of the animal's owner.[354] It is striking that while early written records in Japan recount the killing of wives and servants in order for them to follow a member of the imperial family into death, burial mounds do not contain any such remains. Only the separate pits for the slaughtered horses are evidence of such sacrificial practice (cf. Segawa 1991).[355] Since an edict in the Taika reforms (*Taika no kaishin* 大化改新) of Emperor Kōtoku strictly prohibited the forced sacrifice of relatives and servants to follow the deceased into death, we can assume that the edict outlawed an existing custom. There is evidence of such sacrifices in ancient China. The *Nihon shoki* tells us that Emperor Suinin 垂仁 (r. 29 BCE–70 CE) abolished this custom after realizing its cruelty, and replaced the sacrifice of humans and animals with offering hollow clay figurines called "clay rings" (*haniwa* 埴輪) to accompany the deceased of high social standing. The earliest written records such as chronicles and local gazetteers in Japan support what remains of Kofun-period (ca. 300–538/552) material culture. Numerous clay figurines representing humans and animals have been unearthed. Many museums in Japan conserve *haniwa* of warriors in armor holding swords and bridled horses with or without riders, as well as other figurines representing the daily life of the deceased. The clay objects are often spectacular in design and execution. They were originally arranged in a ring-like pattern, sometimes on several terraces, on top of the burial mounds. Whether they replaced living human and animal sacrifices or not is unclear, and their actual meaning and function remain obscure. However, the figurines are important material records of equestrian culture in a time period when written sources were scant.

The horse-riding lineages from Korea that became powerful in the Yamato state brought with them devastating diseases that the local population had no immunity to, so the fear of horse-riding deities as bringers of pestilences increased. At the same time, the local population would turn to the horse-riding

---

[354] The eighth-century local gazetteer from Harima province recounts the legend of a pond named "Horse tomb pond." The events in the legend are supposed to have taken place during the reign of Emperor Yūryaku 雄略 (r. 456–479). The legend states that a dying man instructed his son that his maid and his horse were to die with him. The son followed his father's wish and built three tombs accordingly. For a translation of this legend, see Aoki (1997, 183); see also Triplett (2004, 30–32). This legend indicates that the practice of funerary sacrifice was at least known in Japan although a legend cannot ultimately prove the historicity of the practice.

[355] Como points out that horses were sacrificed to appease disease-bearing spirits from the seventh century onward. The spirits would use the animals as mounts to speed away (2007, 402). For archaeological finds of horse sacrifices in Japan, see Ueda (1992); for early China, see Lu (1993) and Linduff (2006).

lineages for protection, according to Michael Como (2007, 409). The horse, therefore, was somewhat paradoxically thought of as both a bringer of pestilence and a protector from epidemic disease in ancient and early medieval Japan. Small clay horses (*doba* 土馬) are among objects unearthed from riverbeds and ditches at the boundaries of settlements where they were buried as part of purification rituals in times when epidemics ravaged the land (Farris 2009, 42–47). In about 900, the practice of burying these simple clay figurines disappeared but there is ample evidence of an enduring belief in mounted bringers of infectious disease.[356] Indian Buddhist stories of the horse as a manifestation of the Buddha Śākyamuni in one of his former lives[357] and of the "excellent horse" (Sk. *aśvaratna*, Jp. *mahō* 馬寶) as one of the seven symbols of a world ruler, however, increased esteem for the animal. This is especially evident when the ancient Indian birth tale of the Buddha was combined with an episode from the *Lotus Sutra*: Medieval-period Japanese temple legends and picture scrolls depict Avalokiteśvara saving merchants from man-eating female demons by turning into a flying white horse.[358]

Most of the fifth- and sixth-century horse tombs described above are located in areas named in Fascicle 48 of the early Heian-period *Procedures of the Engi Era* (*Engishiki*) as important centers of horse and cattle breeding: the Kantō area, Shinano, Kai and Suruga provinces, as well as Kyushu. The *Procedures of the Engi Era* is a collection of thousands of rules and procedures for governmental agencies. The procedures aimed to implement the official legal codes and listed taxes – to be paid mainly in natural produce – in exhaustive detail. The compendium makes detailed provisions for wide tracts of land set aside as pastures for horses (and cattle), controlled by a complex bureaucratic system. Horse-keeping, medical care of horses and ceremonial uses of horses[359] already appear in the earliest legal codes, the *Taihō* and *Yōrō Codes*. Equine medicine was codified and the title of "horse doctor" (*ba'ishi* 馬醫師) bestowed, although how equine medicine was actually practiced cannot be gleaned from the lists of

---

356 One horse-riding bringer of epidemics is, for example, the "Bull-Headed Divine King" (Gozu-ten'ō); see also above p. 125.
357 An episode from the *Valāhassa Jātaka* that was translated into Chinese became popular in Heian- and Kamakura-period Japan (Meech-Pekarik 1981, 111n2).
358 See Meech-Pekarik (1981) and Lomi (2011, 169–210).
359 The most important court ceremony was leading around a white horse (*aouma* or *hakuba no sechie* 白馬節会); see Nakada (1990). To this day, some Shinto shrines keep white horses in stables on the shrine precincts and host horse races and other horse-related competitions. The offering of living horses to shrines was replaced by offering wooden statues of horses and votive tablets with paintings of the animal, the so-called "picture horses" (*ema* 絵馬).

penal and administrative laws. Since the *Procedures of the Engi Era* describes an elaborate system in place in the early tenth century, equestrian culture must have developed over a long period of time and involved diverse groups in different regions (Shira'ishi 2016, 96–97). Of particular importance for the history of horse medicine and care in Japan were compendia written in Chinese on the six domesticated animals (*liu chu* 六畜) – horse, ox, sheep, pig, chicken and dog – of which only books with a direct bearing on local animal usage went into wide circulation. Classics on the pig and the chicken did not play a central role in Japan because the Japanese did not breed these animals that were commonly eaten in China. Manuals on the care of larger mammals became popular as oxen and horses provided civilians and the military with transportation and were used in agricultural labor.[360] Hunting for game remained legal and popular although emperors decreed hunting (and fishing) prohibitions from time to time. In regions with extensive horse breeding, horsemeat was rather common. It was rare in most other regions, and even regarded as poisonous.[361]

The practice of equine medicine becomes more concrete in the ninth century with the first writings of veterinarians in Japan who had studied in China and brought back classics such as the Tang-dynasty *Collection of Remedies for Blood Horses by Stable Grooms* (Ch. *Simu anjiji*, Jp. *Shiboku ankishū* 司牧安驥集) by Li Shi 李石 (786–847). The Captain of the Imperial Guards of the Left, Taira Nakakuni 平中國 (dates unknown) was one such student. He published a compilation on horse care in 804 and is considered the founder of Heian-period Nakakuni-style equine medicine, which became especially influential with the eighteenth head of that school, Fujiwara Masachika 藤原政近 (dates unknown), also known under his Buddhist name Shinkai Nyūdō 心海入道.[362] He

---

360 Dairy products were part of the human diet in ancient (and medieval) Japan. For the practice of keeping pets in medieval Japan, see Ambros (2012, 2–3). For an excellent overview on human-animal relationships in Japanese history and through the present day, see Ambros (2012, 17–50). For animal care and religious aspects such as funerary practices, see Kenney (2004).
361 Grumbach shows that different approaches to animal killing, animal sacrifice and meat-eating existed in medieval Japanese society (2005); on horses see Grumbach (2005, 74, 79–80; 84–85n63).
362 See the classic histories of veterinary medicine in Japan by Shira'i ([1944] 1979) and Nakamura (1980). For the medical treatment of horses in early Japan, see Suzuki (1984). The Japanese Society of Veterinary History (Nihon jūigaku-shi gakkai) compiled a biographical dictionary of veterinary medicine in Japan that also includes veterinarians from historical periods (2007). For early historical overviews, see Froehner (1943) who mainly discusses veterinary medicine of the modern period and catalogues Japanese horse books from the University Library in Berlin,

lived in the early sixteenth century when horses became ever more important because of the constant warfare at that time. As he also used Kuwashima 桑島 in his personal name, his students determined that his school would henceforth be called Kuwashima-style horse medicine. Fujiwara Nakatsuna 藤原仲綱 (dates unknown), another military officer, revived the Kuwashima style in the late sixteenth century and many important medical works on horses were compiled by him and his students. In fact, the Kuwashima school became the most important veterinary institution until the end of the Tokugawa period.

Among the Heian-period Chinese classics that Nakatsuna and his students made available for a wider audience in the late medieval and early modern period by transcribing them into *kana* and inserting numerous charts and images were the *Essentials for Horse Doctors* (*Ba'i daigo* 馬医醍醐, 1551) and the *Collection of Remedies for Horses in Syllabic Script* (*Kana Ankishū* 仮名安驥集, 1604). The latter was composed at a Buddhist temple by Hashimoto Dōha 橋本道派 (dates unknown) in collaboration with a monk named Ikkan Wakō 一閑和尚 (dates unknown) and an unnamed doctor (Shira'i 1944, 46–47).

This indicates a close collaboration between veterinarians and Buddhist institutions. This chapter introduces selected sources that demonstrate the relationship between Buddhism and veterinary medicine, focusing on equine medicine. It also outlines certain Buddhist practices, including horse-headed deities for the protection and healing of animals and husbandmen.

7.1 The *Scroll of Equine Medicine* (1267)

The *Scroll of Equine Medicine* (*Ba'i sōshi emaki*), introduced in the preceding chapter, is evidence that caring for the valuable horse involved esoteric knowledge of plants. The scroll also contains images of divine figures related to healing horses and a short postscript after the section on the seventeen plants. The beginning of the scroll consists of a section with ten "image units" showing drawings of ten deities. All are legendary and mythical figures related to the healing of horses or animals in general. Small text boxes in the upper left-hand corner of each image unit state the deity's name and dates which have a special liturgical meaning. The image units also contain mantras and *dhāraṇī* and indicate the names of attendants and the deities' horses but they do not include any explanatory text as such. In some cases, the original Buddhist deity is also mentioned.

---

and Burns (1948). For more recent overviews, see von den Driesch and Peters ([1989] 2003, 55–63) (Japan is included in the chapter on China), Matsuo (2005) and Kozasa (2010).

Displaying the name of the original Buddhist deity is in line with the common belief that each local Japanese god or other divinity is a manifestation of a Buddha or bodhisattva. The drawings are executed beautifully and the horses look life-like and full of energy. The divine figures depicted in the scroll are, in order of their appearance:[363]

Hakuraku (Bole) 伯楽

Iō Hōyaku (Yiwang Fayao) 医王法薬

Raikō (Laigong) 頼公, standing for Leigong 雷公

Tōgun (Dongqun) 東群

Ten (Tian) 天

Ōnamuchi 大汝

Ōryō (Wangliang) 王良

Hongai (Fan Gai) 幡蓋, standing for Fan Kuai 樊噲

Shinnō (Shennong) 神農

Echigo no Tansuke 越後丹介.

The scroll must have been damaged at some point because the first figure, Hakuraku (Bole) is not shown. We can only see his two spritely horses in their stable. Bole was a Zhou-dynasty (seventh century BCE) Chinese cattle doctor who possessed an excellent knowledge of horses. In fact, Bole is the alleged author of important horsemanship manuals that predicted the character of a horse by the shape of hair whorls in its fur and other physiognomic features.[364] For this expertise, he was, according to legend, named after a star in the constellation

---

363 As the majority of them are of Chinese origin, Chinese transcriptions of the names are added.
364 See Harrist (1997) for a study of Bole's "horse physiognomy" in Chinese visual culture. The prediction of the horse's character and the fate of its owner by interpreting the shape of the animal's hair whorls is also an important feature of Tibetan horse books that in part go back to Sanskrit compendia attributed to Śālihotra, the legendary founder of hippiatry in India; see Blondeau (1972) and Maurer (1995, 2001). This kind of divination is also found in Chinese horse classics (Maurer and von den Driesch 2006, 356–357); see also Heerde (1999, 26–27); for an overview on the imagery of Chinese horse books, see Buell et al. (2018); for the practice of interpreting patterns in nature and in animals, see Ambros (2012, 27). For contemporary Tibetan rituals for the protection of horses in connection with medical treatment, see Craig (2006).

of the Heavenly Horse.³⁶⁵ In the *Scroll of Equine Medicine*, his mantras are dedicated to the Medicine Buddha (Sk. Bhaiṣajyaguru) and bodhisattva Avalokiteśvara. Accordingly, this famous Chinese horse specialist is firmly included in Buddhism.

Iō Hōyaku (Yiwang Fayao), which means "Medicine-king Dharma Medicine," is shown as a Buddhist monk holding a vajra staff and a prayer chain. Above his head, we see a picture of Buddha Amitābha (or another Buddha) which is said to be Iō Hōyaku's original form.³⁶⁶ His mantra is dedicated to Amitābha. The name of his attendant, a young man in the clothes of a novice with a shorn head who seems to be feeding the magnificent black horse, is Dharma Master Impassioned (Aizen 愛染) (Sk. Rāga), another indication of a close connection to esoteric Buddhism.

The next three, Leigong,³⁶⁷ Tōgun (Dongqun) and Ten (Tian), look nearly identical. They are dressed as Chinese noblemen or officials, complete with hats and wooden staffs, sitting on mats that look as though they were fashioned from animals' pelts. Such mats indicate the high position of the male figures. Except for Leigong, it remains a mystery who these figures are. Their names seem rather generic: Tōgun (Dongqun) means Eastern Herd and the third figure, Heaven, or just Deity, *ten* (*tian*) also being the established translation of the Sanskrit *deva* (god).

The figure after the three Chinese gods is labeled as Ōnamuchi (fig. 5, left). The picture shows a female mediumistic dancer (*miko*) handling a small double-sided drum. Her body posture indicates that she is dancing a ritual dance. The *miko*'s expression of entrancement and the long straggling hair make her look like a possessed shamanic medium. Both the dancer and her female attendant are on a straw mat. Such a mat traditionally marks a sacred activity. The attendant who is called Kotori, meaning Little Bird, is kneeling in front of the *miko* passing her a book. Both are dressed in white robes and are barefoot. The principal figure of this image unit is the only one from the Shinto (*jindō*) tradition.³⁶⁸ In fact, Ōnamuchi is one of the most important Shinto gods. Ōnamuchi is a male

---

365 In Japan, *hakuraku* became the general term for horse and cattle doctors.
366 Mitsu'i surmises, in light of a 1503 manuscript that he examined (see above p. 160), that "Medicine-king Dharma Medicine" may actually be the name of a medicine that monks administered to the afflicted horses and not the name of the Buddhist monk depicted in the drawing (1994, 446; 448) – a view not shared here.
367 Leigong, Thunder Duke, is connected to the Yellow Thearch (Emperor) and thus to medicine.
368 Although Buddhism and Shinto were practiced in combination until the modern era, this image unit with the Shinto god does not feature any Buddhist element such as a mantra.

7.1 The *Scroll of Equine Medicine* (1267) — 171

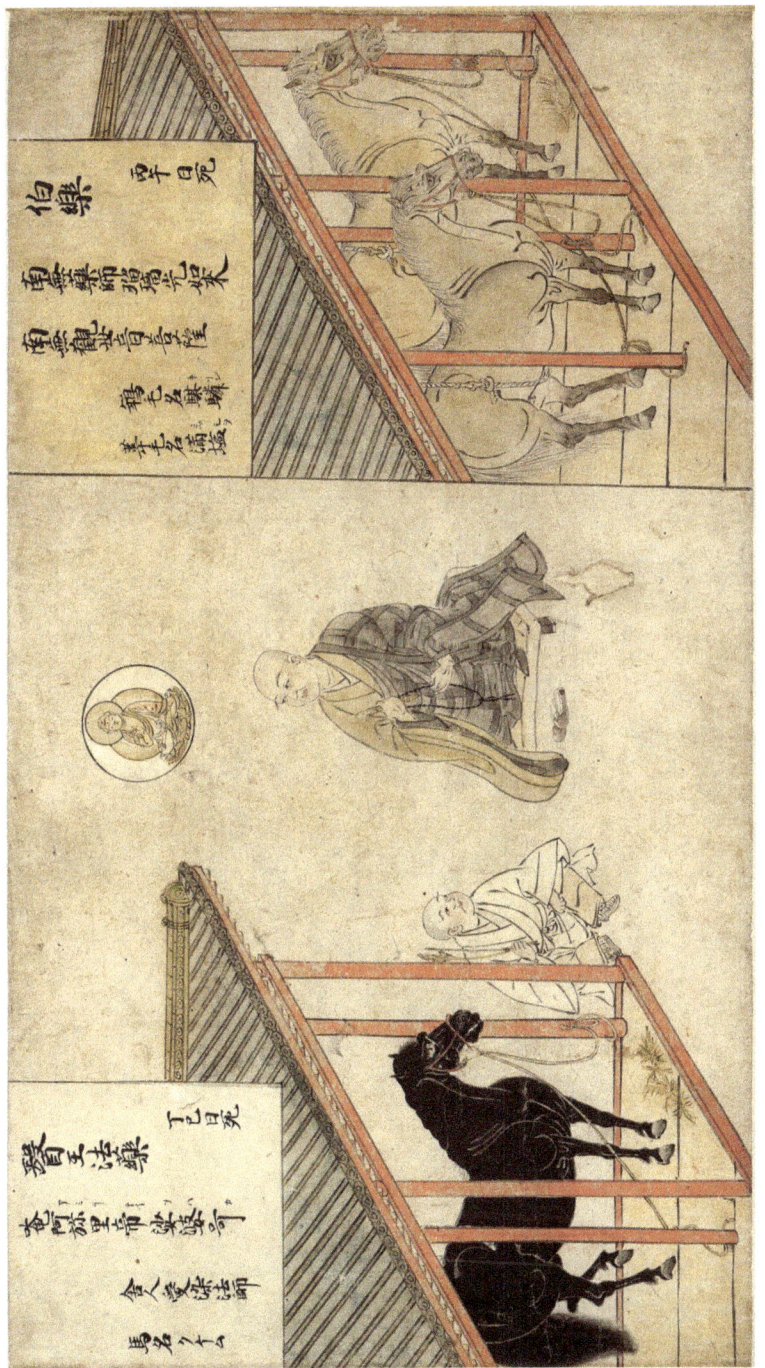

Fig. 4. *Scroll of Equine Medicine* (detail, Iō Hōyaku and Leigong), ink and color on paper, 29.6 x 610.2 cm, Tokyo National Museum (sign. A-10479), ©Tokyo National Museum.

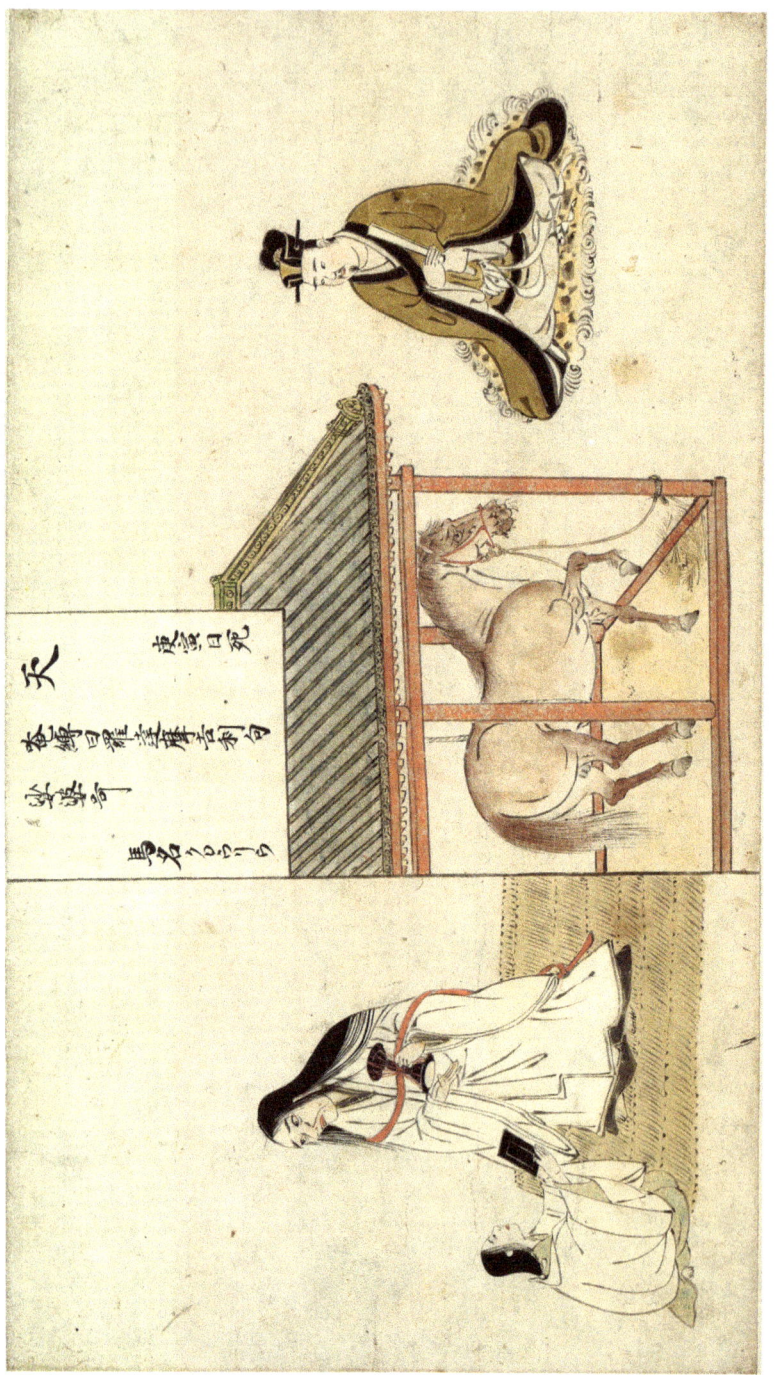

Fig. 5. *Scroll of Equine Medicine* (detail, Ten [Tian] and Ōnamuchi), ink and color on paper, 29.6 × 610.2 cm, Tokyo National Museum (sign. A-10479), © Tokyo National Museum.

god, venerated as Ōkuninushi 大国主, Great Land Lord, for creating Japan and the world. This deity was probably not included in the scroll for his world creation powers but for a well-known episode from the *Kojiki* myths. In the story, a mischievous hare, the White Hare of Inaba, becomes seriously injured and Ōnamuchi advises him to wash his wounds in cold freshwater and roll his flayed body in cattail pollen (*kaba, gama* 蒲).[369] This treatment proved successful and, in the end, the white hare manifests as a deity. This episode is evidently of great interest to animal doctors. As Shinto gods are rarely depicted, and if they are, they are usually depicted in the form of courtiers or court ladies, the *miko* shown here may be representing Ōnamuchi through her mediumistic dance. As evidenced by an early sixteenth-century ritual formula for the empowerment of a horse healing decoction, Ōnamuchi was thought to be a source of healing power for horses.[370]

Ōryō, meaning King Good, a reference to one of the divine kings of the Chinese Zhou dynasty, and Fan Kuai, a second-century BCE Chinese general, are depicted as two men dressed in vermillion-colored robes holding a wooden ceremonial staff and a fan respectively. Both are identified with bodhisattva Ākāśagarbha through their mantra. Fan Kuai also has a second mantra, which hails bodhisattva Samantabhadra.

Shinnō (Shennong), the Divine Husbandman, may be the best-known of the ten figures. In Chinese tradition, he is the mythical founder of agriculture and the healing arts. As a cultural hero, he showed the first people how to plow and how to use medicinal herbs. Without the name given in the box in the left-hand corner, the Divine Husbandman cannot be recognized. He is usually depicted as a hairy wild mountain man with horns and clad in a coat of leaves, with a medicinal plant in his mouth. In the *Scroll of Equine Medicine*, however, he is formally dressed like a Japanese court official. He sits leisurely on a handsome chair holding a brush in his hand like a scholar. Across from him stands a powerful looking black horse. The box with the text is the only one colored in red as if to emphasize the significance of this deity. His long *dhāraṇī* contains small glosses with numbers presumably to aid recitation.

The final figure, Echigo no Tansuke, has the same *dhāraṇī* as the Divine Husbandman. He looks like a Japanese nobleman from the time the scroll was created, with his splendid robes and elegant hat. In his hand he holds a riding whip and he sits on a decorated *tatami* (woven rice straw) mat. The god's name contains a place name, Echigo, which is one of the old provinces of Japan, located

---

[369] The plant's pollen is used as a hemostatic in Chinese-style medicine.
[370] See above p. 161.

on the north shore of the main island far from the capital. The characters of his personal name mean "mercury," an important ingredient in longevity medicines, and "to care for," again an evocative name in the context of this scroll. As he has the same *dhāraṇī* as the Divine Husbandman, the god is clearly connected to this mythical founder of herbal medicine. A short text praising Echigo no Tansuke is provided next to the *dhāraṇī:* "The protector god of travelers, fervently revered in Kai province,[371] works wonders in fixing wicker suitcases, palanquins, horses and clog supports[372]." As a protector god of travelers (*sae no kami* 塞の神), he is a god of boundaries and translocal spaces. He is connected, even identified, with the Road Ancestor God (*dōsojin* 道祖神).[373] The belief in wayside and boundary gods was and is still bound to a particular locality but over time the gods' capacities became more and more complex as local ideas were exchanged and became translocal themselves, as Kura'ishi emphasizes in his studies on the phenomenon (2005, 10 – 16). The boundary god's capacity included the protection of horses as he was believed to ride back and forth to fend off malign influences such as epidemics. The scroll mentions concrete items apart from the horse, here a medium of transport for human travelers. As a protector of road-faring, concrete items such as suitcases, palanquins and the typical stilted clogs for walking, which were important to travelers at the time, fall into the realm of his wondrous powers.

Just looking at the pictures, one can recognize multi-layered traditions, including deities from India, China and Japan. The images are not in chronological order; the mythological deities come first followed by those of a more historical nature, as per tradition. The two parts of the scroll (deities and plants) have a similar layout: The image is in the center, while the text is subordinate to the image and adds meaning to it. The text also conveys meaning visually, making use of pictographic and ideographic characters, as well as phonetic script. Words from three languages – Sanskrit, Chinese and Japanese – are used.

The third and final part of the scroll contains a text of fourteen lines that reveals the work's actual function. The postscript lists a lineage of ten Chinese mythical healers and healing divinities that, curiously, differ from the ten deities pictured in the first part of the scroll. In addition to the Divine Husbandman,

---

371 Kai is not far south of Echigo but is not a neighboring province.
372 This word, consisting of the syllable *ha*, could also mean blades.
373 We know from a tenth-century Japanese dictionary that *dōsojin* was called *tamuke no kami* (太無介乃加美) in indigenous Japanese using the character 介 phonetically. This character is most commonly read as *suke* in personal names. It is therefore likely that the name in the scroll is a general designation of the wayside god.

Bole, Thunder Duke and Eastern Herd, the postscript also lists Yellow Thearch (Emperor), Jīvaka, Bian Que 扁鵲,[374] Zaofu 造父[375], Yaqian 雅遣[376] and Qin 秦[377].

After a (fictive) Chinese date that falls in the Tang dynasty, the author of the scroll makes it clear that the content is to be kept secret: "This knowledge should not be passed on carelessly, and those who are not noble should not receive this transmission." Then follows a list of ritual objects probably used as part of the empowerment ceremony or as part of other rituals conducted in relation to the healing of horses. The list of ritual objects contains "hawk feather arrows (seven), silk, a short-sleeved kimono, a horse, an ox, a great sword, a sword, a suit of armor, a deer skin, a waistband, a monkey skin, the five grains (seven each)."[378] The list includes weapons, animals and animal parts. No explanation is given with regard to what to do with these objects but we are informed that "further details are found in the liturgical text(s)." The objects largely point to cavalry culture and myths connected to the horse.[379] The mention of "silk" is reminiscent of the legend of a human girl and a horse who became the patron deity of the silkworm and therefore of sericulture.[380] Monkeys and horses also enjoyed a close relationship in Japanese culture as well in the past, when live monkeys or parts of dead monkeys were kept in stables as talismans for the protection of the stabled horses.

The postscript ends with instructions for the safe transmission of the scroll to protect the secret knowledge contained within and a dated dedication: "Given to Tadayasu, Third Officer of the Seventh Rank of the Imperial Guards, on the twenty-sixth day, first month of the fourth year of the Bun'ei era." As we can see clearly from his title, the receiver of the scroll was a low-ranking samurai. It can be assumed that Tadayasu must have been a practicing veterinarian who cared for cavalry horses. The name of the bestower of the scroll, however, indicates a connection to Buddhist practice: Sai Amidabutsu. He instructs Tadayasu in the postscript with the following words:

---

374 Bian Que is a legendary physician from the time of the Yellow Thearch. The scroll uses an unusual first character that includes the radical for bird. The second character of his name is also bird-related and means "magpie." See also p. 89.
375 According to Chinese mythology, Zaofu was a most accomplished charioteer, immortalized along with his eight-headed team of horses as a stellar constellation (Cepheus).
376 It is unclear what this figure is.
377 Qin stands for Qin shihuang 秦始皇, the first Chinese Thearch (Emperor); see below p. 180.
378 Prayer texts from early Japan mention similar objects used for appeasing violent spirits. See, for example, Como (2007, 402), quoting the English translation by Phillipi (1990, 70).
379 Mitsu'i correlates the items to those used in a ceremony in 676 CE. Similar items were used then as offerings on the altar (1994, 453; table 454).
380 See Lomi (2011, 236–237) and Como (2005).

> The orally transmitted empowerment into the Dharma medicine presented in its entirety in this scroll must not be easily passed on to anyone. If your apprentice passes away, leaving this world where death comes to old and young alike, then the scroll should be returned to me. If I, Sai Amidabutsu, should die without leaving any apprentices, then this scroll should be burnt and the ashes should be spread.

Since the scroll is still extant and in rather good condition, one can assume that they did have apprentices although the instructions must have been neglected at some point since the scroll in its digital version is now viewable by all who have access to the internet and so can potentially be passed on to everyone. The scroll places the new apprentice in the (Chinese and Indian) lineage that is mentioned in the postscript. The Tang dynasty date guarantees additional authority and legitimacy. The actual ritual may have been conducted by Sai Amidabutsu himself, the transmitter of the secret scroll, who was probably a "secular" veterinarian rather than a trained Buddhist priest although he may have become a monk after retiring from a military career as a veterinarian.

The scarcity of textual information and the choice of textual detail and imagery in this "secret" scroll leads us to conclude that it was used in the context of an oral transmission and empowerment ritual and the scroll itself can be said to be an object of ritual empowerment. The oral transmission may have included mythological explanations for each of the deities in the first part of the scroll which are legendary, semi-historical or divine figures forming the lineage of horse veterinarians in Japan. The figures of the deities are rendered, with the exceptions of Iō Hōyaku who is depicted as a Buddhist monk and Ōnamuchi who looks like a possessed *kami* shrine maiden (*miko*), very stereotypically as Chinese or Japanese scholars – including the Divine Husbandman who is usually depicted as a primordial wild man chewing on a sprig. These images of scholars emphasize that the healing power and blessings manifest in spiritually advanced humans or indigenous deities not only in China but also in Japan. Through the rituals, the ritualist can gain access to these blessings for his "patients," the horses, no matter where he is located. There is a strong emphasis on drawing a connection to the Buddhist cosmos and the healing empowerment of Buddhist deities because of the mantras, *dhāraṇī* and liturgical dates. The images of the deities in the scroll may have functioned as a register for memorizing the names and incantations that were important in the ritual. The comparison with a manuscript text from the sixteenth century in the previous chapter showed that the original purpose of the *Scroll of Equine Medicine* went beyond mere mnemonic purposes. Along with the empowerment of an apprentice in the veterinarian arts, it may have provided the new horse doctor with a formula and ritual instructions to concoct an all-healing medicinal drug.

7.2 Horse Medicine of the Anzai School

Various premodern hippiatric texts in the tradition of the Japanese Anzai school and based on the Tang-dynasty work *Collection of Remedies for Blood Horses by Stable Grooms* connect healing to Buddhist cosmological thinking in a different way. The first example, entitled *Equine Medicine Scroll of the Anzai School* (*Anzai-ryū ba'i emaki* 安西流馬医絵巻), is an undated work consisting of one illustrated manuscript scroll. The second is an illustrated book dating from 1589 with the nearly identical title *Equine Medicine Book of the Anzai School* (*Anzai-ryū ba'isho* 安西流馬医書).[381] Both works are kept in the Veterinary Archives of Azabu University. The manuscripts are also "secret" records (*hidensho*) but otherwise quite different from the aforementioned scroll from the Tokyo National Museum. They combine explanatory text with "charts" – tables and graphic images such as anatomical charts – and are clearly a combination of Chinese veterinary knowledge and esoteric Buddhist ideas. Anzai (or Ansai), mentioned in the title of the two works, is the name of a clan of horse veterinarians in Komagane in Shinano province (today Nagano Prefecture) which used to be an important horse breeding area.

The *emaki* scroll basically consists of sections of *Collection of Remedies for Blood Horses by Stable Grooms* but is composed as a guide through an esoteric Buddhist way of healing by combining it with the Chinese ideas of the Five Phases and other correlative thinking such as the influence of the four seasons on the "organs." This correlative system is very similar to the one found in human medical works as demonstrated above in the ophthalmological treatise.[382] First, the scroll from the Anzai school shows a table of the Five Phases that is typical for the Tendai Buddhist medical tradition, followed by an image of a five-colored Sanskrit syllable "A" that embodies Vairocana Buddha which indicates a strong link with Shingon. This syllable is connected with lines to a five-storied pagoda, the head and then the hand of the Buddha, a horse and the internal organs of a horse followed by a chart of the five sets of physical phenomena of a horse and finally, a horse with five colored sections (see fig. 6).

These images are then followed by a short explanatory text after which more images are shown: a schematic rendition of the horse's development in the womb and five-storied pagodas with combinations of the organs that explain the benign or harmful influences of the four seasons (see fig. 7). Again, a

---

381 For a short description of this book, see Shira'i (1944, 75–75).
382 See also, for example, the image in Michel-Zaitsu (2017, 137, fig. 73).

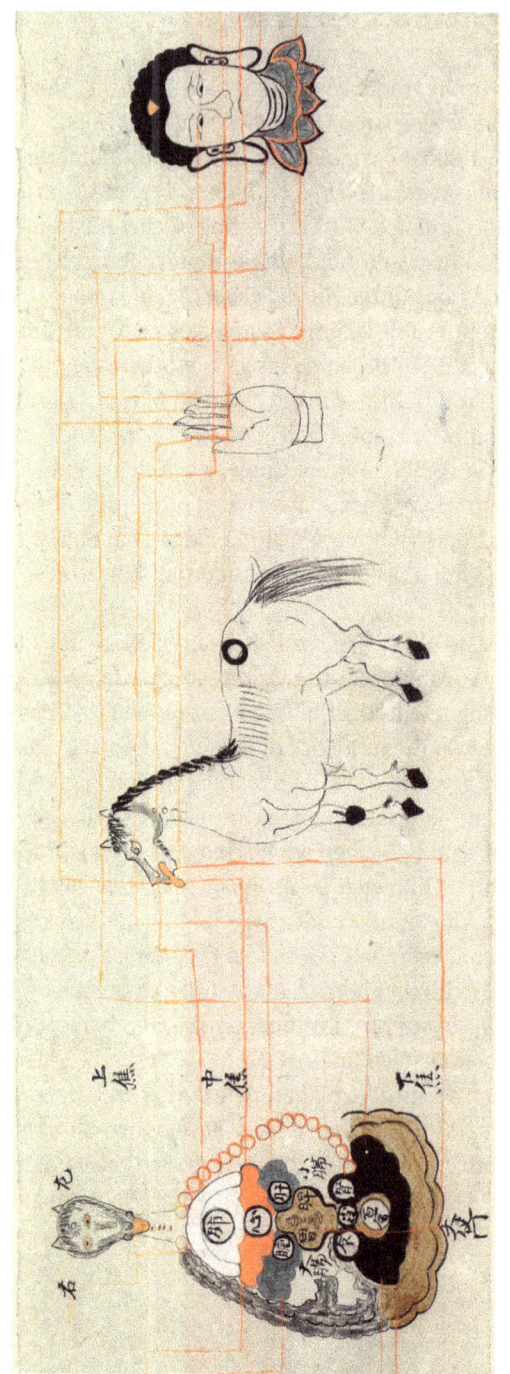

Fig. 6. *Equine Medicine Scroll of the Anzai School (Anzai-ryū ba'i emaki)* (detail, lines link the Buddha's head and hand to the horse's body and organs), ink and color on paper, one scroll, undated, Veterinary Archives of Azabu University.

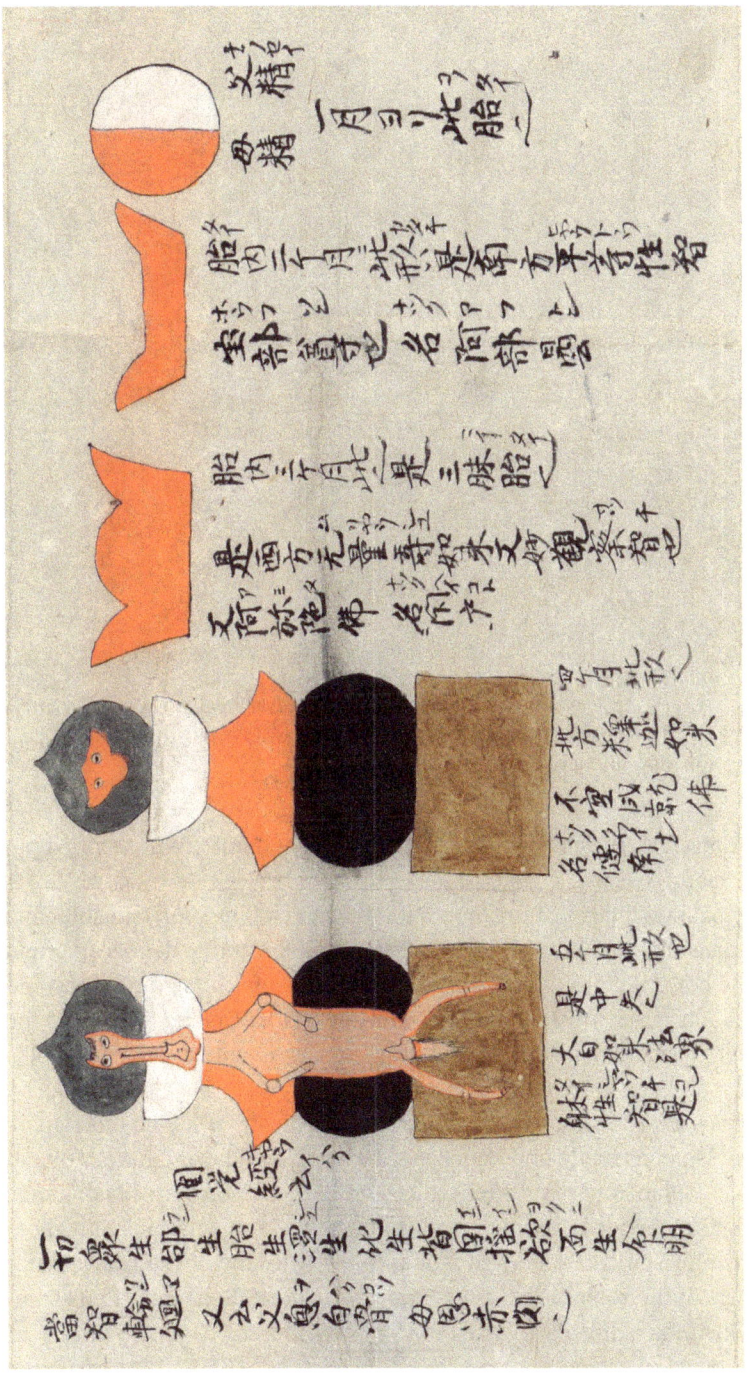

Fig. 7. *Equine Medicine Scroll of the Anzai School (Anzai-ryū ba'i emaki)* (detail, a horse from conception to birth modeled on Buddhist embryology), ink and color on paper, undated scroll, Veterinary Archives of Azabu University.

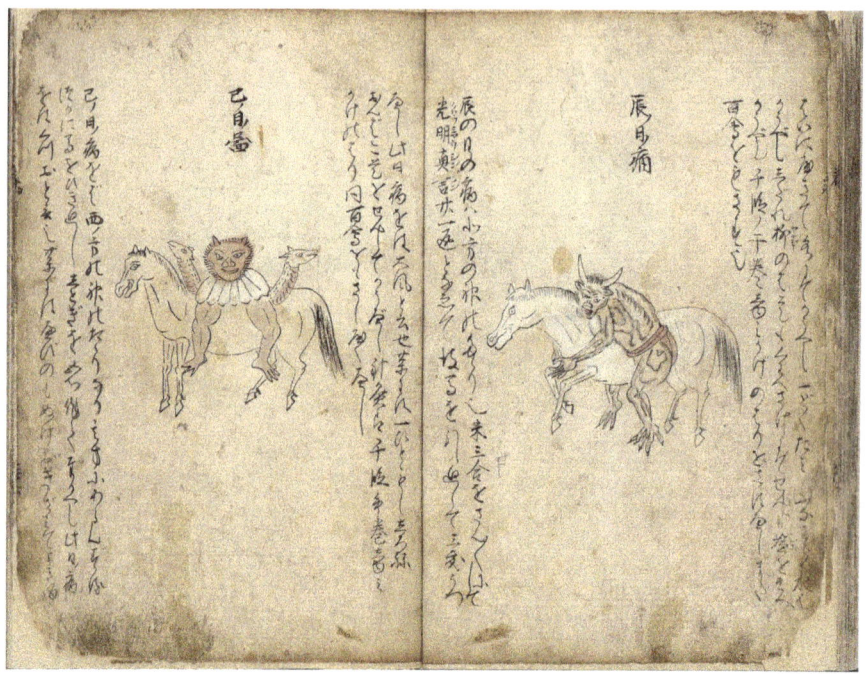

Fig. 8. *Equine Medicine Book of the Anzai School* (*Anzai-ryū ba'isho*) (detail, right: spirit of the day of the dragon, left: spirit of the day of the snake), 1589, bound manuscript book, 27 cm, Veterinary Archives of Azabu University.

short text is inserted, which emphasizes that the mention of the five-storied pagodas is secret knowledge.

Crudely painted images of the first Chinese Thearch (Emperor) Qin shihuang 秦始皇, a horse and Bole lead into a lengthy section of text that details an origin legend of the horse divinity, starting with an image of a falcon in a tree. The end of the scroll comprises a list of the horse's Zang and Fu Organs (including the "gall bladder" a horse does not have) that serves as a summary of the scroll's content.

The *Equine Medicine Book of the Anzai School*, which is executed much more carefully and is not as crude and sketchy as the *emaki* scroll, contains additional sections with explanatory texts after the legend of the falcon with illustrations. The final section provides remedies against afflictions from nefarious influences caused by twelve spirits. Each spirit is associated with one of the twelve Sino-Japanese days of the zodiac. The spirits appear in different shapes, often as animals or monstrous beings (see fig. 8).

Other examples have a substantial section with instructions for Japanese disciples which must have been used in teaching the art of treating horses.[383] The *emaki* scroll, however, is fairly useless as a guide for medical practitioners or learners. It was most probably also an object given to new practitioners on the occasion of ritual empowerment and initiation into "secret knowledge." The framework of textual sections and quotes extracted from the Tang Chinese classic text gave the Japanese Buddhist medical and ritual object great authority.

Mura'i and Matsuo (1974) describe yet another example, one of the last copies of the Anzai scrolls, which dates to 1710, during the period of transition to European models of veterinary medicine. The scroll was copied from a 1579 work written by Ansai Harima no kami 安西幡摩守 (dates unknown).[384] The sections of this work closely follow the two mentioned above: the diagram of the Five Phases, anatomical charts of the "organs," images of a horse's body, a horse's head, the Buddha's head, a five-storied pagoda and the syllable "A" all connected with lines. Explanatory notes and the correlatory diagrams of interrelationships follow. Two pictures show acupuncture points on the horse's body. The last section outlines the history of the work and the history of the school, lists the most important causes for disease and adds some advice for students. It then states the name of the founder and provides a lineage chart of his successors. The individual authorities listed in the chart differ significantly from the thirteenth-century *Scroll of Equine Medicine* in that the initial founding figures are all historical Buddhist monks. The Anzai school sees the Indian scholar monk Memyō Bosatsu 馬鳴菩薩 (Sk. Aśvaghoṣa Bodhisattva) as its founder. No medical work written by this prolific monk is known. However, his name may be his sole qualification for serving as the founder of the Japanese veterinary school. The name of this monk, Aśvaghoṣa, literally means "Horse-voiced."[385] His successor was Dharma Master of the Three Collections [of Buddhist scrip-

---

[383] See the translation of a 1635 print of a horse classic by the veterinarian Michael Heerde into German (1999). The illustrated print is kept at the Bayerische Staatsbibliothek (Bavarian National Library). See also Froehner (1943). Dr. Elizabeth Kenney reported at a conference we both attended, on a 1568 manuscript scroll she is working on that is held at the Library of the University of California San Francisco. The scroll contains images and texts such as the ones shown in fig. 8 below.

[384] Mura'i and Matsuo explain that the scroll was discovered only in January 1972. It was in the possession of the Sasako 笹古 family who has long resided in Komagane, Nagano Prefecture, an area famous for horse breeding. It is now held at Shinshō University, Nagano Prefecture, Japan. For images of this text, see Mura'i and Matsuo (1974, 254–255, fig. 1–12); von den Driesch and Peters (2003, 57, fig. 2–2).

[385] In China, this illustrious Buddhist figure became closely connected with the horse-headed goddess of sericulture; see Lomi (2011, 236).

tures] (*Sanzō hosshi* 三藏法師) of Tang China, a rather generic title that probably refers to the famous Chinese pilgrim monk Xuanzang 玄奘 (602–664) who had travelled to India. A high-ranking monk from Kokawadera Temple[386] finally brought the precious veterinary knowledge from China to Japan.[387]

It would seem that the Chinese texts offered Japanese veterinarians different options for the production of manuals for different purposes, with some used more in ritual contexts and others in more medical contexts: The "ritual" texts, therefore, may not have been studied but functioned like certificates for a successful transmission of expert knowledge. In contrast, texts containing additional details on the application of medicines and other therapies for the treatment of horses seem to have been produced as medical manuals to be read and studied and not as "ritual certificates." Not all texts based on *Collection of Remedies for Blood Horses by Stable Grooms* incorporated Buddhistic elements, however. Manuscripts and prints of the unabridged horse classic without these elements continued to be circulated in both Japan and China in the early modern period.[388]

To summarize, the illustrated manuscripts introduced above served as compendia for veterinarians who practiced hippiatry with the blessings of compassionate and all-powerful Buddhist deities and other formidable divine figures taken from various traditions. This combined knowledge system was increasingly supplanted by knowledge systems introduced by European veterinarians who started to exert their influence in early eighteenth-century Japan.

7.3 A Temple Hospital for Horses

As indicated above, care for animals in Japan was regulated by the ancient administrative codes. The system of equine and bovine medicine was inscribed in the *Legal Codes for Stables and Pastures* (*Kumoku-ryō* 厩牧令). While horse and cattle experts and veterinarians administered medical care to the animals, every

---

386 The scroll says 粉川僧正, providing the reading "Funsen" as the name of the "bishop" (*sōjō* 僧正) (1975, 255, fig. 12) but it is probably the name of the temple, now written with the characters 粉河 and read *kokawa*. It could also be a place name (Matsuo 2005, 11).
387 Mura'i et al. described and analysed further examples of such materials ([1961] 1994, [1977] 1994).
388 A rare collection of horse books from early twentieth-century China has recently been incorporated into the collection of veterinary manuscripts at the Staatsbibliothek zu Berlin – Preußischer Kulturbesitz (Berlin National Library), see catalogue under Sammlung Unschuld/ Ramey. Many of these manuscripts have already been digitized.

cavalryman knew how to apply the set of five recognized treatments: moxibustion, acupuncture, medicines, incantations (*juri* 呪理) and magical technology (*jutsuri* 術理) (Shira'i 1944, 47). Three of the treatments can be said to be of a secular nature while two methods are in the field of religion. By the seventeenth century, all samurai warriors were trained in these methods, meaning that laymen had expert knowledge of spells and rituals usually attributed to Buddhist monastics. The five treatments focused on the well-being of animals in order to keep them fit for human use. However, there were also efforts to promote animal welfare in line with the Buddhist ideal of compassion, which was critical of the exploitation and killing of animals. Famously, Shogun Tokugawa Tsunayoshi 徳川綱吉 (1626–1706) ordered that shelters be built for "useless" horses and stray dogs. Laws prohibiting the ill treatment of animals were also issued, which displayed a strong sense of Buddhist compassion (Bodart-Bailey 2006, 130). In medieval Japan, such an engagement predominantly came from the Shingon Ritsu reformed esoteric Buddhist movement established by Eison briefly introduced above. While Eison himself and most of his disciples largely engaged in bestowing lay precepts to sufferers of leprosy and building bathhouses, his disciple Ninshō 忍性 (also Ryōkan-bō 良観房, 1217–1303) was one of the outstanding monastic physicians of the Kamakura period. In 1267, Ninshō founded Gokurakuji Temple 極楽寺 in the city of Kamakura that had some decades before, in 1192, become the new seat of the military government under the Hōjō family. In fact, this temple enjoyed the patronage of the Hōjō family. It was built as the Hōjō family temple following Ninshō's counsel.

As with any decent-sized Buddhist temple Gokurakuji boasted many functional buildings in addition to the main Buddha halls, *kami* shrines and pagodas. By 1283, the temple housed traditional Buddhist welfare institutions such as a home for elderly monks, a dispensary, an infirmary and a bathhouse. In 1287, Ninshō established a hospital (*ryōbyōjo* 療病所), mainly intended for those with leprosy, in Kuwagayatsu 桑谷. He emulated Shōtoku Taishi who had famously opened four welfare institutions – a dispensary, a hospital, a "field of compassion" (*hiden'in*) for the relief of the poor and needy, and a "field of respect" (*kyōden'in* 敬田院) for the elderly[389] (Wajima 1959, 129). A detailed map dated Genkō 元亨 era year 2 (1322) shows the entire precinct of Gokurakuji Temple including buildings outside of the temple wall proper (Kameya 2012, 36–37; fig. 1, 2). At the lower edge of the well-preserved map, we see a rus-

---

[389] The two "fields," producing good merit and happiness, traditionally form a set (*nifukuden* 二福田). A set of three "fields" includes in addition the "field of gratitude" (*onden* 恩田) for repaying the kindness of teachers and parents. See above p. 139.

tic-looking building labeled as "Sakanoshita Horse Hospital" (Sakanoshita babyōya 坂下馬病屋). It is situated below the southernmost temple gate in a mountainous landscape. According to the temple chronicles, Ninshō also established this horse hospital. He is reported to have visited it frequently even when he was very old. The monk would attach a slip of paper with the "mantra of light" (kōmyō shingon 光明真言)[390] to an animal's neck, recite the mantra and pray for the animal's healing and salvation. He would also give medicine to the animals there, caress them and talk to them as he would to humans. His devotion to suffering horses is connected to the great vow he took at the age of 57 to act as a true bodhisattva. Ninshō vowed to care for the sick and suffering and engage in relief work and welfare and, lastly, to refrain from riding horses. He swore that he would not only help beggars but also relieve the pain of cows and horses abandoned at the roadside. He pledged to gather medicinal herbs in places most difficult to reach and that he would pick these herbs even if his life came into danger (Kameya 2012, 38). This vow is in line with the reforms his teacher Eison initially instigated but his actions differed somewhat from Eison's in that Ninshō created a system of various welfare institutions from donations as well as taxes.[391] As with other monastics in the Shingon Ritsu school, Ninshō gained high prestige and social capital through these actions[392] during his lifetime and enjoyed great appreciation after his death: Emperor Godaigo 後醍醐 (r. 1318–1332/1339) bestowed the posthumous title of Bodhisattva on him. The monk was also popularly thought to be the Buddha King of Healing. Whether the medical facilities and the skill of the monastic physicians at Gokurakuji far surpassed those of the official court medicine (kan'i 官医) at the time (Kameya 2012, 38) or not may be debated but this institution certainly must have been exceptional. It also seems likely that monastics cared for animals in a medical as well as in a religious capacity at places like Gokurakuji Temple's horse hospital.

As with the circulation and production of materia medica outlined in the previous chapter, veterinary knowledge was clearly present at Buddhist temples in general. We also find texts written by Buddhist monks about the healing of animals: The Shingon monk Gyōyo 行誉 (dates unknown) compiled a seven-vol-

---

390 This is the dhāraṇī of Vairocana Tathāgata that according to tradition dispels all evils through the light of the Buddha. The text next to the image of the spirit on the right in fig. 8 above recommends the recitation of this dhāraṇī.
391 See Quinter on differences between Eison's and Ninshō's views (2015, 47–51).
392 Ninshō's actions also incited much criticism from contemporaries such as the monk Nichiren 日蓮 (1222–1282), see Wajima (1959, 132–133). On Ninshō's social work, especially with outcasts (hinin), see Yoshida (1983). For an assessment of Ninshō's welfare system from the perspective of present-day welfare studies, see Hidaka (2009).

ume encyclopedia he called *Selections from a Dust Bag* (*Ainōshō* 壒囊鈔) in 1445 or 1446. The encyclopedia deals with the meaning of things and with etymology. "Dust" in the title is a Buddhist technical term meaning "mundane things." The text is presented in a question-and-answer format and is a reworking of a much earlier encyclopedia entitled *Rubbish Bag* (*Chiribukuro* 塵袋, 1264–1288) which had eleven volumes and 620 entries in total.[393] Later, in 1532, someone who called himself "a certain monk" revised and expanded both works which then appeared under the title of *Rubbish [Bag] with Selections from a Dust Bag* (*Jin ten ainōshō* 塵添壒囊鈔).[394] This twenty-volume work was distributed in print from the seventeenth century and gained widespread popularity.

This example shows that knowledge about the world of things and words, and creating a certain knowledge order was of great concern to Buddhist monastics. As one would expect, the compilers included a lot of knowledge about Buddhist temples, Shinto shrines and related terminology. But does *Rubbish [Bag] with Selections from a Dust Bag* provide a Buddhistic interpretation of equine medicine? The section on equine medicine is found under the entry of "horse doctor," *hakuraku*. After explaining the term, the compilers add a short explanation of the origin legend of the first horse doctor in China, Bole, followed by a brief reference to the ceremonial use of white horses, a list of several recipes for horse medicines and an outline of the connections between the horse's organs and the seasons, etc., gleaned from the Ankishū tradition. The encyclopedia entry on *hakuraku* does mention several formulae among them a panacea (*hiyaku*). The doctor is to sprinkle the medicine on the horse's body. The text uses the Buddhist term for the ritual sprinkling in a consecration ritual (*kanjō*, Sk. *abhiṣeka*), and one is supposed to use mantras while pouring the medicine onto the horse.

As Lomi has already noted (2011, 245), it is astonishing, however, that the encyclopedia makes no mention of the Horse-headed Avalokiteśvara (Batō or Mezu Kannon 馬頭観音) who was believed to protect these animals. Interestingly, this manifestation of the bodhisattva neither appears in the various scrolls mentioned above. However, the Horse-headed Kannon did play a major role as protector of animals in Japan from the Heian period on. Its role changed significantly over the centuries as Lomi (2011) and others have shown. The contemporary Batō Kannon cult for pets and racehorses goes back to early modern devel-

---

393 According to one explanation, the *Rubbish Bag* encyclopedia goes back to a monk called Ryōin 良胤 (dates unknown) who was active at Kanshōji Temple 勧勝寺 in Edo, the same monastery in which Gyōyo lived. Ryōin must have been among the first generation of monks there as the temple was founded in 1252.
394 See Bailey (1960, 34–35, 39) on these premodern Japanese classified reference works.

opments when this deity was widely identified as a horse protector and commonly revered in memorial rituals for beloved horses while in the centuries before, rituals involving this deity were performed by specialized monastics in temples and palaces and were intended to provide general protection from calamities.

7.4 The Horse-headed Kannon as Protector of Animals

In esoteric Buddhism, fierce-looking deities were incorporated into rather complicated systems of manifestations of the Buddha's awakened mind. In one such system, the Horse-headed One, Hayagrīva, a demonic being revered in ancient India, came to be considered one of the powerful "Holders of (esoteric) Knowledge" (*vidyādhara*) or "King of Knowledge" (*vidyārāja*). These beings personify a certain Buddha or bodhisattva. In this case, the Horse-headed One personifies Avalokiteśvara, the bodhisattva of all-encompassing compassion.[395] Various Buddhist sutras describe the Horse-headed Avalokiteśvara as having multiple arms, multiple heads with wrathful faces and a white or green horse head on his crown. Images of him appear in the Womb-World Mandala in Japan. The Horse-headed Avalokiteśvara, or Batō Kannon in Japanese, initially appeared in Japan as a secondary deity, following the Chinese Buddhist tradition. The figure gradually became a primary deity in Japan. The reference to a beast, in this case the horse, indicates the deity's power to assist the practitioner in overcoming beastly thoughts and actions (Lomi 2011, 54) in rituals in which the deity was revered as the primary object of worship.

The emphasis on the protection of animals and animal husbandmen derives from a significant change in a particular popular Buddhist practice; a repentance ritual that includes six forms of Avalokiteśvara. The practice aims at overcoming the three main hindrances to awakening – passion, aggression and ignorance – in the six realms of birth. The Shingon monk Ningai 仁海 (951–1046) is assumed to have replaced the form of the bodhisattva in charge of the animal realm with the Horse-headed Avalokiteśvara, most probably because of the feature of the horse's head in the bodhisattva's crown. In the Heian and Kamakura periods, impressive standing and seated statues and paintings used as primary images in rituals as well as more simple ones for private worship abounded.[396] The step

---

[395] See the comprehensive works on Hayagrīva in India, China and Japan by van Gulik (1935) and Lomi (2010) on rituals of the Horse-headed Avalokiteśvara in contemporary Japan.
[396] The earliest extant statue is from the early eighth century. For the history of Batō Kannon imagery, see Lomi's doctoral dissertation (2011).

to connect the Horse-headed Avalokiteśvara to memorial rituals for favorite horses or those animals that died in the service of their human owners seems to have been made in the late medieval period. The favorite horse of a local ruler or military officer was increasingly seen as an "excellent horse" in the Buddhist tradition (Lomi 2011, 108). Small round stone steles began to appear, marking places at the roadside where pack and draft horses or favorite mounts had perished or are thought to be best memorialized. The steles usually show a relief of the bodhisattva and short inscriptions such as the name of the bodhisattva or the characters for "beloved horse." The practice became increasingly popular with the increasing use of horses. Thousands of these markers from the Edo and Meiji periods still line the smaller country roads – a testimony to the care for the well-being of these animals in both the present and the next life.[397] The tradition of erecting round stone steles along the roads or at crossings to revere the popular boundary deities had clearly been conflated with erecting steles to revere the protector of horses by the early Edo period, not least because both the boundary gods and the horse are not only connected with travel but also with fecundity.[398] The reference to the boundary god in the *Scroll of Equine Medicine*, Echigo no Tansuke, does not point to the horse-headed bodhisattva whatsoever as far as we can tell from the source itself, meaning that the connection between the boundary gods and the bodhisattva had not yet become natural in the thirteenth century when the scroll was created.

***

Returning to the quotation at the beginning of the chapter, Buddhist temples in early Japan owned horses. If one escaped, the law prescribed that this loss needed to be reported to the ministerial bureau in charge and that a public notice must be put up. This particular notice states that a stallion has escaped from the famous Sarusawa-ike pond next to Kōfukuji Temple 興福寺 which is mentioned with its colloquial name Yamashina Temple. Modern-day visitors to the pond in Nara that the stallion ran away from will find no horses, only half-tame deer. But that is another story. The monastic staff of Kōfukuji and other temples in early Japan used horses as beasts of burden to swiftly deliver people

---

397 Kyburz presents his fieldwork in an important horse-breeding area in Japan and devotes several chapters to horse-related rituals and imagery (1987, 189–228; 239–243; see also fig. 26 a, b, 27 a, b and 29 a, b of stone steles of Batō Kannon, and a talismanic horse skull, fig. 31 a).
398 The boundary gods often have a phallic form or depict a couple in sexual union emphasizing the gods' protection of the boundaries between the sexes and their successful procreation. See Turnbull (2015, 274–323), including numerous images from his field survey.

and messages to distant places. The fact that the animals suffered while serving humans would not have escaped their attention. The monastic staff considered birth as a beast (*chikushō*), to be the result of mistreating or killing animals in one's former life. Seeing an animal suffer was thus regarded as a natural condition and as exceedingly negative. As the animal realm is one of three unfortunate birth realms – the others being the realms of the hungry ghosts and the hells – the life of a beast, whether a horse, a bird or an insect, is not expected to be pleasant. On a more abstract level, the birth realms are regarded as psychological states, and the state of the animal is one of ignorance and paranoia. Only a human can gain ultimate insight so birth as a human is seen as fortunate. In this view, it is important to emphasize a fundamental difference between humans and animals and underscore a divide. Even belonging to the human species did not mean that one inevitably belonged to human society in medieval Japan, however. The designation of beggars, ex-convincts and prostitutes as "non-persons" or "non-humans" (*hinin*) is a powerful reminder of social discrimination. In addition to the "non-humans," those working in hereditary professions involving the killing of animals and the fashioning of leather and other animal products were also not included in "normal" human society. They were designated as "defiled ones" (*eta* 穢多) and forced to live in segregated communities well into the modern age. In the early modern period, *eta* were given a Buddhist ordination name after death – a common practice – ending in the character for "beast" (*chiku* 畜).[399]

It was also the case that the Buddhist teachings aimed at saving all sentient beings (*issai shujō* 一切衆生), not differentiating between individual humans, or between humans and animals. According to this view, all sentient beings suffer and are in need of liberation from suffering. The sources such as the various illustrated manuscripts and the activities of the Shingon Ritsu reform movement analyzed above primarily express this view. Some sentient beings were regarded as requiring greater assistance to achieve salvation. To this end, social action was often guided by distinctions between fortunate and unfortunate births or privileged and unprivileged courses of life. While horses were considered precious, this did not, ultimately, result in them receiving better treatment. As horses were born into an unfortunate birth realm – one regarded as being full of pain – humans had an excuse for exploiting the animal.

---

[399] On these discriminatory practices in Buddhism, see Bodiford (1996); Ambros (2012, 36–37).

Conclusion: Boundaries, Maps and Types of Othering

When I commenced my research, I hypothesized that Buddhist monastics ceased all involvement in healing the physical body in the Edo period. I surmised that in this period, which is regarded as a phase of increasing secularization, monastics stopped practicing medicine, a practice categorized as essentially worldly (Sk. *laukika*), and focused their attention on the non-worldly domain (Sk. *lokōttara*), while secular physicians took on the monastics' role in medical care.

However, this topical survey has demonstrated that Buddhist monastics continued to provide medical services into the early modern period. They also provided healing with spells, incantations, amulets and panacea. These practices can be labeled as "magic," or "religious" if magic is deemed a subcategory of "religion." The fact that the monastics did not relinquish all healing practices to secular physicians shows that they did not regard these practices as exclusively worldly (*laukika*). Instead, they were seen as belonging to the world of Buddhism and as being beneficial for the liberation of all beings. The services provided by monastics in the esoteric Buddhist tradition continued to include *kaji* – the moment in rituals when the practitioner and the divinity are mutually empowered, resulting in healing and protection from disease – and the monastics' religious and medical services at the deathbed. The question of a categorical change in the early modern period was, however, not the focus of this book, though it may be the subject of future publications.

My study explored how modern scholars have viewed the role of Buddhism in the history of medicine. I found that scholars with an interest in narrating the history of "traditional medicine" regard Buddhism as a hindrance to the development of Chinese-style medicine in Japan. Ophthalmologist and scholar Ogawa Kenzaburō 小川劍三郎 (1870–1933), one of the pioneers of Western medicine in Meiji Japan, for example, categorizes the Buddhistic ophthalmological chart used by the Majima school (see fig. 1) as typical for premodern medicine in general. Ogawa argues that the monks did not simply use the chart to praise the virtues of the Buddha and impress the ignorant lay believer but strove to apply the contemporary philosophical models outlined in the chart. Ogawa writes that in addition to expounding the theory of the Five Buddhas as guardians of the Five Viscera linked to the five parts of the human eye, which he deems to be essentially irrelevant to the medical healing of sight-related diseases, the Majima school also expounded serious principles based on empirical observation (Ogawa 1971, 57–58). Okuzawa Yasumasa, whose work I discussed in Chapter 4, takes up a corresponding line of argument to Ogawa.

Ishihara Akira (1961), quoted in Mura'i et al. (1994, 466), similarly argues that the anatomical charts (*jintai kaibōzu* 人体解剖図) "went beyond the necessity for medical treatment and consisted of abstractions explained from the view of Buddhist tenets. General medical writings [containing such Buddhist tenets] of the [late medieval] period did discuss disease but [we can observe] a decline in the tendency to mix in Buddhist theory. Empirical medical technique was noted down based on medical theory from the Song dynasty onward, and basic medical knowledge more or less could not be suppressed by the restrictions of Buddhist theory any longer."

As we know from my survey in the chapters above, such charts existed for the exposition of knowledge of the human body and also of the body of the horse. Students of human medicine, ophthalmology or equine medicine used Buddhistic charts well into the early modern period. My study did not set out to expose a critical shift from "unnecessary" Buddhist theory to "useful" Chinese-style empiricist medical theory as part of modernization. I explored both premodern Japanese "Buddhism" and "medicine" in conjunction, based on the claim that the semantic classification of the two fields of social interaction is intrinsically connected with the way society is structured. My overall interest was to track the mode of differentiation between religion and its other, the mode that – speaking with Christoph Kleine (2018) and others – constitutes *secularity*, and more concretely, to highlight forms and arrangements for distinguishing between Buddhism and medicine.

In order to highlight forms and arrangements for distinguishing between Buddhism and medicine, this concluding chapter briefly summarizes the aspirations and *motivations* of social actors in the two fields. The concluding chapter outlines the *functions* of practices in the two fields and the particular *services* the social actors provided. It then gives a brief overview of the *institutions* involved, and details some of the prevalent interpretations and *ideas* that circulated and informed the practices. This is followed by an assessment of how my findings might lead to a reconsideration of categories such as "religion" and "medicine," and a brief typology of boundary making.

Distinguishing between Buddhism and Medicine

In both Buddhism and medicine, the motivation is to heal the sick, to fight sickness and eradicate it once and for all. The goal of religion in contrast to medicine is, however, to strive for universal healing, and achieve whatever counts as salvation. Medicine aspires to recover and conserve health, and to ensure physical and mental well-being. Here, little can be added to what the sociologist Niklas

Luhmann stated: That the system of religion and the system of medicine both attend to the same matter – sickness – but then find differing solutions for coping with contingency specific to each system. In premodern Japanese society, salvation in Buddhism was the same as liberation from sickness. In numerous Buddhist texts that were in use in Japan, liberation from sickness is synonymous with liberation from all suffering. Social actors in both Buddhism and mountain asceticism, which I have only mentioned cursorily in this book, aimed to achieve a radical transformation – overcoming mortality and physical decline – through rituals, particular body techniques and dietetics.

In Japan, longevity was considered important as it gave Buddhists more time to achieve awakening. Longevity practices, developed in ancient India and China, were immensely popular, as were ascetic practices to attain superhuman powers. According to tradition, a person who attained superhuman powers (Sk. *siddhi*) was free of physical suffering and no longer hindered by the limitations of the physical body. End-of-life practices were also connected to liberation from physical suffering. Their function was to prepare the dying for birth in the Pure Land, a place devoid of sickness and pain. End-of-life practices mainly centered on uttering the name (*nenbutsu* 念仏) of the Buddha Amitābha. Buddhists in the tradition of the monk Nichiren 日蓮 (1222–1282) considered it important to repeat the title of the *Lotus Sutra* (*daimoku* 題目), a practice to be observed during one's life and particularly at the moment of death. Manuals for palliative care also include instructions on alleviating pain and helping the dying to cope with emotions of fear and regret. Interestingly, texts such as the *Flower of Eternity* (*Chiyomigusa* 千代見草) attributed to Shinshōin Nichion 心性院日遠 (1572–1642) suggest a division of labor between the ordained who engage in palliative care and priests who specialize in exorcism: While the monks and nuns were to prepare a special diet for the dying, treat pain and chant Buddhist recitations, the text counsels calling priests well versed in driving away the demons with *darani* spells just before the moment of death. This was meant to prevent demons from entering the weakened body of the dying patient.[401] The text required different social actors to combine palliative care, Buddhist recitations and "magical" spells and prepare the dying for a transformation and liberation from suffering for good. All of the social actors, including the patients and their families, were part of the field of religion.

Sponsoring or conducting rituals for the enlightenment (*bodai*) of a deceased family member by ensuring birth in the Pure Land tie in epistemological-

---

[401] A full translation of a 1719 edition of the *Flower of Eternity* (*Chiyomigusa*) is found in Asuka 2003, 21–55; for the passage about driving away demons in the dying, see Asuka 2003, 47.

ly with the idea of the model social action of "sowing good seeds in a field of merit." Model social action has also been linked with eradicating the eight kinds of suffering – birth, old age, sickness, death and the four kinds of psychological suffering resulting from these four. The monastic physician Yūrin made this connection in the foreword to his major compilation of medical knowledge. The topical survey frequently found compassionate action such as medical healing with acupuncture, sponsoring medical facilities, pharmacies and hospices addressed as fields for producing good merit and happiness (fukuden). Various lists of Fields of Merit include offerings and actions that counted as especially worthy. One set of eight Fields of Merit includes, for example, the building of roads, wells, canals and bridges. Others include tending to the sick and caring for animals. Making offerings and serving the buddhas and the monastic community are clearly within the sphere of religion while building roads or caring for animals are not necessarily so. They can be regarded as a secular pursuit. Claiming that these actions too belong to the sphere of Mahāyāna Buddhism enhanced the good reputation of Buddhism and emphasized its universal validity.

Following the principle of the Chinese model, attainment of happiness and well-being as well as the prolongation of life were central to medicine in Japan. Elaborate instructions for nourishing life (yōjō) abounded, and the more Confucian preoccupation with what could be understood as a form of temperance leading to a morally proper life increased in the Edo period.

Buddhist institutions ranged from the large state-sponsored monasteries in urban centers to modest mountain temples. Religious institutions in general included *kami* shrines and centers of mountain asceticism. Buddhist institutions were not only used by the monastic community but also by lay people who came to pray for protection from disease and for healing among other benefits. People also visited Buddhist temples in order to make use of their medical services.

Mahāyāna Buddhism, of which esoteric Buddhism is one strand, prescribes that members of the monastic community aspire to engage in caring for all suffering beings. The institutional engagement of scholar-monks and, we assume, scholar-nuns was so influential that today, we speak of "monastic doctors" (sōi) in premodern Japan. During the formation of the state in the eighth century, an official Bureau of Medicine (Ten'yakuryō) was created and court physicians were trained and employed following the Chinese model. Japanese laws gave preference to students from particular families and, as with other callings, the medical profession was maintained, in contrast to China, as a family profession. In Buddhist institutions, where monastics were supposed to be celibate, medical knowledge was passed from master to disciple. In the secular institutions, medical knowledge ideally passed from father to son. In reality, monastic doctors often shared blood ties and sometimes non-monastic doctors passed on their knowledge to adopted family members, often their sons-in-law, and so via the female line. On the epistemological level, the classifying distinction here was linked to sexual reproduction: Non-reproduction as an expression of purity of the monastic community, and successful reproduction as the fulfillment of the role of the worldly householders.

Passing on medical knowledge within Buddhism and its monastic communities was conceptually tied to salvation and the alleviation of suffering. This conceptual link is missing in the field of medicine and the activities of the secular doctors, although these doctors may have been pious lay Buddhists. Their profession did not require them to care for their patients with religious rituals. The experience and the charisma ascribed to both monastic and secular doctors are of significance here. Other healers in the field of religion who were only loosely connected to Buddhist temples worked freelance, attracting patients, or customers, with their particular charisma and the miracle healing reputation of their profession.

The chapters above mention numerous religious practices and healing rituals. The prestige of Buddhist temples increased when pilgrims reported successful healing they had experienced in connection with the temple's site, their objects of worship and the monastics' activities. Most of those pilgrimage sites were connected to the Medicine Buddha (Yakushi Nyorai) and the bodhisattva Avalokiteśvara (Kannon Bosatsu). A pilgrimage to a certain temple could simultaneously become a journey to a temple hospital, in which the pilgrim, now a patient, could be treated. It is important to stress that a good reputation increased the social capital of monastic doctors or temple founders, often revered as living Buddhas or bodhisattvas. This increase in social capital contributed directly to the temple's economic growth and prosperity.

From the ninth century, monks and nuns as nurses and charismatic healers and, later, monastic physicians were in direct competition with secular doctors in elite circles. Access to knowledge and ritual power in the field of Buddhism was restricted and only possible through initiation. Expertise in the field of medicine in the secular realm was equally strictly controlled and the social control mechanism of initiation reserved medical knowledge for a selected elite. The initiatory structure prevailed although the "secret" and coveted knowledge must have been in wider circulation than the texts would have one believe.

Medical theories reached Japan from Korea and China and, mainly via Buddhist texts, from India during different phases in history. Over the centuries, plural and in many ways autonomous medical traditions formed in Japan. Medical healing in Japan was clearly based on the Chinese system of correspondence that includes the Five Phases, yin and yang and the notion of qi. The combination of the Chinese system of correspondence with specific esoteric Buddhist conceptions is a noteworthy occurrence in Japan. Such combinatory theoretical models abound in texts that are clearly ascribed by the creators and copyists of the texts as belonging to medical healing, showing one of the many overlaps between Buddhism and medicine.

If we regard these various aspirations and motivations, practices, institutions and ideas in the two fields of social interaction as forms and arrangements for distinguishing between religion and medicine, we can see that monastic doctors and secular doctors shared the exact same forms and arrangements except that the office of a monastic doctor required religious ordination. However, monastic ordination in Japan, with the notable exception of the Shingon Ritsu reform movement, resembled lay ordination, which created a rather permeable boundary between the monastic and lay communities. In the course of my survey, I observed a significant overlap between Buddhism and medicine when it came to healing as a social act. A man treating a patient with acupuncture was only *coincidentally* a monk. The act of treatment with acupuncture in itself did not require the acupuncturist to be ordained or not ordained. His profession did not compel him to be a monastic. The man could be a lay Buddhist or agnostic. Looking at the reverse scenario, a secular doctor could hardly be found conducting a Buddhist ritual. This is no coincidence as religion is distinct from medicine in regard to the practice of rituals and ceremonies. Officiating a Buddhist ritual without being ordained or initiated would be regarded as an act of insolence, perhaps even as a criminal act. However, the study of sources concerned with animal health, for example, teaches us that veterinarians who were in the military and so clearly in a secular sphere were trained to have spells and incantations – "magical techniques" – in their repertoire. Given the wide dissemination of ritual knowledge within the circles of self-ordained novices, we can conclude that such techniques were indeed widespread.

Returning to the question of secularity – the mode of differentiation between religion and its other, here medicine and care – in premodern Japan, the emic classification of *laukika-lokōttara* remained significant throughout the period that was studied although it was not as prominent as other classifications in the sources explored. Examining the perception of the physical body in premodern Japan as linked to a wider scenario of a path towards obtaining buddhahood and thereby a universal liberation from suffering provided access to terminologies and taxonomies in the contemporary sources.

Types of Othering

Drawing boundaries, distinguishing and differentiating involve discursive practices such as othering. The result of boundary making is a "map" of the perceived social and cosmological reality. Maps should not be confused with the actual territory. In research, mapping involves religious, progressive or nationalist views of the territory. Taking the map of the "empire as a universe" to be territory, for example, results in a number of problems when studying Buddhism and medicine in early and medieval Japan today. The collective cognitive map that emerged in early Japan consisted of a central hub within a network of places of *kami* worship and state protection. The members of the Yamato family clan who conquered the lands did not replace the existing network, but incorporated Chinese-style forms of religion, authority, and health care into it, negotiating the existing "map." Boundaries as integral features of a map represent discursive strategies of legitimization. However, when an incorporation regime is in place, boundaries can become so entrenched as to not be a subject of negotiation any longer. They cannot even be considered any more, as we have seen in the case of the early ninth-century attempt at reforming the state starting with medicine. Heijō Tennō and his team sought to "x-corporate" medicine from a system that felt alien or "foreign" but, in fact, the *Classified Prescriptions of the Daidō Period* is firmly located within the system and works only because of the boundaries drawn by Heijō's early predecessors. If we are looking for a simple binary opposition in the mode of differentiation between Buddhism and medicine here, we see a native-foreign paradigm connected to a pure-impure binary.

Apart from the problem of drawing temporal boundaries and written history following periodization into political eras, we face the challenge of relating the history of a translocal religion to a set of ideas and practices pertaining to health and well-being that we call medicine. Official ambassadors, occasional visitors, immigrants, merchants and perhaps also stowaways overcame the geographical boundaries while travelling from and to the island archipelago and created a pluralistic and dynamic society in early Japan where Buddhism and a new style of medicine were incorporated. If we were to compare this combination of Buddhist and medical concerns, then it would be of more use to compare it not with the modern situation in Japan but with a combination in a comparable culture that worked with the principles and practices of esoteric Buddhist healing such as Tibet. Although there seems not to have been any direct exchange between Japan and Tibet, the shared esoteric Buddhist culture would in my view make a comparison of boundary making in the two countries worthy of consideration.

Othering of those who negotiate boundaries from within the worlds of Buddhism and medicine involves the idea of heresy. In early Japan, ideas of heresy existed in both systems of religion and medicine. Buddhist monks and nuns were prohibited by law from curing sickness with Daoist spells and charms. Doing so would have been heretical and punishable. As for heterodoxies in medicine, addressed as quackery, we find a significant passage in the twelfth-century *Scroll of Illness and Deformities* (*Yamai no sōshi*). In the illustrated scroll, a comment regarding someone who performs eye surgery unsuccessfully with the patient going completely blind can be interpreted to mean that the surgeon was a charlatan or a quack. In Japanese Buddhism, talismanic practices quite clearly existed within the boundaries of organized religion and thus were part of religious (and magical) orthodoxy. In addition, sources such as the *Ishinpō*, viewed as secular and properly medical, include quotations from Buddhist medical sources and sections on Daoist talismans and spells as outlined in the chapters above. The boundaries are particularly difficult to discern and to cast the findings into a simple binary is even less feasible.

This book focused on social acts and how social actors produced and circulated legitimate knowledge. In the course of the topical survey, I observed the persistent drawing of boundaries between the accomplishments of men and women. Most of the secondary research material surveyed presents the history of medicine and Buddhism, including historiographical writing on Buddhist medicine, as a series of utterances and activities effected by men. The production and circulation of healing knowledge involved various specialists in society, from men and women of the learned elite to the local diviners. It is to be hoped that many more sources will be discovered, and that their consideration will allow Buddhism and medicine to be studied with greater balance and nuance than I have accomplished so far.

Timeline

Timeline

China		Korea					Japan
Neolithic Period ca. 7000–1600 BCE							Jōmon ca. 10,000–300 BCE
Shang ca. 1500–1000 BCE		Mulmun 1500–300 BCE					
Western Zhou 1046–771 BCE							
Eastern Zhou 770–221 BCE	Spring and Autumn 770–476 BCE						
	Warring States 475–221 BCE						
Qin 221–206 BCE		Jin-guk 3rd–2nd c. BCE					Yayoi ca. 300 BCE–300 CE
Western Han 206 BCE–25 CE		Buyeo 2nd BCE–494 CE					
Eastern Han 25–220		Old Silla 57 BCE–935 CE	Goguryeo 37 BCE–668 CE	Baekje 18 BCE–660 CE	Gaya/Mimana 42/370–562 CE		
Six Dynasties 220–589	Three Kingdoms 220–265						Kofun ca. 300–538/552
	Jin 265–420						
	Southern and Northern Dynasties 420–589						Asuka 538–710
	Sui 581–618						
Tang 618–907		United Silla 668–935		Balhae 698–926			Nara 710–794

Events in Japan mentioned in the volume
(names with asterisk indicate male individuals)

Suinin* (r. 29 BCE–70 CE) allegedly replaces sacrifice of humans and animals with "clay rings" (*haniwa*)

Central Asian horse breed introduced via Korea (end of 4th c.)

Use of the Chinese writing system (5th c.)

Korean doctors practice and teach in Japan (5th–6th c.)

Official inception of Buddhism (6th c.)

Direct contact with China (6th c.)

Supporters of Buddhism:
Suiko (r. 592–628)
Kamitsumiya* (Shōtoku Taishi, ca. 573–622)

Taika reforms (*Taika no kaishin*) of Kōtoku* (r. 645–654 CE)

Tenmu* (r. 673–686) commissions building of Yakushiji Temple

Jitō (r. 690–697) completes Yakushiji Temple

Taihō Code (*Taihō ritsuryō*, 701/703), composed by Fujiwara no Fuhito* (658/659–720) and Osakabe* (d. 705) on the order of Monmu* (r. 697–707)

Genmei 元明 (r. 707–715) builds capital of Nara

Chronicle of Ancient Matters (*Kojiki*) compiled (712)

Yōrō Code (*Yōrō ritsuryō*, 718), includes *Administrative Laws for Monks and Nuns* (*Sōni-ryō*) and *Legal Codes for Stables and Pastures* (*Kumoku-ryō*, for equine and bovine medicine)

Bureau of Medicine (Ten'yakuryō) in the capital

Record of Japan (*Nihon shoki*, 720) compiled during Genshō's reign (715–724)

Full incorporation of Buddhism into Japan by Shōmu* (r. 724–749) and Kōmyō (701–760)

Timeline

China			Korea		Japan	
					Heian 794–1185	Early Heian 794–894
Five Dynasties 907–960			Later Baekje 892–936	Later Goguryeo 901–918		Late Heian (Fujiwara) 894–1185
Northern Song 960–1126	Liao 916–1125	Jin 1115–1234	Goryeo 918–1392			
Southern Song 1127–1279					Kamakura 1185–1333 Kenmu restoration 1333–1336	

Events in Japan mentioned in the volume (names with asterisk indicate male individuals)
Completion of Tōdaiji Temple in 747
Kōmyō founds Hokkeji Temple with dispensary for free medicines (*seyakuin*), medical facilities (*hiden'in*) and bathhouse (*karafuro, yokushitsu*)
Kōmyō bequeaths sixty different kinds of medicinal substances of plant, animal and mineral origin to Tōdaiji Temple, kept at Shōsōin repository, *Memorandum of Medicines* (*Shuju yakuchō*, 756)
Activities of "nurse monks" at the imperial court; healing of Kōken (r. 749–758)
South Medicinal Plant Garden (Minami yakuen) near Nara, 749
Full monastic ordination introduced by Jianzhen* (Jp. Ganjin, 688–763)
Kūkai* (Kōbō Daishi, 773–835) establishes practice of the two *maṇḍala*
Records of Japan, Continued (*Shoku Nihongi*, 797)
Classified Prescriptions of the Daidō Period (*Daidō ruijuhō*, 808) on the order of Heijō* (r. 806–809)
Ninmyō* (r. 833–850) establishes medicinal garden in Kyoto
Shinzei* (800–860) conducts healing rituals for Montoku* (r. 850–858)
Later Records of Japan, Continued (*Shoku Nihon kōki*, 869)
Collection of Remedies for Blood Horses by Stable Grooms (Ch. *Simu anjiji*, Jp. *Shiboku ankishū*) by Li Shi* (786–847) introduced
First writings by veterinarians on equine medicine (9th c.)
Taira Nakakuni* (dates unknown) compiles work on horse care (804)
Procedures of the Engi Era (*Engishiki*, 927) listing over fifty different medicinal herbs
Japanese Names for the Materia Medica (*Honzō wamyō*, 901–923) by court physician Fukane Sukehito* (dates unknown)
Essentials of Medicine (*Ishinpō*, 982–984) compiled by court physician Tanba Yasuyori* (912–995)
The Great Mirror (*Ōkagami*, 11th c.): Record of Fujiwara no Takaie's* (979–1044) treatment by a Chinese ophthalmologist Record of Sanjō's* 三条 (r. 1011–1016) fatal illness
Personal notes on illnesses and treatments in court nobles' diaries: Kujō Kanezane* (1149–1207), *Record of Jade Leaves* (*Gyokuyō-ki*) Fujiwara Sadaie* (1162–1241), *Record of the Full Moon* (*Meigekki*)
Fujiwara Ken'i* (1072–ca. 1169) compiles *materia medica* compendia
Formulae for Longevity and Curing (*Chōsei ryōyōhō*, 1184) by Rengi* (dates unknown)
Scroll of Illness and Deformities (*Yamai no sōshi* 病草紙), 12th c.
Record on Drinking Tea for Nourishing Life (*Kissayōjōki*, 1211) by Myōan Eisai* (1141–1215)
Shinnyo (1211–?) rebuilds Chūgūji Temple
Ninshō* (1217–1303) founds Gokurakuji Temple in 1267 with hospital (1287); site of the Sakanoshita Horse Hospital (*Sakanoshita babyōya*)
Rubbish Bag (*Chiribukuro*, 1264–1288), encyclopedia

China	Korea	Japan
Yuan 1271–1368		Muromachi (Ashikaga) 1336–1573
Ming 1368–1644	Joseon 1392–1897	Azuchi-Momoyama 1573–1600
Qing 1644–1911		Edo (Tokugawa) 1600–1868
		Meiji 1868–1912
Republic of China 1912–1949	Korean Empire 1897–1910	Taishō 1912–1926
	Chōsen (colonial period) 1910–1945	Shōwa 1926–1989
People's Republic of China 1949– Republic of China/Taiwan 1949–	Democratic People's Republic of Korea 1948– Republic of Korea 1948–	Heisei 1989–2019
		Reiwa 2019–

Events in Japan mentioned in the volume
(names with asterisk indicate male individuals)

Scroll of Equine Medicine (*Ba'i sōshi emaki*, 1267)

Kajiwara Shōzen* (1265–1337) writes *Book of the Simple Physician* (*Ton'ishō*, 1303/4) and *Myriad Relief Formulae* (*Man'anhō*, 1315)

Seigan* (d. 1379) involved in ophthalmology at Iōzan Yakushiji Temple in Majima

Period of civil strife (1467–1568)

Ashikaga Academy (Ashikaga gakkō) restored

Selections from a Dust Bag (*Ainōshō*, 1445 or 1446) by Gyōyo* (dates unknown)

Rubbish [Bag] with Selections from a Dust Bag (*Jin ten ainōshō*, 1532), encyclopedia

Fujiwara Masachika* (dates unknown) a.k.a. Shinkai Nyūdō founds Kuwashima-style horse medicine (early 16th c.)

Essentials for Horse Doctors (*Ba'i daigo*, 1551)

Equine Medicine Book of the Anzai School (*Anzai-ryū ba'isho*, 1589)

Fujiwara Nakatsuna* (dates unknown) revives Kuwashima style of equine medicine (late 16th c.)

Direct exchange between Japan and Europe, Catholic mission (1549–1639)

Secret Transmission about the Final Mystery of the Eye (*Meigan gokui hiden*, 1575)

Flower of Eternity (*Chiyomigusa*), attributed to Shinshōin Nichion* (1572–1642)

Manase Dōsan* (1507–1594) active in revival of forms of Chinese-style medicine

Increasing emancipation of Japanese medicine from Chinese models

Establishment of Dutch trade post near Nagasaki (1641)

Dutch School (*rangaku*) of science, technology and medicine

Neo-Confucian engagement in various fields of learning including medicine

Collection of Remedies for Horses in Syllabic Script (*Kana Ankishū*, 1604)

Tokugawa Tsunayoshi* (1626–1706) orders the construction of animal shelters

Adoption of new medical system modeled on German medicine (late 19th c.)

List of Images

Fig. 1   Buddhistic eye theory, colored illustration from a manuscript on ophthalmology, *Secret Transmission about the Final Mystery of the Eye* (*Meigan gokui hiden*), 1575, Okusawa Collection. Source: Mishima et al. (2004, 100, fig. 6–7).

Fig. 2   "Diagram of the Five Spheres," from *Essential Subtleties on the Silver Sea* (*Yinhai jingwei*), compiled 14th/15th century in China; early modern print. Source: Kovacs and Unschuld (1998, 134).

Fig. 3   *Scroll of Equine Medicine* (detail, the first three plants), ink and color on paper, 29.6 × 610.2 cm, Tokyo National Museum (sign. A-10479), ©Tokyo National Museum.

Fig. 4   *Scroll of Equine Medicine* (detail, Iō Hōyaku and Leigong), ink and color on paper, 29.6 × 610.2 cm, Tokyo National Museum (sign. A-10479), ©Tokyo National Museum.

Fig. 5   *Scroll of Equine Medicine* (detail, Ten [Tian] and Ōnamuchi), ink and color on paper, 29.6 × 610.2 cm, Tokyo National Museum (sign. A-10479), ©Tokyo National Museum.

Fig. 6   *Equine Medicine Scroll of the Anzai School* (*Anzai-ryū ba'i emaki*) (detail, lines link the Buddha's head and hand to the horse's body and organs), ink and color on paper, undated scroll, ©Veterinary Archives of Azabu University.

Fig. 7   *Equine Medicine Scroll of the Anzai School* (*Anzai-ryū ba'i emaki*) (detail, a horse from conception to birth modeled on Buddhist embryology), ink and color on paper, one scroll, undated, ©Veterinary Archives of Azabu University.

Fig. 8   *Equine Medicine Book of the Anzai School* (*Anzai-ryū ba'isho*) (detail, right: spirit of the day of the dragon, left: spirit of the day of the snake), 1589, bound manuscript book, 27 cm, ©Veterinary Archives of Azabu University.

Bibliography

Note: Chinese and Japanese names of authors and editors of publications in Japanese are written in line with the East Asian convention of writing the family name followed by the given name.

Abbreviations

KT   *Kokushi taikei* 国史大系. 17 vols. Kokushi Taikei Henshūkai, 1897–1901. Several reprints. Yoshikawa Kōbunkan, 1998–2002.
NKBT *Nihon koten bungaku taikei* 日本古典文學大系. 102 vols. Iwanami Shoten, 1957–1967.
NKZ   *Nihon koten zenshū* 日本古典全集. Nihon Koten Zenshū Kankōkai (note: no volume numbers).
SNKT *Shin Nihon koten bungaku taikei* 新日本古典文学大系. 106 vols. Iwanami Shoten, 1989–2005.
T   Print version: *Taishō shinshū daizōkyō* 大正新脩大蔵経. 88 vols. Taishō Issaikyō Kankōkai, 1924–1932.
      Online version: SAT Daizō kyō Text Database (SAT 大正新脩大蔵経テキストデータベース). 2015 version. University of Tokyo. http://21dzk.l.u-tokyo.ac.jp/SAT.
T zuzō Print version: *Taishō shinshū daizōkyō zuzō* 大正新脩大蔵経図像. 12 vols. Taisho Issaikyō Kankōkai, 1933–1935.
      Online version: SAT Taishō zō Image Database (SAT 大正蔵図像 DB). University of Tokyo. http://dzkimgs.l.u-tokyo.ac.jp/SATi/images.php.

Primary Sources

Transcribed Titles

Anzai-ryū ba'i emaki 安西流馬医絵巻 [Basho no koto shimeshi hidari ni 馬書之事しめし左に] (*Equine Medicine Scroll of the Anzai School*), undated scroll, Veterinary Archives of Azabu University, available at: http://turf.azabu-u.ac.jp/htmls-201202/items/M002.html and http://id.nii.ac.jp/1112/00003002/ (last accessed 15 March 2019).

Anzai-ryū ba'isho 安西流馬医書 (*Equine Medicine Book of the Anzai School*), 1589, manuscript book, Veterinary Archives of Azabu University, available at: http://turf.azabu-u.ac.jp/htmls-201202/pages/S002/S002_001.html and http://id.nii.ac.jp/1112/00002964/ (last accessed 15 March 2019).

Ba'i daigo 馬医醍醐 (*Essentials for Horse Doctors*), 1551, Kuwajima Shin'emon no jō nakatsuna 桑島新右衛門尉仲綱, manuscript book, 4 vols, Veterinary Archives of Azabu University.

Ba'i sōshi emaki 馬医草紙絵巻 (*Scroll of Equine Medicine*), 1267, illustrated scroll, Tokyo National Museum (A-10479). See Triplett et al. (2019).

Batō nenju giki 馬頭念誦儀軌 (*Ritual Manual for the Supplication of the Horse-headed Kannon*), short for *Shō Kayakakiribaku Dainuō jō Daishinken kuyō nenju giki hōbon* 聖賀野紇哩縛大威怒王立成大神驗供養念誦儀軌法品 (*Ritual and Offerings for the Great Fierce Vidyārāja, the Holy Hayagrīva*), T 1072 A, attributed to Amoghavajra (705–774). See van Gulik (1935, 85–94).

Bencao gangmu 本草綱目 (*Compendium of Materia Medica*), 1596, Li Shizhen 李時珍 (1518–1593).

Besson zakki 別尊雜記 (*Assorted Notes on Individual Deities*), T zuzō 3007.

Bussetsu daizō shōkyō ketsubon-kyō 仏説大蔵真経血盆経 (*The Buddha's Correct Sutra on the Bowl of Blood*). List of manuscripts and prints in Japan, see Takemi (1983, 231).

Bussetsu goōkyō 佛説五王經 (*Sutra of Five Kings as Told by the Buddha*), T 523, trans. in the Eastern Jin 東晋 period (317–420).

Bussetsu iyu-kyō 佛説醫喩經 (*Sutra on the Medical Simile as Told by the Buddha*), T 219, trans. Dānapāla (d. 1017), late tenth century.

Bussetsu tennyo jōbutsu-kyō 仏説転女成仏経 (*Sutra on Transforming Women into Buddhas*), Heian period (794–1185). See Meeks (2010, 303–304), Blair (2016, 274–278) and Nishiguchi (2014, 259–260).

Bussetsu tennyoshin-kyō 佛説轉女身經 (*Sutra of the Buddha's Sermon on Transforming the Female Body*), T 564, trans. Dharmamitra (356–442).

Butsumo daikujaku myōō-kyō 佛母大孔雀明王經 (*Sutra of the Buddha Mother Great Peacock Wisdom King*), T 982, trans. Amoghavajra. See Des Jardins (2011, 201–263).

Chiyomigusa 千代見草 (*Flower of Eternity*), ca. seventeenth century, attributed to Nichion. See Nichion (1973).

Dai Birushana jōbutsu-kyō sho 大毘盧遮那成佛經疏 (*Commentary on the Sutra of the Grand Resplendent One*), T 1796, Yixing (683–727), between 721 and 747.

Daidō ruijuhō 大同類聚方 (*Classified Prescriptions of the Daidō Period*), 808, Abe Manao 安倍真直 (dates unknown) and Izumo Hirosada 出雲広貞原 (dates unknown). See Maki (1985).

Eiga monogatari 栄華物語 (*A Tale of Flowering Fortunes*), 1028–1107, NKZ (1934). See McCullough and McCullough (1980).

Engishiki 延喜式 (*Procedures of the Engi Era*), 927, NKZ (1927–1929).

Faju piyu jing 法句譬喩經 (*Sutra of Dharma Phrases and Parables*), T 211.4.575b-609b, trans. Dharmatrāta (dates unknown) et al., fourth century.

Fanshi yaohan 番視瑤函 (*Repeated Views from a Box of Precious Jade*), 1644.

Garbhāvakrānti-sūtra (*Sutra on Entering the Womb*), various Chinese trans.: *Bussetsu hōtai-kyō* 佛説胞胎經 (*Sutra on the Embryo in Utero*), T 317, trans. Dharmarakṣa, 303; *Bussetsu nyūtaizō-kyō* 佛説入胎藏會 (*Sutra on Entering the Womb*), T 310 (= *Ratnakūṭa-sūtra*), trans. Yijing, 710; *Butsui Anan setsu shotai-e* 佛爲阿難説處胎會 (*Sutra Spoken to Ānanda on Abiding in the Womb*), T 310, trans. Bodhiruci (fl. fifth/sixth century); *Nanda Avadāna* (*Nanda innen* 難陀因縁): contains a version of the *Nyūbotai-kyō* 入母胎經 (*Sutra on Entering the Mother's Womb*), T 1451 (= *Mūla-sarvāstivāda vinaya*), trans. Yijing, 703–710. See Kritzer (2014).

Gochizō hishō 五智蔵秘抄 (*Secret Treatise on the Repository of Quintuple Wisdom*), 1261, manuscript, one scroll, Ninnaji temple archives, Japan. See Dolce (2016).

Gyokuyō-ki 玉葉記 (*Record of Jade Leaves*), Kujō Kanezane 九条兼実 (1149–1207), 1164–1200. See Kunaichō shoryōbu (1994–2013).

Heike monogatari 平家物語 (*The Tale of the Heike*), fourteenth century, NKBT 32, 33 (1959, 1960).

Hoke-kyō, Hokke-kyō 法華經 (*Lotus Sutra*), short for *Myōhō renge kyō* 妙法蓮華經 (*Sutra of the Lotus of the Wonderful Dharma*), T 262, trans. Kumārajīva (344–413).

Honzō wamyō 本草和名 (*Japanese Names for the Materia Medica*), 901–923, Fukane Sukehito 深江輔仁 (dates unknown), NKZ (1926).

Huangdi neijing 黄帝内經 (*Inner Canon of the Yellow Emperor*), ca. third–first century BCE.

Ichigo daigyō himitsushū 期大要祕密集 (*Secrets of the Crucial Moment of Death*), Kakuban 覺鑁 (1095–1134). See Kakuban ([1977] 1989).

Ishinpō 醫心方 (*Essentials of Medicine*), 982–984, Tanba Yasuyori 丹波康頼 (912–995), NKZ (1935). See Hsia et al. (1986) and Maki (1993–2012).

Jin ten ainōshō 塵添壒囊鈔 (*Rubbish [Bag] with Selections from a Dust Bag*), 1445/46. See Gyōyo (1968, 1972).

Jūju-ritsu 十誦律 (*Ten Recitations Vinaya*), T 1435.

Kan Yakuō Yakujō nibosatsu-kyō 観藥王藥上二菩薩經 (*Sutra on the Visualization of the Two Bodhisattvas, King of Healing and Supreme Healer*). T 1161. See Birnbaum (1979, 115–148).

Kana Ankishū 仮名安驥集 (*Collection of Remedies for Horses in Syllabic Script*), 1604, Hashimoto Dōha 橋本道派 (dates unknown) with Ikkan Wakō 一閑和尚 (dates unknown), print, 4 vols (incomplete), Veterinary Archives of Azabu University.

Kanreiroku 感靈録 (*Records of Gratitude to the Numinous*), ninth century, fragmented. See Kawase (1958) and Tsuji (1981).

Kegon-kyō 華嚴經, Sk. *Avamtamsaka-sūtra* (*Flower Ornament Sutra*), T 278, 279, 293, trans. Buddhabadra (fl. fifth century), ca. 420, Śikṣānanda (652–710), ca. 699 and Prajñā in 800; trans. of Śikṣānanda's version (T 279), see Cleary (1984).

Keiteki-shū 啓迪集 (*Collection of Writings of the Keiteki [Academy]*), 1574, Manase Dōsan 曲直瀨道三 (1507–1594). See Manase (1979).

Kissayōjōki 喫茶養生記 (*Record on Drinking Tea for Nourishing Life*), 1211, Myōan Eisai 明菴榮西 (1141–1215). See Benn (2015, 145–171).

Kojidan 古事談 (*Conversations About Ancient Matters*), 1212–1215, Minamoto Akikane 源顕兼 (1160–1215), SNKT 41 (2005).

Kojiki 古事記 (*Chronicle of Ancient Matters*), 712, NKBT 1 (1966).

Konjaku monogatarishū 今昔物語集 (*Collection of Stories That are Old Today*), SNKT 33–37 (1993–1999).

Konkōmyō-kyō 金光明經 (*Sutra of Golden Light*), short for *Konkōmyō saishōō-kyō* 金光明最勝王經 (*Sovereign Kings of the Golden Light Sutra*), T 665, trans. by Yijing 義淨 (635–713).

Kōyōshō, Yakushushō 香要抄, 藥種抄 (*Compendium of Incense, Compendium of Drugs*), twelfth century, Fujiwara Ken'i 藤原兼意 (1072–ca. 1169), Tenri Library; Kyōu Library (Kyōu Shooku 杏雨書屋). See Mori (1977).

Mahāprajñāpāramitāśāstra, Jp. *Dai chido-ron* 大智度論 (*Treatise on the Perfection of Wisdom*), T 1509, attributed to Nāgārjuna, trans. Kumārajīva. See Lamotte (1944–1980).

Mahāvairocana-sūtra, Jp. *Dai Birushana jōbutsu jinben kaji-kyō* 大毘盧遮那成佛神變加持經 (*Sutra of the Grand Resplendent One*), T 848, trans. Śubhakarasiṃha (637–735) with Yixing in 724.

Maka sōgi-ritsu 摩訶僧祇律 (Mahāsāṃghika vinaya), T 1425.

Man'anhō 万安方 (*Myriad Relief Formulae*), 1315, Kajiwara Shōzen 梶原性全 (1265–1337). See Kajiwara (1986a).

Meigan gokui hiden 明眼極意秘伝 (*Secret Transmission about the Final Mystery of the Eye*), 1575, manuscript, Okusawa Collection.

Meigekki 明月記 (*Record of the Full Moon*), Fujiwara Sadaie 藤原定家 (1162–1241). See Fujiwara; Tsuji, ed. (1971).

Michuan yanke longmu zong lun 秘傳眼科龍木總論 (*Secretly Passed Down Nāgārjuna's Comprehensive Discourse on Ophthalmology*), twelfth century, Baoguang 葆光道人 (dates unknown).

Nankai kiki naihō den 南海寄歸内法傳 (*A Record of Buddhist Practices Sent Home from the Southern Sea*), T 2125, by Yijing. See Kleine (2017).

Nihon ryōiki 日本靈異記 (*Miraculous Stories from Japan*), ninth century, Kyōkai 景戒 (dates unknown). See Nakamura (1973).

Nihon shoki 日本書紀 (*Record of Japan*), 720, NKBT 67, 68 (1965–1967).

Nihonkoku genzai shomokuroku 日本國見在書目録 (*Catalogue of Extant Texts in the Country of Japan*), 891. Fujiwara no Sukeyo 藤原佐世 (847–897). See Fujiwara; Yajima, ed. (1984).

Ōkagami 大鏡 (*The Great Mirror*), eleventh century, NKBT 21 (1960). See McCullough (1980).

Ryōji byō-kyō 療痔病經 (*Sutra on Relieving Sores*), T 1325.

Ryūju bosatsu ganron, Ch. *Longshu pusa yanlun* 龍樹菩薩眼論 (*Nāgārjuna Bodhisattva's Ophthalmological Treatise*), fragmented.

Sanshō ruijūshō 産生類聚抄 (*Encyclopedia of Childbirth*), ca. 1318, Kanazawa Bunko (ms 5–3–1). See Andreeva (2017b).

Senju sengen darani-kyō 千手千眼陀羅尼經 (*Dhāraṇī of the Bodhisattva With a Thousand Hands and Eyes*), T 1060. See Reis-Habito (1993) and Giddings (2017).

Senju sengen kanzeon bosatsu jibyō gōyaku-kyō 千手千眼觀世音菩薩治病合藥經 (*Sutra on the Use of Medicinal Herbs for Healing by the Thousand-eyed, Thousand-hands Avalokiteśvara*), T 1059.

Shaku Egi kanshoku kaizatsu ron 釈慧義寒食解雑論 (*Various Theories on Cold Foods by Shi Huiyi*), T 2059.

Shengji zonglu 聖濟總錄 (*Comprehensive Treatise on the Sage's Advice*), 1111–1117/8.

Shennong bencaojing jizhu 神農本草經集注 (*Variorum of the Divine Husbandman's Classic of Materia Medica*), ca. Han Dynasty (206 BCE–220 CE). See Yang (2007).

Shenshi yaohan 審視瑤函 (*Precious Manual of Ophthalmology*), 1644, Fu Renyu 傅仁宇 (dates unknown). See Fu (1977).

Shibun-ritsu 四分律 (*Four-Part Vinaya*), T 1428. See Bodhi Translation Committee (2015).

Shinshū honzō 新修本草 (*Revised Materia Medica*), fragmented. See Kunaichō shoryōbu (1983).

Shoku Nihon kōki 続日本後紀 (*Later Records of Japan, Continued*), 869. KT 3 (2000).

Shoku Nihongi 続日本紀 (*Records of Japan, Continued*), 797, SNKT 12–16 (1989–1998)

Shuju yakuchō 種々藥帳 (*Memorandum of Medicines*, 756). See Shibata (2000, 23–24, table A and B) and Yoneda (2000).

Shutsu sanzō kishū 出三藏記集 (*Compilation of Notes on the Translation of the Tripitaka*), T 2145, Sengyou 僧祐 (445–518), ca. 515.

Shutsuyō-kyō 出曜經 (*Sutra of the Appearance of Light*), T 212, Zhu Fonian 竺佛念 (fl. fourth century), trans. completed in 374.

Simu anjiji 司牧安驥集 (*Collection of Remedies for Blood Horses by Stable Grooms*), Li Shi 李石 (786–847).

Suśruta saṃhitā (*Compendium of Suśruta*), ca. 250–500 CE. See Bhishagratna ([1907] 1916).

Taiping shenghui fang 太平聖恵方 (*Holy Prescriptions for Universal Relief in the Taiping Era*), 992.

Ton'ishō 頓医抄 (*Book of the Simple Physician*), 1303/4, Kajiwara Shōzen. See Kajiwara (1986b).

Uma no yamai mishiru koto 馬之病見知事 (*Well-known Diseases of the Horse*), 1513, Raichū 賴忠 (dates unknown), manuscript.

Unshitsu-kyō 温室經 (*Bathhouse Sutra*), T 701, short for *Bussetsu unshitsu senyoku shusō-kyō* 温室洗浴衆僧經 (*Sutra Spoken by the Buddha on Bathing the Sangha in the Bathhouse*), trans. Dharmarakṣa (ca. 233–311). See Salguero (2017b, 84–91).

Vajraśekhara-sūtra (*Sutra of the Entering into the Vajra World*), *Kongōchō yuga chū ryakujutsu nenju-kyō* 金剛頂瑜伽中略出念誦經 (*Sutra for Recitation Abridged from the Vajraśekhara Yoga*), T 866, trans. Vajrabodhi (671–741).

Vimalakīrti-sūtra, short for *Vimalakīrtinirdeśa-sūtra* (*Yuimakitsu shosetsu-kyō* 維摩詰所説經) (*Vimalakīrti Sutra*), T 475, trans. Kumārajīva.

Waitai biyao 外台秘要 (*Arcane Essentials of the Imperial Library*), Wang Tao 王燾 (ca. 670–755), 752.

Yamai no sōshi 病草紙 (*Scroll of Diseases and Deformities*), 1193. See Akiyama et al. (1997).

Yamato honzō 大和本草 (*Japanese Materia Medica*), 1708–1709, Kaibara Ekiken 貝原益軒 (1630–1714). See Kaibara (1911).

Yifang leiju 醫方類聚 (*A Collection of Various Medical Prescriptions*), Jin Limeng 金礼蒙 (fl. fourteenth/fifteenth century), 1445.

Yinhai jinwei 銀海精微 (*Essential Subtleties on the Silver Sea*), attributed to Sun Simiao 孫思邈 (580–682 CE). See Kovacs and Unschuld (1998).

Yōgācārabhūmi-śāstra, Jp. *Yuga shiji ron* 瑜伽師地論 (*Discourse on the Stages of Concentration Practice*), T 1579.30.279–882, trans. Xuanzang 玄奘 (602–664) between 646 and 648.

Yōrō-ryō 養老令 (*Yōrō Code*), ca. 718–722. See Dettmer (2009–2015).

Yūrin fukudenhō 有林福田方 (*Fields of Merit Formulae*), 1363, Kitano Yūrin 北野有隣 (d. 1410), NKZ (1936).

Zhubing yuanhou lun 諸病源候論 (*Treatise on the Origins and Symptoms of Diseases*), compiled by Chao Yuanfang 巢元方 (550–630).

Translated Titles

A Collection of Various Medical Prescriptions (*Yifang leiju* 醫方類聚), Jin Limeng 金礼蒙 (fl. fourteenth/fifteenth century), 1445.

A Record of Buddhist Practices Sent Home from the Southern Sea (*Nankai kiki naihō den* 南海寄歸內法傳), T 2125, by Yijing. See Kleine (2017).

A Tale of Flowering Fortunes (*Eiga monogatari* 栄華物語), 1028–1107, NKZ (1934). See McCullough and McCullough (1980).

Arcane Essentials of the Imperial Library (*Waitai biyao* 外台秘要), Wang Tao 王燾 (ca. 670–755), 752.

Assorted Notes on Individual Deities (*Besson zakki* 別尊雜記), T *zuzō* 3007.
Bathhouse Sutra (*Unshitsu-kyō* 温室經), T 701, short for *Sutra Spoken by the Buddha on Bathing the Sangha in the Bathhouse* (*Bussetsu unshitsu senyoku shusō-kyō* 温室洗浴衆僧經), trans. Dharmarakṣa (ca. 233–311). See Salguero (2017b, 84–91).
Book of the Simple Physician (*Ton'ishō* 頓医抄), 1303/4, Kajiwara Shōzen. See Kajiwara (1986b).
Catalogue of Extant Texts in the Country of Japan (*Nihonkoku genzai shomokuroku* 日本國見在書目録), 891. Fujiwara no Sukeyo 藤原佐世 (847–897). See Fujiwara; Yajima, ed. (1984).
Chronicle of Ancient Matters (*Kojiki* 古事記), 712, NKBT 1 (1966).
Classified Prescriptions of the Daidō Period (*Daidō ruijuhō* 大同類聚方), 808, Abe Manao 安倍真直 (dates unknown) and Izumo Hirosada 出雲広貞原 (dates unknown). See Maki (1985).
Collection of Remedies for Blood Horses by Stable Grooms (*Simu anjiji* 司牧安驥集), Li Shi 李石 (786–847).
Collection of Remedies for Horses in Syllabic Script (*Kana Ankishū* 仮名安驥集), 1604, Hashimoto Dōha 橋本道派 (dates unknown) with Ikkan Wakō 一閑和尚 (dates unknown), print, 4 vols (incomplete), Veterinary Archives of Azabu University.
Collection of Stories That are Old Today (*Konjaku monogatarishū* 今昔物語集), SNKT 33–37 (1993–1999).
Collection of Writings of the Keiteki [Academy] (*Keiteiki-shū* 啓迪集), 1574, Manase Dōsan 曲直瀬道三 (1507–1594). See Manase (1979).
Commentary on the Sutra of the Grand Resplendent One (*Dai Birushana jōbutsu-kyō sho* 大毘盧遮那成佛經疏), T 1796, Yixing (683–727), between 721 and 747.
Compendium of Incense, Compendium of Drugs (*Kōyōshō, Yakushushō* 香要抄, 藥種抄), twelfth century, Fujiwara Ken'i 藤原兼意 (1072–ca. 1169), Tenri Library; Kyōu Library (Kyōu Shooku 杏雨書屋). See Mori (1977).
Compendium of Materia Medica (*Bencao gangmu* 本草綱目), 1596, Li Shizhen 李時珍 (1518–1593).
Compendium of Suśruta (*Suśruta saṃhitā*), ca. 250–500 CE. See Bhishagratna ([1907] 1916).
Compilation of Notes on the Translation of the Tripitaka (*Shutsu sanzō kishū* 出三藏記集), T 2145, Sengyou 僧祐 (445–518), ca. 515.
Comprehensive Treatise on the Sage's Advice (*Shengji zonglu* 聖濟總錄), 1111–1117/8.
Conversations About Ancient Matters (*Kojidan* 古事談), 1212–1215, Minamoto Akikane 源顕兼 (1160–1215), SNKT 41 (2005).
Dhāraṇī of the Bodhisattva With a Thousand Hands and Eyes (*Senju sengen darani-kyō* 千手千眼陀羅尼經), T 1060. See Reis-Habito (1993) and Giddings (2017).
Discourse on the Stages of Concentration Practice (*Yōgācārabhūmi-śāstra*, *Yuga shiji ron* 瑜伽師地論), T 1579.30.279–882, trans. Xuanzang 玄奘 (602–664) between 646 and 648.
Encyclopedia of Childbirth (*Sanshō ruijūshō* 産生類聚抄), ca. 1318, Kanazawa Bunko (ms 5–3–1). See Andreeva (2017b).
Equine Medicine Book of the Anzai School (*Anzai-ryū ba'isho* 安西流馬医書), 1589, manuscript book, Veterinary Archives of Azabu University, available at: http://turf.azabu-u.ac.jp/htmls-201202/pages/S002/S002_001.html and http://id.nii.ac.jp/1112/00002964/ (last accessed 15 March 2019).
Equine Medicine Scroll of the Anzai School (*Anzai-ryū ba'i emaki* 安西流馬医絵巻 [*Basho no koto shimeshi hidari ni* 馬書之事しめし左に]), undated scroll, Veterinary Archives of

Azabu University, available at: http://turf.azabu-u.ac.jp/htmls-201202/items/M002.html and http://id.nii.ac.jp/1112/00003002/ (last accessed 15 March 2019).

Essential Subtleties on the Silver Sea (*Yinhai jinwei* 銀海精微), attributed to Sun Simiao 孫思邈 (580–682 CE). See Kovacs and Unschuld (1998).

Essentials for Horse Doctors (*Ba'i daigo* 馬医醍醐), 1551, Kuwajima Shin'emon no jō nakatsuna 桑島新右衛門尉仲綱, manuscript book, 4 vols, Veterinary Archives of Azabu University.

Essentials of Medicine (*Ishinpō* 醫心方), 982–984, Tanba Yasuyori 丹波康頼 (912–995), NKZ (1935). See Hsia et al. (1986) and Maki (1993–2012).

Fields of Merit Formulae (*Yūrin fukudenhō* 有林福田方), 1363, Kitano Yūrin 北野有隣 (d. 1410), NKZ (1936).

Flower of Eternity (*Chiyomigusa* 千代見草), ca. seventeenth century, attributed to Nichion. See Nichion (1973).

Flower Ornament Sutra (*Kegon-kyō* 華嚴經, Sk. *Avamtamsaka-sūtra*), T 278, 279, 293, trans. Buddhabadra (fl. fifth century), ca. 420, Śikṣānanda (652–710), ca. 699 and Prajñā in 800; trans. of Śikṣānanda's version (T 279), see Cleary (1984).

Four-Part Vinaya (*Shibun-ritsu* 四分律), T 1428. See Bodhi Translation Committee (2015).

Holy Prescriptions for Universal Relief in the Taiping Era (*Taiping shenghui fang* 太平聖恵方), 992.

Inner Canon of the Yellow Emperor (*Huangdi neijing* 黄帝内經), ca. third–first century BCE.

Japanese Materia Medica (*Yamato honzō* 大和本草), 1708–1709, Kaibara Ekiken 貝原益軒 (1630–1714). See Kaibara (1911).

Japanese Names for the Materia Medica (*Honzō wamyō* 本草和名), 901–923, Fukane Sukehito 深江輔仁 (dates unknown), NKZ (1926).

Later Records of Japan, Continued (*Shoku Nihon kōki* 続日本後紀), 869. KT 3 (2000).

Lotus Sutra (*Hoke-kyō, Hokke-kyō* 法華經), short for *Sutra of the Lotus of the Wonderful Dharma* (*Myōhō renge kyō* 妙法蓮華經), T 262, trans. Kumārajīva (344–413).

Mahāsāṃghika vinaya (*Maka sōgi-ritsu* 摩訶僧祇律), T 1425.

Memorandum of Medicines (*Shuju yakuchō* 種々薬帳, 756). See Shibata (2000, 23–24, table A and B) and Yoneda (2000).

Miraculous Stories from Japan (*Nihon ryōiki* 日本靈異記), ninth century, Kyōkai 景戒 (dates unknown). See Nakamura (1973).

Myriad Relief Formulae (*Man'anhō* 万安方), 1315, Kajiwara Shōzen 梶原性全 (1265–1337). See Kajiwara (1986a).

Nāgārjuna Bodhisattva's Ophthalmological Treatise (*Ryūju bosatsu ganron*, Ch. *Longshu pusa yanlun* 龍樹菩薩眼論), fragmented.

Precious Manual of Ophthalmology (*Shenshi yaohan* 審視瑤函), 1644, Fu Renyu 傅仁宇 (dates unknown). See Fu (1977).

Procedures of the Engi Era (*Engishiki* 延喜式), 927, NKZ (1927–1929).

Record of Jade Leaves (*Gyokuyō-ki* 玉葉記), Kujō Kanezane 九条兼実 (1149–1207), 1164–1200. See Kunaichō shoryōbu (1994–2013).

Record of Japan (*Nihon shoki* 日本書紀), 720, NKBT 67, 68 (1965–1967).

Record of the Full Moon (*Meigekki* 明月記), Fujiwara Sadaie 藤原定家 (1162–1241). See Fujiwara; Tsuji, ed. (1971).

Record on Drinking Tea for Nourishing Life (*Kissayōjōki* 喫茶養生記), 1211, Myōan Eisai 明菴栄西 (1141–1215). See Benn (2015, 145–171).

Records of Gratitude to the Numinous (*Kanreiroku* 感霊録), ninth century, fragmented. See Kawase (1958) and Tsuji (1981).

Records of Japan, Continued (*Shoku Nihongi* 続日本紀), 797, SNKT 12–16 (1989–1998)

Repeated Views from a Box of Precious Jade (*Fanshi yaohan* 番視瑤函), 1644.

Revised Materia Medica (*Shinshū honzō* 新修本草), fragmented. See Kunaichō shoryōbu (1983).

Ritual Manual for the Supplication of the Horse-headed Kannon (*Batō nenju giki* 馬頭念誦儀軌), short for *Ritual and Offerings for the Great Fierce Vidyārāja, the Holy Hayagrīva* (*Shō Kayakakiribaku Dainuō jō Daishinken kuyō nenju giki hōbon* 聖賀野紇哩縛大威怒王立成大神験供養念誦儀軌法品), T 1072 A, attributed to Amoghavajra (705–774). See van Gulik (1935, 85–94).

Rubbish [Bag] with Selections from a Dust Bag (*Jin ten ainōshō* 塵添壒嚢鈔), 1445/46. See Gyōyo (1972, 1968).

Scroll of Diseases and Deformities (*Yamai no sōshi* 病草紙), 1193. See Akiyama et al. (1997).

Scroll of Equine Medicine (*Ba'i sōshi emaki* 馬医草紙絵巻), 1267, illustrated scroll, Tokyo National Museum (A-10479). See Triplett et al. (2019).

Secret Transmission about the Final Mystery of the Eye (*Meigan gokui hiden* 明眼極意秘伝), 1575, manuscript, Okusawa Collection.

Secret Treatise on the Repository of Quintuple Wisdom (*Gochizō hishō* 五智蔵秘抄), 1261, manuscript, one scroll, Ninnaji temple archives, Japan. See Dolce (2016).

Secretly Passed Down Nāgārjuna's Comprehensive Discourse on Ophthalmology (*Michuan yanke longmu zong lun* 秘傳眼科龍木總論), twelfth century, Baoguang 葆光道人 (dates unknown).

Secrets of the Crucial Moment of Death (*Ichigo daigyō himitsushū* 期大要祕密集), Kakuban 覺鑁 (1095–1134). See Kakuban ([1977] 1989).

Sutra of Dharma Phrases and Parables (*Faju piyu jing* 法句譬喩經), T 211.4.575b-609b, trans. Dharmatrāta (dates unknown) et al., fourth century.

Sutra of Five Kings as Told by the Buddha (*Bussetsu goōkyō* 佛説五王經), T 523, trans. in the Eastern Jin 東晋 period (317–420).

Sutra of Golden Light (*Konkōmyō-kyō* 金光明經), short for *Konkōmyō saishōō-kyō* 金光明最勝王經 (*Sovereign Kings of the Golden Light Sutra*), T 665, trans. by Yijing 義淨 (635–713).

Sutra of the Appearance of Light (*Shutsuyō-kyō* 出曜經), T 212, Zhu Fonian 竺佛念 (fl. fourth century), trans. completed in 374.

Sutra of the Buddha Mother Great Peacock Wisdom King (*Butsumo daikujaku myōō-kyō* 佛母大孔雀明王經), T 982, trans. Amoghavajra. See Des Jardins (2011, 201–263).

Sutra of the Buddha's Sermon on Transforming the Female Body (*Bussetsu tennyoshin-kyō* 佛説轉女身經), T 564, trans. Dharmamitra (356–442).

Sutra of the Entering into the Vajra World (*Vajraśekhara-sūtra*), *Sutra for Recitation Abridged from the* Vajraśekhara Yoga (*Kongōchō yuga chū ryakujutsu nenju-kyō* 金剛頂瑜伽中略出念誦經), T 866, trans. Vajrabodhi (671–741).

Sutra of the Grand Resplendent One (*Mahāvairocana-sūtra*, Jp. *Dai Birushana jōbutsu jinben kaji-kyō* 大毘盧遮那成佛神變加持經), T 848, trans. Śubhakarasiṃha (637–735) with Yixing in 724.

Sutra on Entering the Womb (*Garbhāvakrānti-sūtra*), various Chinese trans.: *Sutra on the Embryo in Utero* (*Bussetsu hōtai-kyō* 佛説胞胎經), T 317, trans. Dharmarakṣa, 303; *Sutra on Entering the Womb* (*Bussetsu nyūtaizō-kyō* 佛説入胎藏會), T 310 (= *Ratnakūṭa-sūtra*), trans. Yijing, 710; *Sutra Spoken to Ānanda on Abiding in the Womb* (*Butsui Anan setsu shotai-e* 佛爲阿難說處胎會), T 310, trans. Bodhiruci (fl. fifth/sixth century); *Nanda Avadāna* (*Nanda innen* 難陀因緣): contains a version of the *Sutra on Entering the Mother's Womb* (*Nyūbotai-kyō* 入母胎經), T 1451 (= *Mūla-sarvāstivāda vinaya*), trans. Yijing, 703–710. See Kritzer (2014).

Sutra on Relieving Sores (*Ryōji byō-kyō* 療痔病經), T 1325.

Sutra on the Medical Simile as Told by the Buddha (*Bussetsu iyu-kyō* 佛説醫喩經), T 219, trans. Dānapāla (d. 1017), late tenth century.

Sutra on the Use of Medicinal Herbs for Healing by the Thousand-eyed, Thousand-hands Avalokiteśvara (*Senju sengen kanzeon bosatsu jibyō gōyaku-kyō* 千手千眼觀世音菩薩治病合藥經), T 1059.

Sutra on the Visualization of the Two Bodhisattvas, King of Healing and Supreme Healer (*Kan Yakuō Yakujō nibosatsu-kyō* 観薬王薬上二菩薩經). T 1161. See Birnbaum (1979, 115–148).

Sutra on Transforming Women into Buddhas (*Bussetsu tennyo jōbutsu-kyō* 仏説転女成仏経), Heian period (794–1185). See Meeks (2010, 303–304), Blair (2016, 274–278) and Nishiguchi (2014, 259–260).

Ten Recitations Vinaya (*Jūju-ritsu* 十誦律), T 1435.

The Buddha's Correct Sutra on the Bowl of Blood (*Bussetsu daizō shōkyō ketsubon-kyō* 仏説大蔵真経血盆経). List of manuscripts and prints in Japan, see Takemi (1983, 231).

The Great Mirror (*Ōkagami* 大鏡), eleventh century, NKBT 21 (1960). See McCullough (1980).

The Tale of the Heike (*Heike monogatari* 平家物語), fourteenth century, NKBT 32, 33 (1959, 1960).

Treatise on the Origins and Symptoms of Diseases (*Zhubing yuanhou lun* 諸病源候論), compiled by Chao Yuanfang 巢元方 (550–630).

Treatise on the Perfection of Wisdom (*Mahāprajñāpāramitāśāstra*, Jp. *Dai chido-ron* 大智度論), T 1509, attributed to Nāgārjuna, trans. Kumārajīva. See Lamotte (1944–1980).

Variorum of the Divine Husbandman's Classic of Materia Medica (*Shennong bencaojing jizhu* 神農本草經集注), ca. Han Dynasty (206 BCE–220 CE). See Yang (2007).

Various Theories on Cold Foods by Shi Huiyi (*Shaku Egi kanshoku kaizatsu ron* 釈慧義寒食解雜論), T 2059.

Vimalakīrti Sutra (*Vimalakīrti-sūtra*, short for *Vimalakīrtinirdeśa-sūtra* [*Yuimakitsu shosetsu-kyō* 維摩詰所説經]), T 475, trans. Kumārajīva.

Well-known Diseases of the Horse (*Uma no yamai mishiru koto* 馬之病見知事), 1513, Raichū 頼忠 (dates unknown), manuscript.

Yōrō Code (*Yōrō-ryō* 養老令), ca. 718–722. See Dettmer (2009–2015).

Secondary Sources

Abe, Ryūichi. 1999. *The Weaving of Mantra: Kūkai and the Construction of Esoteric Buddhist Discourse.* New York: Columbia University Press.

Abé, Ryūichi. 2015. "Revisiting the Dragon Princess: Her Role in Medieval Engi Stories and Their Implications in Reading the *Lotus Sutra.*" *Japanese Journal of Religious Studies* 42.1, 27–70.

Akiyama Ken 秋山虔 et al. 1997. "Yamai no sōshi 病草紙." In *Nihon emaki taisei* 日本絵巻大成 7, edited by Komatsu Shigemi 小松茂美. Tōkyō: Chūō Kōron Sha.

Ambros, Barbara. 2012. *Bones of Contention: Animals and Religion in Contemporary Japan*. Honolulu: University of Hawai'i Press.

Ambros, Barbara. 2015. *Women in Japanese Religions*. New York: New York University Press.

Ambros, Barbara. 2016. "A Rite of Their Own: Japanese Buddhist Nuns and the *Anan kōshiki*." *Japanese Journal of Religious Studies* 43.1, 207–250.

Andreeva, Anna. 2014. "Childbirth in Aristocratic Households of Heian Japan." *Dynamis* 34.2, 357–376.

Andreeva, Anna. 2016. "Lost in the Womb: Conception, Reproductive Imagery, and Gender in the Writings and Rituals of Japan's Medieval Holy Men." In *Transforming the Void: Embryological Discourse and Reproductive Imagery in East Asian Religions*, edited by Anna Andreeva and Dominic Steavu. Sir Henry Wellcome Asian series 16, 420–478. Leiden; Boston: Brill.

Andreeva, Anna. 2017a. "Childbirth in Early Medieval Japan: Ritual Economies and Medical Emergencies in Procedures During the Day of the Royal Consort's Labor." In *Buddhism and Medicine: An Anthology of Premodern Sources*, edited by C. Pierce Salguero, 336–350. New York: Columbia University Press.

Andreeva, Anna. 2017b. "Explaining Conception to Women? Buddhist Embryological Knowledge in the *Sanshō ruijūshō* 産生類聚抄 (*Encyclopedia of Childbirth*, ca. 1318)." *Asian Medicine* 12, 170–202.

Andreeva, Anna. 2018. "Devising the Esoteric Rituals for Women: Fertility and the Demon Mother in the *Gushi nintai sanshō himitsu hōshū*." In *Women, Rites, and Ritual Objects in Premodern Japan*, edited by Karen M. Gerhart, 53–88. Leiden; Boston: Brill.

Andreeva, Anna, and Dominic Steavu, eds. 2016. *Transforming the Void: Embryological Discourse and Reproductive Imagery in East Asian Religions*. Sir Henry Wellcome Asian series 16. Leiden; Boston: Brill.

Aoki, Michiko Yamaguchi. 1997. *Records of Wind and Earth: A Translation of Fudoki, with Introduction and Commentaries*. Monograph and occasional paper series 53. Ann Arbor, MI: Association for Asian Studies.

Arnold, Edwin. 1879. *The Light of Asia, or, The Great Renunciation (Mahābhinishkramana): Being the Life and Teaching of Gautama, Prince of India and Founder of Buddhism (as Told in Verse by an Indian Buddhist)*. London: Trübner.

Arnold, Edwin. 1891. *The Light of the World, or, The Great Consummation*. London: Longmans, Green.

Asahina Yasuhiko 朝比奈泰彦, ed. 1955. *Shōsōin yakubutsu* 正倉院薬物. Ōsaka: Shokubutsu Bunken Kankōkai.

Asuka, Ryōko. 2003. *La médecine traditionnelle japonaise. Traduites, présentées et annotées par Asuka Ryōko (avec la collaboration de Christophe Cauvin, Sophie Houdart et Elisabeth Gautier)*. Oeuvres classiques du Bouddhisme japonais 3. Paris: L'Harmattan.

Azuma Ushio 東潮. 2016. "Torai no bunka to yon-go seiki no kokusai kankei 渡来の文化と四・五世紀の国際関係." In *Kiba bunka to kodai inobēshon* 騎馬文化と古代のイノベーション, edited by Kodaishi shinpojiumu "Hakken, kenshō Nihon no kodai" henshū iinkai 古代史シンポジウム「発見・検証日本の古代」編集委員会, Shira'ishi Ta'ichirō 白石太一郎, Suzuki Yasutami 鈴木靖民, et al. 2. 252–275. Tōkyō: Kadokawa Shoten.

Bailey, Don Clifford. 1960. "Early Japanese Lexicography." *Monumenta Nipponica* 16.1/2, 1–52.
Balkwill, Stephanie. 2016. "The Sūtra on Transforming the Female Form: Unpacking an Early Medieval Chinese Buddhist Text." *Journal of Chinese Religions* 44.2, 127–148.
Bartholomew, James R. 1989. *The Formation of Science in Japan: Building a Research Tradition.* New Haven: Yale University Press.
Bartlett, Harley Harris, and Hide Shohara. 1961. *Japanese Botany During the Period of Woodblock Printing.* Los Angeles: Dawson's Book Shop.
Beghi, Clemente. 2011. "The Dissemination of Esoteric Scrptures in Eighth-century Japan." In *Esoteric Buddhism and the Tantras in East Asia,* edited by Charles D. Orzech, Henrik Hjort Sørensen and Richard Karl Payne. Handbook of oriental studies Section four, China, 24, 661–682. Leiden; Boston: Brill.
Benn, James A. 2015. *Tea in China: A Religious and Cultural History.* Honolulu: University of Hawai'i Press.
Beukers, Harm, Antoine M. Luyendijk-Elshout, M. E. Van Opstall, et al., eds. 1991. *Red-hair Medicine: Dutch–Japanese Medical Relations.* Niewe Nederlandse Bijdragen tot de Geschiedenis der Geneeskunde en der Natuurwetenschappen 36. Amsterdam: Atlanta.
Bhishagratna, Kunjalal. [1907] 1916. *An English Translation of the Sushruta samhita: Based on Original Sanskrit Text, With a Full and Comprehensive Introd., Additional Texts, Different Readings, Notes, Comparative Views, Index, Glossary and Plates.* Chowkhamba Sanskrit studies 30. Varanasi: Chowkhamba Sanskrit Series Office.
Birnbaum, Raoul. 1979. *The Healing Buddha.* Boulder, CO: Shambhala.
Blair, Heather. 2016. "Mothers of the Buddhas: The *Sutra on Transforming Women into Buddhas* (*Bussetsu Tennyo Jōbutsu Kyō*)." *Monumenta Nipponica* 71.2, 263–293.
Blondeau, Anne-Marie. 1972. *Matériaux pour l'étude de l'hippologie et de l'hippiatrie tibétaines [à partir des manuscrits de Touen-houang].* Genève; Paris: Droz.
Bodart-Bailey, Beatrice M. 2006. *The Dog Shogun: The Personality and Policies of Tokugawa Tsunayoshi.* Honolulu: University of Hawai'i Press.
Bodhi Translation Committee, trans. 2015. *Four-Part Vinaya, Collection of Rules for the Nun.* Bodhi Foundation for Culture and Education. Available at http://dharmaguptakavinaya.wordpress.com (last accessed 23 Nov. 2018).
Bodiford, William. 1996. "Zen and the Art of Religious Prejudice: Efforts to Reform a Tradition of Social Discrimination." *Japanese Journal of Religious Studies* 23.1/2, 1–27.
Bodiford, William M. 2005. "Bodhidharma's Precepts in Japan." In *Going Forth: Visions of Buddhist vinaya; Essays Presented in Honor of Professor Stanley Weinstein,* edited by William M. Bodiford. Studies in East Asian Buddhism 18, 185–209. Honolulu: University of Hawai'i Press.
Borup, Jørn. 2004. "Zen and the Art of Inverting Orientalism: Buddhism, Religious Studies and Interrelated Networks." In *New Approaches to the Study of Religion* 1, edited by Peter Antes, Armin W. Geertz and Randi R. Warne. Religion and reason 42, 451–487. Berlin; New York: De Gruyter.
Bouchy, Anne. 1992. *Les oracles de Shirataka, ou, La sibylle d'Ōsaka: vie d'une femme spécialiste de la possession dans le Japon du XXe siècle.* Arles: Éditions Philippe Picquier.
Bowers, John Z. 1970. *Western Medical Pioneers in Feudal Japan.* Baltimore, MD: Johns Hopkins Press.

Bowring, Richard John. 1982. *Murasaki Shikibu, Her Diary and Poetic Memoirs: A Translation and Study.* Princeton, NJ: Princeton University Press.
Bowring, Richard John. 2005. *The Religious Traditions of Japan, 500–1600.* Cambridge: Cambridge University Press.
Buck-Albulet, Heidi. 2016. "Empfängnis und Geburt des Buddha: Zwei Erzählungen aus dem *Konjaku monogatari*." In *Werden und Vergehen: Betrachtungen zu Geburt und Tod in japanischen Religionen*, edited by Birgit Staemmler. Bunka/Wenhua: Tuebingen East Asian studies 24, 13–39. Berlin: Lit.
Buell, Paul D., Timothy May, and David Ramey. 2018. "Chinese Horse Medicine: Texts and Illustrations." In *Imagining Chinese Medicine*, edited by Vivienne Lo and Penelope Barrett, 315–326. Leiden: Brill.
Burnouf, Eugène. 1884. *Introduction à l'histoire du Buddhisme indien.* Bibliothèque orientale 3. Paris: Maisonneuve.
Burnouf, Eugène; Katia Buffetrille, and Donald S. Lopez. trans. 2010. *Introduction to the History of Indian Buddhism.* Chicago, IL: The University of Chicago Press.
Burns, Kenneth F. 1948. "The History of Veterinary Medicine in Japan." *Journal of the American Veterinary Medical Association* 113 (858), 226–230.
Chan, Chi-Chao. 2010. "Couching for Caract in China." *Survey of Ophthalmology* 55.4, 393–398.
Chen, Ming. 2005. "Zhuan Nü Wei Nan 轉女為男, Turning Female to Male: An Indian Influence on Chinese Gynaecology?" *Asian Medicine: Tradition and Modernity* 1.2, 315–334.
Cleary, Thomas F. 1984. *The Flower Ornament Scripture: A Translation of the Avatamsaka Sutra.* Boulder, CO; New York: Shambhala Publications.
Como, Michael. 2005. "Silkworms and Consorts in Nara Japan." *Asian Folklore Studies* 64.1, 111–131.
Como, Michael. 2007. "Horses, Dragons, and Disease in Nara Japan." *Japanese Journal of Religious Studies* 34.2, 393–415.
Como, Michael. 2008. *Shōtoku: Ethnicity, Ritual, and Violence in the Japanese Buddhist Tradition.* Oxford; New York: Oxford University Press.
Como, Michael. 2010. *Weaving and Binding: Immigrant Gods and Female Immortals in Ancient Japan.* Honolulu: University of Hawai'i Press.
Como, Michael. 2015. "Daoist Deities in Ancient Japan: Household Deities, Jade Women and Popular Religious Practice." In *Daoism in Japan: Chinese Traditions and Their Influence on Japanese Religious Culture*, edited by Jeffrey L. Richey. Routledge studies in Taoism, 24–36. London; New York: Routledge.
Cooper, William C., and Nathan Sivin. 1973. "Man as a Medicine: Pharmacological and Ritual Aspects of Drugs Derived from the Human Body." In *Chinese Science: Explorations of an Ancient Tradition*, edited by Nathan Sivin and Shigeru Nakayama. MIT East Asian science series 2, 203–272. Cambridge, MA: MIT Press.
Craig, Sienna R. 2006. "Windhorses and Dharma Warriors: The Religious, Historical, and Cultural Significance of Horse Protection Rituals in Mustang, Nepal." In *Horses and Humans: The Evolution of Human-equine Relationships*, edited by Sandra L. Olsen, M. A. Littauer and Ingrid Rea. BAR international series 1560, 339–354. Oxford: Archaeopress.

de Visser, M[arinus] W[illem]. 1980. *The Goddess Mahāmāyūrī in China and Japan*, English adaptation by Sushama Lohia, New Delhi. Studies in Indo-Asian art and culture 6, Śata-Pitaka series 259. New Delhi: International Academy of Indian Culture.

Deal, William E., and Brian Douglas Ruppert. 2015. *A Cultural History of Japanese Buddhism*. Wiley-Blackwell guides to Buddhism. Malden, MA: Wiley Blackwell.

Demiéville, Paul. 1937. "Byō." In *Hōbōgirin; dictionnaire encyclopédique du bouddhisme d'après les sources chinoises et japonaises*, edited by Paul Demiéville, 224–265. Tokyo: Maison franco-japonaise.

Demiéville, Paul. 1985. *Buddhism and Healing [=Hōbōgirin entry on "Byō", transl. by Mark Tatz]*. Lanham, MD: University Press of America.

Des Jardins, J.-F. Marc. 2011. *Le sūtra de la Mahāmāyūrī: rituel et politique dans la Chine des Tang (618–907)*. [Quebec City]: Les Presses de l'Université Laval.

Deshpande, Vijaya. 1999. "Indian Influences on Early Chinese Ophthalmology: Glaucoma as a Case Study." *Bulletin of the School of Oriental and African Studies* 62.2, 306–322.

Deshpande, Vijaya. 2000. "Ophthalmic Surgery: A Chapter in the History of Sino-Indian Medical Contacts." *Bulletin of the School of Oriental and African Studies* 63.3, 370–388.

Deshpande, Vijaya. 2003–2004. "Nāgārjuna and the Chinese Medicine." *Studia Asiatica* 4/5. 243–259.

Despeux, Catherine, ed. 2010a. *Médecine, religion et société dans la Chine médiévale: Étude de manuscrits chinois de Dunhuang et de Turfan*. 3 vols. Paris: Collège de France.

Despeux, Catherine. 2010b. "Hygiène de vie et longévité à Dunhuang." In *Médecine, religion et société dans la Chine médiévale: Étude de manuscrits chinois de Dunhuang et de Turfan* 2, edited by Catherine Despeux, 769–870. Paris: Collège de France.

Dettmer, Hans Adalbert. 1972. *Die Urkunden Japans vom 8. bis ins 10. Jahrhundert*. Wiesbaden: Harrassowitz.

Dettmer, Hans A[dalbert]. 2009–2015. *Der Yōrō-Kodex*. Veröffentlichungen des Ostasien-Instituts der Ruhr-Universität Bochum 55, 1–4. Wiesbaden: Harrassowitz.

Dettmer, Hans A[dalbert]. 2010. *Der Yōrō-Kodex: Die Gebote; Übersetzung des Ryō no gige, Teil 2 Bücher 2–10*. Veröffentlichungen des Ostasien-Instituts der Ruhr-Universität Bochum 55, vol. 2. Wiesbaden: Harrassowitz.

Dolce, Lucia. 2016. "The Embryonic Generation of the Perfect Body: Ritual Embryology from Japanese Tantric Sources." In *Transforming the Void: Embryological Discourse and Reproductive Imagery in East Asian Religions*, edited by Anna Andreeva and Dominic Steavu. Sir Henry Wellcome Asian series 16, 253–310. Leiden; Boston: Brill.

Drott, Edward R. 2010. "Gods, Buddhas, and Organs: Buddhist Physicians and Theories of Longevity in Early Medieval Japan." *Japanese Journal of Religious Studies* 37.2, 247–273.

Dumas, Raechel. 2013. "Historicizing Japan's Abject Femininity: Reading Women's Bodies in *Nihon Ryōiki*." *Japanese Journal of Religious Studies* 40.2, 247–275.

Dutt, Sukumar. [1961] 1988. *Buddhist Monks and Monasteries of India: Their History and Their Contribution to Indian Culture*. Delhi: Motilal Banarsidass.

Eck, Diana. [1981] 1985. *Darśan: Seeing the Divine Image in India*. Chambersburg, PA: Anima Books.

Egami Namio 江上波夫. 1984. *Kiba minzoku kokka – Nihon kodaishi eno apurōchi* 騎馬民族国家―日本古代史へのアプローチ. Chūkō shinsho 中公新書 147. Tōkyō: Chūō Kōron Sha.

Eisenstadt, Shmuel N. 1996. *Japanese Civilization: A Comparative View*. Chicago; London: The University of Chicago Press.

Evans-Pritchard, Edward E. [1937] 1950. *Witchcraft, Oracles and Magic Among the Azande*. Oxford: Clarendon Press.

Evans-Pritchard, Edward E. [1965] 1970. *Theories of Primitive Religion*. Oxford: Clarendon Press.

Fan, Ka Wai. 2005. "Couching for Cataract and Sino-Indian Medical Exchange from the Sixth to the Twelfth Century AD." *Clinical and Experimental Ophthalmology* 33.2, 188–190.

Farris, William Wayne. 1998. *Sacred Texts and Buried Treasures: Issues in the Historical Archaeology of Ancient Japan*. Honolulu: University of Hawai'i Press.

Farris, William Wayne. 2009. *Daily Life and Demographics in Ancient Japan*. Michigan monograph series in Japanese studies 63. Ann Arbor, MI: Center for Japanese Studies, The University of Michigan.

Faure, Bernard. 1996. *Visions of Power: Imagining Medieval Japanese Buddhism*. Princeton, NJ: Princeton University Press.

Faure, Bernard. 1998. *The Red Thread: Buddhist Approaches to Sexuality*. Princeton, NJ: Princeton University Press.

Faure, Bernard. 2003. *The Power of Denial: Buddhism, Purity, and Gender*. Princeton, NJ: Princeton University Press.

Faure, Bernard. 2016a. *Gods of Medieval Japan Volume 1: The Fluid Pantheon*. Honolulu: University of Hawai'i Press.

Faure, Bernard. 2016b. *Gods of Medieval Japan Volume 2: Protectors and Predators*. Honolulu: University of Hawai'i Press.

Fiordalis, David. 2017. "Stories of Healing from the *Section on Medicines* in the Pāli *Vinaya*." In *Buddhism and Medicine: An Anthology of Premodern Sources*, edited by Pierce Salguero, 118–124. New York: Columbia University Press.

Frazer, James George. [1911] 1926. *The Golden Bough: A Study in Magic and Religion, Part II*. London: Macmillian.

Fritsch, Ingrid. 1996. *Japans Blinde Sänger im Schutz der Gottheit Myōon-Benzaiten*. München: Iudicium.

Froehner, Reinhard. 1943. "Zur altchinesisch-japanischen Pferdeheilkunde." *Deutsche Tierärztliche Wochenschrift/Tierärztliche Rundschau* 27/28, 272–276.

Fu Renyu 傅仁宇. 1977. *Shenshi yaohan* 審視瑤函. Shanghai: Shanghai renmin weisheng chubanshe.

Fujikawa Yū 富士川游. [1899] 1980. *Nihon ganka ryakushi* 日本眼科略史. Fujikawa Yū chosakushū 1 (Tōyō igaku, igaku bunkashi) 富士川游著作集 第1巻 (東洋医学・医学分科史). Kyōto: Shinbunkaku Shuppan.

Fujikawa, Yu. 1911. *Geschichte der Medizin in Japan. Kurzgefaßte Darstellung der Entwicklung der japanischen Medizin mit besonderer Berücksichtigung der europäischen Heilkunde in Japan*. Tokyo: Kaiserlich Japanisches Unterrichtsministerium, Tokio.

Fujikawa, Yu. [1934] 1978. *Japanese Medicine*. New York: AMS Press.

Fujiwara no Sukeyo 藤原佐世; Yajima Genryō 矢島玄亮, ed. 1984. *Nihonkoku genzai shomokuroku: shūshō to kenkyū* 日本国見在書目録: 集証と研究. Tōkyō: Kyūko Shoin.

Fujiwara Sadaie 藤原定家; Tsuji Hikosaburō 辻彦三郎, ed. 1971. *Meigekki* 明月記. Shiryō sanshū, kigai (koki rokuhen) 18 史料纂集、期外[古記録編] 18. Tōkyō: Zoku Gunsho Ruijū Kanseikai.

Fukuda, Akira 福田晃, Araki Hiroyuki 荒木博之, and Yamashita Kin'ichi 山下欣一, eds. 1999. *Fugeki, mōsō no denjō sekai* 巫覡・盲僧の伝承世界. Tōkyō: Miyai Shoten.

Fukunaga Katsumi 福永勝美. 1990. *Bukkyō igaku jiten: ho, Yōga* 仏教医学事典: 補・ヨーガ. Tōkyō: Yuzankaku Shuppan.

Furth, Charlotte. 1999. *A Flourishing Yin: Gender in China's Medical History, 960–1665*. Berkeley, CA: University of California Press.

Garrett, Frances. 2005. "Ordering Human Growth in Tibetan Medical and Religious Embryologies." In *Textual Healing: Essays on Medieval And Early Modern Medicine*, edited by Elizabeth Lane Furdell, 31–52. Leiden; Boston: Brill.

Garrett, Frances. 2008. *Religion, Medicine and the Human Embryo in Tibet*. Critical studies in Buddhism. New York: Routledge.

Gell, Alfred. 1998. *Art and Agency: An Anthropological Theory*. Oxford; New York: Clarendon Press.

Georges, Robert A., and Michael Owen Jones. 1995. *Folkloristics: An Introduction*. Bloomington: Indiana University Press.

Giddings, William J. 2017. "The Sūtra on the Dhāraṇī of the Vast, Complete, and Unobstructed Great Compassion of the Bodhisattva Avalokiteśvara with a Thousand Hands and a Thousand Eyes." In *Buddhism and Medicine: An Anthology of Premodern Sources*, edited by Pierce Salguero, 252–285. New York: Columbia University Press.

Giebel, Rolf W. 2005. *The Vairocanāsaṃbodhi Sūtra, Translated from the Chinese (Taishō Volume 18, Number 848) by Rolf W. Giebel*. BDK English Tripiṭaka series. Berkeley, CA: Bukkyō Dendō Kyōkai and Numata Center for Buddhist Translation and Research.

Goble, Andrew Edmund. 2011. *Confluences of Medicine in Medieval Japan: Buddhist Healing, Chinese Knowledge, Islamic Formulas, and Wounds of War*. Honolulu: University of Hawai'i Press.

Göhlert, Christian. 2014. "Anzan kigan: Rituelle Geburtspraktiken in Japan im Wandel der Zeit." *Asiatische Studien/Études Asiatiques* 68.1, 189–232.

Golzio, Karl-Heinz. 2010. *Die Ausbreitung des Buddhismus in Süd- und Südostasien: Eine quantitative Untersuchung auf der Basis epigraphischer Quellen*. Religionswissenschaft 16. Frankfurt am Main: Peter Lang.

Goodley, Dan. [2011] 2017. *Disability Studies: An Interdisciplinary Introduction*. Los Angeles, CA; London: Sage.

Gorai Shigeru 五来重, ed. 1986. *Yakushi shinkō* 薬師信仰. Minshū shūkyo-shi sōsho 民衆宗教史叢書 12. Tōkyō: Yūzankaku Shuppan.

Gorai Shigeru 五来重. 2007–2009. *Gorai Shigeru chosakushū* 五来重著作集. Kyōto: Hōzōkan.

Granoff, Phyllis. 2011. "The Buddha as the Greatest Healer: The Complexities of a Comparison." *Journal Asiatique* 299.1, 5–22.

Groemer, Gerald. 2001. "The Guild of the Blind in Tokugawa Japan." *Monumenta Nipponica* 56.3, 349–380.

Groemer, Gerald. 2016. *Goze: Women, Musical Performance, and Visual Disability in Traditional Japan*. New York: Oxford University Press.

Groner, Paul. 1989. "The *Lotus Sutra* and Saichō's Interpretation of the Realization of Buddhahood with This Very Body." In *The Lotus Sutra in Japanese Culture*, edited by George J. Tanabe Jr. and Willa Jane Tanabe, 53–74. Honolulu: University of Hawai'i Press.

Groner, Paul. 2002. "Vicissitudes in the Ordination of Japanese 'Nuns' during the Eighth through the Tenth Centuries." In *Engendering Faith: Women and Buddhism in Premodern Japan*, edited by Barbara Ruch. Michigan monograph series in Japanese studies 43, 65–108. Ann Arbor, MI: Center for Japanese Studies, University of Michigan.

Groner, Paul. 2005. "Tradition and Innovation: Eison's Self-Ordinations and the Establishment of New Orders of Buddhist Practioners." In *Going Forth: Visions of Buddhist vinaya; Essays Presented in Honor of Professor Stanley Weinstein*, edited by William M. Bodiford. Studies in East Asian Buddhism 18, 210–235. Honolulu: University of Hawai'i Press.

Grumbach, Lisa. 2005. *Sacrifice and Salvation in Medieval Japan: Hunting and Meat in Religious Practice at Suwa Jinja*. Ph.D. dissertation. Stanford, CA: Stanford University.

Grünhagen, Celine. 2013. *Geschlechterpluralismus im Buddhismus: zur Tragweite westlicher Wissenschaftskonstruktionen am Beispiel frühbuddhistischer Positionen und des Wandels in Thailand*. Studies in Oriental religions 66. Wiesbaden: Harrassowitz.

Gyōyo 行誉; Hamada Atsushi 浜田敦, and Satake Atsuhiro 佐竹昭広, eds. 1968. *Jin ten ainōshō; Ainōshō* 塵添壒嚢鈔; 壒嚢鈔. Tōkyō: Rinsen Shoten.

Gyōyo 行誉. 1972. *Jin ten ainōshō* 塵添壒嚢鈔. Dai Nihon bukkyō zensho 大日本佛教全書 93. Tōkyō: Butsusho Kankōkai Hensan.

Haldar, Jñanrañjan. 1992. *Development of Public Health in Buddhism*. Delhi: Indological Book House.

Hand, Wayland D. 1980. *Magical Medicine: The Folkloric Component of Medicine in the Folk Belief, Custom and Ritual of the Peoples of Europe and America*. Berkeley, CA: University of California Press.

Harrison, Peter. 2006. "'Science' and 'Religion': Constructing the Boundaries." *The Journal of Religion* 86.1, 81–106.

Harrist, Robert E. Jr. 1997. "The Legacy of Bole: Physiognomy and Horses in Chinese Painting." *Artibus Asiae* 57.1/2, 135–156.

Hart, Robert. 1999. "Beyond Science and Civilization: A Post-Needham Critique." *East Asian Science, Technology, and Medicine* 16: 88–114.

Hattori Toshiyoshi [Toshirō] 服部敏良. 1945. *Nara jidai igaku no kenkyū* 奈良時代醫學の研究. Tōkyō: Tōkyōdō.

Hattori Toshirō 服部敏良. 1955. *Heian jidai igaku no kenkyū* 平安時代医学の研究. Tōkyō: Kuwana Bunseidō.

Hattori Toshirō 服部敏良. 1964. *Kamakura jidai igakushi no kenkyū* 鎌倉時代医学史の研究. Tōkyō: Yoshikawa Kōbunkan.

Hattori Tōrō [Toshirō] 服部敏良. 1971. *Muromachi Azuchi Momoyama jidai igakushi no kenkyū* 室町安土桃山時代医学史の研究. Tōkyō: Yoshikawa Kōbunkan.

Hattori Toshirō 服部敏良. 1978. *Edo jidai igakushi no kenkyū* 江戸時代医学史の研究. Tōkyō: Yoshikawa Kōbunkan.

Hattori Toshiyoshi [Toshirō] 服部敏良. [1968] 1982. *Bukkyō kyōten o chūshin toshita Shaka no igaku* 仏教経典を中心とした釈迦の医学. Nagoya: Reimei Shobō.

Haudricourt, André Georges, and Georges Métailié. 1994. "De l'illustration botanique en Chine." *Ètudes chinoises* 13.1–2, 381–416.

Heerde, Michael, ed. and trans. 1999. *Pferdebehandlung mit traditioneller chinesischer Veterinärmedizin (TCVM): Der "Pferdeklassiker."* Stuttgart: Sonntag.

Heidegger, Simone. 1995. *Die Frau im japanischen Buddhismus der Kamakura-Zeit.* Copenhagen: Seminar for Buddhist Studies.

Heidegger, Simone. 2006. *Buddhismus, Geschlechterverhältnis und Diskriminierung: Die gegenwärtige Diskussion im Shin-Buddhismus Japans.* Studies in Modern Asian Religions/Religiöse Gegenwart Asiens 4. Münster: Lit.

Heirman, Ann, and Mathieu Torck. 2012. *A Pure Mind in a Clean Body: Bodily Care in the Buddhist Monasteries of Ancient India and China.* Gent: Academia Press.

Heirman, Ann, Carmen Meinert, and Christoph Anderl, eds. 2018. *Buddhist Encounters and Identities Across East Asia.* Dynamics in the history of religions 10, edited by Volkhard Krech and Licia Di Giacinto. Leiden; Boston: Brill.

Henderson, Gregory, and Leon Hurvitz. 1956. "The Buddha of Seiryōji: New Finds and New Theory." *Artibus Asiae* 19.1, 4–55.

Hidaka Yōko 日高洋子. 2009. "Ninshō to fukushi no ryōiki ni kan suru ikkōsatsu 忍性と福祉の領域に関する一考察." *Saitama gakuen daigaku kiyō (ningen gakubuhen)* 埼玉学園大学紀要(人間学部篇) 9, 145–158.

Hirose Kōjirō 広瀬浩二郎. 1994a. "Chūsei mōsō to Yoshino, Kumano 中世盲僧と吉野・熊野." *Sangaku shugen* 山岳修験 13.3, 33–45.

Hirose Kōjirō 広瀬浩二郎. 1994b. "Nihon bunka-shi to chūsei mōsō (geinōshi nōto) 日本文化史と中世盲僧 (芸能史ノート)." *Geinōshi kenkyū* 芸能史研究 12, 740–56.

Hirose Kōjirō 広瀬浩二郎. 1997. *Shōgaisha no shūkyō minzokugaku* 障害者の宗教民俗学. Akashi raiburarī 明石ライブラリー 2. Tōkyō: Akashi Shoten.

Hirose, Kōjirō 広瀬浩二郎. 1999. "Mōsō kenkyū no igi to kanōsei 盲僧研究の意義と可能性 － 視覚障害者の立場から." In *Fugeki, mōsō no denjō sekai* 巫覡・盲僧の伝承世界, edited by Fukuda Akira 福田晃 and Yamashita Kin'ichi 山下欣一. Tōkyō: Mirai Shoten.

Horton, Sarah J. 2007. *Living Buddhist Statues in Early Medieval and Modern Japan.* New York: Palgrave Macmillan.

Hsia, Emil C. H., Ilza Veith, and Robert H. Geertsma. 1986. *The Essentials of Medicine in Ancient China and Japan: Yasuyori Tamba's Ishimpō, Translated with Introduction and Annotations.* Leiden: Brill.

Hsu, Elisabeth. 2010. "*Qing hao* 青蒿 (Herba *Artemisiae annuae*) in the Chinese materia medica." In *Plants, Health and Healing: On the Interface of Ethnobotany and Medical Anthropology*, edited by Elisabeth Hsu and Stephen Harris, 83–130. New York; Oxford: Berghahn Books.

Huard, Pierre, Zensutsu Oya, and Ming Wang. 1974. *La médecine japonaise des origines à nos jours.* Paris: Dacosta.

Huebotter, Franz. 1932. *Die Sūtra über Empfängnis und Embryologie.* Tokyo: Mitteilungen der Deutschen Gesellschaft für Natur- und Völkerkunde Ostasiens.

Iinuma Kenji 飯沼賢司. 2004. *Hachimanshin to wa nanika* 八幡神とはなにか. Kadokawa sensho 角川選書 366. Tōkyō: Kadokawa Shoten.

Ikeda Matsugorō 池田松五郎. 1929. *Nihon yakugyōshi* 日本薬業史. Tōkyō: Yakugyō Jironsha.

Ishida, Eiichirō 石田英一郎, Oka Masao 岡正雄, Egami Namio 江上波夫, et al. 1958. *Nihon minzoku no kigen: taidan to tōron* 日本民族の起源: 対談と討論. Tōkyō: Heibonsha.

Ishihara Akira 石原明. [1959] 1966. *Nihon no igaku: sono nagare to hatten* 日本の医学: その流れと発展. Tōkyō: Shibundō.
Ishihara Akira 石原明. 1961. *Nihon ni okeru kaibōzu* 日本における解剖図. Tōkyō: Tokushu Bunko Rengō Kyōgikai.
Ishihara, Akira 石原明. 1956a. "Kajiwara Shōzen no shōgai to sono chosho (1) 梶原性全の生涯とその著書 (1)." *Nihon ishi gakkai* 日本医史学会/*Journal of the Japan Society of Medical History* 6.2, 57–68.
Ishihara, Akira 石原明. 1956b. "Kajiwara Shōzen no shōgai to sono chosho (2) 梶原性全の生涯とその著書 (2)." *Nihon ishi gakkai* 日本医史学会/*Journal of the Japan Society of Medical History* 6.4, 139–140.
Ishihara, Akira; Maria-Verena Blümmel, trans. 1999. *Medizinwissenschaft in Japan: Strömungen und Entwicklungen*. Düsseldorfer Arbeiten zur Geschichte der Medizin/Beihefte 12. Düsseldorf: Triltsch.
Ishihara, Akira, and Howard S. Levy. 1968. *The Tao of Sex: An Annotated Translation of the Twenty-eighth Section of The Essence of Medical Prescriptions (Ishimpō)*. Yokohama: Shibundō.
Ishii, Kazuko. 1992. "The Correlation of Verses from the *Sang Hyang Kamahāyānan Mantranaya* with Vajrabodhi's *Jāpa-sūtra*." *Area and Culture Studies* 44, 225–236.
Jannetta, Ann Bowman. 1987. *Epidemics and Mortality in Early Modern Japan*. Princeton, NJ: Princeton University Press.
Jones, William H[enry] S[amuel] [1923] 1945. *Hippocrates and the Corpus Hippocratum*. Oxford: Oxford University Press.
Jones, William Henry Samuel, and Edward Theodore Withington. 1909. *Malaria and Greek history*. Manchester: The University Press.
Jones, William Henry Samuel, Ronald Ross, and George Grigson Ellet. 1907. *Malaria, a Neglected Factor in the History of Greece and Rome*. Cambridge: Macmillan & Bowes.
Jyotirmitra. 1985. *A Critical Appraisal of Āyurvedic Material in Buddhist Literature, with Special Reference to Tripiṭaka, Foreword by G. J. Meulenbeld*. Chaukhambha Sanskrit Series. Varanasi: Jyotiralok Prakashan.
Kaibara Ekiken 貝原益軒. 1911. "Yamato honzō 大和本草." In *Ekiken zenshū* 益軒全集 6. Tōkyō: Ekiken Zenshū Kankōbu.
Kajiwara Shōzen 梶原性全. 1986a. *Man'anpō* 萬安方. Tōkyō: Kagaku Shoin, Kasumigaseki Shuppan.
Kajiwara Shōzen 梶原性全. 1986b. *Ton'ishō* 頓医抄. Tōkyō: Kagaku Shoin, Kasumigaseki Shuppan.
Kajiyama, Yuichi. 1982. "Women in Buddhism." *The Eastern Buddhist* 15.2, 53–70.
Kakuban 覺鑁. [1977] 1989. *Ichigo daigyō himitsushū* 期大要祕密集. Kōgyō Daishi senjutsushū 興教大師撰述集 1, edited by Miyasaka Yūshō 宮坂宥勝, 157–176. Tōkyō: Sankibō Busshorin.
Kameya Tsutome 亀谷勉. 2012. "Wagakuni saigo no dōbutsu seryō shisetsu ka sōi Ninshō no 'babyōya' わが国最古の動物施療施設か 僧医忍性の'馬病屋'." *Nihon jūishigaku zasshi* 日本獣医史学雑誌/*Japanese Journal of Veterinary History* 49: 36–39.
Kandahjaya, Hudaya. 2016. "San Hyan Kamahāyānikan, Borobudur, and the Origins of Buddhism in Indonesia: Networks of Masters, Texts, Icons." In *Esoteric Buddhism in Mediaeval Maritime Asia*, edited by Andrea Acri, 67–112. Singapore: ISEAS Publishing.

Karow, Otto. 1953. "Daidōruijuhō: Klassifizierte Rezepte der Daidōperiode (806–810): ein Beitrag zur Geschichte des Textes und seiner Kritik durch die Kokugakugelehrten." *Monumenta Nipponica* 91, 55–198.

Karow, Otto. 1957. "Textkritische Untersuchungen zum Daidōruijuhō." *Monumenta Nipponica* 13.1/2, 83–100.

Karow, Otto. 1957–1958. "Textkritische Untersuchungen zum Daidōruijuhō (2)." *Monumenta Nipponica* 13.3/4, 284–312.

Karow, Otto. 1958. "Textkritische Untersuchungen zum Daidōruijuhō (3)." *Monumenta Nipponica* 14.1/2, 119–152.

Karow, Otto. 1959. "Textkritische Untersuchungen zum Daidōruijuhō (4)." *Monumenta Nipponica* 15.1/2, 150–175.

Karow, Otto. [1948] 1978. "Das Honzō-Wamyō. Eine japanische Pharmakopoe der Heian-Zeit, und seine Bedeutung für die Geschichte der altjapanischen Medizin". In *Opera Minora: zum 65. Geburtstag*, edited by Otto Karow, Hans Adalbert Dettmer and Gerhild Endress, 195–201. Wiesbaden: Harrassowitz.

Karow, Otto, and Friedrich Weller. 1954. "Das Daidōruijuhō und die Kokugaku." *Monumenta Nipponica* 10, 45–64

Katō Yasuaki 加藤康昭. 1974. *Nihon mōjin shakaishi kenkyū* 日本盲人社会史研究. Tōkyō: Miraisha.

Katsuura Noriko 勝浦令子. 2003. *Kodai, chūsei to josei to bukkyō* 古代・中世の女性と仏教. Nihonshi riburetto 日本史リブレット 16. Tōkyō: Yamakawa Shuppansha.

Katsuura Noriko 勝浦令子. 2007. "Nihon kodai ni okeru gairai shinkōkei san'e ninshiki no eikyō: Honzōsho to mikkyō kyōten no kentō o chūshin ni 日本古代における外来信仰系産穢認識の影響: 本草書と密教経典の検討を中心に." *Shiron* 史論 60, 28–45.

Kawada Yōichi 川田洋一, ed. 1976. *Bukkyō shisō to igaku* 仏教思想と医学. Tōkyō: Tōyo Tetsugaku Kenkyūsho.

Kawada Yōichi 川田洋一, ed. 2013. *Bukkyō kango to kanwa kea* 仏教看護と緩和ケア. Seimei tetsugaku nyūmon 生命哲学入門 3. Tōkyō: Daisan Bunmei Sha.

Kawase Kazuma 川瀬一馬. 1958. *Nihon kanreiroku: kyūan sannen shō* 日本感靈録: 久安三年鈔. Sakamoto Ryūmon bunko fukusei sōkan 阪本龍門文庫覆製叢刊 1. Yoshino: Ryūmon Bunko.

Kenney, Elizabeth. 2004. "Pet Funerals and Animal Graves in Japan." *Mortality* 9.1, 42–60.

Khan, Mohammed Abdul Mujeeb. 2016. *Early Japan and the Continental Medical Literary Tradition: Tanba no Yasuyori's Conceptualization of Medicine in Ishinpō*. Ph.D. dissertation. Cambridge: University of Cambridge.

Kimura Yōjirō 木村陽二郎. 1973. "Nakamura Tekisai no 'Kinmō zuan' ni tsuite 中村惕斎の訓蒙図彙について." *Kyōyō gakka kiyō (Tōkyō daigaku kyōyō gakubu)* 教養学科紀要 (東京大学教養学部) 5: 105–131.

Kinski, Michael. 2005. "Materia Medica in Edo Period Japan: The Case of Mummy: Takai Ranzan's *Shokuji kai*, Part Two." *Japonica Humboldtiana. Jahrbuch der Mori-Ōgai-Gedenkstätte, Humboldt-Universität zu Berlin* 9, 55–170.

Kippenberg, Hans Gerhard. 1978. "Zur Kontroverse über das Verstehen fremden Denkens." In *Magie: Die sozialwissenschaftliche Kontroverse über das Verstehen fremden Denkens*, edited by Hans Gerhard Kippenberg and Brigitte Luchesi. Suhrkamp-Taschenbuch Wissenschaft 674. 9–51. Frankfurt am Main: Suhrkamp.

Kippenberg, Hans Gerhard and Brigitte Luchesi, eds. 1978. *Magie: Die sozialwissenschaftliche Kontroverse über das Verstehen fremden Denkens*. Suhrkamp-Taschenbuch Wissenschaft 674. Frankfurt am Main: Suhrkamp.

Kitagawa, Joseph Mitsuo. 1989. "Buddhist Medical History." In *Healing and Restoring: Health and Medicine in the World's Religious Traditions*, edited by Lawrence E. Sullivan, 9–32. New York; London: Macmillan.

Kleine, Christoph. 1996. *Hōnens Buddhismus des Reinen Landes: Reform, Reformation oder Häresie?* Religionswissenschaft 9. Frankfurt am Main; New York: Peter Lang.

Kleine, Christoph. 2012. "Buddhist Monks as Healers in Early and Medieval Japan." *Japanese Religions (Special Issue: Religion and Healing in Japan, edited by Christoph Kleine and Katja Triplett)* 37.1–2, 13–38.

Kleine, Christoph. 2017. "Health Care in Indian Monasteries: Selections from Yijing's *Record of the Inner Law Sent Home from the Southern Seas*." In *Buddhism and Medicine: An Anthology of Premodern Sources*, edited by Pierce Salguero, 145–159. New York: Columbia University Press.

Kleine, Christoph. 2018. *The Secular Ground Bass of Pre-modern Japan Reconsidered: Reflections upon the Buddhist Trajectories towards Secularity*. Working Paper Series of the HCAS "Multiple Secularities – Beyond the West, Beyond Modernities" 5. Available at http://ul.qucosa.de/api/qucosa%3 A23479/attachment/ATT-0/.

Kleine, Christoph, and Katja Triplett. 2012. "Introduction to 'Religion and Healing in Japan'." *Japanese Religions (Special Issue: Religion and Healing in Japan, edited by Christoph Kleine and Katja Triplett)* 37.1–2, 1–12.

Kodaishi shinpojiumu "Hakken, kenshō Nihon no kodai" henshū iinkai 古代史シンポジウム「発見・検証日本の古代」編集委員会, Shira'ishi Ta'ichirō 白石太一郎, Suzuki Yasutami 鈴木靖民, et al., eds. 2016. *Kiba bunka to kodai inobēshon* 騎馬文化と古代のイノベーション. 発見・検証日本の古代. Tōkyō: Kadokawa Shoten.

Kōdate, Naomi. 2004. "Aspects of *Ketsubonkyō* Belief." In *Practicing the Afterlife: Perspectives from Japan*, edited by Susanne Formanek and William R. LaFleur. Beiträge zur Kultur- und Geistesgeschichte Asiens 42, 121–143. Wien: Verlag der Österreichischen Akademie der Wissenschaften.

Kohn, Livia, ed. 2000. *Daoism Handbook*. Handbook of oriental studies, China 14. Leiden: Brill.

Kosoto Hiroshi 小曽戸洋. 1999. *Kanpō no rekishi: Chūgoku, Nihon no dentō igaku* 漢方の歴史: 中国・日本の伝統医学. Ajia bukkusu あじあブックス 11. Tōkyō: Taishūkan Shoten.

Kovacs, Jürgen, and Paul U. Unschuld. 1998. *Essential Subtleties on the Silver Sea: The Yin-hai jing-wei: A Chinese Classic on Ophthalmology*. Comparative studies of health systems and medical care 38. Berkeley, CA: University of California Press.

Kozasa Manabu 小佐々学. 2010. "Nihon zairaiba to seiyōba – jūiryō no shinten to nichiō jūigaku kōryūshi 日本在来馬と西洋馬 —獣医療の進展と日欧獣医学交流史—." *Nihon jūishi-kai zasshi* 日本獣医師会雑誌/*Journal of the Japan Veterinary Medical Association* 64.6, 419–428.

Kritzer, Robert. 2009. "Life in the Womb: Conception and Gestation in Buddhist Scripture and Classical Indian Medical Literature." In *Imagining the Fetus: The Unborn in Myth, Religion, and Culture*, edited by Vanessa R. Sasson and Jane Marie Law, 73–89. Oxford; New York: Oxford University Press.

Kritzer, Robert. 2014. *Garbhāvakrāntisūtra: The Sūtra on Entry into the Womb*. Studia Philologica Buddhica monograph series 31. Tokyo: International Institute for Buddhist Studies.

Kuhn, Thomas S. 1975. *The Structure of Scientific Revolutions*. International encyclopedia of unified science 2, 2. Chicago: University of Chicago Press.

Kunaichō shoryōbu 宮内庁書陵部, ed. 1983. *Shinshū honzō* 新修本草. Tōkyō: Tosho Ryōshōkan/Kunaichō Shoryōbu.

Kunaichō shoryōbu 宮内庁書陵部, ed. 1994–2013. *Kujō Kanezane-bon Gyokuyō* 九条家本玉葉. Tōkyō: Tosho Ryōshōkan/Kunaichō Shoryōbu.

Kunaichō Shōsōin jimusho 宮内庁正倉院事務所, and Shibata Shōji 柴田承二, eds. 2000. *Zusetsu Shōsōin yakubutsu* 図説正倉院薬物. Tōkyō: Chūō Kōron Sha.

Kura'ishi Tadahiko 倉石忠彦. 2005. *Dōsojin shinkō no keisei to tenkai* 道祖神信仰の形成と展開. Tōykō: Ōkawa Shobō.

Kuriyama, Shigehisa. 1998. *The Expressiveness of the Body and the Divergence of Greek and Chinese Medicine*. New York: Zone Books.

Kyburz, Josef A. 1987. *Cultes et croyances au Japon: Kaida, une commune dans les montagnes du Japon central*. Paris: Maisonneuve et Larose.

Lamotte, Étienne. 1944–1980. *Le traité de la grande vertu de sagesse de Nāgārjuna (Mahāprajñāpāramitāśāstra)*. Louvain: Université de Louvain, Institut Orientaliste.

Langenberg, Amy Paris. 2017. *Birth in Buddhism: The Suffering Fetus and Female Freedom*. Routledge critical studies in Buddhism. London: Routledge.

Lee, Jen-Der. 2005. "Childbirth in Early Imperial China." *Nan Nü* 7.2, 216–286.

Lee, Jen-der. 2012. "*Ishinpo* and Its Excerpts from *Chanjing*: A Japanese Medical Text as a Source for Chinese Women's History." In *Overt and Covert Treasures: Essays on the Sources for Chinese Women's History*, edited by Clara Wing-chung Ho, 185–215. Hong Kong: Chinese University Press.

Leslie, Charles, ed. 1976. *Asian Medical Systems: A Comparative Study*. Berkeley, CA: University of California Press.

Leuchtenberger, Jan C. 2013. *Conquering Demons: The 'Kirishitan,' Japan, and the World in Early Modern Japanese Literature*. Ann Arbor, MI: University of Michigan, Center for Japanese Studies.

Levering, Miriam. 1982. "The Dragon Girl and the Abbess of Mo-Shan: Gender and Status in the Ch'an Buddhist Tradition." *Journal of the International Association of Buddhist Studies* 5.1, 19–35.

Linduff, Katheryn M. 2006. "Imaging the Horse in Early China: From the Table to the Stable." In *Horses and Humans: The Evolution of Human-equine Relationships*, edited by Sandra L. Olsen, M. A. Littauer and Ingrid Rea. BAR international series 1560, 303–322. Oxford: Archaeopress.

Lloyd, Geoffrey E[rnest] R[ichard]. 1991. *Methods and Problems in Greek Science*. Cambridge: Cambridge University Press.

Lloyd, G[eoffrey] E[rnest] R[ichard]. 1996. *Adversaries and Authorities: Investigations into Ancient Greek and Chinese Science*. Ideas in context 42. Cambridge; New York: Cambridge University Press.

Lloyd, G[eoffrey] E[rnest] R[ichard], and Nathan Sivin. 2002. *The Way and the Word: Science and Medicine in Early China and Greece*. New Haven, CT: Yale University Press.

Lo, Vivienne, and Christopher Cullen, eds. 2005. *Medieval Chinese Medicine: The Dunhuang Medical Manuscripts.* London; New York: RoutledgeCurzon.

Lock, Margaret M. 1980. *East Asian Medicine in Urban Japan: Varieties of Medical Experience.* Berkeley, CA: University of California Press.

Lomi, Benedetta. 2010. "The Iconography of Ritual: Images, Texts and Beliefs in the Batō Kannon Fire Offering." In *Grammars and Morphologies of Ritual Practices in Asia (Section II)*, edited by Lucia Dolce, Gil Raz and Katja Triplett. Ritual dynamics and the science of ritual 1, 557–575. Wiesbaden: Harrassowitz.

Lomi, Benedetta. 2011. *The Precious Steed of the Buddhist Pantheon: Ritual, Faith and Images of Batō Kannon in Japan.* Ph.D. dissertation. London: School of Oriental and African Studies.

Lomi, Benedetta. 2014. "Dharanis, Talismans, and Straw-Dolls Ritual Choreographies and Healing: Strategies of the *Rokujikyōhō* in Medieval Japan." *Japanese Journal of Religious Studies* 41.2, 255–304.

Lomi, Benedetta. 2017. "The Ox-Bezoar Empowerment for Fertility and Safe Childbirth: Selected Readings from the Shingon Ritual Collection." In *Buddhism and Medicine: An Anthology of Premodern Sources*, edited by C. Pierce Salguero, 351–357. New York: Columbia University Press.

Lu, Liancheng. 1993. "Chariot and Horse Burials in Ancient China." *Antiquity* 67 (257), 824–838.

Ludvik, Catherine. 2007. *Sarasvatī: Riverine Goddess of Knowledge: From the Manuscript-carrying vīṇā-player to the Weapon-wielding Defender of the Dharma.* Leiden; Boston: Brill.

Luhmann, Niklas. 1982. *Funktion der Religion.* Frankfurt am Main: Suhrkamp.

Lurie, David B. 2011. *Realms of Literacy: Early Japan and the History of Writing.* Harvard East Asian monographs 335. Cambridge, MA; London: Harvard University Press.

Ma Jixing 馬継興. 1985. "'Ishinpō' chūteki koigaku bunken shotan 『医心方』中的古医学文献初探." *Nihon igaku-shi zasshi* 日本医史学雑誌 31.3, 326–371.

Mabbett, Ian. 1998. "The Problem of the Historical Nāgārjuna Revisited." *Journal of the American Oriental Society* 118.3, 332–346.

Macé, Mieko. 2013. *Médecins et médecine dans l'histoire du Japon: aventures intellectuelles entre la Chine et l'Occident.* Collection Japon. Paris: Les Belles Lettres.

Machi, Senjurō. 2014. "The Evolution of 'Learning' in Early Modern Japanese Medicine." In *Listen, Copy, Read: Popular Learning in Early Modern Japan*, edited by Matthias Hayek and Annick Horiuchi. Brill's Japanese studies library 46, 164–204. Leiden; Boston: Brill.

Maekawa Fumio 前川文夫. 1975. "Bai-no-sōshi no shokubutsu ni tsuite 馬医草紙の植物について." *Shokubutsu kenkyū zasshi* 植物研究雑誌/*Journal of Japanese Botany* 50.3, 24–26.

Maitre, Claude Eugène. 1925. "Une inscription japonaise de l'an 623." In *Études asiatiques, publiées à l'occasion du vingt-cinquième anniversaire de l'École française d'Extrême-Orient*, edited by École francaise d'Extrême-Orient, 403–430. [Paris]: G. Van Oest.

Maki Sachiko 槙佐知子, ed. and trans. 1985. *Daidō ruijuhō: zenshaku seikai* 大同類聚方: 全訳精解. Tōkyō: Heibonsha.

Maki Sachiko 槙佐知子, ed. and trans. 1993–2012. *Ishinpō: Maki Sachiko zenshaku seikai* 医心方: 槙佐知子全訳精解. Tōkyō: Chikuma Shobō.

Maki Sachiko 槇佐知子, ed. and trans. 1995. *Taikyō shussan hen* 胎教出産篇. Ishinpō: Maki Sachiko zenshaku seikai 医心方: 槇佐知子全訳精解 22. Tōkyō: Chikuma Shobō.
Maki Sachiko 槇佐知子, ed. and trans. 1996. *Jibi inkō ganshi hen* 耳鼻咽喉眼歯篇. Ishinpō: Maki Sachiko zenshaku seikai 医心方: 槇佐知子全訳精解 5. Tōkyō: Chikuma Shobō.
Maki Sachiko 槇佐知子, ed. and trans. 1997. *Fujin shobyō hen* 婦人諸病篇. Ishinpō: Maki Sachiko zenshaku seikai 医心方: 槇佐知子全訳精解 21. Tōkyō: Chikuma Shobō.
Maki Sachiko 槇佐知子, ed. and trans. 1998. *Sanka chiryō, girei hen* 産科治療・儀礼篇. Ishinpō: Maki Sachiko zenshaku seikai 医心方: 槇佐知子全訳精解 23. Tōkyō: Chikuma Shobō.
Maki Sachiko 槇佐知子. 2000. *Yamai kara kodai o toku:* Daidō ruijuhō *tansaku* 病から古代を解く:『大同類聚方』探索. Tōkyō: Shinsensha.
Malinowski, Bronislaw. [1925] 1955. "Magic, Science and Religion." In *Science, Religion and Reality*, edited by Joseph Needham, 19–84. New York: Braziller.
Malinowski, Bronislaw. 1926. *Crime and Custom in Savage Society*. London: Paul.
Manase Dōsan 曲直瀬道三. 1979. *Keiteiki-shū* 啓迪集. Kinsei kanpō igakusho shūsei 近世漢方医学書集成, Manase Dōsan 曲直瀬道三 1–2, edited by Ōtsuka Yoshinori 大塚敬節 and Yakazu Dōmei 矢数道明. Tōkyō: Meicho Shuppan.
Manieri, Antonio [Maniēri Antonio マニエーリ アントニオ]. 2012. "*Wamyōruijushō* 'Gyūba no ke' mon no honbun『和名類聚抄』「牛馬毛」門の本文." *Gaikokugogaku kenkyū* 外国語学研究 13, 1–7.
Marcon, Federico. 2015. *The Knowledge of Nature and the Nature of Knowledge in Early Modern Japan*. Studies of the Weatherhead East Asian Institute, Columbia University. Chicago; London: The University of Chicago Press.
Maruyama Yumiko 丸山裕美子. 1998. *Nihon kodai no iryō seido* 日本古代の医療制度. Rekishigaku sōsho 歴史学叢書. Tōkyō: Meicho Kankōkai.
Masamune Atsuo 正宗敦夫. 1936. "Fukudenhō kaidai 福田方解題." In *Yūrin fukudenhō* 有林福田方. Nihon koten zenshū 日本古典全集. Tōkyō: Nihon Koten Zenshū Kankōkai.
Matisoff, Susan. 1978. *The Legend of Semimaru, Blind Musician of Japan*. New York: Columbia University Press.
Matsuo Shin'ichi 松尾信一. 2005. "Nihon ba'ishi – kodai yori bakumatsu, ishin zengo made 日本馬病史―古代より幕末・維新前後まで―." *Nihon jūishigaku zasshi* 日本獣医史学雑誌 4, 21–21.
Maurer, Petra. 1995. "The Horse Book of the Prince of Jharkot." *Kailash* 17.3–4, 147–156.
Maurer, Petra H. 2001. *Handschriften zur tibetischen Hippiatrie und Hippologie*. Beiträge zur Zentralasienforschung 8. Bonn: VGH Wissenschaftsverlag.
Maurer, Petra, and Angela von den Driesch. 2006. "Tibetan 'Horse Books' from the High Himalayas." In *Horses and Humans: The Evolution of Human-equine Relationships*, edited by Sandra L. Olsen, M. A. Littauer and Ingrid Rea. BAR international series 1560, 355–361. Oxford: Archaeopress.
Mauss, Marcel. 1923/24. "Essai sur le don. Forme et raison de l'échange dans les sociétés archaïques." *L'Année Sociologique*, 130–186.
May, Jasques. 1967. "Chinkiyaku." In *Hōbōgirin; dictionnaire encyclopédique du bouddhisme d'après les sources chinoises et japonaises*, edited by Paul Demiéville, 329–335. Tokyo: Maison franco-japonaise.

Mayanagi Makoto 真柳誠. 1993. "Chūgoku honzō to Nihon no juyō 中国本草と日本の受容." In *Chūgoku honzō zuroku* 中国本草図録 9, edited by Xiao Peigen 蕭培根 and Mayanagi Makoto 真柳誠 (trans.), 218–229. Tōkyō: Chūō Kōron Sha.

Mazars, Sylvain. 2008. *Le bouddhisme et la médecine traditionnelle de l'Inde*. Médecines d'Asie, savoirs & pratiques. Paris: Springer.

McBride II, Richard D. 2011. "Esoteric Buddhism and its Relation to Healing and Demonology." In *Esoteric Buddhism and the Tantras in East Asia*, edited by Charles D. Orzech, Henrik Hjort Sørensen and Richard Karl Payne. Handbook of oriental studies section four, China 24, 208–214. Leiden; Boston: Brill.

McCullough, Helen Craig, trans. 1980. *Ōkagami, the Great Mirror: Fujiwara Michinaga (966–1027) and his Times, a Study and Translation*. Princeton: Princeton University Press.

McCullough, Helen Craig, and William H. McCullough, trans. 1980. *A Tale of Flowering Fortunes: Annals of Japanese Aristocratic Life in the Heian Period*. Stanford, CA: Stanford University Press.

Meech-Pekarik, Julia. 1981. "The Flying White Horse: Transmission of the Valāhassa Jātaka Imagery from India to Japan." *Artibus Asiae* 43.1/2, 111–128.

Meeks, Lori R. 2007. "In Her Likeness: Female Divinity and Leadership at Medieval Chūgūji." *Japanese Journal of Religious Studies* 34.2, 351–392.

Meeks, Lori R. 2010. *Hokkeji and the Reemergence of Female Monastic Orders in Premodern Japan*. Studies in East Asian Buddhism 23. Honolulu: University of Hawai'i Press.

Métailié, Georges. 2015. *Traditional Botany: An Ethnobotanical Approach*. Biology and biological technology, science and civilisation in China series part 4, vol. VI. Cambridge: Cambridge University Press.

Meulenbeld, G. Jan. 1999. *A History of Indian Medical Literature*. Groningen oriental studies 15. Groningen: E. Forsten.

Michel-Zaitsu, Wolfgang. 2017. *Traditionelle Medizin in Japan von der Frühzeit bis zur Gegenwart*. München: Kiener Verlag.

Mishima, Saiichi, Yakoh Chiba, Akio Majima, et al. 2004. *The History of Ophthalmology in Japan*. Hirschberg history of ophthalmology; The monographs. Oostende: Jean-Paul Wayenborgh.

Mitsu'i Takaosa 三井高孟. [1968] 1994. "Emaki ni himerareta rekishi 絵巻に秘められた歴史." In *Bagaku: Uma o bungaku suru* 馬学: 馬を科学する, edited by Matsuo Shin'ichi 松尾信一. Uma no bunka sōsho 馬の文化叢書 7, 442–462. Yokohama: Baji Bunka Zaidan.

Miura Saburo 三浦三郎. 1980. *Kusuri no minzokugaku: Edo jidai senryū ni miru* くすりの民俗学: 江戸時代川柳にみる. Tōkyō: Ken'yukan.

Miyata, Nana. 2012. *Die Übernahme der chinesischen Kultur in Japans Altertum. Kultureller Wandel im innen- und außenpolitischen Kontext*. Bunka/Wenhua: Tuebingen East Asian studies 22. Berlin: Lit.

Moerman, D. Max. 2015. "The Buddha and the Bathwater: Defilement and Enlightenment in the *Onsenji engi*." *Japanese Journal of Religious Studies* 42.1, 71–87.

Mori Shikazō 森鹿三. 1977. *Kaidai* 解題: *Ken'i* 兼意, *Kōyōshō; Yakushushō* 香要抄; 藥種抄. Tenri Toshokan zenpon sōsho washo no bu 天理図書館善本叢書和書之部 31. Tōkyō: Yagi Shoten; Tenri: Tenri University Press.

Mori Shikazō 森鹿三. 1999. *Honzōgaku kenkyū* 本草學研究. Ōsaka: Takeda Kagaku Shinkō Zaidan Kyōu Shooku.

Mrozik, Susanne. 2007. *Virtuous Bodies: The Physical Dimensions of Morality in Buddhist Ethics*. Oxford: Oxford University Press.

Mukharji, Projit Bihari. 2014. "Vishalyakarani as *Eupatorium ayapana:* Retro-botanizing, Embedded Traditions, and Multiple Historicities of Plants in Colonial Bengal, 1890–1940." *The Journal of Asian Studies* 73.1, 65–87.

Mura'i Hideo 村井秀夫, and Matsuo Shin'ichi 松尾信一. 1974. "Jūi kankei makimono ni kan suru kenkyū 1 Nagano-ken Komagane, Sasako no Anzai-ryū Anki makimono ni tsuite 獣医関係巻物に関する研究 1長野県駒ヶ根, 笹古家の安西流安驥巻物について." *Shinshū daigaku nōgaku-bu kiyō* 信州大学農学部紀要 11.2, 245–258.

Mura'i Hideo 村井秀夫, Matsuo Shin'ichi 松尾信一, and Shira'i Tsunesaburō 白井恒三郎. [1961] 1994. "Ba'i makimono (Bunroku yonnen) ni tsuite 馬医巻物（文禄四年）について." In *Bagaku: Uma o bungaku suru* 馬学: 馬を科学する, edited by Matsuo Shin'ichi 松尾信一. Uma no bunka sōsho 馬の文化叢書 7, 537–538. Yokohama: Baji Bunka Zaidan.

Mura'i Hideo 村井秀夫, Matsuo Shin'ichi 松尾信一, and Shira'i Tsunesaburō 白井恒三郎. [1977] 1994. "Ba'i emaki no ruikei ni tsuite 馬医絵巻の類型について." In *Bagaku: Uma o bungaku suru* 馬学: 馬を科学する, edited by Matsuo Shin'ichi 松尾信一. Uma no bunka sōsho 馬の文化叢書 7, 463–472. Yokohama: Baji Bunka Zaidan.

Nagai Akiko 永井彰子. 2002. *Nikkan mōsō no shakai-shi* 日韓盲僧の社会史. Tōkyō: Ashi Shobō.

Nagai Yoshinori 永井義憲. 1966. "Nihon kanreiroku no senja to seiritsu 日本感霊録の撰者と成立." In *Nihon bukkyō bungaku kenkyū* 日本仏教文学研究, edited by Nagai Yoshinori 永井義憲, 147–154. Tōkyō: Toyoshima Shobō.

Nagai Yoshinori 永井義憲. 1985. "*Minami Hokkeji korōden* ni tsuite 『南法華寺古老伝』について." In *Nihon bukkyō bungaku kenkyū* 日本仏教文学研究, edited by Nagai Yoshinori 永井義憲. Shintensha kenkyū sōsho 新典社研究叢書 12, 716–728. Tōkyō: Shintensha.

Nakada Takeshi 中田武司. 1990. *Aouma no sechie kenkyū to shiryō* 白馬節会研究と資料. Tōkyō: Ōfūsha.

Nakamura Yōkichi 中村洋吉. 1980. *Jōigaku-shi* 獣医学史. Tōkyō: Yōkendō.

Nakamura, Kyoko M. 1973. *Miraculous Stories from the Japanese Buddhist Tradition: The Nihon ryōiki of the Monk Kyōkai*. Monograph series 20. Cambridge, MA: Harvard University Press.

Nakanishi Atsuo 中西淳朗. 2005. "Isō Obinata Daijō no ryakuden 医僧・大日方大乗の略伝." *Nihon ishi gakkai* 日本医史学会/*Journal of the Japan Society of Medical History* 51.2, 240–241.

Nakano, Hatayoshi 中野幡能. 1985. *Usagū* 宇佐宮. Nihon rekishi sōsho 日本歴史叢書 37. Tōkyō: Yoshikawa Kōbunkan.

Nakao Takashi 中尾堯, and Imai Masaharu 今井雅晴, eds. 1983. *Chōgen, Eison, Ninshō* 重源・叡尊・忍性. Tōkyō: Yoshikawa Kōbunkan.

Nakayama Shigeru 中山茂. 1974. *Rekishi toshite no gakumon* 歴史としての学問. Tōkyō: Chuō Kōron Sha.

Nakayama, Shigeru. 1984. *Academic and Scientific Traditions in China, Japan, and the West*, Translated by Jerry Dusenbury. Tokyo: University of Tokyo Press.

Nakayama, Shigeru. 2007. "Thomas Kuhn: A Historian's Personal Recollections." *Historia scientiarum. Second Series: International Journal of the History of Science Society of Japan* 17.1, 49–53.

Nakayama Shigeru 中山茂. 2013. *Paradaimu to kagaku kakumei no rekishi* パラダイムと科学革命の歴史. Kōdansha gakujutsu bunko 講談社学術文庫 2175. Tōkyō: Kōdansha.

Nakayama Tarō 中山太郎. 1934. *Nihon mōjin-shi* 日本盲人史. Tōkyō: Shōwa Shobō.

Nakayama Tarō 中山太郎. 1936. *Zoku Nihon mōjin-shi* 続日本盲人史. Tōkyō: Shōwa Shobō.

Nakazumi Yukinobu 中泉行信, Nakazumi Yukihito 中泉行史, and Saitō Yoshio 斎藤仁男. 1985. "Bunko no mado kara: ganka sho-ryūha no hidensho 文庫の窓から 眼科諸流派の秘伝書 (38)." *Ganshō ganka* 臨床眼科 39.2, 228–229.

Nakazumi Yukinobu 中泉行信, Nakazumi Yukihito 中泉行史, and Saitō Yoshio 斎藤仁男. 1987a. "Bunko no mado kara 'Ganka Ryūmoku-ron' (1) 文庫の窓から「眼科龍木論」（１）." *Ganshō ganka* 臨床眼科 41.10, 1196–1197.

Nakazumi Yukinobu 中泉行信, Nakazumi Yukihito 中泉行史, and Saitō Yoshio 斎藤仁男. 1987b. "Bunko no mado kara 'Ganka Ryūmoku-ron' (2) 文庫の窓から「眼科龍木論」（２）." *Ganshō ganka* 臨床眼科 41.11, 1268–1269.

Naoki, Kōjirō. 1988. "The Nara State." In *Ancient Japan*, edited by Delmer M. Brown. The Cambridge history of Japan 1, 268–316. Cambridge; New York: Cambridge University Press.

Nattier, Jan. 2009. "Gender and Hierarchy in the Lotus Sūtra." In *Readings of the Lotus Sūtra*, edited by Stephen F. Teiser and Jacqueline I. Stone, 83–106. New York: Columbia University Press.

Nei Kiyoshi 根井浄. 1976. "Shugendō no iryō ni tsuite 修験者の医療について." *Indogaku Bukkyōgaku kenkyū* 印度學佛教學研究/*Journal of Indian and Buddhist Studies* 24.2, 893–896.

Nei Kiyoshi 根井浄. 1980. "Toyama baiyaku to shugenja ni tsuite 富山売薬と修験者について." *Indogaku Bukkyōgaku kenkyū* 印度學佛教學研究/*Journal of Indian and Buddhist Studies* 28.2, 624–625.

Nichion. 1973. "Chiyomigusa 千代見草." In *Kinsei bukkyō no shisō* 近世佛教の思想, edited by Kashiwabara Yūsen 柏原祐泉 and Fujii Manabu 藤井学. Nihon shisō taikei 日本思想大系 57, 397–453. Tōkyō: Iwanami Shoten.

Nihon gakushiin 日本学士院, ed. 1955–1964. *Meiji-zen Nihon igaku-shi* 明治前日本医学史. Tōkyō: Nihon Gakujutsu Shinkōkai.

Nihon ganka gakkai hyakushūnen kinen hensan iinkai 日本眼科学会百周年記念誌, ed. 1997. *Nihon ganka no rekishi* 日本眼科の歴史. Tōkyō: Nihon Ganka Gakkai.

Nihon jūigaku jinmei jiten hensai iinkai 日本獣医学人名事典編纂委員会, ed. 2007. *Nihon jūigaku jinmei jiten: Nihon jūigaku-shi gakkai sōritsu 35 shūnen kinen* 日本獣医学人名事典: 日本獣医史学会創立35周年記念, *Biographical dictionary of veterinary medicine in Japan*. Tōkyō: Nihon jūigaku-shi gakkai, The Japanese Society of Veterinary History.

Nihonyanagi Kenji 二本柳賢司. 1994. *Bukkyō igaku gaiyō* 佛教医学概要. Kyōto: Hōzōkan.

Nihonyanagi Kenji 二本柳賢司. 1996. "Gomahō ni okeru gohō goyaku gokō no igakuteki kōka (1) 護摩法における五宝五薬五香の医学的効果(一)." *Mikkyōgaku* 密教学 3, 267–108.

Nihonyanagi Kenji 二本柳賢司. 1997a. "Nihon mikkyō igaku to yakubutsugaku 日本密教医学と薬物学." In *Rekishi no naka no yamai to igaku* 歴史の中の病と医学, edited by Yamada Keiji 山田慶兒 and Kuriyama Shigehisa 栗山茂久, 545–566. Kyōto: Kokusai Nihon bunka kenkyū sentā; Shibundō.

Nihonyanagi Kenji 二本柳賢司. 1997b. "Gomahō ni okeru gohō goyaku gokō no igakuteki kōka (2) 護摩法における五宝五薬五香の医学的効果(二)." *Mikkyōgaku* 密教学 33, 101–132.

Nishiguchi Junko 西口順子. 1998. "Jōbutsu-setsu to josei 成仏説と女性." In *Josei to shūkyō* 女性と宗教, edited by Kojima Kyōko 児島恭子 and Shiomi Minako 塩見美奈子, 329–354. Tōkyō: Yoshikawa Kōbunkan.

Nishiguchi Junko 西口順子. 2014. "'Tennyo jōbutsu kyō' ni tsuite「転女成仏経」について." In *Chūsei kaiga no matorikkusu* 中世絵画のマトリックス, edited by Sano Midori 佐野みどり et al., 254–275. Tōkyō: Seikansha.

Nishioka, Yōko 西岡陽子. 2000. "Chijin mōsō no denshō shishō – 'Chijin-kyō' oyobi shakumon ni tsuite – 地神盲僧の伝承詞章ー「地神経」および釈文についてー" In *Zaichi denshō no sekai (Nishi Nihon)* 在地伝承の世界(西日本), edited by Iwase Hiroshi 岩瀬博, Fukuda Akira 福田晃 and Watanabe Shōgo 渡辺昭五. Kōza Nihon no denshō bungaku 講座日本の伝承文学 8, 299–312. Tōkyō: Mirai Shoten.

Nobel, Johannes, ed. 1937. *Suvarṇabhāsottamasūtra. Das Goldglanz-Sūtra: ein Sanskrittext des Mahāyāna-Buddhismus; Nach den Handschriften und mit Hilfe der tibetischen und chinesischen Übertragungen.* Leipzig: Harrassowitz.

Nobel, Johannes. [1944] 1958, ed. and trans. *Suvarṇaprabhāsottamasūtra. Das Goldglanz-Sūtra: ein Sanskrittext des Mahāyāna-Buddhismus; die tibetischen Übersetzungen mit einem Wörterbuch.* Leiden: E.J. Brill; Stuttgart: W. Kohlhammer.

Nobel, Johannes. 1951. *Ein alter medizinischer Sanskrit-Text und seine Deutung.* Supplement to the Journal of the American Oriental Society. Baltimore: The Society.

Norbeck, Edward, and Margaret Lock, eds. 1987. *Health, Illness, and Medical Care in Japan: Cultural and Social Dimensions.* Honolulu: University of Hawai'i Press.

Oberländer, Christian. 1995. *Zwischen Tradition und Moderne: Die Bewegung für den Fortbestand der Kanpō-Medizin in Japan.* Medizin, Gesellschaft und Geschichte/Beiheft 7. Stuttgart: Steiner.

Obinata Daijō 大日方大乗. 1958. *Bukkyō igaku* 佛教医学. Tōkyō: Sankō Shuppansha.

Obinata Daijō 大日方大乗. 1962. *Bukkyō eiseigaku* 仏教衛生学. Tōkyō: Sankō Shuppansha.

Obinata Daijō 大日方大乗. 1965. *Bukkyō igaku no kenkyū* 仏教医学の研究. Tōkyō: Kasama Shobō.

Obinata Daijō 大日方大乗. 1966. *Bukkyō kangogaku* 仏教看護学. Tokyo: Kasama Shobō.

Offermanns, Jürgen. 2002. *Der lange Weg des Zen-Buddhismus nach Deutschland: vom 16. Jahrhundert bis Rudolf Otto.* Lund studies in history of religions 16. Stockholm: Almquist & Wiksell.

Ogata Nobuo 小形信夫. 2003. "Iwate no bosama, itako ni tsuite 岩手の盲僧・巫女について." In *Fugeki, mōsō no denjō sekai* 巫覡・盲僧の伝承世界, edited by Fukuda Akira 福田晃 and Yamashita Kin'ichi 山下欣一, 257–272. Tōkyō: Mirai Shoten.

Ogawa Kenzaburō 小川剣三郎. [1904] 1971. *Nihon gankashi, kōhon* 日本眼科学史: 稿本. Kyōto: Shibunkaku.

Ōharu chōshi henshū iinkai 大治町史編集委員会, ed. 1979. *Ōharu chōshi* 大治町史. Ōharu-chō (Aichi-ken): n/a.

Ohnuki-Tierney, Emiko. 1984. *Illness and Culture in Contemporary Japan.* Cambridge: Cambridge University Press.

Ohnuma, Reiko. 2000. "The Story of Rūpāvatī: A Female Past Birth of the Buddha." *Journal of the International Association of Buddhist Studies* 23.1, 103–145.

Ohnuma, Reiko. 2001. "Woman, Bodhisattva, and Buddha." *Journal of Feminist Studies in Religion* 17.1, 63–83.

Oka Masao 岡正雄, Yawata Ichirō 八幡一郎, Egami Namio 江上波夫, et al. 1948. "Nihon minzoku bunka no genryū to Nihon kokka no keisei (zadankai) 日本民族文化の源流と日本国家の形成(座談会)." *Minzokugaku kenkyū* 民族學研究 13.3, 207–277.

Okimori Takuya 沖森卓也, and Satō Makoto 佐藤信, eds. 1994. *Jōdai mokkan shiryō shūsei* 上代木簡資料集成. Tōkyō: Ōfū.

Okuzawa Yasumasa 奥沢康正. 1997. "Me'ishi-tachi no hidensho to ryūha 目医師達の秘伝書と流派." In *Rekishi no naka no yamai to igaku* 歴史の中の病と医学, edited by Yamada Keiji 山田慶兒 and Kuriyama Shigehisa 栗山茂久, 195–228. Kyōto: Kokusai Nihon Bunka Kenkyū Sentā.

Ooms, Herman. 2009. *Imperial Politics and Symbolics in Ancient Japan: The Tenmu Dynasty, 650–800*. Honolulu: University of Hawai'i Press.

Ooms, Herman. 2015. "Framing Daoist Fragments, 670–750." In *Daoism in Japan: Chinese Traditions and Their Influence on Japanese Religious Culture*, edited by Jeffrey L. Richey. Routledge studies in Taoism, 37–59. London; New York: Routledge.

Otsuka, Yasuo. 1976. "Chinese Traditional Medicine in Japan." In *Asian Medical Systems: A Comparative Study*, edited by Charles Leslie, 322–340. Berkeley, CA: University of California Press.

Otto, Bernd-Christian, and Michael Stausberg. eds. 2013. *Defining Magic: A Reader*. Sheffield: Equinox.

Paul, Diana Y. 1979. *Women in Buddhism: Images of the Feminine in the Mahāyāna Tradition*. Berkeley, CA: Asian Humanities.

Phillipi, Donald. 1990. *Norito*. Princeton, NJ: Princeton University Press.

Piggott, Joan R. 1997. *The Emergence of Japanese Kingship*. Stanford, CA: Stanford University Press.

Powell, Margaret, and Masahira Anesaki. 1990. *Health Care in Japan*. London; New York: Routledge.

Pradel, [Chari] María del Rosario. 2016. *Fabricating the Tenjukoku Shūchō Mandara and Prince Shōtoku's Afterlives*. Japanese visual culture 17. Leiden; Boston: Brill.

Pye, Michael. 1996. "Syncretism: Buddhism and Shinto on One Island." In *Religions in Contact. Selected Proceedings of the Special IAHR Conference held in Brno, August 23–26, 1994*, edited by Iva Dolezalova, Bretislav Horyna and Dalibor Papousek, 159–162. Brno: Czech Society for the Study of Religions.

Quinter, David. 2015. *From Outcasts to Emperors: Shingon Ritsu and the Mañjuśrī Cult in Medieval Japan*. Brill's Japanese studies library 50. Leiden; Boston: Brill.

Rambelli, Fabio, and Eric Robert Reinders. 2012. *Buddhism and Iconoclasm in East Asia: A History*. London; New York: Bloomsbury.

Reis-Habito, Maria D. 1993. *Das Dhāraṇī des grossen Erbarmens des Bodhisattva Avalokiteśvara mit tausend Händen und Augen: Übersetzung und Untersuchung ihrer textlichen Grundlage sowie Erforschung ihres Kultes in China*. Monumenta Serica/Monograph series 27. Nettetal: Steyler.

Reißenweber, Heidrun Helga. 1994. *Arzneipflanzengärten in Japan: Wandel und Kontinuität in der Arzneikunde der Edo-Zeit (1600–1868): Zum gesellschaftlichen, ökonomischen und weltanschaulichen Kontext naturkundlichen Wissens*. Ph.D. dissertation. Munich: Ludwig Maximilians University.

Robson, James. 2011. "Formation and Fabrication in the History and Historiography of Chan Buddhism." *Harvard Journal of Asiatic Studies* 71.2, 311–349.

Rosenfield, John M. 1986. "Introduction: Tōdai-ji in Japanese History and Art." In *The Great Eastern Temple: Treasures of Japanese Buddhist Art from Tōdai-ji [exhibition held at The Art Institute of Chicago from June 28 to September 7, 1986]*, edited by Yukata Mino and John M. Rosenfield, 17–31. Chicago; Bloomington, IN: Art Institute of Chicago; Indiana University Press.

Rosner, Erhard. 1989. *Medizingeschichte Japans*. Handbuch der Orientalistik 5, Japan 3.5. Leiden: E.J. Brill.

Ruch, Barbara, ed. 2002. *Engendering Faith: Women and Buddhism in Premodern Japan*. Michigan monograph series in Japanese studies. Ann Arbor, MI: Center for Japanese Studies, University of Michigan.

Ruch, Barbara. 1977. "Medieval Jongleurs and the Making of a National Literature." In *Japan in the Muromachi Age*, edited by John Hall and Takeshi Toyoda, 279–309. Los Angeles, CA: University of California Press.

Ruch, Barbara. 1990. "The Other Side of Culture in Medieval Japan." In *Medieval Japan*, The Cambridge History of Japan 3, edited by Kozo Yamamura, 500–543. Cambridge: Cambridge University Press.

Sakai Shizu 酒井シヅ. 1982. *Nihon no iryō-shi* 日本の医療史. Tōkyō: Tōkyō Shoseki.

Salguero, C. Pierce. 2009. "The Buddhist Medicine King in Literary Context: Reconsidering an Early Example of Indian Influence on Chinese Medicine and Surgery." *History of Religions* 48.3, 183–210.

Salguero, C. Pierce. 2013. "'On Eliminating Disease': Translations of the Medical Chapter from the Chinese Versions of the Sūtra of Golden Light." *ejournal of Indian Medicine* 6, 21–43.

Salguero, C. Pierce. 2014. *Translating Buddhist Medicine in Medieval China*. Encounters with Asia Philadelphia: PENN/University of Pennsylvania Press.

Salguero, C. Pierce. 2015. "Reexamining the Categories and Canons of Chinese Buddhist Healing." *Journal of Chinese Buddhist Studies* 28, 35–66.

Salguero, C. Pierce, ed. 2017a. *Buddhism and Medicine: An Anthology of Premodern Sources*. New York: Columbia University Press.

Salguero, C. Pierce. 2017b. "Karma in the Bathhouse: The Sūtra on Bathing the Sangha in the Bathhouse." In *Buddhism and Medicine: An Anthology of Premodern Sources*, edited by C. Pierce Salguero, 84–91. New York: Columbia University Press.

Sanford, James H. 2006. "Breath of Life: The Esoteric Nembutsu." In *Tantric Buddhism in East Asia*, edited by Richard K. Payne, 161–189. Boston: Wisdom Publications.

Schiefsky, Mark John. 2005. *Hippocrates: On Ancient Medicine, Translated with Introduction and Commentary*. Studies in ancient medicine 28. Leiden: Brill.

Schuster, Nancy. 1981. "Changing the Female Body: Wise Women and the Bodhisattva Career in Some *Mahāratnakūṭasūtras*." *Journal of the International Association of Buddhist Studies* 4.1, 24–69.

Segawa Yoshinori 瀬川芳則. 1991. "Umakai shūdan no kami matsuri 馬飼集団の神祭り." In *Kofun jidai no kenkyū 3: Seikatsu to saishi* 古墳時代の研究 3—生活と祭祀, edited by Ishino Hironobu 石野博信, Iwasaki Takuya 岩崎卓也, Kawaki Kunihito 河上邦彦, et al., 122–130. Tōkyō: Yūzankaku.

Sharf, Robert H. 1996. "The Scripture on the Production of Buddha Images." In *Religions of China in Practice*, edited by Donald S. Lopez. Princeton readings in religions, 261–267. Princeton, NJ: Princeton University Press.

Sharf, Robert H., and Elizabeth Horton Sharf, eds. 2001. *Living Images: Japanese Buddhist Icons in Context*. Stanford, CA: Stanford University Press.
Shibata Shōji 柴田承二. 2000. "Shōsōin yakubutsu to sono kagakuteki chōsa 正倉院薬物とその化学的調査 Introduction – Shosoin and the Old Drugs Stored Therein." In *Zusetsu Shōsōin yakubutsu* 図説正倉院薬物, edited by Kunaichō Shōsōin jimusho 宮内庁正倉院事務所 and Shibata Shōji 柴田承二, 9 – 24. Tōkyō: Chūō Kōron Sha.
Shin, Chang-Geon. 2016. "The Formation and Development of the Self-Image of Kampō Medicine in Japan: The Relationship Between Showa-Period Kampō and Science." In *Essays on the History of Scientific Thought in Modern Japan*, translated by Christopher Carr and M.G. Sheftall, edited by Osamu Kanamori, 235 – 267. Tokyo: Japan Publishing Industry Foundation for Culture.
Shinkawa Tokio 新川登亀男. 1999. *Dōkyō o meguru kōbō: Nihon no kunnō, dōshi no hō o agamezu* 道教をめぐる攻防：日本の君王、道士の法を崇めず. Ajia bukkusu あじあブックス 13. Tōkyō: Taishūkan Shoten.
Shinmura Taku 新村拓. 1985. *Nihon iryō shakaishi no kenkyū. Kodai chūsei no minshū seikatsu to iryō* 日本医療社会史の研究.古代中世の民衆生活と医療. Tōkyō: Hōsei Daigaku Shuppankyoku.
Shinmura Taku 新村拓, ed. 2006. *Nihon iryō-shi* 日本医療史. Tōkyō: Yoshikawa Kōbunkan.
Shinmura Taku 新村拓. 2013. *Nihon bukkyō no iryō-shi* 日本仏教の医療史. Tōkyō: Hōsei Daigaku Shuppankyoku.
Shirahata, Yōzaburō. 2016. *Daimyo Gardens, translated by Imoto Chikako and Lynne E. Riggs*. Nichibunken monograph series 19. Kyoto: International Research Center for Japanese Studies.
Shira'i Mitsutarō [Kōtarō] 白井光太郎. [1891] 1934. *Nihon hakubutsu-gaku nenpyō* 日本博物学年表. Tōkyō: Ōka shoten.
Shira'i Mitsutarō. [1926] 2011. "A Brief History of Botany in Old Japan." In *Scientific Japan, Past and Present. Prepared [by the National Research Council of Japan] in Connection with the Third Pan-Pacific Science Congress, Tokyo, 1926*, edited by Pacific Science Congress, 213 – 227. Tokyo: [Jigyokudō; Maruzen] Nabu Press.
Shira'i Tsunesaburō 白井恒三郎. [1944] 1979. *Nihon jūigaku-shi* 日本獣医学史. Tōkyō: Bun'eidō.
Shira'ishi Ta'ichirō 白石太一郎. 2016. "Nihon rettō no kiba bunka wa donoyōni shite hajimattanoka 日本列島の騎馬文化はどのようにして始まったのか." In *Kiba bunka to kodai inobēshon* 騎馬文化と古代のイノベーション, edited by Kodaishi shinpojiumu "Hakken, kenshō Nihon no kodai" henshū iinkai 古代史シンポジウム「発見・検証日本の古代」編集委員会, Shira'ishi Ta'ichirō 白石太一郎, Suzuki Yasutami 鈴木靖民, et al. 2: 88 – 103. Tōkyō: Kadokawa Shoten.
Sōda Hajime 宗田一. 1981. *Nihon meiyaku – baiyaku no bunka-shi* 日本の名薬−売薬の文化史. Tōkyō: Yasaka Shobō.
Sōda Hajime 宗田一. 1993. *Toraiyaku bunka-shi* 渡来薬文化史. Tōkyō: Yasaka Shobō.
Sōda Hajime 宗田一. [1989] 2017. *Zusetsu, Nihon iryō bunka-shi* 図説・日本医療文化史. Kyōto: Shibunkaku Shuppan.
Sonoda, Kōyū. 1988. "Early Buddha Worship." In *Ancient Japan*, edited by Delmer M. Brown. The Cambridge History of Japan 1. 359 – 414. Cambridge, UK; New York: Cambridge University Press.

Sonoda, Kyoichi. 1988. *Health and Illness in Changing Japanese Society.* Tokyo: Tokyo University Press.
Sonoda Kyōichi 園田恭一. 2010. *Shakaiteki kenkō-ron* 社会的健康論. Tōkyō: Tōshindō.
Sonoda, Hidehiro, and S. N. Eisenstadt, 1998. *Japan in a Comparative Perspective.* International symposium 12. Kyoto: International Research Center for Japanese Studies.
Soysal, Yasemin Nuhoğlu. 1994. *Limits of Citizenship: Migrants and Postnational Membership in Europe.* Chicago, IL: University of Chicago.
Stone, Jacqueline and Mariko Namba, eds. 2008. *Death and the Afterlife in Japanese Buddhism.* Honolulu: University of Hawai'i Press.
Strickmann, Michel. 2002. *Chinese Magical Medicine,* edited by Bernard Faure. Stanford, CA: Stanford University Press.
Sugitatsu Yoshikazu 杉立義一. 1991. *Ishinpō no denrai* 医心方の伝来. Kyōto: Shibunkaku Shuppan.
Sugiyama Jirō 杉山二郎. 1994. *Tenpyō no Perujia-jin* 天平のペルシア人. Tōkyō: Seidosha.
Sunim, Hae-ju. 1999. "Can Women Achieve Enlightenment? A Critique of Sexual Transformation for Enlightenment." In *Buddhist Women Across Cultures,* edited by Karma Lekshe Tsomo, 123–141. New York: State University of New York Press.
Suzuki Shōei 鈴木昭英, ed. [1993] 2016. *Bukkyō geinō to bijutsu* 仏教芸能と美術. Bukkyō minzokugaku taikei 仏教民俗学大系 5. Tōkyō: Meicho Shuppan.
Suzuki Takeo 鈴木建夫. 1984. "Kodai uma no shitsubyō to ba'i ni tsuite 古代馬の疾病と馬医について." In *Ritsuryōsei to kodai shakai* 律令制と古代社会, edited by Takeuchi Rizō sensei kiju kinen ronbunshū kankōkai 竹内理三先生喜寿記念論文集刊行会, 110–130. Tōkyō: Tōkyōdō Shuppan.
Suzuki, Daisetz Teitaro. [1927] 1949. *Essays in Zen Buddhism (First Series).* The complete works of D.T. Suzuki. London: Rider.
Suzuki, Yui. 2012. *Medicine Master Buddha: The Iconic Worship of Yakushi in Heian Japan.* Japanese visual culture 3. Leiden; Boston: Brill.
Suzuki, Yui. 2014. "Twanging Bows and Throwing Rice: Warding off Evil in Medieval Japanese Birth Scenes." *Artibus Asiae* 74.1, 17–41.
Tada Iori 多田伊織. 2010. "Shiryō shōkai *Ishinpō* shoin *Sōshinhō* shūitsu – tōajia ni denpa shita bukkyō igaku no shosō 史料紹介『医心方』所引『僧深方』輯佚-東アジアに伝播した仏教医学の諸相." *Nihon kenkyū* 日本研究 41.3, 411–444.
Takeda kagagaku shinkō zaidan Kyōu shooku henshū 武田科学振興財団杏雨書屋編集, ed. 2015. *Manase Dōsan to kinsei Nihon iryō shakai* 曲直瀬道三と近世日本医療社会. Tōkyō: Takeda Kagagaku Shinkō Zaidan.
Takemi, Momoko. 1983. "'Menstruation Sutra' Belief in Japan." *Japanese Journal of Religious Studies* 10.2–3, 229–246.
Tambiah, Stanley Jeyaraja. 1984. *The Buddhist Saints of the Forest and the Cult of Amulets: A Study in Charisma, Hagiography, Sectarianism, and Millennial Buddhism.* Cambridge studies in social anthropology 49. Cambridge: Cambridge University Press.
Tambiah, Stanley Jeyaraja. 1990. *Magic, Science, Religion, and the Scope of Rationality.* The Lewis Henry Morgan lectures 1984. Cambridge; New York: Cambridge University Press.
Tanihara Hidenobu 谷原秀信. 2013. "Hyōshi no kaisetsu: Nihon de saisho no ganka senmon'i: Majima Seigan to Majima-ryū ni tsuite 表紙の解説 日本で最初の眼科専門医: 馬島清眼と馬島流について." *Ganka* 眼科 55.9, 977–983.

Tatsukawa Shōji 立川昭二. 1979. *Kinsei yamai no sōshi: Edo jidai no byōki to iryō* 近世病草紙: 江戸時代の病気と医療. Heibonsha sensho 平凡社選書 63. Tōkyō: Heibonsha.

Thomas, Keith. [1971] 1980. *Religion and the Decline of Magic: Studies in Popular Beliefs in Sixteenth- and Seventeenth-century England*. 4th ed. London: Weidenfeld & Nicolson.

Tonomura, Hitomi. 2007. "Birth-giving and Avoidance Taboo: Women's Body Versus the Historiography of Ubuya." *Japan Review* 19: 3–45.

Töpfer, Susanne. 2014. "The Physical Activity of Parturition in Ancient Egypt: Textual and Epigraphical Sources." *Dynamis* 34.2, 317–335.

Torigoe Yasuyoshi 鳥越泰義. 2005. *Shōsōin yakubutsu no sekai: Nihon no kusuri no genryū wo saguru* 正倉院薬物の世界: 日本の薬の源流を探る. Heibonsha shinsho 平凡社新書 296. Tōkyō: Heibonsha.

Totman, Conrad. 2000. *A History of Japan*. The Blackwell History of the World. Oxford: Blackwell.

Toyoshima Osamu 豊島修. 1990. *Kumano shinkō to shugendō* 熊野信仰と修験道. Tōkyō: Meicho Shuppan.

Triplett, Katja. 2001. *Prinz Goldglanz auf der Reise durch Himmel und Höllen: Zwei japanische Bildrollen des Bishamon no honji aus dem 16. Jahrhundert im Kölner Museum für Ostasiatische Kunst*. Indica et Tibetica 42/Arbeitsmaterialien zur Religionsgeschichte 16. Marburg: Indica-et-Tibetica-Verlag.

Triplett, Katja. 2004. *Menschenopfer und Selbstopfer in den japanischen Legenden: das Frankfurter Manuskript der Matsura Sayohime-Legende*. Studies in modern Asian religions/Religiöse Gegenwart Asiens 2. Münster: Lit.

Triplett, Katja. 2010a. "Gründungslegenden in der Erinnerungspflege japanisch-buddhistischer Tempel am Beispiel des Tsubosakasan Minami Hokkeji." In *Geschichten und Geschichte: Historiographie und Hagiographie in der asiatischen Religionsgeschichte*, edited by Max Deeg, Oliver Freiberger and Christoph Kleine. Historia religionum 30, 140–180. Uppsala: Almqvist & Wiksell.

Triplett, Katja. 2010b. "Esoteric Buddhist Eye-healing Rituals in Japan and the Promotion of Benefits." In *Grammars and Morphologies of Ritual Practices in Asia (Section II)*, edited by Lucia Dolce, Gil Raz and Katja Triplett. Ritual Dynamics and the science of ritual 1, 485–497. Wiesbaden: Harrassowitz.

Triplett, Katja. 2012. "Magical Medicine? – Japanese Buddhist Medical Knowledge and Ritual Instruction for Healing the Physical Body." *Japanese Religions (Special Issue: Religion and Healing in Japan, edited by Christoph Kleine and Katja Triplett)* 37.1–2, 63–92.

Triplett, Katja. 2013. "Healing Rituals in Contemporary Japanese Esoteric Buddhism as Acts of Individual and Collective Purification." In *Purification: Religious Transformations of Body and Mind*, edited by Gerhard Marcel Martin and Katja Triplett, 107–117. London: Bloomsbury Publishing.

Triplett, Katja. 2013–2014. "Hippiatry and Ritual Healing: Considering Japanese Buddhist Illustrated Manuscripts on Equine Medicine." *CSJR Newsletter* 26/27, 21–23.

Triplett, Katja. 2014. "For Mothers and Sisters: Care of the Reproductive Female Body in the Medico-ritual World of Early and Medieval Japan." *Dynamis* 34.2, 337–356.

Triplett, Katja. 2016. "Wissen und Wunder: 'Erleuchtung und das Bild des asiatischen Buddhismus im 19. und 20. Jahrhundert." In *Erleuchtung. Kultur- und Religionsgeschichte eines Begriffs*, edited by Almut-Barbara Renger, 367–395. Freiburg: Herder.

Triplett, Katja [Toripuretto Katiya トリプレットカティヤ]. 2017a. "Fōretchi-hon 'Sayohime' kaidai, honkoku フォーレッチ本「さよひめ」解題・翻刻." In *Sekkyō – hito wa shinbutsu ni nani wo takusō to suru nowa* 説経 一人は神仏に何を托そうとするのか, edited by Kōbe joshi daigaku koten geinō kenkyū sentā 神戸女子大学古典芸能研究センター, 275–323. Osaka: Izumi Shoin.

Triplett, Katja. 2017b. "Using the Golden Needle: Nāgārjuna Bodhisattva's *Ophthalmological Treatise* and Other Sources in the *Essentials of Medical Treatment*." In *Buddhism and Medicine: An Anthology of Premodern Sources*, edited by Pierce Salguero, 543–548. New York: Columbia University Press.

Triplett, Katja. 2017c. "The Making and Unmaking of Religious Objects: Sacred Waste Management in Comparative Perspective." In *Materiality in Religion and Culture (Tenri University – Marburg University Joint Research Project)*, edited by Saburo Shawn Morishita. Marburger Religionswissenschaft im Diskurs 2, 143–154. Zürich: Lit.

Triplett, Katja. 2018. "Approaching Emptiness: Buddhist Pilgrimage in Japan." In *Approaching the Sacred: Pilgrimage in Historical and Intercultural Perspective*, edited by Ute Luig. Berlin Studies of the Ancient World 49, 59–89. Berlin: Edition Topoi. Available at urn: nbn:de:kobv:188-fudocsdocument000000027524–4 (last accessed 23 Nov. 2018).

Triplett, Katja. 2019a. "Potency by Name? 'Medicine Buddha Plant' and Other Herbs in the Japanese *Scroll of Equine Medicine* (*Ba'i sōshi emaki*, 1267)." *Himalaya* (Special issue "Approaching Potent Substances in Medicine and Ritual Across Asia," edited by Barbara Gerke und Jan van der Valk) 39.1, 189–207. Available at https://digitalcommons.macalester.edu/himalaya/vol39/iss1/12 (last accessed 25 Aug. 2019).

Triplett, Katja. 2019b. "Buddhist Monastic Physicians' Encounters with the Jesuits in Sixteenth- and Seventeenth-Century Japan, As Told from Both Sides." In *Buddhism and Medicine: An Anthology of Modern and Contemporary Voices*, edited by Pierce Salguero, 3–15. New York: Columbia University Press.

Triplett, Katja, Barbara Gerke, and Jan van der Valk. 2019. "Gallery: Potent Substances in a Thirteenth Century Japanese Scroll Painting." *Himalaya* (Special issue "Approaching Potent Substances in Medicine and Ritual Across Asia," edited by Barbara Gerke und Jan van der Valk) 39.1, 4–8. Available at https://digitalcommons.macalester.edu/himalaya/vol39/iss1/5 (last accessed 25 Aug. 2019).

Tsuji Eiko 辻英子. 1981. *Nihon kanreiroku no kenkyū* 日本感霊録の研究. Tōkyō: Kasama Sōsho.

Tsukahara, Togo. 1993. *Affinity and Shinwa Ryoku: Introduction of Western Chemical Concepts in Early Nineteenth-century Japan*. Amsterdam: Gieben.

Turnbull, Stephen. 2015. *Japan's Sexual Gods: Shrines, Roles, and Rituals of Procreation and Protection*. Leiden: Brill.

Tweed, Thomas A. 2005. "American Occultism and Japanese Buddhism: Albert J. Edmunds, D. T. Suzuki, and Translocative History." *Japanese Journal of Religious Studies* 32.2, 249–281.

Ueda Masaaki 上田正昭. 1992. "Satsu gyūma shinkō no kōsatsu 殺牛馬信仰の考察." In *Kamigami no saishi to denshō: Matsumae Takeshi kyōju koki kinen ronbunshū* 神々の祭祀と伝承―松前健教授古稀記念論文集, edited by Ueda Masaaki 上田正昭, 19–34. Tōkyō: Tōmeisha.

Ueda Sanpei 上田三平. [1930] 1972. *Nihon yakuen-shi no kenkyū* 日本薬園史の研究. [Takadamachi: n/a] Tōkyō: Watanabe shoten.

Ueki Masatoshi 植木雅俊. 2013. *Bukkyō no naka no danjokan—genshi bukkyō kara Hokekyō ni itaru jendā byōdō no shisō* 仏教のなかの男女観―原始仏教から法華経に至るジェンダー平等の思想. Tōkyō: Iwanami Shoten.

Ueno Masuzō 上野益三. [1948] 1973. *Nihon hakubutsugaku-shi* 日本博物学史. Tōkyō: Heibonsha.

Unschuld, Paul U. 1985a. *Medicine in China: A History of Ideas*. Comparative studies of health systems and medical care. Berkeley, CA: University of California Press.

Unschuld, Paul U. 1985b. "Kataraktoperationen im alten China." *Deutsches Medizinhistorisches Museum* 5, 62–66.

Unschuld, Paul U. 1986. *Medicine in China: A History of Pharmaceutics*. Comparative studies of health systems and medical care. Berkeley, CA: University of California Press.

Ury, Marian Bloom. 2002. "Nuns and Other Female Devotees in *Genkō shakusho* (1322), Japan's First History of Buddhism." In *Engendering Faith: Women and Buddhism in Premodern Japan*, edited by Barbara Ruch. Michigan monograph series in Japanese studies 43, 189–207. Ann Arbor, MI: Center for Japanese Studies, University of Michigan.

Vandenreydt, Sarah. 2011. "'Bouddhisme' entre 'philosophie' et 'religion'. Discours savants et dynamiques sociales en Angleterre (1875–1900)." *Asiatische Studien/Études Asiatiques* 65.1, 241–264.

Vickers, Brian, ed. 1984. *Occult and Scientific Mentalities in the Renaissance*. Cambridge: Cambridge University Press.

van Gulik, Robert Hans. 1935. *Hayagrīva: The Mantrayānic Aspect of Horse-cult in China and Japan*. Leiden: E.J. Brill.

von den Driesch, Angela, and Joris Peters. [1989] 2003. *Geschichte der Tiermedizin: 5000 Jahre Tierheilkunde*. Stuttgart: Schattauer.

Wajima Yoshio 和島芳男. 1959. *Eison, Ninshō* 叡尊・忍性. Tōkyō: Yoshikawa Kōbunkan.

Waldschmidt, Anne. 2017. "Disability Goes Cultural: The Cultural Model of Disability as an Analytical Tool." In *Culture – Theory – Disability: Encounters Between Disability Studies and Cultural Studies*, edited by Anne Waldschmidt, Hanjo Berressem and Moritz Ingwersen. Disability studies: Body – power – difference 10. 19–27. Bielefeld: Transcript.

Walley, Akiko. 2015. *Constructing the Dharma King: Hōryūji Shaka Triad and the Birth of the Prince Shōtoku Cult*. Leiden: Brill.

Williams, Duncan Ryuken. 2004. "Esoteric Waters: Meritorious Bathing, Kōbō Daishi, and Legends of Hot Spring Foundings." *Bulletin of the Research Institute of Esoteric Buddhist Culture (Special issue)* 2, 195–216.

Williams, Duncan Ryūken. 2005. *The Other Side of Zen: A Social History of Sōtō Zen: Buddhism in Tokugawa Japan*. Buddhisms. Princeton, NJ: Princeton University Press.

Wilson, Liz. 1996. *Charming Cadavers: Horrific Figurations of the Feminine in Indian Buddhist Hagiographic Literature*. Chicago, IL: The University of Chicago Press.

Winfield, Pamela D. 2005. "Curing with *kaji*: Healing and Esoteric Empowerment in Japan." *Japanese Journal of Religious Studies* 32.1, 107–130.

Wittkamp, Robert F. 2018. "The Body as a Mode of Conceptualization in the *Kojiki* Cosmogony." *Kansai daigaku Tōzai gakujutsu kenkyūjo kiyō* 関西大学東西学術研究所紀要 51, 47–64.

Wulff, Kurt. 1935. "Sang Hyang Kamahāyānan Mantrānaya: Ansprache bei der Weihe buddhistischer Mönche aus dem Altjavanischen übersetzt und sprachlich erläutert von K[urt] Wulff." *Historisk-filologiske Meddelelser. Det Kongelige Danske Videnskabernes Selskab* 21.4.

Yakazu Dōmei 矢数道明. 1982. *Kinsei kanpō igakushi – Manase Dōsan to sono gakutō* 近世漢方医学史: 曲直瀬道三とその学統. Tōkyō: Meicho Shuppan.

Yamada Keiji 山田慶兒, and Kuriyama Shigehisa 栗山茂久, eds. 1997. *Rekishi no naka no yamai to igaku* 歴史の中の病と医学. Kyōto: Kokusai Nihon Bunka Kenkyū Sentā, Shibundō Shuppan.

Yamagiwa Nobuyuki 山極伸之. 2001. "Ritsu-zō ni kitei sarenai shie 律蔵に規定されない四依." *Indogaku bukkyōgaku kenkyū* 印度学仏教学研究/*Journal of Indian and Buddhist Studies* 50.1, 453–447.

Yamamoto, Chikyō, and International Academy of Indian Culture, ed. and trans. 1990. *Mahāvairocana-sūtra: Translated into English from Ta-p'i lu che na ch'eng-fo shen-pien chia-ch'ih ching, the Chinese Version of Śubhākarasiṁha and I-hsing, A.D. 725*. Śatapiṭaka series 359. New Delhi: International Academy of Indian Culture and Aditya Prakashan.

Yamane Michihiro 山根陸宏. 1999. "Kinsei Yamato no Chijin-kyō zatō to sono geinō 近世大和の地神経座頭とその芸能." *Biblia: Bulletin of Tenri Central Library* 110, 58–72.

Yamano Chie 山野智恵. 2011. "Nāgārujuna to ijutsu – *Ryūju ganron* no seiritsu to tenkai ナーガールジュナと医術-『龍樹眼論』の成立と展開" *Journal of Rengeji Institute of Buddhist Studies* 4, 20–44.

Yang, Shou-zhong, trans. 2007. *The Divine Farmer's Materia Medica: A Translation of the Shen Nong Ben Cao Jing*. Boulder, CO: Blue Puppy Press.

Yoneda Yusuke 米田雄介. 2000. "*Shuju yakuchō* ni tsuite 『種々薬帳』について." In *Zusetsu Shōsōin yakubutsu* 図説正倉院薬物, edited by Kunaichō Shōsōin jimusho 宮内庁正倉院事務所 and Shibata Shōji 柴田承二, 25–32. Tōkyō: Chūō Kōron Sha.

Yoshida Fumio 吉田文夫. 1983. "Ninshō no shakai jigyō ni tsuite 忍性の社会事業について." In *Chōgen, Eison, Ninshō* 重源・叡尊・忍性, edited by Nakao Takashi 中尾堯 and Imai Masaharu 今井雅晴, 392–433. Tōkyō: Yoshikawa Kōbunkan.

Yü, Chün-fang. 2001. *Kuan-yin: The Chinese Transformation of Avalokiteśvara*. New York: Columbia University Press.

Zucconi, Laura M. 2007. "Medicine and Religion in Ancient Egypt." *Religion Compass* 1.1, 26–37.

Zysk, Kenneth G. 1991. *Asceticism and Healing in Ancient India: Medicine in the Buddhist Monastery*. New Delhi: Motilal Banarsidass.

Index

Abe 阿部 (718–770), 138; See also Kōken Tennō
abhiṣeka (Jp. *kanjō* 灌頂; consecration), 75, 146, 185
active compassion (*jihi* 慈悲), 9
acupuncture, 70, 83, 91, 108, 123, 141, 158, 181, 183, 192, 194
adhiṣṭhāna, 65
Administrative Laws for Monks and Nuns (*Sōni-ryō* 僧尼令), 66
aggregates (Sk. *skandha*), 72
agriculture, 138, 163, 167, 173
Ainōshō 塵嚢鈔, 185
Aizen 愛染, 170
Ākāśagarbha, 173
Akṣobhya, 26–27, 129
amalā, 79–80, 142
Amaterasu ōmikami 天照大神 (Sun Goddess), 57
Amida 阿弥陀 (Amitābha), 26, 133
Amitābha, 23, 26–27, 133, 151, 170, 191
amulets, 64, 67, 189
Anagarika Dharmapala (1864–1933), 51
Anahobe no Hashihito no Himeko 穴穂部間人皇女 (d. 621/622), 111, 131, 133
Ānanda, 44
anatomical charts (*jintai kaibōzu* 人体解剖図), 177, 181, 190
ancestor veneration, 23, 74
ancestors, 23, 53, 57, 59, 74, 107, 174
animal sacrifice, 165, 167
animals; See also *chiku*; horses, general; *liu chu*
– animal parts, 175
– animal products, 135, 188
– animal sacrifice, 165, 167
– bovine medicine, 182
– cattle, 163, 166, 169–170, 182
– *chikushō* 畜生 (birth as animal), 114
– domestic animals, x, 18–19, 151, 162, 167
– equine medicine, xii, 5, 18–19, 152–158, 161, 163–180
– fishing, 167

– hippiatry, xii, 160, 162–163, 169, 177, 182
– hunting, 167
– leather, 132, 188
– pets, 167, 185
– sericulture, 175, 181
– *tiryag-yoni* (birth as animal), 114
– veterinarians, 18, 152, 167–168, 175–177, 181–182, 194
– veterinary medicine, 5, 158, 163–164, 167–168, 177–182, 184
Ankan 安寬 (dates unknown), 62
Ankishū 安驥集, 167–168, 185
anmaroku 菴摩勒 (*amalā*), 142
anpō 罨法 (poulticing), 122
Ansai Harima no kami 安西幡摩守 (dates unknown), 181
Anzai-ryū ba'isho 安西流馬医書, 177
aouma no sechie 白馬節会 (white horse ceremony), 166
Arcane Essentials of the Imperial Library (*Waitai biyao*, Jp. *Gaidaihiyō* 外台秘要), 86, 88
archaeology, 38, 49, 124, 137, 164–165
Arnold, Edwin (1832–1904), 50–51
ars medicina, 32
Artemisia annua, 157
artemisinin (*qinghaosu* 青蒿素), 39
ascetics, 11–12, 20, 102–103, 107, 128, 135
Ashikaga gakkō 足利学校, 140
Ashuku 阿閦 (Akṣobhya), 26
ashura 阿修羅 (jealous warriors), 114
Assorted Notes on Individual Deities (*Besson zakki* 別尊雜記), 146
astronomy, 76
Asukabehime 安宿媛 (701–760), 128; See also Kōmyō kōgō
asura (jealous warriors), 114
Aśvaghoṣa, 181
aśvaratna ("horse jewel"), 112, 166
authority, ix, 16, 21, 23, 49, 55–57, 68, 104, 149, 176, 181, 195
Avalokiteśvara, xv, 14–15, 68, 79, 85, 90, 104–105, 112, 134, 161, 166, 170, 185–

187, 193; See also Batō Kannon; Horse-headed Avalokiteśvara; Kanjizai; Kannon; Kanzeon; Mezu Kannon; Tsubosaka Kannon
Avatamsaka-sūtra, 59
awakening, 23, 51, 56, 68, 71, 77–78, 81, 107, 119–120, 133, 186, 191
āyurveda, 5–6, 12–13, 142
Azaihime no Mikoto 浅井比売命, 100

Ba'i daigo 馬医醍醐, 168
Ba'i sōshi emaki 馬医草紙絵巻, 152
ba'i 馬醫 (horse medicine, doctor), 163
backache, 123
Baekje (Jp. Kudara) 百済, 56, 62, 137, 139, 144
Baikal skullcap, 89
banana, 155, 157
bathhouse (*karafuro*, *yokushitsu* 浴室), 128–131, 133, 183
bathing, 129–130
Batō Kannon 馬頭観音, 134, 185–187
Batō nenju giki 馬頭念誦儀軌, 134
Bencao gangmu 本草綱目, 145
bencao 本草 (*materia medica*), 135, 145
benefits, xi, 17, 37, 45–46, 79, 105, 129, 131, 151, 192
Benzaiten 弁財天, 99–101, 105–107; See also Chikubushima Benzaiten; Uga-Benzaiten; Myōon
Beop-jang 法藏 (Jp. Hōzō, dates unknown), 62
Besson zakki 別尊雑記, 146
bezoar, 66, 112–113, 126, 133; See also ox bezoar
Bhaiṣajyaguru, 13, 57, 170; See also Medicine Buddha
bhikṣuṇī, 1, 132; See also female monastic order; nuns
Bian Que 扁鵲 (ca. 401–310 BCE), 89, 175
birth; See also conception; embryology; gestation; perinatal care; perinatal rituals; reproduction (sexual)
– as one kind of suffering, 192
– birth in the Pure Land (*ōjō* 往生), 11, 57, 133, 191
– childbirth, 66, 113, 120, 122–123

– delivery, 66, 111–113, 138
– six realms of birth (*rokudō* 六道), 114
biwa hōshi 琵琶法師 (lute-playing priests), 107
blessing formula (*iwai* 祝), 126
blind minstrels, 70, 106
blind priests (*mōsō* 盲僧), 70, 92, 106–108
blindness, ix, 17, 67, 70–71, 73, 76, 79, 87–88, 92–93, 97, 102–103, 105, 108
blood, 26–27, 29, 31, 36, 44, 88, 116, 133, 158, 167, 177, 182, 193
bloodletting, ix, 158
bodai 菩提 (awakening, enlightenment), 128, 191
bodhi (awakening, enlightenment), 1, 23, 51
bodhisattva, xii, 14–15, 21, 46, 68, 79, 81–83, 86–88, 90, 97, 104–105, 107, 112, 114, 117–118, 132, 159, 162, 169–170, 173, 181, 184–187, 193; See also Avalokiteśvara; Yakujō bosatsu; Yakuō bosatsu
Bodhisena (704–760), 6
body; See also corporeality; five principal viscera; Fu Viscera; six hollow viscera; Zang and Fu Viscera; Zang Viscera
– female bodies, 16, 18, 113–115, 119
– human organs, 28
– perfect body, 68, 114, 120, 130
– physical body, xii, 5, 17, 24, 45–46, 78, 88, 162
– reproductive female body, xii, 17, 111–112, 114, 116, 118, 120–126, 128, 130, 132
– transformation of the female body, 115–116
Bole 伯楽, 169, 175, 180, 185
Book of the Simple Physician (*Ton'ishō* 頓医抄), 95
bosama 盲僧 (blind monks), 108
botanical names, 156–158
botany, 5, 136, 152–153
bovine medicine, 182
Brahmans, 6, 12, 90, 109
brain, 89–91
broomcorn millet, 89
Buddha eye (*butsugen* 佛眼), 72, 108
buddhahood, 16, 22, 46, 114–115, 119, 121, 194; See also *jōbutsu*

Buddhism, general
- Asian Buddhism, 1, 14, 16, 23, 48, 71, 113, 115–116
- Buddhism, history of, 20–24
- Buddhist deities, 6, 13, 15, 17, 65, 148, 159, 161, 176, 182
- Buddhist folklore studies, 6, 64–65
- Buddhist legends, 10, 15, 17, 44, 67, 92, 105, 116–117, 130, 147
- Buddhist medicine, 3, 5, 9–13, 15, 28, 46–48, 61–63, 69, 72, 85, 196
- Buddhist sutras, 5, 44, 59, 119, 142, 186
- Buddhist temples, 4–6, 56, 66, 74, 80, 92, 99, 101, 128, 137, 141, 145, 148, 184–185, 187, 192–193
- Chinese Buddhism, 4, 55
- East Asian Buddhism, 1, 14, 16, 71, 113, 115–116
- esoteric (tantric) Buddhism, ix, xi, 3, 16, 27–28, 46, 50, 65, 68–69, 74–78, 82, 109, 134, 146–147, 150–151, 170, 177, 183, 186, 189, 192, 194–195
- Indian Buddhism, 10, 12, 115, 118
- popular Buddhism, 64
- Zen Buddhism, 9, 11, 51–52, 98, 115, 140, 151, 162
Buddhist medicine, 3, 5, 9–13, 15, 28, 46–48, 61–63, 69, 72, 85, 196; See also *Bukkyō igaku*
Bukkyō igaku 仏教医学, 11
Bukkyō minzokugaku 仏教民俗学, 64
Bureau of Horses (Meryō, Uma no tsukasa 馬寮), 163, 192
Bureau of Medicine (Ten'yakuryō 典薬寮), 65, 137, 146, 163
Burnouf, Eugène (1801–1852), 49–50
Bussetsu daizō shōkyō ketsubon-kyō 佛説大蔵真経血盆経, 116
Bussetsu iyu-kyō 佛説醫喩經, 44
Bussetsu tennyo jōbutsu-kyō 佛説転女成仏経, 119–120
Bussetsu tennyoshin-kyō 佛説轉女身經, 115
butsugen 佛眼 (Buddha eye), 72, 108
Butsumo daikujaku myōō-kyō 佛母大孔雀明王經, 112
butter, 1, 18

byakugō 白毫 (*ūrṇā-keśa*; tuft of white hair), 72
byō 病 (sickness), 13, 41–44, 85
byōen 病縁 (cause of disease), 105

calendrical practices, 52
cancer, 122
candana (sandalwood), 134
canthus, 25–26
carp brain, 90
carp gall, 89–90
cassia seed, 89
Catalogue of Extant Texts in the Country of Japan (*Nihonkoku genzai shomokuroku* 日本國見在書目録), 163
cataract couching, 76, 80–82, 87, 91, 93, 95–96, 109; See also cataractopiesis; golden needle (for cataract couching)
cataractopiesis, 80, 90–91, 95
cataracts, 17, 76, 79–80, 87–88, 90–91, 101, 109, 127; See also golden needle (for cataract couching); *qingmang*; *seimō*
cattail pollen (*kaba, gama* 蒲), 173
cattle, 163, 166, 169–170, 182
cattle breeding, 166
cavalry horses, 175
celibacy, 113
Central Asia, 14, 71, 130
Chanjing 産経, 123
charms, 3, 42, 196
chicken, 167
Chijin 地神, 108
chiku 畜 (beast), 188
Chikubushima, 99–101, 105–106
Chikubushima Benzaiten 竹生島弁財天, 99–101, 106
chikushō 畜生 (birth as animal), 114
childbirth, 66, 113, 120, 122–123
children, xv, 17, 60, 97, 112–113, 116, 126, 140
Chinese-style medicine, 9, 12, 15, 26, 28–29, 39–40, 52–53, 55, 57, 61, 64, 122, 141, 158, 160, 173, 189; See also *kanpō*
Chinese-style therapies, 8

chinkiyaku 陳棄藥 (putrefied urine for healing), 150
Chiribukuro 塵袋, 185
Chiyomigusa 千代見草, 191
Chōnin 長仁 (dates unknown), 68, 104–105
Chōsei ryōyōhō 長生療養方, 146
Christian missionaries, 4, 11
Christianity (kirishitankyō 基督教), 62
Christians, ix, 4, 11, 40–41, 48, 62, 141
Chronicle of Ancient Matters (Kojiki 古事記), 63
Chūgūji 中宮寺, 131, 133
cikitsā-vidyā (study of medicine), 21
Cimicifuga simplex, 89
cinnamon, 142
civilization, 13, 32, 36–37
Classic on Obstetrics (Chanjing 產經, Jp. Sankyō), 123–124
Classified Prescriptions of the Daidō Period (Daidō ruijuhō 大同類聚方), 10, 53, 195
cold disease, 161
Collection of Remedies for Blood Horses by Stable Grooms (Simu anjiji 司牧安驥集), 158, 167, 177, 182
Collection of Remedies for Horses in Syllabic Script (Kana Ankishū 仮名安驥集), 168
Collection of Rules for the Nuns, 1
Collection of Stories That are Old Today (Konjaku monogatarishū 今昔物語集), 130
Collection of Writings of the Keiteki [Academy] (Keiteiki-shū 啓迪集), 98
colonialism, 37, 49
compassion, 9, 13, 79, 117, 129, 139, 183, 186; See also jihi
Compendium of Drugs (Yakushushō 薬種抄), 147
Compendium of Essentials on Incense (Kōyōshō 香要抄), 147
Compendium of Essentials on Precious Substances (Hōyōshō 宝要抄), 147
Compendium of Incense and Drugs (Kōyakushō 香薬抄), 148–149
Compendium of Materia Medica (Bencao gangmu, Jp. Honzō kōmoku 本草綱目), 145
Compendium of Suśruta (Suśruta saṃhitā), 29, 31, 73, 81, 120

Compendium of Varieties of Cereals (Kokuruishō 穀類抄), 147
Compilation of Notes on the Translation of the Tripitaka (Shutsu sanzō kishū 出三藏記集), 121
Comprehensive Treatise on the Sage's Advice (Shengji zonglu 聖濟總錄), 87
conception, 23, 63, 84, 121–122, 179, 194
Confucianism, 60, 62
Confucianism (jukyō 儒教), 62
Confucius, 56
consecration, 74–78, 104, 146, 185
Conversations About Ancient Matters (Kojidan 古事談), 147
corporeality, 116, 118
Corpus Hippocraticum, 32
Cortex fraxini, 89
cosmology, 16, 28, 58, 60, 69, 125–126, 163, 177, 195
coughing, 123
court literature, 10
court medicine, 184
Csoma de Kőrös, Alexander (Sándor) (1784? 1842), 50
cultivation, 18, 137–138, 145, 151
cupping, 158
cures, 15, 17, 42, 64–67, 69, 93
curse, 3, 52

Dai'iō 大医王, 104
Daichibō 大智坊, 96
Daidō ruijuhō 大同類聚方, 10, 64
Daigoji Temple 醍醐寺, 147–149
daimoku 題目, 191
Dainichi 大日 (Mahāvairocana), 26
dairy products, 167
Daoism, 15–16, 63, 66–67, 69, 81–82, 87–88, 109, 122, 126, 150, 196
darani 陀羅尼 (Sk. dhāraṇī), 79, 81, 85, 104–105, 127, 191
darśana (vision, sight), 74
deafness, 71, 73
death, ix, 23, 44, 57, 68, 74, 79, 84, 95, 111, 116, 125, 128–129, 139, 149–151, 165, 176, 184, 188, 191–192
Dee, John (1527–1608/9), 39
defilement, 115–116, 130

delusion, 71, 92
Demiéville, Paul (1894–1979), 13, 41–43, 56, 67, 75–76
demonic medicine, 6
demonology, 15, 46
demons, ix, 2, 6, 42, 46, 151, 166, 186, 191
deva, 59, 114, 170
dhāraṇī (Jp. darani 陀羅尼, ju 呪), xv, 46, 79–81, 85, 102, 104–105, 112, 122, 127, 168, 173–174, 176, 184
Dhāraṇī of the Bodhisattva With a Thousand Hands and Eyes, 46, 79
Dharma, xv, 15–16, 18, 21, 41, 59, 102, 112, 117–118, 132, 149–151, 153, 159, 161–162, 170, 176, 181
Dharma medicine (hōyaku 法藥), 153, 159, 161–162, 170, 176
Dharmagupta vinaya, 21
diagnosis, 24, 44, 101
Diamond-World Mandala (Vajradhātu maṇḍala), 27, 78
diarrhea, 88, 144
diet, 84, 167, 191
disability, 10
disability studies, 10
Discourse on the Stages of Concentration Practice (Yōgācārabhūmi-śāstra), 71
diseases, 5, 15, 17, 24, 31–32, 34–36, 41–42, 44, 46, 63, 67, 73, 78–79, 81, 83–85, 87–89, 91–92, 96, 98, 100, 122–123, 129, 143, 151, 160, 165, 189
diseases, general; See also disability; impairment; Wind Illness
– boils, 45, 84, 126, 129
– cancer, 122
– cataracts, 17, 76, 79–80, 87–88, 90–91, 101, 109, 127
– cause of disease, 105
– chronic diseases, 15
– diarrhea, 88, 144
– disease names, 10
– epilepsy, 34
– hot and cold diseases, 41, 161
– leprosy (Hansen's disease), 129
– malaria, 32, 39
– sight-related diseases, 5, 17, 67, 78–79, 81, 83, 85, 87, 89, 91–92, 96, 98, 100, 189
– sores, 14, 44–45, 85
– women's diseases, 84, 122–123
dispensary (seyakuin 施藥院), 13, 62, 129, 135, 138, 183
Divaricate saposhnikovia, 89
divination, 3, 92, 97, 169
divine intervention, 1, 92
doba 土馬, 166
doctors, 6–7, 9, 11, 34, 65, 82, 88, 90–91, 93–94, 96, 98–101, 108–109, 127, 135, 137, 141, 145, 168, 170, 173, 192–194; See also monastic doctor, physician
doctors (kusushi 醫師), 65
dog, 80, 84, 156, 160, 167, 183
Dōgen Kigen 道元希玄 (1200–1253), 115
dōjutsu 道術 ("techniques of the Way"), 67
Dōkyō 道鏡 (d. 772), 62
donation, 17, 99, 129–130, 133, 184
dōsojin 道祖神, 174
dreams, 132
Dunhuang, 14, 71
Dutch School (rangaku 蘭学), 9
dying, 150, 165, 191

ear, 44, 72–73, 83
Earth God (Chijin 地神), 108
Echigo no Tansuke 越後丹介, 169, 173–174, 187
effectiveness, 1–3, 35, 39, 81, 90, 120, 126, 133, 152, 162
efficacy, 17, 39, 56, 79, 136
effigies, 66–67
Egami Namio's 江上波夫 (1906–2002), 164
Egypt, 1, 39
eight causes of suffering, 12
eight fields of merit (hachi fukuden 八福田), 129, 192
Eight Generals (Hasshōgun 八将軍), 125
eight kinds of suffering (hakku 八苦), 129, 192
Eison 叡尊 (1201–1290), 131, 183–184
elixir of immortality, 93
ema 絵馬, 166

Index

emakimono 絵巻物 (picture scrolls), 10
embryology, 68, 119–120, 179
Empedocles, 37
empowerment, 65, 70, 72, 74–76, 78, 80, 82, 84, 86, 88, 90, 109–110, 113, 173, 175–176, 181
Encyclopedia of Childbirth (*Sanshō ruijūshō* 産生類聚抄), 120
Engishiki 延喜式, 139, 145, 166
enjudō 延壽堂, 151
enlightenment (*bodhi*, Jp. *bodai* 菩提), 51, 57, 75, 114–115, 120, 128, 191; See also awakening
entangled histories, 49
En'yū Tennō 円融天皇 (r. 969–984), 123
epidemics, 9, 11, 15, 54, 138, 166, 174
equine medicine, xii, 5, 18–19, 152–158, 161, 163–182, 184–188, 190
Equine Medicine Book of the Anzai School (*Anzai-ryū ba'isho* 安西流馬医書), 177
Essence (*jing*, Jp. *sei* 精), 26–27, 88, 104
Essential Subtleties on the Silver Sea (*Yinhai jinwei* 銀海精微), 28, 30, 90
Essentials for Horse Doctors (*Ba'i daigo* 馬医醍醐), 168
Essentials of Medicine (*Ishinpō* 医心方), 9–10, 17, 81, 122, 125, 145
eta 穢多, 188
Europe, ix, 14, 33–34, 36, 40–41, 49–50, 77, 97–98, 137, 141, 152, 158
Evans-Pritchard, Edward Evan (1902–1973), 38, 125
evil, 68, 71, 116, 125, 184
evil (*jagi* 邪義), 68
excellent horse (Sk. *aśvaratna*, Jp. *mahō* 馬寶), 166, 187
excorcism, 15, 102
expulsion ceremony (*hakken-shiki* 撥遣式), 74
eye, xi, 6, 14, 17, 24–29, 31, 43–44, 46, 67, 70–84, 86–110, 143, 163, 189, 196; See also blindness; cataracts; five rings and eight boundaries (of the eye); ophthalmology
eye (*gen* 眼), 72
eye-opening ceremony (*kaigan kuyō* 開眼供養), 6, 73–75, 77, 80, 143

Fan Kuai 樊噲, 169, 173
Fanshi yaohan 番視瑤函, 98
fecundity, 187
female bodies, 16, 18, 113–115, 119
female hygiene, 121
female monastic order, 121, 131–132
female sexual organ, 117
femininity, 118
fengbing 風病 (Wind Illness), 88
fertility, 112–113, 131
fetus, 120, 123
fever, 36, 84, 123, 134, 161
field of compassion (*hiden'in* 悲田院), 129, 139, 183
field of gratitude (*onden* 恩田), 183
field of respect (*kyōden'in* 敬田院), 183
Fields of Merit (*fukuden* 福田, Sk. *puṇya-kṣetra*), 129, 192
Fields of Merit Formulae (*Fukudenhō* 福田方), 129
Filliozat, Jean (1906–1982), 42
fire, 28–29, 31, 53, 66–67, 89, 104, 130, 150
fire offering ceremony, 66
fishing, 167
Five Agents (*wuxing* 五行), xiii, 28–29
Five Buddhas (*gobutsu* 五仏), 26–27, 29, 97, 189
Five Elements (in Indian medicine), 28, 31
Five Fields of Learning (*pañca-vidyā*), 21
Five Hindrances and Three Subordinations (*goshō sanju* 五障三従), 114
Five Medicines (*goyaku* 五薬), 18, 142, 150
five principal viscera (*zang* 臟), 27
five rings and eight boundaries (of the eye) (*gorin hakkaku* 五輪八廓), 97
Five Spheres (of the eye), 24, 26–30
Five Viscera Five Buddhas (*gozō gobutsu* 五臟五仏), 97
Five Wisdom Buddhas (*gochi nyorai* 五智如來), 27
Flower of Eternity (*Chiyomigusa* 千代見草), 191
Flower Ornament Sutra, 59, 117
folklore studies, 6, 64–65, 70, 125
food, 18, 20, 36, 86, 105, 115, 124–125, 164
food taboos, 124–125

Formulae for Longevity and Curing (*Chōsei ryōyōhō* 長生療養方), 146, 151
Four Noble Truths, 44
Four Supports (*shie* 四依), 1, 18
Four-Part Vinaya, 1, 21–22, 61
Frazer, James George (1854–1938), 38, 124–125
fu mushroom, 155
Fu Viscera, 28, 88
fūbyō 風病 (Wind Illness), 88
fudoki 風土記, 52
Fujikawa Yū 富士川游 (1865–1940), 7–8, 70
Fujiwara Ken'i 藤原兼意 (1072-ca. 1169), 146–148
Fujiwara Masachika 藤原政近 (dates unknown), 167
Fujiwara no Fuhito 藤原不比等 (658/659–720), 128
Fujiwara no Michinori 藤原通憲 (1106–1160), 148
Fujiwara no Sukeyo 藤原佐世 (847–897), 86, 163
Fujiwara no Takaie 藤原隆家 (979–1044), 92–93
Fujiwara Sadaie 藤原定家 (or Teika, 1162–1241), 94, 145
Fujiwara Sadakane 藤原定兼 (dates unknown), 146
Fujiwara 藤原, 53
Fujiwara-kyō 藤原京, 57
fujutsu 巫術 (magical, shamanistic techniques), 67, 82
Fukane Sukehito 深根輔仁 (dates unknown), 144
fukuden 福田 (Fields of Merit), 129, 192
Fukudenhō 福田方, 129
funerary objects, 164
fungus, 77, 157–158
Funsen sōjō 粉川僧正, 182
furanyaku 腐爛藥 (putrid urine for healing), 150
Furusawa Gentai 古澤元泰 (ca. 1762-?), 100–101

gaki 餓鬼 (hungry ghosts), 114
gall bladder, 28, 180
gama 蒲 (cattail), 173
gan 癌 (cancer), 122
Ganjin 鑑真 (Ch. Jianzhen 鑑真, 688–763), 21, 62
Ganron 眼論, 82, 86
garbha, 119–120
Garbhadhātu maṇḍala, 27
Garbhāvakrānti-sūtra, 120
gardening, 138
gazetteers, 52, 130, 165
gen 眼 (eye), 72, 104
Genbō 玄昉 (d. 746), 61
Genmei Tennō 元明天皇 (r. 707–715), 58
Genshō Tennō 元正天皇 (r. 715–724), 58, 102–103, 128
gestation, 68, 119
ghosts, ix, 114, 188
ginger, 89, 151
Ginkakuji 銀閣寺, 140
ginseng, 141–142, 144
glow worm, 89
Go-Shirakawa Tennō 後白河天皇 (r. 1155–1158), 148–149
goblin, 94
gochi nyorai 五智如來 (Five Wisdom Buddhas), 27
Godaigo Tennō 後醍醐天皇 (r. 1318–1332/1339), 184
gods (*ten* 天, Sk. *deva*), 114
gofu 護符 (charms, talismans), 3
gokō 牛黄 (ox bezoar), 66
Gokurakuji Temple 極楽寺, 183
golden needle (for cataract couching), xii, 80, 82, 88, 90–91
golden stylet (*konbei* 金箆, *konchū* 金籌), 75, 81
goma 護摩 (fire offering ceremony), 150
Gorai Shigeru 五来重 (1908–1993), 64–65
gorin hakkaku 五輪八廓 ("five rings and eight boundaries" of the eye), 97
Gosei-ha 後世派, 140
Goseihō-ha 後世方派, 140
goshō sanju 五障三從 (Five Hindrances and Three Subordinations), 114
goyaku 五藥 (Five Medicines), 18
goze 瞽女 (visually impaired female musicians), 107

gozō gobutsu 五臓五仏 (Five Viscera Five Buddhas), 97
Gozu-ten'ō 牛頭天王, 125, 166
Great Medicine King (Dai'iō 大医王, Sk. Vai-dyarāja), 104
Greek medicine, 37, 91
gynecology, 120
Gyōki 行基 (668–749), 139
Gyokuyō-ki 玉葉記, 94
Gyōyo 行誉 (dates unknown), 184

hachi fukuden 八福田 (eight fields of merit), 129
Hachiman 八幡, 102, 138
Haguroha 羽黒派, 107
hakase 博士 ("yin-yang diviner"), 68
hakken-shiki 撥遣式 (expulsion ceremony), 174
hakku 八苦 (eight kinds of suffering), 129
hakuba no sechie 白馬節会 (white horse ceremony), 166
Hakuraku/*hakuraku* 伯楽, 169–170, 185
haniwa 埴輪, 165
hārītakī (*kariroku* 訶梨勒), 79–80, 142, 144
Hashimoto Dōha 橋本道派 (dates unknown), 168
Hasshōgun 八将軍, 125
Hattori Toshirō 服部敏良 (1906–1992), 7–8, 48, 52, 61–62, 102, 141
Hayagrīva, 134, 186
healing, general
– exorcistic healing arts (*ijutsu* 毉術), 102
– faith healing, 1–2
– healing by prayer (*kiryō* 祈療), 11
– medical arts (*ijutsu* 醫術), 62
– miracle healing, 2, 10, 67, 71, 102–103, 105, 193
– religious healing, 1
– this-worldly healing, 18
health care, 9, 11–13, 18, 195
health, general, 24
heart, 25–27, 29, 83, 102, 134
Heijō Tennō 平城天皇 (r. 806–809), 53, 58, 195
Heijō-kyō 平城京 (Nara), 58
Heike monogatari 平家物語, 70
hells (*jigoku* 地獄, Sk. *naraka*), 114

herbal (compendium), 145, 153
herbs, xii, 14, 18, 85, 126, 130, 133, 135, 137–139, 141, 144, 153, 159, 173, 184
heresy, 23, 69, 196
heterodoxy, 1–2, 12, 43, 68–69, 196
hiden'in 悲田院 (field of compassion), 129, 139, 183
hidensho 秘伝書 (secret records), 96, 177
hijiri 聖 (holy person, ascetic), 102, 117
hikeiroku 鞞醯勒 (*vibhītaka*), 142
hinin 非人 ("non-human"), 131–132, 184, 188
hippiatry, xii, 160, 162–163, 169, 177, 182
hippology, 163
history of medicine, 4, 6–9, 13, 32, 53, 62, 64, 70, 109, 189, 196
History of the Tsubosakadera (*Tsubosakadera korōden* 壺坂古老伝), 103
hiyaku 秘薬 (panacea), 161
Hōei 法栄 (dates unknown), 62
Hōgonji 宝厳寺, 99–100
Hōjō Masako 北条政子 (1156–1225), 151
Hokkeji Temple 法華寺, xi, xiv, 99, 103, 121, 128–131, 133
Holder of (esoteric) Knowledge (*vidyādhara*), 186
Holy Prescriptions for Universal Relief in the Taiping Era (*Taiping shenghui fang* 太平聖恵方), 87, 94–95, 97
homa (fire offering ceremony), 150
Hōnen 法然 (1133–1212), 23
honey, 1, 18, 80
Honzō kōmoku 本草綱目, 145
Honzō wamyō 本草和名, 144
honzō 本草 (*materia medica*), 135–136, 144–145
Hōren 法蓮 (dates unknown), 62, 102–103
horse classics, 158, 169
horse doctors (*ba'ishi* 馬醫師), 161, 166, 168, 176, 185
horse hospital, 184
horse rider theory, 164
Horse-headed Avalokiteśvara, 185–187
horses, general; See also animals; *aouma no sechie*; excellent horse; *hakuba no sechie*; horse hospital; Horse-headed

Avalokiteśvara; veterinarians; veterinary
　　　　medicine
– clay horses (*doba* 土馬), 166
– equestrian culture, 164–165, 167
– hippiatry, xii, 160, 162–163, 169, 177, 182
– hippology, 163
– horse, 18, 84, 111, 134, 151, 156–170,
　　　173–182, 184–188, 190
– horse breeding, 166–167, 177, 181
– horse classics, 158, 169
– horse doctors, 161, 166, 168, 176, 185
– horse-headed deities, 168, 185–187
– horsemeat, 167
– racehorses, 185
Hōshō 寶性 (Ratnasaṃbhava), 26
hospices, 151, 192
hospital (*ryōbyōjo* 療病所), 183
hot disease, 161
hot springs, 130
Hōyōshō 宝要抄, 147
Hua Tuo 華佗 (ca. 145–208), 89
Huangdi neijing 黄帝内經, 141
human sacrifice, 106
humans (*ningen* 人間, Sk. *manuṣya*), 114
humors, 12, 36
hungry ghosts (*gaki* 餓鬼, Sk. *preta*), 114
hunting, 167
hygiene, 9, 12–13, 21, 84, 121, 130; See also
　　　bathing; female hygiene

Ichibata-ryū 一畑流, 99
Ichigo daigyō himitsushū 期大要祕密集, 151
igaku 医学 (medicine), 8, 10–11, 61, 64
ijutsu 醫術 (exorcistic healing arts), 102
ijutsu 醫術 (medical arts), 62
Ikkan Wakō 一閑和尚 (dates unknown), 168
illness, 2–3, 8, 11, 13–14, 24, 26, 45, 56,
　　　62, 67–68, 78, 88, 93, 95, 101, 104,
　　　112, 123, 196
immortality, 93, 135, 150
impairment, x, 1, 10, 71, 92, 94–96, 98,
　　　100, 102, 104–108, 110
impurity, 34, 80, 120, 130
Inbe (Imube) 斎部, 53
incantation (*jinju* 神呪), 68
incantations, 3, 17, 41, 45–46, 64–69, 90,
　　　104–105, 176, 183, 189, 194

incense, 143, 145, 147–150
incorporation, 40, 52–55, 57–58, 60,
　　　63–64, 69, 102, 128, 195
incubation ritual (*komori* 籠り), 94, 99
Indian bread, 157–158
Indian medical tradition, 5, 87
infant, 112
infertility, 17
initiation, 1, 16, 46, 75–78, 109, 130, 181,
　　　193
Inner Canon of the Yellow Emperor (*Huangdi
　　　neijing* 黄帝内經), 141
Iōzan Ichibataji 醫王山一畑寺, 99
Iōzan Yakushiji 醫王山薬師寺, 96, 99
iryō 医療 (medical therapeutics), 10
Ise jingū 伊勢神宮, 57
Ise Shrine (Ise jingū 伊勢神宮), 57
Ishihara Akira 石原明 (1924–1980), 8, 83,
　　　94–95, 190
Ishinpō 医心方, 9–10, 17, 82–83, 85–87,
　　　90, 93, 122, 125–127, 145–146, 196
issai shujō 一切衆生 (all sentient beings),
　　　188
itako 巫女 (female medium), 108
iwai 祝 (blessing formula), 126

jagi 邪義 (evil), 68
Japanese Materia Medica (*Yamato honzō* 大
　　　和本草), 145
Japanese Names for the Materia Medica
　　　(*Honzō wamyō* 本草和名), 144
Japanese Society for Oriental Medicine, 8
Java, 22
jealous warriors (*ashura* 阿修羅, Sk. *asura*),
　　　114
Jianzhen 鑑真 (Jp. Ganjin, 688–763), 21, 62
jigoku 地獄 (hells, Sk. *naraka*), 114
jihi 慈悲 (active compassion), 9
Jikun 慈訓 (691?-777), 62
Jin ten ainōshō 塵添壒嚢鈔, 185
jindō 神道 ("way of the gods," Shinto), 55,
　　　170
jing 精 (Essence), 27, 41, 88
jinju 神呪 (incantation), 68
jintai kaibōzu 人体解剖図 (anatomical
　　　charts), 190
jishō 自性 (sense of self), 72

Jishōji 慈照寺, 140
Jitō Tennō 持統天皇 (r. 690–697), 57
Jīvaka, 85, 89, 175
jōbutsu 成仏 (buddhahood), 22, 75–76, 119
Jōgen 成賢 (1162–1232), 148–149
Jōkai 乗海 (1116–1178), 149
Jōkei 貞慶 (1155–1213), 103–104
Jones, William Henry Samuel (1876–1963), 32–37, 125
ju 呪 (spell, incantation), 3, 104
jugon 呪言 (spell, incantation), 65
jukyō 儒教 (Confucianism), 62, 112
jūnishi 十二支 (twelve stems), 125
Jūnishin 十二神, 97

kaba 蒲 (cattail), 173
Kaibara Ekken 貝原益軒 (1630–1714), 145
kaigan kuyō 開眼供養 (eye-opening ceremony), 74
kaji 加持 (Sk. *adhiṣṭhāna*; "assistance"), 65–67, 75, 189
Kajiwara Shōzen 梶原性全 (1265–1337), 15, 95, 149
Kakken 覺憲 (1131–1213), 104
Kakuban 覺鑁 (1095–1134), 151
Kakuzen 覺禪 (1143–?), 113
kami 神, 55, 57–58, 60, 63–65, 100, 112, 130, 174, 176, 181, 183, 192, 195
Kamitsumiya 上宮 (ca. 573–622), 111; See also Shōtoku Taishi; Umayado
Kan Yakuō Yakujō nibosatsu-kyō 觀藥王藥上二菩薩經, 14–15
kan'i 官医 (court medicine), 184
Kan'i 寬意 (1062–1101), 146, 148, 184
Kana Ankishū 仮名安驥集, 168
kanbyōsō 看病僧 ("nurse monks"), 61
Kanjizai 觀自在, 15
kanjō 灌頂 (*abhiṣeka*; consecration), 75, 185
Kannon 觀音, 15, 99–100, 103–106, 133–134, 140, 185–187, 193
kanpō 漢方 (Chinese-style medicine), 8–9, 124, 143
Kanreiroku 感靈錄, 67, 103–104
Kanshōji Temple 勸勝寺, 185
Kanzeon 觀世音, 15
karafuro 浴室 (bathhouse), 129
kariroku 訶梨勒 (*hārītakī*), 142

karma, 111
karmic retribution, 15, 92
Kegon-kyō 華嚴經, 59, 117
Keiteiki-shū 啓迪集 (*Collection of Writings of the Keiteki [Academy]*), 98
ki 氣, 気, xiii, 26–27
kidneys, 25, 27, 83
Kikei Shinzui 季瓊真蘂 (1401–1469), 139
killing of animals, 183, 188
King of Healing, 14–15, 184
King of Knowledge (*vidyārāja*), 186
Kinkakuji 金閣寺, 139
Kinmei Tennō 欽明天皇 (r. 539–571), 56, 111
kirishitankyō 基督教 (Christianity), 62
kiryō 祈療 (healing by prayer), 11
Kissayōjōki 喫茶養生記, 151
Kitano Yūrin 北野有隣 (d. 1410), 129, 192
knowledge transfer, 1, 4, 98
Kōfukuji Temple 興福寺, 163, 187
kofun 古墳, 164–165
koidō 古医道 (ancient Japanese medicine), 64
Kojidan 古事談, 147
Kojiki 古事記, 63, 173
Kōken Tennō 孝謙天皇 (r. 749–758), 62, 138
Kokuruishō 穀類抄, 147
komori 籠り (incubation), 94, 99
Kōmyō kōgō 光明皇后 (659–760), 80, 128–129, 131, 133, 138, 142–143, 184
kōmyō shingon 光明真言 (mantra of light), 184
Kōmyō, Queen Consort; Empress, 80, 128–129, 131, 133, 138, 142–143, 184
Konjaku monogatarishū 今昔物語集, 130
Korea, 52–53, 58, 83, 87, 92, 94, 110, 130, 136, 142, 144, 163, 165, 193
Kōtoku Tennō 孝徳天皇 (r. 645–654), 57, 165
Kōyakushō 香藥抄, 148
Kōyōshō 香要抄, 147
kudokuyu 功德湯 (warm water merit), 130
Kuhn, Thomas (1922–1996), 40
Kujaku myōō 孔雀明王, 112
Kujō Kanezane 九条兼實 (1149–1207), 94
Kūkai 空海 (773–835), 27, 46, 65–66, 69, 76, 112, 148
Kumoku-ryō 厩牧令, 182
kusushi 醫師 (doctors), 65

kyōden'in 敬田院 (field of respect), 183
Kyōkai 景戒 (dates unknown), 103, 108, 118
Kyoto Buddha Eye Association (Kyōto butsugen kyōkai 京都仏眼協会), 108
Kyōto butsugen kyōkai 京都仏眼協会, 108
Kyōu Library (Kyōu Shooku 杏雨書屋), 98, 147–148
Kyōu Shooku 杏雨書屋, 98, 147–148

Later Records of Japan, Continued (*Shoku Nihon kōki* 続日本後紀), 139
laukika, 46, 189, 194
lay Buddhists, 17, 22, 48, 193
leather, 132, 188
Legal Codes for Stables and Pastures (*Kumoku-ryō* 厩牧令), 182
legends, 5–6, 10, 15, 17, 44, 67, 71, 92, 102, 105–106, 116–118, 129–130, 147, 166; See also *setsuwa*
Leigong 雷公, 169–171
leprosy, 13, 129–132, 183
leprosy (Hansen's disease), 129
liberation, 21, 71, 73, 128, 131, 188–189, 191, 194
licorice, 142, 144
Light of Asia, 50
literacy, 55
liu chu 六畜 (the six domestic animals), 167
liver, 25, 27, 29, 83, 91
local gazetteers (fudoki 風土記), 52
logos, 35
lokōttara, 46, 189, 194
longevity, 57, 84, 136, 146, 149, 151, 174, 191
longevity medicines, 174
Longmu yanlun 龍樹眼論 (*Nāgārjuna's Treatise*), 82
Longmu 龍木 (Nāgārjuna), 82, 87
Lotus Sutra, xiii, 59, 61, 99, 107, 114, 117–118, 128, 166, 191
Luhmann, Niklas (1927–1998), 45, 191
lung, xv, 25, 27, 29, 83–84, 107

magea, 34
magic, ix, 2–3, 7, 16, 20–24, 26, 28, 30, 32, 34–43, 66–67, 99, 134, 189
magical cures, 42
magical medicine, xii, 3
magical techniques, 19, 67, 194
Mahābhārata, 6
Mahāmāyūrī vidyārājñī (Jp. Kujaku myōō 孔雀明王), 112
Mahāprajñāpāramitā-śāstra, 73
Mahāsāṃghika vinaya, 61
Mahāvairocana, 26–27, 31, 46, 75, 77
Mahāvairocana-sūtra, 46, 75, 77
Mahāyāna, 14, 21–22, 45, 78, 112, 120, 132, 150, 192
mahō 馬寶 (excellent horse), 166
Majima Seigan 馬島清眼 (d. 1379), 96–98
malaria, 32, 39
Man'anhō 万安方, 95
Manase Dōsan 曲直瀬道三 (1507–1594), xiii, 98, 140–141
mandala (*maṇḍala*), 27, 31, 75, 78, 133, 146, 186
mantra, xiii, 27, 41, 44–45, 74, 134, 161, 168, 170, 173, 176, 184–185
mantra of light (*kōmyō shingon* 光明真言), 184
manuṣya (human being), 114
mappō 末法, 151
masseurs, 70, 108
mastitis, 122
materia medica; See also *bencao*; *honzō*
– fossils, 143
– herbal (compendium), 145, 153
– *materia medica* literature, 5, 61, 144, 159
– metals, 135
– minerals, 135
– plant-based *materia medica*, 5, 135, 144
Matsura Sayohime 松浦さよひめ, 105–107
medical facilities, 129, 184, 192
medical systems, 8, 36, 46
medical therapeutics (*iryō* 医療), 10
medicinal gardens, 5, 134–142, 144, 146, 148, 150, 152, 154, 156, 158, 160, 162
medicinal gardens (*yakuen* 薬園), 137
medicinals, 141–144
Medicine Buddha, xii, 13–14, 57, 65, 97–98, 130, 137, 139, 142, 153, 159, 161–162, 170, 193
medicine, general; See also *āyurveda*; medicinals; medicines
– ancient Japanese medicine, 52, 64

- bovine medicine, 182
- Buddhist medicine, 3, 5, 9–13, 15, 28, 46–48, 61–63, 69, 72, 85, 196
- Chinese medicine, 4, 32, 47–48, 60, 62, 82, 85, 91, 124, 135, 140–141
- Chinese-style medicine, 9, 12, 15, 26, 28–29, 39–40, 52–53, 55, 57, 61, 64, 122, 141, 158, 160, 173, 189
- Christian medicine, 11
- demonic medicine, 6
- Dharma medicine (*hōyaku* 法薬), 153, 159, 161–162, 170, 176
- dietetics, 41, 191
- equine medicine, xii, 5, 18–19, 152–158, 161, 163–182, 184–188, 190
- Greek medicine, 37, 91
- hippiatry, xii, 160, 162–163, 169, 177, 182
- Indian medicine, 6, 12, 42, 52, 61, 80, 98
- Japanese medicine, 7–10, 15, 32, 52, 62, 64, 83, 108
- Japanese-style medicine, 64
- magical medicine, xii, 3
- medicine, definitions, 3
- metaphors, medical, 78, 81
- monastic medicine, 12
- obstetrics, 84, 122–125, 127
- ophthalmology, xii, 25, 28–29, 70–72, 81–83, 86–93, 95–98, 100–101, 108–109, 177, 189–190
- scientific medicine, 2–3, 37, 43
- Sino-Japanese medicine, 8
- surgery, 17, 41, 47, 75–78, 80–81, 85, 90–91, 95, 97–98, 196
- talismanic medicine, 66
- traditional medicine, 9, 189

medicines
- drugs, 21, 39, 45, 88, 91, 135–143, 145–151, 159
- Five Medicines (*goyaku* 五薬), 18, 142, 150
- ingredients, 10, 18, 89, 150
- longevity medicines, 174
- panaceas, 134–136, 138, 140, 142, 144, 146, 148, 150–162, 185, 189
- putrid medicine, 1, 18
- *shōyaku* 生薬 (crude drugs), 143
- substances, xii, 1, 10, 18, 62, 76, 78, 80, 113, 134, 136, 142–144, 147

medicus, 32
meditation, 51, 102
medium (spiritual), 11, 18, 70, 93, 102, 107–108, 170
Meigan gokui hiden 明眼極意秘伝, 24–25, 27, 31
Meigekki 明月記, 94, 145
Memorandum of Medicines (*Shuju yakuchō* 種々薬帳), 143
Memyō 馬鳴 (Aśvaghoṣa), 181
menstruation, 113–114, 116
menstruation sutra, 116
mercuric sulfide, 126
Meryō 馬寮 (Bureau of Horses), 163
metals, 135
Mezu Kannon 馬頭観音, 185
midwifery, 127
midwives, 111
miko 巫女 (shamanic medium), 131, 170, 173, 176
miko 神子, 11
military, 4, 19, 54–56, 67, 98, 140, 163, 167–168, 176, 183, 187, 194
milk, 112, 137; See also dairy products; mother's milk
Minami hokkeji Temple 南法華寺, 99
Minami yakuen 南薬園, 138
minerals, 135
miracles, x, 2, 10, 17, 49, 67, 71, 100, 102–105, 130, 132, 150, 161–162, 193
miraculous cures, 15
Miraculous Stories from Japan (*Nihon ryōiki* 日本霊異記), 103, 117
mistletoe, 157–158
modernity, xi, 7
monasteries, 12, 20, 22, 59, 94, 128, 192
monasteries (*kokubunsōji* 国分僧寺), 128
monastic doctor, physician (*sōi* 僧医), 11, 38, 61–62, 94, 109, 127, 129, 135, 145, 183–184, 192–194
monastic medicine, 12
monastic rules, 20–22
monkey, 163, 175
monks, 6, 11–12, 18–22, 42, 44, 53, 57, 59, 61–62, 66–67, 70, 94–96, 98–99, 101–102, 108–109, 113, 117–118, 128–

132, 134, 142, 146, 149–150, 170, 181, 183–185, 189, 191–193, 196
Monmu Tennō 文武天皇 (r. 697–707), 128
Montoku Tennō 文徳天皇 (r. 850–858), 66
mōsō 盲僧 (blind priest), 92, 108
mother's milk, 80, 89, 135
motherhood, 113
mothers, xii, 17, 80, 119, 131
Mount Tamura Dharma medicine (*Tamurasan hōyaku* 田村山法薬), 161–162
mountain asceticism, 65, 67, 102, 191–192
moxa, 158
moxibustion, 83, 122–123, 158, 183
mugwort, 157–158
mujutsu 巫術 (magical, shamanistic techniques), 67
Mūlasarvāstivādins, 112
mulberry, 151
Murasaki Shikibu 紫式部 (ca. 973–1025), 111
mūrti (physical appearances of a deity), 74
muscles, 26–27, 31
muscles/tendons, 26
mushokushi 無食子 (wasp gall), 144
musicians, 70, 106–107, 109
Mutō-shin 武塔神, 125
Myōan Eisai 明菴栄西 (1141–1215), 151
Myōgen-in 明眼院, 95–96, 98–99, 109
myōjin 明神, 106
myōō 明王 (Wisdom King), 112
Myōon 妙音, 107
Myriad Relief Formulae (*Man'anhō* 万安方), 95
myrobalan, 142
myths, 10, 124, 173, 175

Nāgārjuna, 73, 82–83, 85–88, 97
Nāgārjuna (Longmu 龍木, Longshu 龍樹), 82
Nāgārjuna Bodhisattva's Ophthalmological Treatise (Jp. *Ryūju bosatsu ganron*, Ch. *Longshu pusa yanlun* 龍樹菩薩眼論), 82–83, 87, 97
Nāgārjuna's Treatise, 87
nāginī, 114, 118
Nakarai Zuisaku 半井瑞策 (1522–1596), 123
Nakatomi 中臣, 53
Nakayama Shigeru 中山茂 (1928–2014), 40
naraka (hells), 114

narratives, ix, 5, 99, 101, 104–106, 114, 117, 133
nativism, 53, 63–64
natural laws, 29
Needham, Joseph (1900–1995), 48
Neo-Confucianism, 4, 152
Nepal, 50
Nichiren 日蓮 (1222–1282), 184, 191
Nihon kanreiroku 日本感霊録, 103; See also *Kanreiroku*
Nihon ryōiki 日本霊異記, 103, 117–118
Nihon shoki 日本書紀, 58, 63, 111, 165
Nihon tōyō igakkai 日本東洋医学会, 8
Nihonkoku genzai shomokuroku 日本國見在書目録, 163
Ningai 仁海 (951–1046), 186
ningen 人間 (human being), 114
Ninmyō Tennō 仁明天皇 (r. 833–850), 139
Ninnaji 仁和寺, 146, 148–149
Ninshō 忍性 (1217–1303), 183–184
Nobel, Johannes (1887–1960), 39, 59
non-humans (*hinin* 非人), 131, 188
non-worldly (Jp. *shusse* 出世, Sk. *lokōttara*), 46, 189
noroi 呪 (spell, incantation), 3
nourishing life (Ch. *yangsheng*, Jp. *yōjō* 養生), 150–151, 192
nunneries, 59, 128, 131
nunneries (*kokubun niji* 国分尼寺), 128
nuns, 1, 17–18, 20–22, 42, 53, 56–57, 59, 66–67, 74, 102, 121, 127–128, 131–132, 134, 142, 150, 191–193, 196; See also *Collection of Rules for the Nuns*; female monastic order
nurse monks (*kanbyōsō* 看病僧), 61–62

Obinata Daijō 大日方大乗 (1877–1970), 9
obstetrics, 84, 122–125, 127
offerings, 1, 66, 74–75, 129, 134, 143, 165–166, 175, 192
Ogawa Kenzaburō 小川剣三郎 (1870–1933), 70, 190
oil, 1, 18, 143
oilseed, 89
ōjō 往生 (birth in the Pure Land), 11
Ōkagami 大鏡, 93–94

Okamoto Yūken 岡本由顕 (dates unknown), 123
Ōkuninushi 大国主, 173
omniscience, 35, 49, 72
Ōnamuchi no kami 大己貴神, 63, 161–162, 170, 172–173, 176
onden 恩田 (field of gratitude), 183
ophthalmology, xii, 25, 28–29, 70–72, 81–83, 86–93, 95–98, 100–101, 108–109, 177, 189–190
ordination, 1, 17–18, 20–22, 44, 59, 71, 101, 121, 128, 130–132, 188, 194
orthodoxy, 1–2, 43, 51, 196
Osakabe Shinnō 刑部親王 (d. 705), 128
ox bezoar (gokō 牛黄), 66, 126

pain, 15, 38, 88, 114, 116, 124, 134, 184, 188, 191
panaceas, 134–136, 138, 140, 142, 144, 146, 148, 150–162, 185, 189
pañca-buddha (Five Buddhas), 27
pañca-vidyā (Five Fields of Learning), 21
parasol tree fruit, 89
parturition, 116, 125
Peacock King Dhāraṇī Sutra (Kujakuō jukyō 孔雀王呪經), 112
Peacock Wisdom Queen (Mahāmāyūrī vidyārājñī), 112
pearls, 90
penis, 115
pepper, 144
perinatal care, 127
perinatal rituals, 112
pets, 167, 185
pharmaceutics, 11, 17–18, 52, 66, 95, 135, 137, 144, 146–148
pharmacognosy, 5, 136
pharmacy, 41, 192
Phyllanthus emblica, 142
physis, 37
picture scroll (emakimono 絵巻物), 10
picture scrolls, 10, 95, 106, 151–152, 166
pig, 80, 89, 167
pig gall, 89
pigeon, 89
pilgrimage, 12, 17, 67, 92–93, 98–101, 103, 105, 162, 182, 193

pills, 88–89
plants
– botanical garden, 138
– botany, 5, 136, 152–153
– gardening, 138
– herbal (compendium), 145, 153
– herbal remedy, 162
– herbal treatment, 122
– herbology, 137
– herbs, xii, 14, 18, 85, 126, 130, 133, 135, 137–139, 141, 144, 153, 159, 173, 184
– medicinal gardens, 5, 134–142, 144, 146, 148, 150, 152, 154, 156, 158, 160, 162
– medicinal herbs, 14, 18, 85, 126, 130, 135, 137–139, 153, 173, 184
– plant names, 53, 145, 153, 159–160
– plant-based *materia medica*, 5, 135, 144
– pleasure gardens, 137, 139
– tea plant, 145, 151
poison, 66, 112, 155, 162
pollution, 125, 130
potency, xii, 1, 135
poulticing (anpō 罨法), 122
powder, 88–89, 126
prayer, 1, 11, 13, 50, 52, 56, 67, 100, 125, 133, 170, 175
precepts, 21–22, 62, 75, 113, 121–122, 131–132, 183
Precious Manual of Ophthalmology (Shenshi yaohan 審視瑤函), 90
pregnancy, 68, 84, 107, 113, 116, 122–124
preta (hungry ghosts), 114
prisca theologia, 40
Procedures of the Engi Era (Engishiki 延喜式), 139, 145, 166–167
procreation, 18, 68, 113, 187
puṇya-kṣetra (Field of Merit), 129
Pure Land, 11, 57, 119, 132–133, 140, 191
purification, 53, 67, 130, 166
purity, 34, 80, 130, 193
putrid urine for healing, 18

qi 氣, xiii-xiv, 26–27, 29, 86, 88, 141, 193
Qin shihuang 秦始皇, 175, 180
qinghaosu 青蒿素, 39

qingmang 清盲 ("clear blindness," cataracts), 87
quackery, 1, 36–37, 196

Rāga, 170
rangaku 蘭学 (Dutch studies), 9
ratio, 35
rationality, 38–39
Ratnasaṃbhava, xv, 26–27
recipe, 79, 89–90, 93, 162, 185
Record of Jade Leaves (*Gyokuyō-ki* 玉葉記), 94
Record of Japan (*Nihon shoki* 日本書紀), 58, 63, 111
Record of the Full Moon (*Meigekki* 明月記), 94, 145
Record on Drinking Tea for Nourishing Life (*Kissayōjōki* 喫茶養生記), 151
Records of Gratitude to the Numinous (*Kanreiroku* 感霊録), 67, 103
Records of Gratitude to the Numinous in Japan (*Nihon kanreiroku* 日本感霊録), 103
Records of Japan, Continued (*Shoku Nihongi* 続日本紀), 102, 138–139
relics, 74, 131, 139
remedies, 3, 10, 99, 120, 125, 158, 167–168, 177, 180, 182
Rennyo 蓮如 (1415–1499), 11
Repeated Views from a Box of Precious Jade (*Fanshi yaohan* 番視瑤函), 98
reproduction (sexual), 17, 24, 110, 112, 114, 120, 193
Revised Materia Medica (*Shinshū honzō* 新修本草), 144
rhubarb, 88, 142, 144
rice wine, 161
Ritual Manual for the Supplication of the Horse-headed Kannon (*Batō nenju giki* 馬頭念誦儀軌), 134
Ritual of the Six-syllable Sutra (*rokujikyōhō* 六字経法), 66–67
rituals (*shuhō* 修法), 65
Road Ancestor God (*dōsojin* 道祖神), 174
Rōben 良辯 (689–774), 62
rokudō 六道 (six realms of birth), 114

rokujikyōhō 六字経法 (*Ritual of the Six-syllable Sutra*), 66
Rokuonji 鹿苑寺, 139
Rubbish [Bag] with Selections from a Dust Bag (*Jin ten ainōshō* 塵添壒囊鈔), 185
Rubbish Bag (*Chiribukuro* 塵袋), 185
ryōbyōjo 療病所 (hospital), 183
Ryōin 良胤 (dates unknown), 185
Ryōji byō-kyō 療痔病經, 14, 44–45, 85

sacrifice, 93, 106, 165, 167
sacrificial practice, 165
sae no kami 塞の神, 174
Sagara 娑謁羅, 126
Saichō 最澄 (767–822), 21–22, 27
Sakanoshita babyōya 坂下馬病屋, 184
Sakanoshita Horse Hospital (Sakanoshita babyōya 坂下馬病屋), 184
Śākyamuni, xv, 8, 20, 23, 26–27, 56–57, 74, 166; See also Shaka
śalākā (spatula, rod), 77; See also golden needle (for cataract couching); golden stylet
salvation, 5, 16, 18, 22, 44–45, 57, 115, 120, 131, 133, 184, 188, 190–191, 193
saṃsāra (cycle of birth and death), 44, 113–114
sandalwood (Sk. *candana*, Jp. *sendan* 栴檀), 134, 144
Sang Hyang Kamahāyānan Mantrānaya, 77–78
sangha, 21, 127, 129, 131, 133, 142, 150
Sanjō Tennō 三条天皇 (r. 1011–1016), 93
sanko 三狐 ("three foxes"), 66
Sankyō 産経, 123
Sanshō ruijūshō 産生類聚抄, 120
Sarasvatī, 100
Sarvāstivāda vinaya, 61
Satō Keiun 佐藤慶雲 (dates unknown), 101
satori 悟 (seeing, understanding), 51
saving all sentient beings (*issai shujō* 一切衆生), 188
science, xii, 1–6, 8–9, 16, 24, 29, 32, 34, 37–43, 47–49, 95, 98, 101, 136, 147–148
scientia, 2
scientific medicine, 2–3, 37, 43

scientific revolution, 40
Scroll of Equine Medicine (Ba'i sōshi emaki 馬医草紙絵巻), xii, 152–158, 161, 168–173, 175–176, 181, 187
Scroll of Illness and Deformities (Yamai no sōshi 病草紙), 95, 196
secret, 16, 24–25, 27–28, 31, 43, 68–69, 86, 96–98, 100–101, 104, 109, 126, 146, 148, 150–151, 161, 175–177, 180–181, 193
secret records (hidensho 秘伝書), 28, 43, 97–98, 100
Secret Transmission about the Final Mystery of the Eye (Meigan gokui hiden 明眼極意秘伝), 24–25, 27, 31
Secret Treatise on the Repository of Quintuple Wisdom (Gochizō hishō 五智蔵秘抄), 68–69
seimō 清盲 ("clear blindness," cataracts), 87
Seiryōji Temple 清涼寺, 74
seken 世間 (worldly, secular), 46
sekkyō 説教 (sermon literature), 105
Selections from a Dust Bag (Ainōshō 塵嚢鈔), 185
Semimaru 蝉丸, 106–107
sendan 栴檀 (sandalwood), 134
Sengyou 僧祐 (445–518), 121
Senju sengen kanzeon bosatsu jibyō gōyakukyō 千手千眼觀世音菩薩治病合藥經, 14, 85
sense of self (Sk. svabhāva, Jp. jishō 自性), 72–73
sericulture, 175, 181
sermon literature (sekkyō 説教), 105
setsuwa 説話 (Buddhist legends), 10, 103, 116
sex change, 116, 119–120, 132–133
sexual activity, 17, 113, 115
sexual desire, 120
sexuality, 83–84, 113–114, 116–117, 119–120, 122, 132–133, 187
Shaka 釈迦 (Śākyamuni), 8, 26, 56
shamaness, medium (miko 巫女), 131, 170, 173, 176
shamanic mediums, 70
shamanism, 70, 82, 102, 170
shamanistic techniques, 82

shami 沙彌 (novice), 68, 102, 104
sheep, 161, 167
shelters (for animals), 183
Shengji zonglu 聖濟總錄, 87, 95
Shennong bencaojing jizhu 神農本草經集注, 144
Shennong 神農 (Jp. Shinnō, Divine Husbandman, Farmer), 63–64, 144, 169, 173
Shenshi yaohan 審視瑤函, 90
Shi Sengshen 釈僧深 (ca. 420–502), 86
shido no shami 私度の沙彌 (self-ordained novice), 68, 102
shie 四依 (Four Supports), 18
Shingon mikkyō 真言密教, 27
Shingon Risshū 真言律宗, 131–132, 183–184, 188, 194
Shingon 真言, 27, 65, 78, 112–113, 131–132, 135, 146–147, 149, 151, 177, 183–184, 186, 188, 194
Shinkaku 心覚 (1117–1180), 146, 148–149
Shinkyō-ryū 神教流, 100–101
Shinnō 神農 (Shennong), 144, 169, 173
Shinnyo 真如 (1211-?), 131–133
Shinshōin Nichion 心性院日遠 (1572–1642), 191
Shinshū honzō 新修本草, 144
Shinto, 52, 60, 64, 100, 126, 166, 170, 173, 185
shintō 神道 ("way of the gods," Shinto), 55
Shinzei 信西 (1106–1160), 148–149
Shinzei 真済 (800–860), 65
Shira'i Mitsutarō 白井光太郎 (1863–1932), 152
Shōgen 勝賢 (1138–1196), 148–149
Shōkokuji 相国寺, 140
Shoku Nihon kōki 続日本後紀, 139
Shoku Nihongi 続日本紀, 102
Shōmu Tennō 聖武天皇 (r. 724–749), 55, 58–60, 62, 128–129, 138–139, 142
Shōsōin 正倉院, 80, 129, 142–144
Shōtoku Taishi 聖徳太子, 57, 111, 131, 183
shōyaku 生薬 (crude drugs), 143
Shugendō 修験道, 102, 135
shugenja 修験者 (ascetic), 102
shuhō 修法 (rituals), 65
Shuju yakuchō 種々薬帳, 143

Shukaku Hōshinnō 守覚法親王 (1150–1202), 149
shukke 出家 (renouncing secular life), 113
shūkyō 宗教 (religion), 47
shusse 出世 (non-worldly), 46
Shutsu sanzō kishū 出三藏記集, 121
sickness, 10–11, 13–14, 20, 41, 67, 123, 134, 190–192, 196
Siddhartha Gautama, 20
siddhi (superhuman powers), 135, 191
sight-related diseases, 5, 17, 67, 78–79, 81, 83, 85, 87, 89, 91–92, 96, 98, 100, 189
Silk Road, 22, 71
silkworm, 175
Silla 新羅, 56, 62, 86, 137, 144
Simu anjiji 司牧安驥集, 158, 167, 177, 182
six hollow viscera (Ch. *fu* 腑), 28
skandha ("aggregates"), 72
small and large intestines, 28
Small Item Formulae (*Xiaopin fang* 小品方), 90
smallpox, 138
Sōda Hajime 宗田一 (1921–1996), 8
Soga 蘇我, 56–57, 59
sōi 僧医 (monastic physician), 61, 192
Sōni-ryō 僧尼令 (*Administrative Laws for Monks and Nuns*), 66–67
sorcery, 65
South Medicinal Plant Garden (Minami yakuen 南薬園), 138
Soysal, Yasemin, 54–55, 60
spells, 3, 15, 42, 45–46, 65, 67–68, 85, 105, 112, 125–127, 183, 189, 191, 194, 196
spirits, 4, 15, 46, 93, 97, 165, 175, 180, 184
spleen, 27, 29
stick lac, 144
stomach, 28, 83
Strickmann, Michel (1942–1994), 15, 67
Śubhakarasiṃha (637–735), 76
suffering beings, 9, 15–16, 114, 192
sugar, 1, 18
Suiko Tennō 推古天皇 (r. 592–628), 56, 111
Suinin Tennō 垂仁天皇 (r. 29 BCE–70 CE), 165
Sukunabikona no kami 少名毘古那神, 63
Sun Goddess, 55, 57, 59

Sun Simiao 孫思邈 (580–682 CE), 90
superhuman powers (*siddhi*), 135, 191
supernatural powers, 44
superstition, ix, 1, 7, 31, 34–35, 50, 64, 124
Supreme Healer, 14–15, 44, 63, 82
Supreme Physician, 20
surgery, 17, 41, 47, 75–78, 80–81, 85, 90–91, 95, 97–98, 196
Susanoo-no-mikoto 須佐之男命, 126
Suśruta saṃhitā, 29, 31, 73, 81
Sutra of Golden Light, 57, 59, 61, 85, 128
Sutra of the Buddha Mother Great Peacock Wisdom King (*Butsumo daikujaku myōō-kyō* 佛母大孔雀明王經), 112
Sutra of the Buddha's Sermon on Transforming the Female Body (*Bussetsu tennyoshin-kyō* 佛説轉女身經), 115
Sutra on Entering the Womb (Sk. *Garbhāvakrānti-sūtra*), 120
Sutra on Relieving Sores (*Ryōji byō-kyō* 療痔病經), 14, 44–45, 85
Sutra on the Medical Simile as Told by the Buddha (*Bussetsu iyu-kyō* 佛説醫喩經), 44
Sutra on the Use of Medicinal Herbs for Healing Illness by the Thousand-eyes, Thousand-hands Avalokiteśvara (*Senju sengen kanzeon bosatsu jibyō gōyaku-kyō* 千手千眼觀世音菩薩治病合藥經), 14, 85
Sutra on the Visualization of the Two Bodhisattvas, King of Healing and Supreme Healer (*Kan Yakuō Yakujō nibosatsu-kyō* 観薬王薬上二菩薩經), 14–15
Sutra on Transforming Women into Buddhas (*Bussetsu tennyo jōbutsu-kyō* 仏説転女成仏経), 119–120
sūtra, definition of, 14
Suzuki Daisetsu 鈴木大拙 (1870–1966), 50–52
svabhāva (Jp. *jishō* 自性; sense of self), 72

Tachibana no Toyohi 橘豊日 (518–587), 111
Taihō Code (*Taihō ritsuryō* 大宝律令), 42, 67, 128, 137, 166
Taihō ritsuryō 大宝律令, 42, 67, 128, 137, 166

Taiping shenghui fang 太平聖恵方, 87, 94–95, 97
Taira Nakakuni 平中國 (dates unknown), 167
Taira no Kiyomori 平清盛 (1118–1181), 148
Takeda Science Foundation, 95, 98, 147–148
Taki 多紀, 147
talismanic medicine, 66
talismanic texts, 1, 126
talismans, 3, 45–46, 64, 66, 125–126, 175, 196
Tamurasan hōyaku 田村山法薬, 161
Tanba (no) Yasuyori 丹波康頼 (912–995), 82–83, 86–89, 94, 122–124, 126–127, 146
tantra, ix, 16, 44, 50, 65, 76, 118
tea, 99, 137, 145, 151
tea plant, 145, 151
techniques of the Way (*dōjutsu* 道術), 67
technology, 9, 54–55, 66, 143, 164, 183
Ten Recitations Vinaya, 61
ten 天 (birth realm of the gods), 114
Ten'yakuryō 典薬寮 (Bureau of Medicine), 65, 137, 146, 163, 192
Tendai 天台, 22, 108, 140, 146, 177
tengu 天狗, 94
Tenmu Tennō 天武天皇 (r. 673–686), 57, 62, 128, 137
tennō 天皇 ("heavenly ruler," Emperor, Empress), 111
tennyo 転女 (transformation of "woman"), 119–120
tennyoshin 轉女身 (woman's corporeal transformation), 115, 120
Terminalia bellirica, 142
Terminalia chebula, 142
The Buddha's Correct Sutra on the Bowl of Blood (*Bussetsu daizō shōkyō ketsubonkyō* 仏説大蔵真経血盆経), 116
The Great Mirror (*Ōkagami* 大鏡), 93
The Tale of the Heike (*Heike monogatari* 平家物語), 70
Three Fruits (*triphalā*), 79–80, 142, 150
Tibet, 1, 8, 22, 120, 144, 195
Tōdaiji Temple 東大寺, 6, 59, 62, 80, 104, 128–129, 142–143
tōdōza 当道座 (guild of blind musicians), 107–108

Tokugawa Tsunayoshi 徳川綱吉 (1626–1706), 183
Ton'ishō 頓医抄, 95
torii 鳥居 (shrine gate), 100
Toshitokujin 歳徳神, 126
toxicity, 126
trade, 4, 14–15, 94, 98, 135–136, 141–143, 145, 151
transformation of the female body, 115–116
translation, 4, 13, 23–24, 35, 44, 48, 61, 87, 119–121, 170
Treatise on the Origins and Symptoms of Diseases (*Zhubing yuanhou lun* 諸病源候論), 88
tridoṣa, 12
triphalā (Three Fruits), 142
Triple Burner, 28
Tsubosaka Kannon 壺阪観音, 105–106
Tsubosakadera korōden 壺坂古老伝, 103
Tsubosakadera 壺坂寺, 99, 103–105
tuft of shining white hair (Sk. *ūrṇā-keśa*, Jp. *byakugō* 白毫), 72
Twelve Gods (Junishin 十二神), 97
twelve stems (*jūnishi* 十二支), 125

Udānavarga, 41
Ueda Sanpei 上田三平 (1881–1950), 137–141, 165
Uga-Benzaiten 宇賀弁財天, 100
Ugajin 宇賀神, 100
uji 氏 (lineage), 55
uma no kusushi 馬醫 (horse medicine, doctor), 63
Uma no tsukasa 馬寮 (Bureau of Horses), 163
Uma no yamai mishiru koto 馬之病見知事, 160
Umayado 厩戸 (574–622), 111; See also Kamitsumiya; Shōtoku Taishi
unction ceremony (Sk. *abhiṣeka*, Jp. *kanjō* 灌頂), 75
uranai 占 (divination), 3
urinary bladder, 28
urination, 123
urine, 18, 117, 150; See also *chinkiyaku*; *furanyaku*; putrid urine for healing; urinary bladder; urination

258 — Index

ūrṇā-keśa (Jp. *byakugō* 白毫; tuft of white hair), 72
Uttara-tantra, 31, 81–82, 87

vagina, 117
Vaidyarāja, 104
Vairocana, xv, 27, 59, 129, 142–143, 177, 184
vajra, 76–78, 170
Vajradhātu maṇḍala, 27
Vajraśekhara-sūtra, 46, 78
Variorum of the Divine Husbandman's Classic of Materia Medica (*Shennong bencaojing jizhu* 神農本草經集注), 144
vegetables, 84, 134
veterinarians, 18, 152, 167–168, 175–177, 181–182, 194
veterinary medicine, 5, 158, 163–164, 167–168, 177–182, 184
vibhītaka, 79–80, 142
vidyādhara (Holder of [esoteric] Knowledge), 186
vidyārāja (Jp. *myōō* 明王; Wisdom King), 112, 134, 186
Vimalakīrti-sūtra, xiii, 61
vinaya, 1, 18, 20–22, 61–62, 67, 71, 112, 121–122, 129–132, 142, 150
virtue, 9, 17, 21, 23, 62, 113, 116, 119, 133, 189
Viscum album, 157–158

wahō igaku 和方医学 (Japanese-style medicine), 64
Waitai biyao 外台秘要, 86, 88, 109
Wake 和気, 50, 63, 127, 145–146
warm water merits (*kudokuyu* 功徳湯), 130
wasp gall, 144
water, 26–29, 31, 66, 75, 88–89, 93, 99–100, 112, 130, 161
welfare, 13, 70, 108, 128, 149, 183–184
well-being, 2–3, 24, 56, 58, 62, 112, 136, 142, 183, 190, 192, 195
Well-known Diseases of the Horse (*Uma no yamai mishiru koto* 馬之病見知事), 160
wind, 26–27, 29, 31, 80, 83, 88–89, 91, 93
Wind Illness, 88, 93
Wolfiporia extensa, 157

woman's corporeal transformation (*tennyoshin* 轉女身), 120
womb, 27, 68, 119–120, 122–123, 177, 186
Womb-World Mandala (*Garbhadhātu maṇḍala*), 27, 186
women; See also female bodies; female hygiene; female monastic order; female sexual organ; menstruation; nuns; parturition; womb
– aristocratic women, 17, 113, 121, 128
– mothers, xii, 17, 80, 119, 131
– obstetrics, 84, 122–125, 127
– parturient mothers, 80
– pregnancy, 68, 84, 107, 113, 116, 122–124
– reproductive female body, xii, 17, 111–112, 114, 116, 118, 120–126, 128, 130, 132
– transformation of the female body, 115–116
– women's diseases, 84, 122–123
– women's health, 5, 122
World Health Organization, 24
worms, 83, 115
wuxing 五行 (Five Agents), 28

Xiaopin fang 小品方, 90
Xuanzang 玄奘 (602–664), 182
Yakazu Dōmei 矢数道明 (1905–2002), 9, 98
yakuen 藥園 (medicinal garden), 137–139
yakuen-shi 藥園師 (Medicinal Garden Masters), 137
Yakujō bosatsu 藥上菩薩, 14
Yakuō bosatsu 藥王菩薩, 14
Yakuonji Temple 藥園寺, 139
Yakushi Nyorai 藥師如来, 13, 57, 65, 98–99, 101, 103, 107, 130, 153, 193
Yakushiji Temple 藥師寺, 57, 96, 99, 137
Yakushushō 藥種抄, 147
Yamai no sōshi 病草紙, 95, 196
Yamato, 55, 63, 111, 128, 145, 164–165, 195
Yamato honzō 大和本草, 145
yangsheng 養生 (nourishing life), 150
Yaqian 雅遣, 175
Yellow Thearch (Emperor), 141, 170, 175
Yijing 義淨 (635–713), 13, 44, 57, 59, 85
yin-yang diviners, 111
yin-yang tradition, 105

Yinhai jinwei 銀海精微, 28, 90
Yixing 一行 (683–727), 76–77
Yōgācārabhūmi-śāstra, 72
yōjō 養生 (nourishing life), 150, 192
yokushitsu 浴室 (bathhouse), 129
Yōmei Tennō 用明天皇 (r. 585–587), 111
Yōrō Code (*Yōrō-ryō* 養老令), 53, 66–67, 128, 137–138, 163, 166
Yoshimasa 義政 (1436–1490), 139–140
Yoshimitsu 義満 (1358–1408), 139–140
Yūryaku Tennō 雄略天皇 (r. 456–479), 165

Zang and Fu Viscera, 28, 88
Zang Viscera, 27, 29
Zaofu 造父, 175
zatō 座頭 (visually impaired entertainers), 107, 109
Zhubing yuanhou lun 諸病源候論, 88
zō 蔵 (Sk. garbha), 119–120
zugon 呪言 (incantations, spells), 65

www.ingramcontent.com/pod-product-compliance
Lightning Source LLC
Chambersburg PA
CBHW061935220426
43662CB00012B/1922